BY RACHEL MADDOW

Drift

Blowout

Bag Man

Prequel

PREQUEL

PREQUEL

AN AMERICAN FIGHT
AGAINST FASCISM

RACHEL MADDOW

CROWN
NEW YORK

Copyright © 2023 by Rachel Maddow

All rights reserved.

Published in the United States by Crown, an imprint of the Crown
Publishing Group, a division of Penguin Random House LLC, New York.

CROWN and the Crown colophon are registered trademarks of
Penguin Random House LLC.

Photograph credits appear on page 363.

Hardback ISBN 978-0-593-44451-1
Ebook ISBN 978-0-593-44452-8

PRINTED IN THE UNITED STATES OF AMERICA ON ACID-FREE PAPER

crownpublishing.com

2 4 6 8 9 7 5 3 1

First Edition

Book design by Elizabeth Rendfleisch

For Susan

CONTENTS

AUTHOR'S NOTE

There were millions of words written about the rise of (and fight against) fascism as it was happening in pre–World War II America: material in books, magazines, newspapers, congressional hearings, government investigations, FBI files, trial transcripts, personal correspondence, et cetera. This makes for many big haystacks to search for many hidden needles. Luckily, I had the benefit of a remarkable amount of recent scholarship by really impressive historians who had already done some serious sifting. Among the most important to this book are Steven J. Ross (*Hitler in Los Angeles*), Charles R. Gallagher (*Nazis of Copley Square*), Bradley W. Hart (*Hitler's American Friends*), and Nancy Beck Young (*Why We Fight: Congress and the Politics of World War II*). These four not only are friends to this book but were friends to the podcast that first got me going on this topic.

Outside of that small group, I need to acknowledge a few other historians and writers, all of whom were key to my understanding both specific pieces of this sprawling story and the larger context. These are James Q. Whitman (*Hitler's American Model*), Laura B. Rosenzweig (*Hollywood's Spies*), Mark Lamster (*The Man in the Glass House*), Gerald Horne (*The Color of Fascism*), Rhodri Jeffreys-Jones (*The Nazi Spy Ring in America*), and Steven Watts (*The People's Tycoon*).

I should also mention that there are a bunch of great, very readable contemporaneous sources that you won't regret spending time with if you're lucky enough to find them in used bookstores. I commend to you Henry Reed Hoke (*It's a Secret* and *Black Mail*), John Roy Carlson (*Under Cover*), Michael Sayers and Albert E. Kahn (*Sabotage*), and O. John Rogge (*The Official German Report*). There is also Lawrence Dennis's own published account of being a defendant in the great sedition trial (*A Trial on Trial*). Academic sources and biographies on this topic are spare and sometimes even harder to find than the really old stuff, but there are some great ones out there that were indispensable to this work: Glen Jeansonne (*Women of the Far Right*), Leo P. Ribuffo (*The Old Christian Right*), Donald Warren (*Radio Priest*), Niel M. Johnson (*George Sylvester Viereck*), and Harnett T. Kane (*Huey Long's Louisiana Hayride*).

CAST OF CHARACTERS

(in order of appearance)

GEORGE SYLVESTER VIERECK, German immigrant, American citizen, Nazi agent

PHILIP JOHNSON, American fanboy of Hitler and fascism who became one of the world's most renowned architects

HUEY LONG, Louisiana pol who gave America a 1930s test-drive for dictatorship

LAWRENCE DENNIS, author of *The Coming American Fascism* and similar treatises; a man with an unexpected and hidden personal history

FATHER CHARLES COUGHLIN, the antisemitic Catholic "Radio Priest" with an audience in the tens of millions

ARNOLD ERIC SEVAREID, cub reporter in Minneapolis who went on to become a famous and erudite CBS News commentator

WILLIAM DUDLEY PELLEY, who believed he had been visited by Jesus, multiple times; pined after the job of America's Hitler

HENRY ALLEN, violent white supremacist who once tried to "purchase" the Ku Klux Klan

LESLIE FRY, promoter of the Illuminati, the New World Order, and other fantasies she pitched as real; gave the toxic *Protocols of the Elders of Zion* to Henry Ford

LEON LEWIS, antifascist spymaster of Southern California, American hero

GEORGE DEATHERAGE, American fascist who sought advice from the German embassy, and got it

GENERAL GEORGE VAN HORN MOSELEY, a man big enough to make a play to be the American führer, but small enough that he was not willing to risk his U.S. Army pension to do it

CHARLES B. HUDSON, Nazi-supported antisemitic pamphleteer who came to Washington from Omaha to buck up General Moseley

JOHN C. METCALFE, German American newspaper reporter who went undercover to investigate Nazis all across America

LEON TURROU, FBI special agent who sparked a new kind of cinema in Hollywood

JOHN F. CASSIDY, who led an armed insurrectionist group, complete with automatic rifles from a local U.S. military armory and handmade bombs; considered himself a good, God-fearing Christian

O. JOHN ROGGE, Justice Department prosecutor who was up to his eyeballs in fascist/Nazi treachery for more than a decade

SENATOR ERNEST LUNDEEN (AND HIS WIFE, NORMA), George Sylvester Viereck's first collaborators inside Congress

HARRIET JOHNSON, PHYLLIS POSIVIO, EDWARD CORNEABY, Senate staffers who dropped the dime on the Lundeens

HENRY HOKE, direct-mail advertising guru who helped uncover a remarkable Nazi plot inside Congress

SENATOR BURTON K. WHEELER, powerful U.S. senator with friends in even higher places

SENATOR ROBERT RICE REYNOLDS, rip-roaring pro-fascist pol with some novel ideas about restricting immigration

DILLARD STOKES, *Washington Post* reporter with a knack for being in the right place at the right time

WILLIAM POWER MALONEY, hard-charging and cantankerous Justice Department prosecutor

GEORGE HILL, George Sylvester Viereck's "keyman" inside Congress

REPRESENTATIVE HAMILTON FISH, Hill's boss, who was on good terms with senior officials in Hitler's Germany but detested Franklin Delano Roosevelt

LAURA INGALLS, the most famous and accomplished female pilot living in 1940; also a paid Nazi agent

ELIZABETH DILLING, who did yeoman's work inventing the "Red Scare" long before Joe McCarthy came on the scene, with financial backing from Henry Ford

LOIS DE LAFAYETTE WASHBURN, an antisemitic activist so convinced of her own explosive power that she sometimes called herself T.N.T.

SENATOR WILLIAM LANGER, nicknamed "Wild Bill" for good reason, the best friend a Nazi agent could have in Congress

The House of the Vampire arrived in 1907, with a pinch of Bram Stoker's *Dracula*, a dash of Swinburne, and a major crush on Oscar Wilde. Two of the novella's main characters, Jack and Ernest, were named after the split-personality lead character in Wilde's play *The Importance of Being Earnest*. In *The House of the Vampire,* the hero, Reginald Clarke, is a handsome middle-aged boulevardier, bon vivant, and night prowler. Clarke is also a magnet for impressionable and gifted young males, often ones with fetchingly long eyelashes, and always with "subtler, more sympathetic, more feminine" ways than the general run of men. The book's twenty-two-year-old author, George Sylvester Viereck (he went by Sylvester, which sounded more continental), was himself a pillow-lipped and self-professed sensualist who said he worshipped Wilde as one of his three life models, alongside Napoleon and Christ. "Wilde is splendid," he wrote. "I admire, nay I love him. He is so deliciously unhealthy, so beautifully morbid. I love all things evil! I love the splendor of decay, the foul beauty of corruption." Sylvester, at age seventeen, had struck up an apparently romantic friendship with Wilde's most notorious paramour, Lord Alfred Douglas. Young Viereck also loved to show off the framed violet he said he had plucked from Wilde's grave.

The House of the Vampire is seen today by precisely no one as the world's greatest gay vampire fiction, but it does have the distinction of being the world's first known publication in that now ample oeuvre. Viereck's hero vampire, Reginald, swaggers through the book seducing younger men, gently tugging them away from the unerringly difficult or hag-like women who otherwise seek their attentions. "A tremendous force trembled in his very fingertips," Viereck wrote of Reginald. "He was like a gigantic dynamo, charged with the might of ten thousand magnetic storms." In Viereck's voluptuous, pretentious, deeply stupid romp, Reginald is seeking not blood—like Bram Stoker's original vampire—but something more rarefied. He squeezes from his prey every drop of literary, musical, and aesthetic juice they possess, "absorbing from life the elements essential to artistic completion," as the hero explains. By the novel's close, everybody is drained but vampire Reginald.

"In every age there have been great men—and they became great by absorbing the work of other men," Viereck wrote of his first novel. "My vampire is the Overman of Nietzsche. He is justified in the pilfering of other men's brains."

Viereck loosed his genre-pioneering book on the world in 1907 with considerable hopes. "You've heard of the 'great American novel'?" Viereck wrote to one critic. "Well, I've written it."

The critics did not agree.

"The style of the book was quite impossible," wrote one, "keyed from the first word to the last in the highest pitch of emotion." Still, though, the book did sell some copies, and it even had its own brief run on the stage, in an adaptation by a man who later co-wrote the screenplay for *The Wizard of Oz*.

VIERECK HAD BEEN born in Munich and immigrated to America with his parents in 1896, when he was eleven years old. He had always been drawn to the memory and the landscape of his birthplace. There was mystery and intrigue in Sylvester's family history in Germany, including unproved claims to royal lineage. Viereck's father, Louis, was rumored to be the issue of a brief affair between a famous stage actress in the Prussian royal court and Kaiser Wilhelm I. The kaiser, if he was indeed the father, was in no position to acknowledge this son, and he never did.

Royalty or not, Louis ended up a Marxist, joining the anti-monarch Socialist Party in Germany, and possibly getting involved in a plot to assassinate the kaiser. This tale seems a tad on the nose, in the Oedipal sense, but it is true that Louis was run out of Berlin and then Munich and then all of Germany, on account of his Marxist proclivities. He landed in New York, but not exactly on his feet. Sylvester's father never found much success in the New World. He organized German Americans in support of the presidential candidates William McKinley and Theodore Roosevelt, wrote a forgotten monograph on German-language instruction in American schools, and gave the occasional lecture on German culture and society. For his young son, rife as he was with artistic gifts and a robust, unerring self-confidence in those gifts, Louis was a distant and feckless father. While Louis eventually ended up putting his tail between his legs and going back to Berlin to finish out his days giving lectures, this time about American culture and society, Sylvester, naturalized citizen of the United States, decided to stay put in New York, an electrified city in an up-and-coming country—a place with a trajectory matched to his own arcing ambition.

By the time he was in his mid-twenties (the commercial and critical flop of *The House of the Vampire* notwithstanding), Viereck was recognized as a rising star in American literature. He had published a volume of well-regarded poems. Whispers that he was maybe the grandson of Kaiser Wilhelm I were probably good for sales, and also for contributing to the almost inexplicably fawning publicity he had a knack for attracting. He was "the most widely discussed literary man in the United States today," one glossy middlebrow magazine wrote of Viereck, "unanimously accused of being a genius."

Whatever his gifts in the realm of literature, poetry, or self-promotion, where Viereck truly distinguished himself was as an advocate to the American public for his beloved fatherland, a cause that he took on with crusading passion at the advent of World War I. When a German U-boat torpedoed a New York–bound passenger liner in May 1915, drowning 1,200 civilians, including

124 Americans, Viereck defended Germany for doing it. "The facts absolutely justify the action of the Germans if the *Lusitania* was, indeed, torpedoed by a German submarine," Viereck wrote in a statement to reporters. "Legally and morally there is no basis for any protests on the part of the United States. The *Lusitania* was a British ship. British ships have been instructed by the admiralty to ram submarines and to take active measures against the enemy. Hence every British ship must be considered in light of a warship." Germany "means business," Viereck explained to his fellow Americans, and "does not bluff." It was, to say the least, an unpopular stand in a country enraged by the loss of civilian life on that torpedoed ocean liner.

Just weeks later, Viereck found himself at the center of an even more concentrated fury. While squiring a visiting German official around Manhattan, Viereck managed to leave behind a briefcase full of secret documents on the Sixth Avenue elevated train. The satchel was quickly grabbed by a federal agent who had been tailing them. Its contents were ferried to Washington and then—with the Wilson administration's quiet blessing—leaked to the New York *World,* which released them in installments as a bombshell exposé of Germany's designs on America. The documents in the left-behind briefcase—as showcased in the pages of *The World*—showed vast financial transfers by the German government into a long list of private U.S. bank accounts and detailed discussions among German officials about their efforts to keep American public opinion aligned against the United States joining the world war, to hamper our ability to help our allies, and to generally mess with us in the meantime. The documents showed that Viereck was not just a high-profile pro-German U.S. citizen; he was a paid agent of the German government, which was handsomely bankrolling all his publishing efforts.

After an ensuing furor, Viereck moved to change the name of his pretentious, well-funded, pro-German magazine from *The Fatherland* to the much more corn-fed-sounding *Viereck's American Weekly.* But the damage was done. The documents from the Sixth Avenue El showed that the German government was spending

$2 million per week (in 1915 dollars; nearly $60 million a week today) on propaganda and espionage efforts targeting the United States. They also revealed German government discussions about serious sabotage plans, including using straw buyers to secretly purchase U.S. munitions factories and military supplies to prevent that matériel from being provided to our allies fighting Germany in the war.

It was a pain for the Germans to have this all exposed, and a pain for Viereck personally, particularly after the United States finally joined the war effort in 1917. Viereck had been living with his wife's family in sleepy Mount Vernon, New York, until an angry mob descended on the house and forced him out into the night. He decided he would wait out the conclusion of the war in New York City, where it was easier to blend into the crowd. But he never really did manage to regain the small purchase he had acquired on the American literary scene.

There's a cracking letter in the files of former president Teddy Roosevelt from around this time in which Roosevelt tells Viereck that if he's so much more supportive of Germany than of the United States, then perhaps Viereck is being a bad citizen of both, so maybe he should renounce his American citizenship, piss off back to Germany, and join the German army, which would at least make him useful to one of the two countries. Viereck did no such thing, but you can tell from the letter how much Roosevelt enjoyed telling him to do it. (He leads off by telling Viereck he has "mental shortcomings" and is "unutterably base," and by the end he is just hollering at him to get out: "You are not a good citizen here. But neither are you a good citizen of Germany. You should go home.") Roosevelt also endorsed a move to eject Viereck from the roster of the Poetry Society of America—perish the thought.

After World War I, as he neared his forties and came to realize he was unlikely to ever scale the tiers of fame he desired, Viereck began, vampirically one could say, to cultivate relations with more celebrated men. He shuttled between Europe and America, seeking out famous statesmen, soldiers, doctors, scientists, businessmen, and writers, then persuading them to sit for interviews. "To me the men to whom I have talked and whose thoughts I record are flashes of the great World Brain," he wrote in a collection of these personality profiles. "Some are incandescent in their intensity; in others the divine flame burns more dimly. Their colours are more varied than the spectrum. I am the spectroscope that reveals the stuff of which they are made, or, translating colour into sound, I am the trumpet through which they convey their message."

His first big get was Kaiser Wilhelm II, who was living in exile in Holland after his defeat in the massively deadly, epic war he had started. "In view of your years-long manly struggle for truth and right, I feel no hesitation in authorizing you to publish the impressions you gathered at Doorn as the guest of His Majesty," the kaiser's aide wrote to Viereck. "I do this the more willingly because I know the communications entrusted to you by his majesty will be made use of by yourself in a manner calculated to promote the true, just interests of Germany."

Viereck became an annual visitor to Doorn and a trusted mouthpiece of the kaiser, who often greeted him, Viereck's own son remembered, as "*mon cousin.*" Viereck seemed proud to be able to help the fallen, mostly despised, mostly insane German monarch make sense of why exactly God had abandoned him, the divinely chosen leader of a great nation, in his pursuit of a Christian empire in Europe. The kaiser settled on the shortcomings of the German people as the problem. "We refused in the end to face all risks in preserving faith," Wilhelm II told Viereck. "The German people performed miracles of endurance, but, at the last, they failed. . . . We should have fought to the *very* last carrot, the *very* last man, the *very* last round of munitions. . . . The odds against us, toward the end, were twenty to one. We could still have prevailed, with complete faith in God. We should have trusted in God, not in human logic."

Viereck ended up getting a remarkable number of Great Men to sit down and talk politics, economics, faith, sex, psychology, and general worldview: Henry Ford, Nikola Tesla, Benito Mussolini, Albert Einstein, the military and political generals of the late war. *I am not a journalist,* he would tell them, *I am a poet.* Viereck was "80 percent clever and strong minded, and 20 percent an impenetrable blockhead," the playwright George Bernard Shaw said of him. "He generally brings the 20 percent to bear on me."

But it was Dr. Sigmund Freud who seemed to understand his interviewer best, according to an exchange Viereck recorded. "Our [psychological] complexes are the sources of our weakness," Freud said to Viereck. "They are also often the source of strength."

"I wonder what my complexes are?" Viereck asked.

Freud gently reminded him that a serious assessment could take two or three years of real work, but the father of psychoanalysis did have a quick take on George Sylvester Viereck. "You have sought, year after year, the outstanding figures of your generation, invariably men older than yourself."

"It is part of my work," Viereck reminded Herr Doktor.

"But it is also your preference," Freud replied. "The great man is a symbol. Your search is the search of your heart. You are seeking the great man to take the place of the father. It is part of your father complex."

George Sylvester Viereck did finally settle on—and worship—a particular father figure. The man was five years his junior, an Austrian plebeian whose rise in the kaiser's military ranks during the war topped out low at the rank of corporal. When Viereck met him for an interview in 1923, the man had virtually nothing to say about his past and refused to be photographed for the article Viereck was writing. He appeared more poet than politician, Viereck wishfully noted, and sipped tea or cordials with the polish of a "high brow." But when the thirty-four-year-old housepainter and wannabe messiah shouted the

George Viereck as a young man

beauties of his new political movement—National Socialism—his listener felt an almost physical heat. "His voice filled the room," Viereck wrote, and "cords" on his "forehead stood out threateningly." His eyes flashed "something of the Blonde Beast of Nietzsche." *Like a gigantic dynamo,* the journalist-poet might have been thinking, *charged with the might of ten thousand magnetic storms.* The first words Viereck wrote of the man would prove prophetic: "Adolf Hitler must be handled with care. He is a human explosive."

Hitler was already a divisive figure in his native land, but Viereck suggested the rising pol was welcomed even by his countrymen who were shy to say so. "There is no one in Germany who does not recognize the importance of his emblem, the 'Hakenkreuz,' the ancient swastika, sometimes standing by itself and sometimes superimposed on a cross or a shield, a mystic symbol of militant Germanism," wrote Viereck. He drew applause across the social strata, Viereck claimed. "He overcomes them with his eloquence. He storms their reserve with his passion." Hitler spoke to Viereck of the unfairness of the Treaty of Versailles, which settled World War I and clipped the kaiser's drive for empire, hemming Germany into newer, narrower borders. He then turned to the communist doctrine that now ruled Russia. "The Peace Treaty and Bolshevism are two heads of one monster," Hitler insisted. "We must decapitate both." Decapitating Bolshevism, in Hitler's calculus, required ridding Germany of the "alien in their midst"—the Jews. When Viereck suggested to the younger man that perhaps his sweeping antisemitism might displace many great artists, scientists, manufacturers, and generally esteemed citizens, Hitler disagreed: "The fact that a man is decent is no reason why we should not eliminate him."

In the face of that ominous forecast, Viereck remained neutral on Hitler's politics, but not on his personality: "If he lives, Hitler, for better or for worse, is sure to make history."

Almost ten years later, as Hitler was about to ascend to the chancellorship of Germany, Viereck recycled his interview for the popular U.S. magazine *Liberty* ("America's Best Read Weekly"), with added touches on Germany's need for physically healthy citizens, for the re-expansion of its territories, and, above all, for an arousal of the national spirit, the national pride, the national might. When Hitler's army began to storm across Europe in 1939 and 1940, Viereck was all in. Finally, a Germany that seemed prepared to "fight to the *very* last carrot." Viereck was quick to warn his fellow Americans of the futility of challenging the führer's military machine. Viereck had gazed into Hitler's "magnetic blue eyes," he would write. He deemed it unwise for the United States to test the man's resolve.

THE FÜHRER'S PORTRAIT now held pride of place in Viereck's home office on Riverside Drive in New York City. Of the three dozen photographs of famous acquaintances—including Albert Einstein, Theodore Roosevelt, George Bernard Shaw, Marshal Foch, and Kaiser Wilhelm II—Hitler's was the largest. Hitler, by Viereck's lights, was first in the pantheon of the Great Nietzschean Overmen. "There must be a great crop of oysters before one pearl is born. Millions of flowers grow in the garden to achieve one matchless rose, and billions of men must be born to produce one superman like Goethe, Napoleon, Da Vinci or Hitler," Viereck said, later adding that Hitler "out-Napoleons Napoleon."

By 1940, Viereck had become what he so wanted to be: a reliable servant to his father figure from the fatherland. After his incompetent but earnest try at it in World War I, now in the second war the long-ago poet had positioned himself as the mastermind of one of Hitler's crucial plans for America; he was the center wheel of a propaganda campaign, funded by the German government and its agents in the United States. "Propaganda helped us to power," Joseph Goebbels announced at the Nazi Party congress in 1936. "Propaganda kept us in power. Propaganda will help us conquer the world."

Hitler explained the plan in typically blunt terms: "Our strategy is to destroy the enemy from within, to conquer him through himself." Viereck had literally written a book on the subject in 1930 (dedicated to Dr. Sigmund Freud of all people), assessing the weakness of the kaiser's propaganda campaign in America during the first great war. "We were pikers," Viereck claimed to have been told by one downhearted German officer. "What was a million dollars compared to the stake for which we were playing? For centuries to come, the German people will have to pay for our stinginess. . . . We lacked the vision, the authority, and the inexhaustible funds of the Allies." Viereck specifically castigated his German paymasters for the debacle of the suitcase full of secret documents that he and his visitor left behind on a subway train, as if that were an expenses problem and not just his own sheer idiocy. "If the German Government had provided [the visiting official] with an automobile or a bodyguard, this disaster would have been averted. Governments, reckless in some matters, are at times prodigiously stingy."

But that was last time around. The lead-up to this next world war would be different: lessons learned, no expense to be spared. Nazi Germany poured money and manpower into dividing the American polity, hoping to keep the United States and its arsenal of democracy out of the war in Europe. "America for Americans," as Hitler said in an interview widely published in the United States in 1940, "and Europe for the Europeans." His government blanketed America with isolationist and antisemitic literature. According to records discovered after the war was over, the German Foreign Office rained down on Americans more than 1 million leaflets and postcards, about 2.5 million pamphlets and magazines, and 135,000 books just in the single summer of 1941. The Nazis' Special War Fund expended seemingly endless resources in the effort. When the German embassy was ordered shuttered by President Franklin D. Roosevelt that same summer, the embassy vault still held more than $3.5 million—about $75 million today—in cash.

A good chunk of the German money devoted to this effort passed through the hands of George Sylvester Viereck, who used it to try to exploit a key weakness he had discerned in the American political system. "The more I study the record of foreign propaganda in the United States, the more I am surprised by the long patience of the American Government," he wrote. "While the law requires that the ownership of a newspaper must be fully disclosed, there was nothing to prevent the German government or an individual German from making a present of several million dollars to an American sympathizer; nor was there anything to prevent the sympathizer from making his money talk—for Germany! There is no safeguard which the law can create which human ingenuity cannot circumvent."

Viereck and other Nazi agents doled out cash to myriad publications in the United States, whose editors and publishers then helped the Germans consolidate a mailing list of friendlies and potential friendlies that may have reached into the millions. The Foreign Office in Berlin also funded Nazi shortwave radio stations around the United States, all with the same messaging, which would be nutted up succinctly by one American prosecutor after the war: "The United States is internally corrupt. There is political and economic injustice, war profiteering, plutocratic exploitation, Communist sedition, Jewish conspiracy, and spiritual decay within the United States." American foreign policy was "selfish, bullying . . . and predatory." President Roosevelt was a "warmonger and a liar, unscrupulous, responsible for suffering, and a pawn of Jews, Communists, and Plutocrats." The German army possessed all the strength it needed for victory in Europe. America and Great Britain were sadly lacking in men, material, and morale, and certain to kneel to Germany. The United States, like the rest of the world, was "menaced" by communists and Jews.

That German propaganda campaign, by ground and by air, was facilitated by a cadre of American troops. There was Lawrence Dennis, proud to be known as "the intellectual godfather of American fascism"; his mentee Philip Johnson, later a celebrated modern architect; William Dudley Pelley, who, after founding the Nazi wannabe Silver Shirts, dreamed of being America's own Hitler; the raging white supremacist and antisemite George Deatherage, who vowed that "religion that does not stay within the accepted bounds of Christian morality shall be suppressed." There was also James True, who had professed his admiration for the book burners in Nazified Austria because "filthy books have been published by the hundreds, under the guise of science or 'liberalism' for the debauchery of youth. Quite naturally the first move of the Aryans was to destroy this mental poison. Soon, we predict, we shall have similar book burnings in this country." There was also the handsome brawler Joe McWilliams, who set out to organize angry young men into fascist street-fighting cells. McWilliams called for "an America free of Roosevelt, free of kikes, free of Republicans and free of the Democratic Party which are only the stooges of the Jews. We want in America the same methods and same system that Hitler inaugurated in Germany."

Viereck's homegrown American conspirators and ideological allies also included the exalted, conspiracy-minded U.S. Army general George Van Horn Moseley, the wildly popular antisemite radio preacher Father Charles Coughlin, American businessmen like Henry Ford, and, more unnerving, at least two dozen sitting members of Congress. Congressmen and senators used the special privileges of government office to aid and abet Viereck and the Nazi cause; they colluded with Viereck to produce and distribute more than three million separate pieces of pro-German mailings. Many of these tracts were written by Viereck himself or by the Hitler government in Berlin, and then published in America under the bylines of the willing congressmen.

IN THE YEARS leading up to the U.S. entry into World War II, the American government, American institutions, American democracy itself, was under attack from enemies without and within. The great American fight against fascism that we have inherited as a cornerstone in our country's moral foundation is a fight that didn't happen only overseas in the 1940s. Americans fought on both sides of that divide here at home, too, and their stories will curl your hair. They may also bolster your confidence in our ability to win our modern iterations of those same recurring fights, not to mention the future rounds, too, when this inevitably comes up again on civilization's big democracy chore wheel.

The fight here at home in the 1930s and 1940s is a story of American politics at the edge: a violent, ultra-right authoritarian movement, weirdly infatuated with foreign dictatorships, with detailed plans to overthrow the U.S. government, and even with former American military officers who stood ready to lead. Their most audacious plan called for mounting hundreds of simultaneous armed attacks on U.S. government targets in the immediate aftermath of FDR's likely reelection in 1940. Their attacks would spark chaos and panic, they hoped, and galvanize and radicalize anti-Roosevelt Americans, culminating in an armed takeover of the U.S. government and the installation of something much more like a fascist dictatorship. And as far-fetched as that sounds, these belligerents were doing a lot more than flapping their lips. They had started stealing from federal armories, and had made their plans to raid them, with confederates on the inside ready to help. They had bought weapons by the hundreds and thousands and started building and stockpiling bombs.

The even more incendiary fact was that these would-be insurrectionists enjoyed an astonishing amount of support from federal elected officials who proved willing and able to use their share of American political power to defend the extremists, to derail the Justice Department's efforts to thwart or punish them, and to shield themselves from potential criminal liability when they were found out. In the lead-up to World War II, the U.S. Congress was rife with treachery, deceit, and almost unfathomable actions on the part of people who had sworn to defend the Constitution but who instead got themselves implicated in a plot to end it.

We can look back now, at a distance of more than eighty years, and see that all those American fascists (along with their lies and disinformation, their Hitler love, their white supremacist antisemitic derangement) ended up splintered on a rocky embankment. But in the moment, the lead-up to World War II in America was a much more close-run affair than we want to remember. It was a fast ride through churning and dangerous political rapids, and it wasn't clear at the time exactly who and what were going to survive the journey. A lot of powerful figures in Congress, in the media, in law enforcement, in religious leadership, were bailing hard to keep the fascist boat afloat.

.   .   .

CALCULATED EFFORTS TO undermine democracy, to foment a coup, to spread disinformation across the country, to overturn elections by force of arms with members of Congress helping and running interference—all these things add up to a terrible episode for a country like ours to live through, but they are not unprecedented. Our current American struggle along these lines, it turns out, has a prequel.

And it turns out that the most interesting part of that story is about the Americans—mostly forgotten today—who picked up the slack in this fight against our domestic authoritarians and fascists and heavily armed right-wing militias. People like federal prosecutors William Power Maloney and O. John Rogge; federal lawmen such as Leon G. Turrou and Peter Wacks; Leon Lewis, a Jewish veteran of World War I who ran a dangerous undercover spy operation inside the dens of American Nazis; brave informants like Charles Slocombe, John C. Metcalfe, and Denis Healy, who all took real physical risks; journalists like Dillard Stokes, Arthur Derounian, and the cub reporter Arnold Sevareid; a direct mail advertising consultant turned daring citizen investigator, Henry Hoke. These mostly unremembered Americans stood up and challenged both the fascists and the political figures who were running a protection racket for them. They were not necessarily the people you might expect to be on the front lines, but there they were, standing fast. They won. And they left stories to tell—incredible stories—about how they did it.

PREQUEL

CHAPTER ONE

THE GLASS HOUSE

The reedy and excitable twenty-six-year-old recent Harvard graduate, full of anticipation, was motoring out to an open field in Potsdam, Germany, to attend a Nazi youth rally. Part of the draw for the Harvard man was the chance to see and hear, *in person*, Adolf Hitler, who was then still several months away from ascending to the chancellorship of Germany but already the talk of Europeans and Americans in the know. Another factor in the draw to Potsdam was the opportunity to witness up close the dazzling spectacle reliably on display at Nazi rallies. The American aesthete, who would eventually achieve his own considerable level of celebrity both at home and abroad, was keenly interested in the power of artifice.

The young man had been a lonely outsider, lacerated by cruel juvenile humor for much of his life. He was frail and a stutterer and suffered from a low-grade bipolar disorder called cyclothymia. The accompanying "nervous breakdowns" had already slowed his progress in life. Yes, he went to Harvard, but although he entered with the class of 1927, he did not receive his bachelor of arts until three years after most of his classmates, in June 1930.

Still he had gradually adopted the carriage of a man above it all, buoyed in no small part by the precepts adopted from his favorite philosopher, Friedrich Nietzsche. Nietzsche's siren song was really just one blaring note, and hard to misapprehend: The mass of men was a sorry lot whose most useful quality was the

ability to conform to rules others wrote for them. But, the celebrated nineteenth-century German scholar posited, there was a
small squadron of elites, of demigods, of *Übermenschen* (in English, roughly "supermen") capable of molding the world and all
its human glories because they refused to be bound by convention
or morality or man-made law.

The Harvard man had been raised with what he called "rather
an upper class feeling" about things, so he not only was on the
lookout for these predestined few, the rare *Übermenschen,* but suspected he himself would one day be counted among them. He covered any suspicions of his own "inferiority," one close acquaintance
theorized, by being "personally aggressive."

The menacing martial snap and guttural roar of that Potsdam
youth rally in the fall of 1932 turned out to be something akin to a
tent revival for the young American, a political awakening doubt-
lessly intensified by the invigorating sight—he would later tell his
biographer—of "all those blond boys in black leather" parading by.

The leader of the Hitler Youth, beefy and baby-faced, introduced Hitler to a field of thirty thousand *Jugend* sporting match-
ing brown uniforms, armbands with the new national emblem,
and, pinned over the left breast of the lucky few who could afford
it, a weighty metal badge stamped with swastika and sword.

Fifty thousand onlookers in the overflowing stadium watched
as Hitler came to the stage. Children waved hundreds of big Nazi
flags, and the crowd roared. "We must learn once more to feel as a
nation and act as a nation if we want to stand up before the world,"
the führer of the future told his rapt audience. "Let no German
boy ever bow to an injustice—be proud and defiant and never
yield. . . . Never abandon your people and be more faithful than
ever if [the fatherland] is in the greatest distress and danger." A
reporter in attendance noted that Hitler had to pause here, for
several minutes, while the crowd sounded its approval. "Through
our movement a new and strong generation is growing up that has
new courage and does not surrender."

"You simply could not fail to be caught up in the excitement of it, by the marching songs, by the crescendo and climax of the whole thing," the young American would say of that day, decades later. He was struck by the notion that Adolf Hitler might just be the *Über-Übermensch*, the figure to reshape politics in Germany and beyond. He was also struck with the feeling that he, Philip Johnson, was somehow destined for his own role in this epochal undertaking.

Philip Johnson would go on to become a shaper of sorts, as one of the world's best-known architects. He would dream up and create sleek, dark, unornamented urban skyscrapers that were widely mimicked, as well as his near-miraculous Glass House, never again tried. But in 1932, on that day in Potsdam, Johnson's machined glass-and-steel reputation was all in the future; this was long before he took up his actual life's work as an architect, before he was famous and fêted and seated at

Philip Johnson in the early 1930s

the epicenter of midtown Manhattan's power tables at the Four Seasons Grill Room (he helped design that restaurant too). Back in 1932, on his return to New York from the Hitler Youth rally that stirred his soul, young Philip Johnson's dream was to bring Hitler-style fascism to America.

Johnson's prospects for leading a popular fascist movement to refashion American culture, politics, and government seemed exceedingly dim to those who knew him best. He was "pulsating with new ideas and hopes . . . was wildly impatient, could not sit down," one of his few admirers recalled. But his incessant "quickness and vibration," she implied, could also be grating. Some contemporaries suspected that Johnson would be a man without close friends or even suitable employment, were it not for his money. Philip Johnson had plenty of money. When he was still an undergraduate at Harvard, his father had gifted him a boatload of preferred stock in the Aluminum Company of America (later Alcoa). The stock threw off an annual dividend income of anywhere from $20,000 to $100,000 a month (in today's dollars), depending on the American economy's own bipolar boom-or-bust rhythms.

Johnson picked up a lot of tabs, which often got him what he desired. While not (yet) a practicing architect himself, he became a high-wattage presenter and popularizer of the architectural work of others. He co-curated and provided funding for *Modern Architecture: International Exhibition* and also *Machine Art,* two groundbreaking shows at New York's fledgling Museum of Modern Art introducing Americans to the latest European industrial design and designers. This gave him the chance to celebrate the men he deemed the *Übermenschen* of modern architecture— Walter Gropius, Le Corbusier, and Ludwig Mies van der Rohe among others. He became the head of the Department of Architecture at MoMA, perhaps in part because he could furnish his own salary. He also paid the salary of his personal assistant, and the MoMA librarian, and the publicity director he hired on, Alan Blackburn, who was one of Johnson's few intimate friends from boarding school and Harvard.

His efforts to curate and fund American-style fascism did not run quite as smoothly. Johnson had a lot going on in the early 1930s. He had his job at the museum to tend, as well as negotiations for a retail concession (tentatively named Art, Inc.) in the new Rockefeller Center, inveigling efforts to make himself interior designer to the smart set's filthy rich, and a whirling social life. On warm summer nights Johnson would drive up to Harlem in a friend's open-top Chrysler sedan for assignations with a beautiful and honey-voiced African American cabaret singer. Jimmie Daniels was "a beautiful, beautiful kid," Johnson would wistfully recall years later. The two would stay overnight at an uptown boardinghouse whose owners knew the score. "I tried to have him downtown," Johnson would say. "It didn't work so well."

He and Alan Blackburn often invited friends over to Johnson's duplex apartment, which doubled as a showroom for Mies van der Rohe's modern designs. There, they could belittle President Roosevelt and his milquetoast New Deal all they wanted, or talk of the day when the United States had a bold leader like Hitler. Johnson started compiling a list of young men and women who seemed sympathetic to an American Hitler, and maybe even willing to join his and Blackburn's new organization, the Gray Shirts. (Johnson conceived the Gray Shirts as an American counterpart of Hitler's menacing tip-of-the-spear storm troopers, or Brownshirts, both in style and in substance.) He entrusted this secret list to his personal assistant, Ruth Merrill, and told her to never let it out of her sight. She said the list grew to somewhere between two hundred and three hundred names, though no more than twenty ever showed up at actual meetings of the Gray Shirts.

Miss Merrill regarded the enterprise, right down to the occasional German-language-only get-togethers and Johnson's hiring of a German manservant, Rudolph, as what we now call cosplay— overgrown boys in dress-up. Philip had "a weak character and [an] immature mind," she said. This view was widely shared among people who knew Johnson well; they described him as "flighty" or "rather silly" or "too much of a fool to worry about." Philip Johnson was "harmless," concluded the sheriff of the county in Ohio where Johnson grew up and kept a home. "[He] just has a lot of money and nothing to do but travel around and spend, being a nuisance to himself and everyone else."

There was one figure among Johnson's art world acquaintances who was less forgiving of his antics. Philip's "only real passion," Lincoln Kirstein explained, "was to exert power to tell people what they want."

Kirstein was a mirror image of Philip Johnson from most angles: an almost exact contemporary, Harvard educated, independently wealthy thanks to his father, bisexual, an unflinching aesthete, and a budding arts impresario. While at Harvard, Kirstein had founded the Society for Contemporary Art on campus, as well as a literary magazine that published new poetry by e. e. cummings, T. S. Eliot, Edmund Wilson, and Ezra Pound—before Pound was revealed as a committed fascist himself. While Johnson spent the first years of his professional life introducing Europe's modern design and architecture to America, Kirstein was busy creating an American ballet troupe to rival the best in Europe.

But Kirstein was different from Philip Johnson in one very consequential respect: He was Jewish.

Kirstein's father was close friends with the Harvard law professor Felix Frankfurter, who was already ringing alarm bells in the halls of power in the United States about the unfolding brutality of the Nazis' rule in Germany. Frankfurter spent the 1933–34 academic year at Oxford University in England, where he had a closer view of developments in Europe. "The air here [in England] is charged, albeit in a sober kind of way, with the kind of feeling that preceded 1914," Frankfurter wrote to his friend President Franklin Delano Roosevelt. He also forwarded the president letters from a League of Nations commissioner describing the enormity of recent Nazi decrees making Jews second-class citizens in Germany. In April 1934, Frankfurter published one of the first articles detailing the early consequences of Hitler's Aryan-only policies, which included stripping many Jewish professionals of their positions in academia, law, and medicine. "There is no doubt," Frankfurter wrote, "that the Jew in Germany is doomed."

Lincoln Kirstein could sense ill winds blowing across the Atlantic and into the kinds of upper-class salons of Manhattan that welcomed rich, influential young men like him and Philip Johnson. At a stylish loft on East Fortieth Street one night in 1934, when a wealthy socialite was in her cups and suddenly free from inhibition, she lashed out at a fellow partygoer, who happened to be Jewish. "You live on corruption!" she yelled. "You all ought to be extirpated." The gathering's bohemian hostess described the scene to Lincoln Kirstein the next day. She initially appeared distraught and confided to her young friend that she was afraid that the ugly scenes playing out in Germany "might happen here in America." But she gradually talked herself out of anxiety. The drunk malefactor, she finally explained to Kirstein, was probably overwrought because she had been unsuccessful in her headlong attempts to seduce a man named Lawrence Dennis.

IT WAS PROBABLY no surprise to Kirstein that Lawrence Dennis, an enthusiastic *kochleffel* (pot stirrer), had set the scene in motion. Dennis was a handsome, well-traveled, and unusually compelling figure—a Harvard man like Philip Johnson and Lincoln Kirstein, but a generation older, and with a somewhat mysterious (or at least somewhat fuzzy) life history. He was a former U.S. State Department hand, a sometime stockbroker, an amateur economist, and a political gadfly masquerading as a deeply intellectual theorist.

Dennis's forceful, erudite personality and his rugged, square-jawed good looks had caught the eye of many an excitable middle-aged woman, not to mention Philip Johnson and Alan Blackburn. The incipient urban fascists invited Dennis to lecture at the secret meetings of their still closeted Gray Shirts anytime he was free, and they took his oracular pronouncements to heart. Dennis had invested early in the possibilities of American-style fascism, and he clearly relished the prospect of a violent turning of the tables. "I ask no sympathy and would resent an indication of pity just as I would have neither sympathy nor mercy on thousands of people now in the seats of the mighty if I came to power," Dennis wrote privately to a friend in 1933, on seeing up-from-nothing Hitler take over the chancellorship of Germany. "I should like nothing better than to be a leader or follower of a Hitler who would crush and destroy many now in power. It is my turn of fate now to suffer. It may someday be theirs."

Lawrence Dennis advised Johnson and Blackburn, their handful of fellow Gray Shirts, and anybody else who was listening that if they wanted a fascist government in America they were going to have to play the long game. The best vehicle for that faraway future, as far as Dennis could see, was a recent governor and current U.S. senator from the state of Louisiana, Huey Long. "Smarter than Hitler," Dennis said. "The best example of our nearest approach to a national fascist leader." He also said, characteristically cocksure, "Long reads my stuff."

CHAPTER TWO

"COME TO MY FEAST"

Huey Long was all over the news in 1934—in newspapers, on radio, in newsreels. At a time of global political extremes—fascism, communism, relentless and deepening global economic depression—Long lurked in the wings of American power as the exemplar of just how far out there we might be able to get in this country. By 1934, America had already thrown out the living, breathing debacle that was Herbert Hoover and brought on Roosevelt and his swashbuckling brand of can-do, out-of-my-way, big-*D* Democratic power governance. FDR was radically transforming the economy and the executive branch—maybe even the Supreme Court—with a political force of will that drove his opponents beyond mere outrage. Five years into the Depression, with fascism ascendant in Europe and the future of democracy feeling very much like an open question everywhere, FDR was clearing the electoral field as America's boldest possible president.

Bolder still, though, was Huey Long. Here was both a very American personal success story and a glimpse of what post-democracy strongman rule might look like in the United States, signaled not by a uniformed march on Rome or a Reichstag fire but by a governor who became senator while simultaneously keeping the governor's job, breaking the spine of democracy in his state with the help of a cadre of brass-knuckled bodyguards, engineering kidnappings of his enemies, and defeating or sidestepping multiple impeachments and indictments and investigations, all while soaking up adoration at a muddy rural rally with farmers or in a roaring ballroom full of tuxedoed and gowned admirers, his vast and disparate audiences too in love with his charm to much care what he actually meant. Somehow simultaneously cherubic and menacing in appearance, Huey Long was a populist, a rule breaker, a shockingly gifted orator, and a thug. He once commanded National Guard troops to mount an actual true-blue armed military assault on the municipal government of the largest city in his state. The man launched an armed invasion of New Orleans!—and got away with it. The best contemporaneous biography of Long in Louisiana was subtitled "The American Rehearsal for Dictatorship."

There had rarely been a moment like this in U.S. history. The shifts in the tectonic plates of American politics and governance were thrilling to some, terrifying to others, and felt by all. President Roosevelt and his novel New Deal policies were just beginning to work their way into American society in 1934. The federal government, for the first time in its history, was using its power to provide emergency relief to the tens of millions of Americans whose lives had been destroyed, through no fault of their own, by the stock market crash and the cataclysmic economic disintegration that followed. FDR and his fellow Democrats in Congress were spending money, in a hurry, for the general welfare. They were putting millions of unemployed Americans back to work— with a regular paycheck—remaking the country's roads, bridges, hospitals, schools, water treatment and irrigation facilities, public utilities.

The New Deal was a dangerous and dastardly revolution in American governance to some, and not nearly enough to others. They wanted more, faster. The Communist Party of the United States of America (still, before 1935, taking its marching orders and funding from Moscow) was in that tiny, vocal, and active fringe. There were only maybe twenty thousand party members in the United States in 1934, but they had big ideas. This Depression looked to them like the final crisis of capitalism that Karl Marx had prophesied.

American communists seized this moment to position themselves as the friend and champion of the poor and marginalized: farmworkers, factory workers, struggling shopkeepers, coal miners, and African Americans. Communists were agitating for a forty-hour workweek, higher wages, and robust labor unions open to females, immigrants, and every ethnic minority. They were protesting evictions, leading rent strikes, demanding that landowners in the South give sharecroppers fair pay for their toil. When nine Black teenage boys were wrongfully convicted of rape and sentenced to die in Alabama, it was the CPUSA that paid for lawyers to argue the case up to the U.S. Supreme Court and helped organize mass demonstrations in support of the Scottsboro Boys.

But overall, the numbers were never there. Even after Stalin's "popular front" policy cut loose American Reds from the dictates of Moscow to make common cause with all sorts of native lefty causes, organized communism was never as strong or capable in the United States as its often hysterical critics would have you believe. Not in the 1930s, its period of most rapid expansion (when membership passed fifty thousand, then sixty thousand), and not twenty years later, when the country would frantically self-conflagrate our civil liberties in the panic of our biggest Red Scare. But that's not to say there wasn't a powerful appeal in the idea of a proletarian, more or less multiracial American populism, particularly one with agrarian roots. And particularly at a time of widespread, prolonged economic pain.

Having grown up a part of that marginalized and largely forgotten mass of Americans, Huey Long understood this lesson in his bones. And he

Huey Long leads the LSU marching band.

used it for all it was worth. He had by 1934 emerged as President Franklin Roosevelt's most talented political antagonist and was already building a remarkable grassroots political movement, which he called Share Our Wealth. The basis of Long's Share Our Wealth platform was as simple and straightforward as a biblical edict, and it sure sounded like one. "None shall be too rich, and none shall be too poor," Long would tell his listening audience, occasionally a national audience on the NBC radio network. "America will become a land sharing the fruits of the land, not for the favored few, not to satisfy greed, but that all may live in a land in which the Lord has provided an abundance sufficient for the luxury and convenience of the people in general."

Long was offering a concrete set of policies to help bring this into being: A guaranteed monthly pension for every American over the age of sixty who needed it. A guaranteed college education for all who desired it. "No youth will have to depend on the wealth of his parents to have a college education," he would say, "but on their own energy and their own ability." A guaranteed annual family income equal to a third of the national average. A guaranteed stake, also worth a third of the average family wealth in America: "enough for a home, an automobile, a radio, and the ordinary conveniences." *None too poor!*

Huey Long had a plan to pay for this too, simply by taking the money from where it was stashed. He'd been pointing at it since he first sprinted into public life as a loud, brash, preternaturally talented twenty-four-year-old Louisiana attorney back in 1918. Less than 2 percent of the American citizenry was hoarding more than 60 percent of the total wealth in the country back then, he said, and their share had only grown in the years since, through the economic boom of the 1920s and the frightening upheaval of the ongoing Depression. When he became a senator, Long called for a federal tax on all that accumulated wealth, and not just a progressive tax but an *exponential* tax. The first million was in the clear; the second million would be taxed at 1 percent; the third million 2 percent; the fourth at 4 percent; the fifth at 8 percent; the sixth million at 16 percent; the seventh at 32 percent; the eighth at 64 percent; the ninth million and above at 99 percent.

Long insisted he had no interest in punishing anyone and promised not to strip the rich of their mansions or their yachts or their seaplanes: "I'm gonna leave them with every palace, with every convenience, with every comfort." Depending on the speech, depending on the exact audience and setting, the details of his proposed wealth tax were malleable. The point was to create the perception that he was applying simple Robin Hood–style arithmetic to the problem of economic injustice. He meant to cap individual family wealth at $5 million. Or maybe $50 million. Or maybe three hundred times the wealth of the average household. Never mind the multiplication tables, Huey said it would be simple. Just use federal tax laws to "take the billion-dollar fortunes and strip 'em down to fryin' size." *None too rich!*

Long didn't spend much time parsing numbers and statistics in his speeches, but he did have a genius for painting down-home word pictures to explain the national economy. The Lord, Long insisted, "has called the barbecue. 'Come to my feast,' He said to 125 million American people. But Morgan and Rockefeller and Mellon and Baruch have waltzed up and took 85 percent of the vittles off the table. Now how you gonna feed the balance of the people? What's Morgan and Baruch and Rockefeller and Mellon gonna do with all that grub? . . . When they've got everything on the God's living earth that they can eat and they can wear and they can live in and all that their children can live in and eat and wear and all their children's children can use, then we got to call Mr. Morgan, and Mr. Mellon, and Mr. Rockefeller, and say 'Come back *here*. Put some stuff back on this table *here* that you took away. Leave something else for the American people.' "

That was a red-hot message in 1934, in the lowest trough of the Depression. By the end of its first year, Long's Share Our Wealth Society counted nearly eight million active members, in more than twenty-five thousand separate local clubs across America. At one of Long's speeches in an open field near Des Moines, a crowd twenty thousand strong signaled "Amen!" when he asked if they were for a more equal distribution of wealth.

And unlike most populist pols, the Kingfish, as he liked to be called, had an actual track record of getting things done. In the six and a half years since he had taken power in his home state, the forty-one-year-old Long had delivered twenty-five hundred miles of new paved roads, forty bridges, free textbooks in the public schools, free night schools to teach more than 100,000 illiterate adults to read, and state hospitals to serve everybody in Louisiana, whether they possessed the means to pay their medical bills or not. The state's voter registration increased by 76 percent in a single year after Long forced the Louisiana legislature to repeal the poll tax. He also raised taxes on corporations doing business in the state, especially on the oil companies that had dominated the state legislature for decades.

It was an almost unbelievable record of accomplishment— practical help for regular people, at a time when all the regular people of this country were desperately in need of some practical help. The political story behind how he did it was either exciting or terrifying, depending on the cut of your ideological jib. The bare truth of Huey Long's Louisiana miracle is that he was able to get it all done because he effectively did away with any competing po- litical interests in the state, not to mention any checks and bal- ances on his own power to rule. Long's signature innovation in American power politics was bringing the whole state of Louisi- ana under the control of his political machine. He took total con- trol of all elections in the state. Also all appointed offices. He stacked every level of state government and even local government with people who answered only to him. He used bribes and threats to simply take anything he wanted, including from the state legis- lature. And he reaped the rewards—not just the policy outcomes he dictated as if handed down by a king, but tribute, sent up to said king by every penny-ante official in the state who owed him their job. And they all did. He ran Louisiana like a mob boss. Ev- erybody kicked up to him. He had a piece of everyone's action. And even the credible accusations of kidnapping and attempted murder that followed him around never quite stuck. He had the police and the prosecutors sewn up tight, too.

"I am the Constitution," Long said. "There *may* be smarter men than me, but they ain't in Louisiana."

The Kingfish's program of wildly progressive economics, key to his popularity and to his national political prospects, was a sideshow for Lawrence Dennis. Dennis was in the middle of writing his *Coming American Fascism* book, and Huey Long looked like the proof in the autocratic pudding: "It takes a man like Long to lead the masses," he said. Here was a single man who was harnessing "the discontent of the people" and using every tool available to make himself into an all-powerful figure in his home state. And he was still on the rise! A less cynical man could look at Long's signature policies and call him a figure of the left; for a Lawrence Dennis, what was much more important about Huey was his gleeful grave digging for American democratic norms. This, finally, was a man who not only had the kinds of skills that would be needed to end America's small-*r* republican form of government; he plainly intended to do just that. Dennis also took note of Long's effective use of optics to consolidate political strength. Huey Long understood the power of putting his power on display, traveling with a phalanx of uniformed guards from the Louisiana State Police and a side helping of menacing heavily armed men not in uniform at all, "the skull crushers," Long's own brother called them.

Then, too, there was Long's seemingly limitless appetite for and accretion of authority. "A perfect democracy can come close to looking like a dictatorship," Huey told one reporter, "a democracy in which the people are so satisfied they have no complaint." He was elected to the U.S. Senate in 1930, but insisted he could simultaneously hold on to the governorship until 1932, when he installed his chosen puppet. And why shouldn't he? Who was going to stop him? "Control of a state government at once gives command to public funds, the taxing power to get more, and armed militia, and a judiciary," Dennis explained to interested readers like Philip Johnson. The state militia was the key, according to

Dennis, because it gave a governor like Long a ready-made military organization, with "distinctive uniforms" and a willingness to follow any orders that came from him alone. "Communism in Russia triumphed chiefly because Lenin captured the loyalty of the troops," Dennis reminded his readers. First a state. Then a nation.

PHILIP JOHNSON'S LIFE in New York had begun to get wobbly near the end of 1934. Jimmie Daniels dumped him for a wealthy older man and left for Europe, and the insecure Johnson fretted that his lack of sexual prowess had something to do with it. His interior decorating business catering to the city's nouveaux riches was going nowhere. He was losing sway at the Museum of Modern Art, where Lincoln Kirstein had started warning its key trustees, including Nelson Rockefeller and his mother, that the museum was in danger of being "tarred with the Fascist brush." Kirstein's whispered misgivings had also helped scuttle the Art, Inc., concessions at Rockefeller Center. Johnson's standing in New York was at a low, and he was working himself into a full-on snit about it.

The time was perfect for Johnson to fall headlong under the ideological spell of Huey Long. With Lawrence Dennis in his ear and Long on his mind, Johnson could practically conjure that Hitlerian Potsdam scene shimmering to life on the American horizon. Things will be different "when the revolution comes," he started to tell friends and acquaintances, who rarely understood what the hell he was talking about. Johnson spoke of becoming one of Huey Long's key brain trusters or his minister of fine arts. At his most manic, Johnson's personal assistant Ruth Merrill recalled, he speculated that he, Philip Johnson, might himself end up being the American Hitler. "Johnson felt the fate of this country rested on his shoulders," Merrill later told FBI investigators, "and that by joining with Huey Long he could eventually depose Long from control of the country and gain it for himself."

So just before the winter solstice in 1934, Philip Johnson and Alan Blackburn summoned a reporter from the *New York Herald*

Tribune to Johnson's Museum of Modern Art office for an exclusive. The "adventurers, with an intellectual overlay," explained to the newspaperman that they were taking a sabbatical from MoMA to start a new political movement. They were calling it the National Party, and they were lighting out for Louisiana the very next day to sign on Huey Long as their new leader.

Johnson and Blackburn revealed the National Party's seemingly idiotic slogan to the reporter ("The need is for one party"), as well as the snazzy new pennants they had designed—blazoned with aerodynamic flying-wedge emblems—which they would be mounting on Johnson's automobile. They also laid out their new party's platform, which consisted in its entirety of "direct action" and "more emotionalism" in government. No policy at all, just feelings. And action! Lots of action. Johnson said they wanted nothing but courage and loyalty from their followers, the kind of courage and loyalty that gangsters John Dillinger and Al Capone inspired, he explained. And they talked all of this through with the reporter while leafing through firearms catalogs and choosing the weapons they might take with them on the road. "Mr. Johnson favored a submachine gun," the *Herald Tribune* reported, "but Mr. Blackburn preferred one of the larger types of pistol."

The next day the pair of twentysomethings attached their flying-wedge felt pennants to the fenders of Johnson's baronial twelve-cylinder Packard touring car, loaded it with volumes of Shakespeare, Machiavelli, Nietzsche, Dennis, and weapons catalogs (if not the actual weapons yet), and headed south to offer their services to Huey Long.

Lincoln Kirstein, for one, was not unhappy to hear that Johnson and Blackburn had bailed on New York. Kirstein had managed to keep his sense of humor about their weird fascist buccaneering, but that had changed when he stopped by their office to needle the pair by announcing his new membership in the Communist Party, that great bogeyman of the American right. The adventurers were in no mood for joking. Blackburn asked for

Kirstein's latest address and then threatened to have him beaten up. Kirstein laughed it off at the time, but what he could not shake for years was the memory of Johnson's nastiest remark to him: "He told me I was number one on his list for elimination in the coming revolution."

CHAPTER THREE

UMWEGE

If you were a young German attorney looking to make your mark in the all-powerful Nazi Party in 1933, turns out Fayetteville, Arkansas, was a surprisingly auspicious place to be. As part of their crusade to make daily life intolerable for German Jews, the Nazis by then had started enacting a double-edged plan: generating menacing political and cultural cues that encouraged widespread, consistent, and murderous intimidation of Jewish citizens by fellow Germans while also drafting civil and criminal codes that placed all persons of Jewish heritage outside the privileges and protections of the state. Toward that latter aim, one particular foreign country offered a road map of sorts. And so, in 1933, the German Foreign Office dispatched a young man named Heinrich Krieger to the University of Arkansas School of Law.

"Awful it may be to contemplate, but the reality is that the Nazis took a sustained, significant, and sometimes even eager interest in the American example of race law," James Q. Whitman wrote in his landmark 2017 book, *Hitler's American Model*. "Nazi lawyers regarded America, not without reason, as the innovative world leader in the creation of racist law."

Whitman's book made a splash when it was first published in 2017, but his central finding would hardly have been news to the millions of people living under the yoke of legal segregation in the American South in the 1930s. *The Pittsburgh Courier*—then the nation's most widely circulated African American newspaper—

published an editorial in 1933 titled "Hitler Learns from America." Langston Hughes put it more poetically in 1937: "Fascists is Jim Crow peoples, honey."

When young Heinrich Krieger was sent to the American South to take notes for the führer, he was quick to see how the United States could provide a sort of conceptual prototype for new German law. Jim Crow laws segregating Black Americans and stripping them of legal and political rights were just one of the many bulwarks in American law constructed for the protection of white people from the "lower races." In his carrel at the law library in Fayetteville, Krieger was in a catbird's seat for studying all kinds of finely crafted American statutory racial hierarchy. He was able to conduct a comprehensive study of more than thirty states whose laws and courts forced Black Americans into second-class citizenship, as well as U.S. federal law governing immigration, Indian treaties, and treatment of people in America's new territorial acquisitions.

In the book that grew out of his year in Arkansas, *Das Rassenrecht in den Vereinigten Staaten* (Race law in the United States), Krieger laid out his case that "race protection" had been a crucial motivator in the construction of America's tiered system of justice. He wasn't out on some weird Germanic limb in doing so; a long line of revered statesmen and political figures had essentially admitted the same. Theodore Roosevelt, for instance, might have castigated Sylvester Viereck as a German agent who should bounce back to Berlin instead of hounding his fellow Americans here, but in his broader view of the human condition Roosevelt saw white Americans and white Germans as allies in an ongoing war between the races in which the white (Anglo-Saxon) man was bound to fight against all comers: Blacks, the Irish (at least until he needed the Irish vote), Slavs, Latins, and Asians. "From the United States and Australia the Chinaman is kept out because the democracy, with much clearness of vision, has seen that his presence is ruinous to the white race," Roosevelt had written in 1894. "The whole civilization of the future owes a debt of gratitude greater than can be expressed in words to that democratic policy which has kept the temperate zones of the new and newest worlds a heritage for the white people."

A crowning achievement in the march of "civilization," Roosevelt had opined in his book *The Winning of the West*, was the white triumph over the vast Native population in North America. The conquered peoples, Roosevelt asserted without any actual knowledge, lived an existence "but a few degrees less meaningless, squalid and ferocious than that of the wild beasts." (Hitler also took note of that empire-building march with the U.S. cavalry as the spear's point. Americans had "gunned down the millions of Redskins to a few hundred thousand," he said, "and now keep the modest remnant under observation in a cage.")

When he had become president in 1901, Theodore Roosevelt was still in full cry on the topic of race. His fellow (white) citizens lacked a proper appreciation of the perils at hand, he harangued audiences large and small, or the "courage" to do something about it. White Americans were mixing their genes too freely with other folks, inviting "race suicide." Roosevelt badgered white women to have more (100 percent pure) white babies. This was "warfare of the cradle," Roosevelt would say, and "fundamentally infinitely more important than any other question in this country."

Teddy Roosevelt was a standout, but Krieger had no shortage of material to work with from a long line of U.S. presidents. Both Thomas Jefferson and Abraham Lincoln had expressed hopes that all people of African descent living in the United States would one day be shipped overseas. "The two races, equally free, cannot live in the same government," asserted Jefferson, who lived in fear of a slave revolt. Krieger could also point to American presidents of more recent vintage. Woodrow Wilson in 1913 had resegregated the federal workforce by law, purging Black Americans from the best and best-paying government jobs. Calvin Coolidge in 1924 had signed into law radical restrictions on immigration, but not before publishing a stinging little essay in *Good Housekeeping* magazine titled "Whose Country Is This?" Immigration restrictions, Coolidge wrote under the *Good Housekeeping* Seal of Approval, were a necessary first step in walling off white America

from "the vicious, the weak of body, the shiftless or the improvident." These types, he implied, could be identified by nationality
and skin color. "There are racial considerations too grave to be
brushed aside for any sentimental reasons," Coolidge wrote. "Biological laws tell us that certain divergent people will not mix or
blend. . . . The unassimilated alien child menaces our children."

The architect of Coolidge's 1924 immigration restrictions was
a wealthy eugenicist lawyer who went on to form the American
Coalition of Patriotic Societies, whose slogan was "Keep America
American." In 1936, a leader of the group was given an honorary
doctorate by a Nazi-affiliated German university for his advance-
ment in North America of racial eugenics—the fake science of
preserving racial purity. When Hitler's final solution hit full pace
in Europe, the same American Coalition of Patriotic Societies
would lead the charge to block Jewish refugees from coming to
America.

The chair of Public Law in Munich, home city of the Nazi
Party, praised Coolidge's restrictive immigration quotas as exemplary law, writing in a 1933 article that Coolidge's approach "represents a carefully thought-through system that first of all protects
the United States from the eugenic point of view against inferior
elements trying to immigrate."

German national and all-round white man that he was, Heinrich Krieger himself had no trouble gaining a visa to the United
States and admission to one of its government-financed institutions of higher learning. At Fayetteville, he turned out to be an
incisive observer, and his research ultimately identified the central
tension in American race law and life: How do you legally privilege white men as a "ruling race" in a land in which the written
Constitution—and quite explicitly the Fourteenth Amendment—
guarantees equal protection of the law to all, regardless of skin
color?

For Krieger, the genius of the American legal system was in
how it allowed for the circumvention of this obvious contradiction
by use of juridical *Umwege* (pronounced UM-vee-guh), secret and
twisting passageways of reasoning that led to whatever outcome

was politically desirable. Krieger understood this would be a bit of a revelation to legal scholars and practitioners in Germany, where they operated within the limits of civil law—a mechanical system in which the written statutes and codes were not at all fungible. In the United States, where common law held sway, judges had (and have) more room to maneuver.

On matters of race, Krieger explained to his Nazi legal cohorts, the American system of justice took all the room it needed. It was a bouillabaisse of "artificial line-drawing, partly by statute, partly by the courts," spiced with illogic, arbitrariness, and incoherence. Exhibit A was a series of U.S. Supreme Court decisions in the Insular Cases, handed down in the aftermath of the Spanish-American War. The result of that war—the U.S. deathblow to what remained of the Spanish Empire—had turned heads all over Europe and delivered to America a new and far-flung set of territories including Puerto Rico, Guam, Hawaii, and the Philippines and all the (brown-skinned) inhabitants therein, inhabitants who were clearly due the rights and privileges enjoyed by mainland Americans. Clearly, that is, until the U.S. Supreme Court held, despite straightforward language in the Constitution to the contrary, that the federal government was not bound to confer these rights on these particular noobs. ("The Constitution follows the flag," Secretary of War Elihu Root famously quipped when the court announced its unreasoned decision, "but doesn't quite catch up with it.") These islands and their likely ungovernable and unassimilable "alien races" *belonged* to the United States, the court opined, but were not *a part of it*. Puerto Ricans, for example, the justices explained nonsensically, were "foreign to the United States in a domestic sense." Which is exactly as dumb as it sounds.

But not without value, if you just looked at it the right way. "At first glance," one German legal scholar had already written, the U.S. Supreme Court pronouncements appeared "exceedingly motley, almost confusing, especially to an eye that is accustomed to German decisional law." But if you allow the *Umwege* to do their work on you, American race law's secret passageways can lead you beyond the strict, narrow limitations of the actual text of the law and into the more expansive vaults of intuition: "As we study it more deeply and reflect on it in an unbiased way, however, we must concede that there is a wealth of life and immediacy in these decisions, a thorough intellectual and juristic examination of the material from the most varied points of view, a penetrating recourse to the ultimate questions, an impartial formulation of the arguments for and against, and a proud appeal to the living legal intuitions for the American people that lie behind them, which reveal the high legal and political talents and the cultivation of the people of the Union." In other words, Americans had found ways—on matters of race—to use the law to justify just about anything they wanted to do. Leave the egalitarian, idealistic language on the books, but interpret that language however you need to, to justify any policy that just feels right.

The Nazis were in love with this idea. It meant you didn't have to spell out your eliminationist plans in black and white; you just needed to act on those plans, with compliant and complacent lawyers writing artfully around the worst of your intentions and with courts providing assurance that they would get what you were going for *intuitively* and the law wouldn't get in your way.

The fruits of Krieger's labor at the University of Arkansas proved most useful to the Nazi-dominated Ministry of Justice and

A lynching in America, 1935

its adjuncts throughout the German government, who were tasked with accelerating the alienation of all Jews in Germany, and who wanted the law on their side to help. "The Jews in Germany represent a thoroughly extraordinary economic power," one councillor at the German Ministry of Justice explained that year. "As long as they have a voice in economic affairs in our German Fatherland, as they do now, as long as they have the most beautiful automobiles, the most beautiful motorboats, as long as they play a prominent role in all pleasure spots and resorts, and everywhere that costs money, as long as all this is true I do not believe that they can really be segregated from the body of the German *Volk* in the absence of statutory law." So, just regulations enforcing different rules for Jews would not be enough. The Nazis needed to criminalize Jewishness itself. But how, exactly?

Here is where Krieger's investigation into U.S. law proved to be of most practical assistance. Indian laws, immigration laws, Jim Crow laws in America, were all based on one basic idea: that the "superior" white race must be walled away and protected from all others. If everyone in power agrees on that as your tacit starting assumption and also your ultimate goal, you can *Umwege* your way there through almost any picayune black-letter dispute. Define the races under law (any vague stab at it will do—judges will know what you mean), mandate the separation of the races or enact any other race-based rule in order to protect one group from the other, and, voilà, the ranking of racial superiority and the justified subjugation of one race by another will be encoded in law firmly enough to empower any racist improvising by the necessary authorities while still giving the impression of legality. With these rules backed up in criminal statutes, state violence could be employed to keep the proverbial peace, to impose domination of one race over another, all under color of law.

America offered so many examples of how it could be done. Yes, the U.S. Constitution had its grandiloquent promise of equal protection of the law, but in practical application that concept yielded easily before the imperative of race protection. You didn't have, for example, explicit strictures in twentieth-century U.S. law providing that Black Americans and white Americans would have different enumerated rights when it came to marriage. Nevertheless, interracial marriage in much of America was a criminal offense, punishable by fines or imprisonment. Even without a systematic effort to uniformly define "white" or "Black" in some sciencey-sounding way (the Nazis noted that Nevada specifically mentioned "Ethiopians" in its law, while other states referred to "African descent"), just committing to the idea that the criminal law could be used to enforce barriers between the races was enough. Judges would know what to do. All in the well-understood spirit of protecting whiteness from imagined genetic incursion. The explicit assurance of "equal protection" of the law was simply elided, ignored by Americans who invented and sustained these legal constructs, confident that the legal system would allow what was needed, regardless.

Here, for the Nazis, was a template for the taking. The racist goals of the Nazi government were well understood; those values were to be pursued in the law whether the inherited German legal system prescribed or proscribed them. German jurists and Nazi Party officials were encouraged to approach their work, as Whitman notes, "in the spirit of Hitler."

"American race legislation certainly does not base itself on the idea of racial difference," one German criminal law expert noted in a crucial June 1934 internal debate about how to put German law to the task of achieving Hitler's aims for the Jews. "But to the extent this legislation is aimed against Negroes and others, [it is based] absolutely certainly on the idea of the inferiority of the other race, in the face of which the purity of the American race must be protected." White Americans, with segregation, were simply protecting themselves against a lesser, alien race "attempting to gain the upper hand." The Jews in Germany, a senior official in Hitler's Ministry of Justice explained, "must be kept enduringly apart," a task that "can only be achieved through statutory measures that forbid absolutely all sexual mixing of a Jew with a German, and impose severe criminal punishment."

The American experience in "race protection," in using the law to create a criminally enforced racially organized social structure, had given Nazi lawyers a great jumping-off point. What followed was their Law for the Protection of German Blood and German Honor, passed in September 1935:

> Marriages between Jews and citizens of German or kindred blood are forbidden.
>
> Marriages concluded in defiance of this law are void, even if, for the purposes of evading this law, they were concluded abroad. . . .
>
> Sexual relations outside marriage between Jews and nationals of German or kindred blood are forbidden.

Violators faced a year in prison, hard labor, and fines.

A second law, passed two months later, stripped Jews of German citizenship and all political rights. A Jew, as defined by this new statute, was "anyone who is descended from at least three grandparents who are racially full Jews" or anyone "who is descended from two full Jewish grandparents if (a) he belonged to the Jewish religious community at the time this law was issued, or joined the community later, (b) he was married to a Jewish person, at the time the law was issued, or married one subsequently, (c) he is the offspring of a marriage with a Jew, which was contracted after the Law for the Protection of German Blood and German Honor became effective, (d) he is the offspring of an extramarital relationship with a Jew, and will be born out of wedlock after July 31, 1936."

THE OTHER NOTABLE move the Nazi-controlled Reichstag made at its session in September 1935, as Whitman points out, was to formally adopt the swastika as the official symbol of the new Germany. The swastika had long been the symbol of the Nazi Party, but now the national legislature was weighing the adoption of the swastika as the emblem of the German nation. The United States figured in that decision too. Back in July of that year, while the head Nazis were still settling on their new flag's final design, a powerful new German ocean liner, the SS *Bremen,* entered its berth at Pier 86 in New York, flying an outsized swastika. Plenty of people in America already understood exactly what the insignia represented. A crowd of nearly two thousand New Yorkers, variously described in the ensuing police and newspaper reports as "rioters" or "Communist sympathizers," gathered to demonstrate displeasure. The melee briefly turned violent. The protesters beat one police officer; a city detective shot one of the demonstrators in the groin.

Five of the protesters managed to board the *Bremen,* fend off the ship's crew, haul down the flag, and toss it unceremoniously into the Hudson River. The crowd roared approval. "What a beautiful sight it was," said one young American woman who was there that night, "to see the flag, in the spotlight, go downriver." German officials were incensed and lodged an official protest through diplomatic channels. The U.S. Department of State released a statement offering regret that the "German national emblem" had not "received the respect to which it was entitled."

The Germans were even more livid when a local New York City magistrate released all but one of the flag maulers without sanction from the notorious holding prison the Tombs and then used the occasion to lecture Adolf Hitler and company. Judge Louis B. Brodsky went out of his way to explain that many regarded this new emblem of Germany as a "black flag of piracy" and believed that the SS *Bremen* had engaged in a "gratuitously brazen flaunting of an emblem which symbolizes all that is antithetical to American ideals of the God given and inalienable rights of all peoples to life, liberty, and the pursuit of happiness." The judge's long speech from the bench took aim at the Nazis' "war on religious freedom . . . the suppression of the blessed trinity of free speech, freedom of the press and lawful assembly, the degradation of culture, an international menace threatening freedom; a revolt against civilization—in brief, if I may borrow a biological concept, an atavistic throw-back to premedieval, if not barbaric, social and political conditions."

The German ambassador issued another formal protest in response. The Nazi commissar of justice railed against "the characteristic Jewish impudence of Magistrate Brodsky of New York," crowing that "the time is past that the German people can be insulted by Jews."

The U.S. secretary of state, Cordell Hull, somehow felt obliged to apologize to Germany for Judge Brodsky, calling the judge's opinion "unfortunately" worded and saying that from the perspective of the U.S. government "it is to be regretted."

The Nazi minister of propaganda, Joseph Goebbels, confided to his diary that week, "The Judge Broudski [*sic*] in New York has insulted the German national flag. . . . Our answer: In Nuremberg the Reichstag will meet and declare the swastika flag to be our sole national flag." In his speech introducing the laws, Hermann Göring denounced Judge Brodsky by name and called him an "uppity Jew." Hitler took time in his own Nuremberg speech to publicly thank President Franklin Delano Roosevelt and his administration for being "thoroughly decent and honorable" in denouncing Brodsky's recent comments. But he also took time to suggest that if the United States and its friends didn't bring "international Jewish agitation" to heel, the laws in the Reich might become even more harsh.

CHAPTER FOUR

"LOUISIANA WAS NOT QUITE READY"

The Hitler-adoring, would-be-fascist aesthete Philip Johnson arrived in Louisiana's capital swelled with his own youthful imaginings. Johnson and his lackey, Alan Blackburn, full of big dreams, nosed their National Party pennant–flying Packard into Baton Rouge in the first days of 1935, when Nazis in Germany were still working out their first run of explicitly antisemitic law. Johnson and Blackburn hoped to hitch their wagon to the shooting star of American politics, the U.S. senator Huey Long, who was already making noise about challenging Franklin Delano Roosevelt in the next year's presidential election.

Johnson was convinced that Senator Long would immediately recognize the many useful talents he and Blackburn could bring to the Kingfish's Share Our Wealth political operation. The two could write political speeches (Harvard men, after all), or art direct and produce stylish pamphlets and publications (just look at what they'd done for architecture and design of the so-called International Style). They could even create stages and backdrops for Long's raucous, immense political rallies (Johnson had seen the nuts and bolts of those awe-inspiring sets, firsthand, in Potsdam).

Problem was, they couldn't get an audience with Long. Huey Long was a very hard man to get to meet in 1935. In fact, he was pretty much unreachable.

Not that Philip Johnson didn't know where Huey Long was at almost any time. From anywhere in Baton Rouge, at all hours of the night, Philip Johnson or anyone could see the beacon of light glowing brightly, twenty-four stories high, atop the art deco capitol that towered above the city streets. Huey Long had won the funding for that pricey capitol building in his term as governor, and even though his official job was in Washington, D.C., now, he still reserved a top floor of the capitol in Baton Rouge as his personal apartments. The Olympian altitude, he explained, set him above the pollen and the dust that had long plagued his sleep.

When the Kingfish did emerge from his suites, you could barely see him for the ever-growing cadre of armed men surrounding him, a scene that screamed "dictator" in any language. From the single Louisiana state trooper he had been assigned at the start of his first year as governor, Long's protection detail grew quickly to include at least a dozen troopers. In early 1935, as the Kingfish's supporters whispered about rumored marplots and assassination cabals, the head of Louisiana's Bureau of Criminal Identification kept adding additional state police to the detail. That ever-growing group was further supplemented by civilian toughs who caught Long's eye.

Long's little traveling personal army was not armed in any uniform way, but they were *amply* armed. Murphy Roden, a former state trooper, had a .38-caliber Colt super-automatic tucked into his suit jacket. Joe Messina, a slow-witted two-hundred-pound side of beef with deep-set, wary eyes and a canine devotion to Long—the Kingfish had plucked Messina from his lowly job as house detective at a seedy hotel—carried a small-caliber pistol in one pocket and a blackjack in another. George McQuiston sported a snub-nosed revolver and, on special occasions, a sawed-off shotgun haphazardly concealed inside a paper bag.

These musclemen were not merely for show, as they had demonstrated with increasing frequency—often against reporters who worked for what Long sometimes called the "lyinnewspapers." In the final legislative session of 1934, Long's guards arrested two newspapermen who tried to enter the (unlawfully) closed senate chamber. When the photographer Leon Trice snapped a picture of Long bickering with a state representative in the public lobby outside the house chamber, Huey's enforcers sucker-punched Trice and threw him ass over elbows down a flight of marble stairs. Another newsman reported that Senator Long had "stood by laughing" at the sight of Trice's head bouncing down the steps.

Trice got it worse six months later, not long after Philip Johnson had arrived in Louisiana. In the first week of February 1935, Trice took an innocuous photograph of Senator Long disembarking from a train in New Orleans. Messina, according to a wire service reporter at the scene, "rushed the slender 125-pound Leon Trice, fists flailing. He shouted, 'Put down that . . . thing.' Messina slugged Trice in the face as Trice pleaded: 'Don't do that, Joe.' Huey said not a word. He stalked with an impressive air to a group of waiting automobiles and, surrounded by his bodyguards, sirens screaming, drove away at terrific speed down Canal Street, ignoring all traffic lights."

Witnesses said Messina had first beaten Trice with his bare fists and, after the defenseless photographer had fallen, with his blackjack. The beating was so brutal that Trice had to be taken to the hospital, and the district attorney in New Orleans was moved to file charges of assault with the intent to murder against Messina.

The senator's motley semiofficial protective cohort stood by the doors of the legislative chambers in the capitol as the Boss prowled the floor, buttonholing lawmakers, demanding that they pass his bill to, say, transfer all authority rightfully exercised by the City of New Orleans to the administration of Governor Oscar K. Allen, which is to say to the Long political machine. "We have a Governor [Allen] who weeps about it like a woman," noted one informed wag in Baton Rouge, "and serves, like a dishwasher in a restaurant serves his master." When that particular bill did pass, as Huey's bills always did, it gave the Long machine direct control of all the thousands of patronage jobs to be distributed in the state's one true metropolis. This meant yet more control, more power, and not incidentally a huge new haul of kickbacks from the wage earners, whether sincerely appreciative or simply strong-armed.

Long's bodyguards remained at the senator's side whenever he strode across the travertine marble floor of the capitol rotunda, down the forty-eight steps at the front of the building (one for every state in the Union), and into his already purring limousine. The bodyguard retinue was always there in Long's motorcade, too—sirens wailing—with the Kingfish sitting pretty in the padded backseat, smoking his ten-inch cigar.

The men kept a wary eye on other shoppers as Senator Long was measured and fitted for his custom-made silk shirts and double-breasted suits at Godchaux's department store on Canal Street. They kept bawdy revelers away from Huey's table at the Roosevelt Hotel bar. The Roosevelt was the city's first post-Prohibition nightspot to admit women, and the bar's owner, Seymour Weiss, encouraged the loveliest young salesclerks from Godchaux's to stop in after a long day's work. Huey was happy to invite a few of them over to his table to partake of his favorite drink, the Ramos Gin Fizz, which features heavy cream, egg whites, orange flower water, and then a squirt of seltzer to add "a touch of effervescence" to the gin. All the bartenders knew exactly how to mix it to the Kingfish's specs.

Long's hair-trigger security detail was particularly watchful when the Roosevelt's owner, Seymour Weiss, stopped by the senator's table. Weiss was Huey's key bagman in the Big Easy, and he often came by with sacksful of cash from companies that wanted a crack at state contracts for highways, bridges, hospitals, schools, and other public works projects, all of which Long controlled.

PHILIP JOHNSON DIDN'T know much about the mechanics of politics, but he intuited enough to realize that it might not be wise to directly approach Long without benefit of an actual and formal invitation. Johnson and Blackburn never did get an audience with Long on their first tour of Baton Rouge. But they didn't give up. When they found out that Long was decamping from Louisiana to D.C. to check in on his day job in the Senate, Johnson and Blackburn temporarily ditched their Packard touring car and hopped on the Kingfish's train north. The pair then took rooms in the Broadmoor hotel in Washington, just a few floors below Long's suites, where the senator liked to meet visiting foreign dignitaries while still in his purple silk pajamas.

Still, despite Johnson's and Blackburn's unmistakable show of enthusiasm and fealty, Long had no use for them. He was already long on bootlickers and flatterers, and fine for money, having just pocketed $350,000 in "legal fees" from Louisiana's Tax and Public Service Commissions, not to mention his under-the-Roosevelt-Hotel-table take from Seymour Weiss and his flood of kickbacks from state employees. The Kingfish did finally agree to a meeting with the strange boys living downstairs from him, sometime around February 1935, but that was as far as it went. When Alan Blackburn leaked a story to a Washington reporter that he and Philip Johnson had mastered a new piece of technology that would be the perfect complement to Huey Long's indefatigable communication skills (the Visomatic slideshow machine), the Kingfish did not take the bait. He reportedly also had a look at some of Johnson's amateur attempts at speechwriting and tossed them aside.

Philip Johnson did have a vaguely substantive meeting with Senator Long's personal secretary, but it did not go well. Johnson was still shaking his head about the episode almost sixty years later, in an interview he gave when the American Academy of Achievement bestowed upon him its Golden Plate Award. Turns out an actual practitioner of power politics was not that much interested in Johnson's rhetoric, or art direction, or new communications technology, or pseudo-fascist theory. "One of [Senator Long's] people said to me, I'll never forget this, 'How many votes do you control?'" Johnson remembered. The answer would be two for sure, his and Blackburn's, and maybe a dozen other Gray Shirts' up in New York City. The way Long's people saw it, Philip Johnson and his sidekick were a couple of pikers, fascists manqué who didn't have the foggiest notion what it required to actually *accrue* power. The way Johnson saw it, unsurprisingly, the shortcoming was on Long's side, and not Johnson's. "He was so individual and chaotic that there was no way of getting along," Johnson said.

By the dog days of summer 1935, Johnson was contemplating

whether to take the advice of Long's secretary, who had told him to ship out to his hometown in Ohio and try a run for Congress under the Share Our Wealth banner. While Johnson and Blackburn had ceased following Long around like excited little pups, the pair was still paying very close attention to the press coverage of his every movement. They were pleased to see that Long was hinting at a third-party run for the presidency in 1936. Even if he was unable to outright win election and remake the presidency in the fashion of his all-powerful consulship in Louisiana, Johnson figured at least his candidacy would likely split the Democrats down the middle. This would deny Roosevelt reelection, and maybe even open the country up to a political free-for-all that could be exploited. And in the lead-up to that chancy presidential campaign season, Long already appeared to have embarked on a project to sow a little chaos.

On the morning of September 8, 1935, according to reports, Huey was back in Baton Rouge, busy whipping votes in a special legislative session he had called. He was about to jam through a bill making it illegal—punishable by fines and imprisonment—for federal officers to exercise any authority in Louisiana that was not explicitly granted by the Constitution of the United States. In blunt terms, Huey was threatening that any federal government officials coming into the state of Louisiana would risk arrest and imprisonment for doing so. It was a big F-U to FDR, and to the whole idea of the sovereignty of the U.S. government. "The broadest and boldest defiance of Federal authority since the Civil War," wrote a reporter for the United Press syndicate.

Bulletins in the next day's newspapers, September 9, 1935, were even more dramatic, but for an entirely different reason: Huey Long had been gut shot the night before, at around 8:30 P.M., while walking through the rotunda of the Louisiana State Capitol. Initial reports were as odd as they were alarming. The suspected assailant was identified as an apolitical twenty-eight-year-old ear, nose, and throat specialist who was scheduled to do two tonsillectomies the next day. The doctor had allegedly slipped inside the iron ring of Long's bodyguards and fired one shot, at point-blank range. The bullet, praise be, had missed all major organs. Doctors had given the Kingfish a series of blood transfusions, according to initial reports, and performed an operation to stop the hemorrhaging. The medical professionals didn't have a lot to say, but Long's political team insisted he would pull through.

So the general public, and Philip Johnson among them, was not well prepared at all for the next day's news bulletin: Senator Huey Long, the ruler of Louisiana and the would-be ruler of the United States, had died of his wounds.

A picture of Huey Long looms over Louisiana's gubernatorial inauguration the year after Long's death.

The day of his funeral in Baton Rouge, more than a hundred thousand of Long's admirers waited in the wet, boiling heat for a glimpse of the passing coffin filled with his mortal remains. "All day men and women fought for a place near the grave, shoving and tugging against the ropes that police and guardsmen used to hold them back," one reporter wrote of the scene. "Every fifteen minutes or so an elderly man or woman would crumple quietly to the ground." A six-year-old girl was nearly trampled in the crush of the crowd. While members of the LSU marching band, in sunsplashed purple-and-gold uniforms, beat out a baleful dirge, and pallbearers shouldered the casket down the forty-eight steps of the capitol, one old-timer fell to his knees. "I don't care," said the man. "I'd just as soon die for Huey."

A representative from Long's Share Our Wealth Society, the Reverend Gerald L. K. Smith, was the featured speaker in the heat that day. Smith was characterized as "a viper," "a leech," "anti-Christian," and "anti-God" by a fellow clergyman (and this was one of his allies), but he was almost as talented an orator as Long himself. Smith knew how to rile a crowd, from any pulpit or podium, and he certainly did that day. Huey Long "died for us," he told the overheated assembly. "The ideals which he planted in our hearts have created a gnawing hunger for a new order. This hunger and pain, this parching thirst for better things can only be healed and satisfied by the completion of that victory toward which he led us. . . . I was with him when he died. I said 'Amen' as he breathed his last. His final prayer was this: 'Oh, God, don't let me die. I have a few more things to do.'"

NEWSPAPERMEN AND POLITICAL observers weren't sure what to make of Huey Long's strange and unexpected death, and they were even more divided on how to sum up his life. Huey Long was a deeply corrupt public figure, hungry for power and money, and remarkably adept at accruing both. But the single idea he rode to political power—that America needed to confront economic inequality and injustice head-on—had enormous appeal. As did the schools and hospitals and toll-free bridges and roads he built. Neither did Long seek to divide Americans, except by class. He loudly proclaimed himself the champion of the have-nots, who are after all much more numerous than the haves. He had "a streak of deep sincerity, a sympathy by no means hypocritical, with the sufferings of the dispossessed, which brought a popular following his other qualities could never have commanded," *The Washington Post* editorialized. However, the *Post* went on, "in the career of Huey Long is epitomized the essential weakness of democracy—the pathetic willingness of the electorate to trust a glib tongue and a dynamic personality. Quite justifiably he was called a forerunner of American Fascism."

Huey's death, by chance, happened the same week the Reichstag enacted the Nuremberg Laws and raised high its swastika flag, and so the German führer was on the front pages also, and in the minds of journalists and readers alike. "That Huey built roads and bridges and provided free schoolbooks nobody will deny, but nobody knows how much they cost or how much money was stolen in the process," wrote one nationally syndicated columnist. "Huey was gradually copying the Hitler state, but Louisiana was not quite ready for blood purges and internment camps."

CHAPTER FIVE

"HE HAD A VERY HIGH OPINION OF ME"

The bells began to ring out across Nuremberg on the afternoon of September 8, 1936, announcing the arrival of the führer at the fourth annual Nazi Party congress—the "Rally of Honor." The city had swelled to a temporary population of 1.5 million, triple its normal size. Thousands of special trains had been rolling into the rail yards for days, disgorging party officials, district leaders, cadres of uniformed Nazi youth, members of the Women's Labor Service and *Bund Deutscher Mädel* (the League of German Girls), soldiers from infantry, artillery, and armor, and the ubiquitous Brownshirts, or storm troopers. The twenty-five-thousand-man *Schutzstaffel* was making its debut in Nuremberg that week and drawing plenty of attention in their menacing jet-black uniforms. The newly outfitted SS troops were on hand for dignitary protection, crowd control, and general-use head cracking. Freshly mounted loudspeakers at the train station were still barking out instructions to the new arrivals, herding them toward their assigned tent camps, and keeping the platforms clear for the next train.

Private homes and public inns were stuffed full; the tent cities and the hastily constructed wooden barracks ringing the medieval city were nearing capacity also. The core of the city teemed with newcomers that day. "All day long streets have been filled with marching Storm Troops, Special Guards, party leaders, and Hitler youth," wrote an American newspaperman on hand to report on the Nazi congress. He estimated 200,000 political workers, 90,000 storm troopers, and 50,000 Hitler Youth. "Together [they] will produce later that mass hysteria that hypnotizes both participants and spectators."

When the bells signaled the arrival of Hitler, the sea of Nazis washed toward city hall to catch a glimpse. A fascist-leaning history professor from American University in Washington (in Nuremberg for research of an academic nature, no doubt) caught sight of a tall, square-jawed American man whom he recognized as an ideological compatriot. "I have a very vivid impression of you striding down the streets of Nuremberg," the professor later wrote to Lawrence Dennis. "I wanted to catch up with you but you were lost in the crowd and my search was in vain." Dennis's biographer Gerald Horne would later write that in that moment America's most outspoken fascist "symbolically melted into the Nazi mass."

Poor Philip Johnson, left leaderless by the death of Huey Long a year earlier, was now stuck in Chicago, forty-five hundred miles away and still looking for his place in *any* authoritarian movement, while his ideological guru, Lawrence Dennis, was in Nuremberg, invited into the engine room of the global fascist enterprise. Dennis was one of a few hundred foreign diplomats, dignitaries, and "thought leaders" the Nazis had deemed sufficiently sympathetic to Hitler's politics to warrant an invitation to observe the proceedings in person. Dennis was already well known to officials up and down the line at the German embassy in Washington, where they maintained a growing file of newspaper clippings by and about the erudite American.

Lawrence Dennis's biographical file alone must have seemed full of possibility to the Nazi officials posted in the United States. He had spent much of his youth in Europe, was fluent in French and German, and had passable Spanish. His time on the Continent had delayed his formal education, but Dennis had finally graduated from the elite prep school Phillips Exeter Academy in 1915, and after a brief sojourn as a junior officer in the American Expeditionary Force in wartime France he got his Harvard degree in 1920, at age twenty-six. He counted among his prized acquaintances a son of Theodore Roosevelt's, a scion of the estimable Brown Brothers Harriman banking concern, and Joseph P. Kennedy Sr., the wildly successful financier who had just served as the first chairman of the new Securities and Exchange Commission and was soon to be confirmed as U.S. ambassador to Great Britain.

Dennis had spent nearly a decade as a diplomat in training in the U.S. State Department. His first foreign posting was in Bucharest in 1920 (where he was accorded the decoration of the Order of the Star of Romania from his host government), and from there he distinguished himself in the revolutionary hot spots of Haiti, Honduras, and Nicaragua. Though he never rose above the rank of chargé d'affaires, Dennis was asked to go mano a mano with several Latin American strongmen and would-be revolutionaries whom the Coolidge administration deemed less than hospitable to American interests in general and American commercial interests in particular. Despite his success there, Dennis left the State Department unexpectedly in 1926, in a huff, complaining on his way out the door about a promotion system that favored connections and upper-class manners to actual abilities and intellect. His squawking got him a good bit of ink in newspapers across the country, and he leaned into the role of a well-informed and mordant social critic.

Dennis testified to Congress and spoke to reporters about American business interests' insistence on stripping Latin American nations of their sovereignty and then fouling up their national finances to a fare-thee-well. He took a cynical scythe to American sweet talk about democracy. "We have founded recent American policy in Nicaragua on the naïve assumption that what Nicaragua mainly needs is fair elections and freedom from revolutions," he preached. "As a matter of fact, among the things Nicaragua most needs are not electoral and civil policing, but primary instruction, sanitation, means of communications, and a better economic structure. . . . These, however, are not exported in the soldier's knapsack."

By the end of 1930, Lawrence Dennis had turned full-time to writing political treatises based on what he had seen at the crossroads of American foreign policy, domestic politics, and private banking. He liked attention, and he liked to shock his audience. Expounding angrily on American hypocrisy and the shortcomings of American democracy got him the reactions he desired. (He would have been a real star on Substack.)

Dennis entered the field of political philosophy at an opportune moment for someone who self-identified as a "maverick" and a "dissenter." The waves of economic disaster that roiled the country and the world after the stock market crash of 1929 (Dennis had prophesied the crash, according to Dennis) opened the field for radical new notions about ripping out existing political systems at their roots and remaking the world in an entirely new image. By the time Hitler rose to power in 1933, Dennis was evangelizing for a strong, unimpeded central government of intellectual and technical elites to plan and run the American economy for the long haul, with no heed for the next fast-approaching election cycle. He cultivated a reputation as an astute and fearless champion of European-style fascism as the irresistible next (and preferred) means of American governance.

So it's no wonder that whenever Lawrence Dennis came to Washington to, say, make a speech at the Shoreham Hotel ballroom—"Is Fascism in the United States Inevitable?"—German diplomats would invite him to dinner to flatter him and fill him in on all the latest exciting happenings in Berlin. It was not hard to see why Lawrence Dennis had been marked as a potentially very useful tool of the Nazi cause in the United States. And Dennis seemed more than happy to play that role.

By the season of the 1936 "Rally of Honor" for Hitler in Nuremberg, the Dennis file at the German embassy bulged not only with clippings about his various speaking engagements up and down the Eastern Seaboard but also with reviews of his most recent book, *The Coming American Fascism.* "Until Mr. Dennis arrived on scene," one reporter noted at the time, "American fascism did not have a prophet."

Lawrence Dennis was both an outspoken proponent of Hitler-style authoritarianism and an avowed isolationist, opposed to

American involvement in foreign wars, especially any war in Europe against Hitler. Simultaneous advocacy of these two copacetic positions was clearly no coincidence, but Dennis portrayed it as if it were. "I took my isolationism from George Washington's Farewell Address and from a long line of classics," he would say. He counted among his friends the most committed isolationists in the U.S. Congress.

The Hitler government's special summons to Nuremberg was the cherry on top of what had been a fascinating months-long string-gathering sojourn in Europe for Dennis, in the summer of 1936. By his own later description, Dennis had been received and celebrated by intellectual, diplomatic, and political elites from one side of the Continent to the other. The most consequential political theorist of the day, the economist John Maynard Keynes, had invited the American to lunch to discuss ideas. The famous British economist "had a very high opinion of me," Dennis bragged. "I was very greatly touched by the fact that he had read my book and read my stuff."

Dennis also had an informal chin-wag with one of the leading left-wing thinkers in Britain, who was also one of his occasional debating opponents, the former MP John Strachey. (Strachey was likely unaware of his wife's lusty pursuit of Dennis back in New York a few years earlier.) As he did with Keynes, Dennis bragged on Strachey's attentions. He "thought very highly of me," Dennis said, and "had read my latest book and considered it a thoroughly sound and adequate exposition of the subject."

Dennis was also received by government officials in Paris who were just then taking stock of Hitler and his regime. "There were no pro-German French," Dennis found, "but there were many French who were against their getting into war and wanted to be neutral." In Moscow, Dennis was shown around by George Kennan, a future architect of American Cold War policy, who was then a thirty-two-year-old chargé d'affaires. Kennan hosted Dennis for meals, took him on the party circuit, and updated him on the current state of the pseudoscience we would eventually call Kremlinology.

Dennis also made a brief but useful visit to Rome. The Mussolini government, having been given a pass by world leaders when it seized Ethiopia by military force just a few months earlier, was clearly tightening its alliance with Hitler and "wanted America to stay out of" any future war in Europe. Mussolini granted Dennis a private one-on-one meeting that lasted an hour, and although Il Duce was close-lipped ("cautious but friendly," in Dennis's telling), Dennis nevertheless deemed it a success. "I just wanted to be able to say that I had met him or seen him," Dennis explained.

All those meetings paled in comparison to the invitation to the Nazi Party's Nuremberg show of strength; this was where the real action was in Europe that summer. "Leaving now for Nuremberg," he wrote home to his wife, Eleanor, at the beginning of September, "where the world will be told where it gets off and what's going to happen, or, at least, where it could be so told by der Fuehrer."

Eleanor Simson Dennis was home in America that summer, tracking her husband across Europe. "They must love you over there for your understanding," she had written to Lawrence from the couple's farmhouse in the Berkshires in Massachusetts. In another, she seemed to gush. "When this reaches you, you will be in Deutschland," she wrote, "right in the heart and pulse of that wonderful nation where men are he-men and women are so womanly. . . . Be nice to all the Germans for me and especially to those brave women who are making babies for Hitler and being slaves so happily and willingly to their men."

Mrs. Dennis had trained in ballet in France and was running her own dance academy in New York City when the couple met a few years earlier. But by the summer of 1936, that dance school was in the rearview mirror. She was living at the family's ramshackle farmhouse in rural Becket, Massachusetts, trying to make ends meet on her husband's spotty income (thank God for occasional checks from Dennis's gazillionaire devotee, Philip Johnson), minding a two-year-old daughter, and about to deliver a second child. All mostly on her own. In fact, when Dennis extended his stay in Europe to watch the Nazis at work and play, he missed the birth of his second daughter, which occurred on September 6, 1936, two days before the opening of the Nuremberg congress.

Dennis's stated views on women and society were about what you might expect ("the paramount objectives of public policy, so far as women are concerned, should be to make good wives and mothers and not to make as many soft berths as possible for old maids and thus to put a premium on the avoidance of marriage"). That blunt, bitter tone wasn't reserved for his pronouncements on gender relations. It was part of what made Dennis the leading spokesman for fascism in America in 1936, and also an exemplar of why certain people found comfort in authoritarian ideology. One big appeal of fascism, if nothing else, was its unapologetic embrace of cruelty. Cruelty toward others, coupled with hypersensitivity toward any slight to oneself.

Reading Dennis's books, articles, and interviews, listening to tapes of his lectures and debates, you get a feeling for a man acutely aware of any affront, cloaking personal insecurity with an armor of certitude. And then that mean streak. "Human nature has not changed materially under liberal capitalism," he wrote in 1935. "The masses have not the intelligence or the humanity, nor the winners the magnanimity, which liberal assumptions have postulated." Lawrence Dennis put on a clinic in name-dropping (Keynes "had a very high opinion of me"); elitism ("Social order requires government and administration by a ruling class or power-exercising class which must always be an aristocracy of management, however selected. . . . For the masses, the school is a necessary process to enable them to read signs and advertisements"); and feigned insouciance ("I'm not very emotional anyway, and I couldn't share the American pro-British and anti-German" feeling).

Dennis, would-be *Übermensch*, often described himself as a man who operated outside the realm of passion—which suggested an extreme lack of self-awareness or a deep need to hide his true self. Anne Morrow Lindbergh, the gimlet-eyed wife of America's hero flier and notable Nazi sympathizer Charles Lindbergh, spent hours in Dennis's company talking political philosophy and parsing world events, but never really got a handle on what was driving him. "He was rather reserved and extremely sensitive," she wrote of Dennis. "His brilliance carries you along 'with the greatest of ease.' I only find myself disturbed by that curious downward pout of the mouth that is almost like the terrible mouths of the Greek masks for tragedy. He has suffered, this man, been badly hurt—why, I don't know, and it seems to have left him with that curious grimace (terribly revealing, changing a whole face in a flash) and with no love of mankind as such."

Lawrence Dennis entering court

"We aren't concerned with moral issues," he had explained in one public debate. "The idea of fascism is to make the show run. In other words, any problem is small if you set up the right machinery to meet it." That a very large number of people might get chewed up in the works of that machinery was either beside the point for Lawrence Dennis, or exactly the point.

THE NAZI CONCLAVE Dennis witnessed in Nuremberg was conceived and designed to show the rest of the world just how powerful Hitler's authoritarian machinery had become. The national economy was humming again, the führer insisted; the German people, united as never before, had been resurrected. Germans would no longer hang their heads in shame at their defeat in the recent world war or live under the restrictions placed on them by the Treaty of Versailles. They had, in defiance of that treaty, built the most powerful military in all of Europe and had already begun to reclaim territory that rightfully belonged to the German people. "What would our opponents have said had I then prophesized that during these four years Germany would have shaken off the chains of the slavery of Versailles, that the Reich would have regained its defense freedom," Hitler said in his opening speech at the Rally of Honor. "Had I predicted all these things four years ago I would have been exposed to the derision of the world and branded a madman. Yet in these brief four years all these things have happened, and who would now dare to reproach us for looking back upon these developments with a feeling of pride and satisfaction?"

The totality of Germany's newfound military power was on display throughout the week. On the third morning of the Rally of Honor, the reconstituted German *Luftwaffe* appeared without warning in the skies above Nuremberg—four hundred weaponized airships in all: scout planes, followed by heavy bombers, then dive-bombers, and then sleek new monoplane fighters. "Jubilant thousands waved and cheered as the glittering fighting fleet, created since Hitler scrapped the Versailles Treaty 18 months ago, dipped through the cloudless sky over the Reichsfuehrer's hotel," observed one reporter.

The flyover was just a warm-up for the display of military maneuvers on the final day of the congress. The drone of planes could be heard before they appeared over the parade grounds that morning, while loudspeakers announced their arrival: the *Horst Wessel* squadron, the *Richthofen*, the *Immelmann*. They flew in, performing choreographed turns and dives until, in climax, a gaggle of seventeen fighter planes appeared on the horizon and then scudded over the gathering in a swastika formation. Tens of thousands of German soldiers then rushed the parade ground. The mounted cavalry rode in through the gates, followed by light artillery and heavy batteries, booming away; then the infantry, covered by artillery and machine gun fire, and supported by columns of tanks, chased a mock enemy off the field.

When the shooting was all done, Adolf Hitler's voice cut through the smoke-filled air above the faux battlefield. "As I see you before me, I feel, I know, that this guard defends us against all dangers and threats," he said. "Germany is once more worthy of its soldiers, and I know you will be worthy soldiers of the Reich! . . .

Grave times may come. You will never waver, never lose course, never prove cowardly! We all know that heaven is not gained by half measures! Freedom has no use for cowards! The future belongs to the brave alone!"

This martial spectacle was meant not just for fellow Germans in attendance but for an international audience. It clearly hit its mark, judging from the coverage of the day. "No other country, not excluding Russia, can produce so great a mass of men of similar intelligence and equal physique, ready or almost ready, to take the field," wrote a *New York Times* reporter, clearly impressed by what he had witnessed. "And once more there comes over the beholder the stunning conviction of Germany's unequalled strength."

Lest their intended audiences miss the sharper point of this exercise, the Nazis were very clear about exactly where this firepower was aimed: at the great threat to all free men, the communist scourge, those "Bolshevist Jews," as Hitler called them.

Antisemitism was hotter and meaner than ever in Germany in the summer of 1936. The Nazi Party congress in Nuremberg was said to be considering more new laws to forbid Jews in Germany to own or inherit private property. "Last summer I found many still believing that the Nazis might moderate and allow German Jews, at least, economic rights," an American pastor living in Berlin explained. "But this summer finds Jews in Germany even despairing of their future in business."

There was a clear shift happening just then. Nazi Party efforts to bully Jews into leaving the country were well under way, but the program appeared to be turning into something even more menacing. The American clergyman reported that government officials in southern Bavaria, and even in Berlin, were refusing to renew the passports of Jews living in Germany. "If Germany wants us to leave," said one confused Jewish rabbi in Berlin, "they should make it possible for us to go."

Lawrence Dennis got a close look at what was happening that week in Nuremberg, having been invited into the Nazi family circle. His minder for the festivities was a protégé of Joseph Goebbels, Ulrich von Gienanth, who was angling for a high-level assignment in America. Dennis also received his own small team of uniformed storm troopers to escort him through a carefully planned daily schedule of meals, private meetings, and public events. "These young Nazi elite guards assigned to act as our hosts and guides lived with us in our hotel," Dennis later explained. "They had breakfast with us around 8, bundled us off . . . to the first function of the day around 9 . . . and brought us home around midnight. We were with them the best part of eighteen hours a day."

The führer even agreed to a brief private interview with Dennis. In private, up close, Dennis found the German dictator unimpressive. Hitler's talents, he decided, were instinctual and ran to propaganda and political showmanship. Not that Dennis diminished them; there was clearly something to be learned, he later wrote, by watching Hitler ply his dark art. The führer had united the normally fractious German polity around a set of common (and mostly invented) enemies. "Hitler was able to exploit with guile the gullibility of the 'best' people, and with the utmost sincerity the patriotism of the nationalists who wanted to see Versailles avenged," Dennis wrote. "The anti-communist line got the capitalists, the anti-Versailles line got the army and the nationalists, the anti-Semitic line got the masses as well as the classes."

Dennis's main interlocutors in Germany in 1936—Goebbels, Alfred Rosenberg, Rudolf Hess, and Hermann Göring—were more to his liking. They seemed to be thinking men, even intellectuals. "They didn't try to propagandize the prominent Americans that they met with," Dennis later explained. "They made up their propaganda more for the masses. They were very tactful and diplomatic, I thought." They made sure Dennis understood where their interests met his, and that was in keeping America on the sidelines of any war in Europe.

At one point, and this has been corroborated by both Dennis and his contacts in Germany, Dennis suggested that the Nazis' treatment of the Jews was not advancing that critical mission. It looked bad. Maybe they didn't have to be so straightforward about the whole business, he suggested. To strip Jews of citizenship and property rights, they didn't need overt laws that just came right out and said that. "Why don't you treat the Jews more or less as we treat the Negroes in America?" he asked.

"The strongest thing they said to me was, 'You Americans mind your own business, and we'll mind ours. You leave ours alone; we'll leave yours alone,'" Dennis explained years after the fact. "Of course, I couldn't strongly disagree with that."

CHAPTER SIX

BULLET HOLES

When Philip Johnson strolled into the Keck & Keck architecture office in Chicago in August 1936, the principals of the firm were nowhere to be found. So Johnson breezed over to the desk of the firm's twenty-five-year-old chief draftsman, Robert Bruce Tague, speaking as he approached. "We were never formally introduced," he said, and then asked about the work Tague was doing. "What's interesting?" The two men made a little small talk about the projects the firm had on the drawing board. Tague's bosses, the Keck brothers, were the only name architects in Chicago designing and constructing modern buildings in the so-called International Style. They had already built the Crystal House and the House of Tomorrow, and Tague was at that moment working on the Cahn House in Lake Forest (which Mrs. Cahn liked to call "the House of the Day After Tomorrow"). These sleek, flat-roofed residences were revelations in Middle America—like no homes anybody had ever seen, designed with both comfort and durability in mind. The Kecks employed industrial materials. The most dramatic of all the projects, the Crystal House, was three floors of glass, stood up by a concrete and steel exoskeleton. These were also the first houses in the country to employ something called solar heating.

Philip Johnson, as the former head of architecture exhibitions at the Museum of Modern Art, had been among the few unreserved champions of this strange new style of building, so Tague was happy to talk shop with him. He assumed the brothers Keck would feel obliged to do Johnson a favor, if that's what Johnson was here for. Johnson in fact wasted little time before making his ask. He needed something constructed, he explained to Tague, and in a hurry.

He already had the thing designed in his head, but with no training in draftsmanship he was himself incapable of making a proper drawing of the colossal structure he had in mind. Johnson simply started describing what he wanted, talking fast, while Tague bent over his drafting table, sketching the thing to life: It was a massive platform, which consisted of a series of bright white four-by-eight drywall panels, seamlessly joined, to make a backdrop forty feet wide and twenty-eight feet high. There was a narrow stage about ten feet high, running the length of the platform. Another ten or so feet above that was a small pulpit, big enough for just one man, who would appear to be floating in air, high above his audience. At the top of the backdrop, Johnson wanted seven pairs of brackets placed at four-and-a-half-foot intervals, each pair sturdy enough to fasten a pole holding an enormous American flag rising another ten feet high. The brackets needed to be able to withstand the strongest wind blowing off Lake Michigan.

Tague had a pretty good idea why Johnson wanted them to build this dramatic platform, and for whom. In the very small community of modern architecture, Johnson's reputation as an ultra-right zealot preceded him. The draftsman and his bosses knew that after his failed Louisiana sojourn to try to attach himself to Huey Long, and then Long's assassination, Johnson had gone to work for Father Charles Coughlin, the "radio priest" whose national audience at the time numbered in the tens of millions. The shift of allegiance made sense; Coughlin had been one of Long's spurs and crucial allies for a planned third-party presidential run against Roosevelt. Coughlin had formed his own nascent political party just about the same time Long was making his famous "barbecue speech"—*Come to my feast!* The two men shared an economic program that leaned heavily on government control, the teachings of Jesus Christ, and the vilification of bankers. Long's "Share Our Wealth" pamphlets included an excerpt from Coughlin's 1932 sermon—a "discourse on Increased Wealth and Decreased Wages." By the summer of 1935, the increasingly militant, media-savvy priest with a huge and growing following was already moving toward booming Huey Long for president. In fact, on the day Long was shot, President Roosevelt had summoned Father Coughlin to the Summer White House in Hyde Park, New York, to try to dissuade Coughlin from backing Long. Word of Long's death arrived at Hyde Park only a few hours before Coughlin did, so there ended up being considerably less at stake in their conversation that day. But even so, the president kept the appointment. He considered Coughlin a loose cannon, rolling loaded around the ship of state. Which of course he was, and which was exactly what drew Philip Johnson's interest. Coughlin, Johnson later said, "seemed the most dynamic populist at the time."

By the summer of 1936, Coughlin had begun a national speaking tour opposing Roosevelt's reelection. Coughlin, a stout, combustible, forty-four-year-old fireplug of a man, was not shy in his tactics, or in his rhetoric. He had been insisting for months that Roosevelt was a "betrayer" and a "liar." The president was in thrall to Reds, he said; he was practically handing the country over to the commies.

One stop on Coughlin's tour was a Labor Day weekend rally at Riverview Park in Chicago, and that's why Johnson wanted this strange big white platform festooned with the flag brackets. "Fred Keck was a good Democrat, a Roosevelt man," Tague recalled many years later. "Of all things he wouldn't want to do. But he couldn't turn down Philip Johnson very well."

The erection of the platform would be proof to Johnson that he really was, at long last, making a vital contribution to the political cause. After Huey Long's assassination, Johnson and Blackburn had struggled to find their purpose. First, they took the advice of Long's aide and piloted Johnson's banner-waving Packard to New London, Ohio, where Johnson entered the primary campaign for a seat in the state legislature. His family had a sterling reputation in the area. Philip's father was the pride of New London—a successful attorney living in Cleveland who never forsook his roots. He was a founder of the main bank in the town and maintained a seat on its board and sympathy with its depositors. On the strength of his family name, Philip won his primary campaign with relative ease. But as New London became reacquainted with the younger Johnson, he began to wear out his welcome.

Still in his twenties, having never had a paying job, filthy rich thanks only to his father, and with no background in politics or governance, Johnson nevertheless reckoned himself, à la Nietzsche, one of the favored few. He behaved as if the citizens of New London, Ohio, were lucky to have him back home to set them straight. Johnson had "taken it upon himself to endeavor to decimate the policies of this town without consent or approval of anyone, other than himself," an official at the town bank later explained, "and in such a manner that it has become very distasteful to the businessmen of this vicinity."

By June 1936, with the general election still five months away, Johnson and New London were pretty well fed up with each other. So Johnson simply abandoned the town (and his campaign for the state legislature) and put his shoulder to the wheel of a bigger cause: Father Coughlin's battle royale against FDR.

The way Johnson envisioned the Father Coughlin Labor Day event in Chicago, it would re-create the pageantry of a Hitler rally, not unlike the Hitler Youth rally he'd attended in Potsdam four years earlier. "The police were all pro-Coughlin, especially the Irish," Johnson told Coughlin's biographer fifty years after the fact. "We said, 'We want the sirens and all the trimmings,' so we went into Chicago with sirens blasting! We had a photograph of Father Coughlin sixty feet high. . . . The great field was so crowded you couldn't move." The paid attendance, according to the Coughlin organization, was around 80,000, but reporters on hand estimated the crowd at nearer to 150,000.

Beyond the impressive crowd size, however, at least as compared with the political pageants staged by the Nazis, Johnson's designed tableau ended up a little wan. For one thing, Hitler's rally

Father Charles Coughlin on the stage designed by Philip Johnson

makers made sure to keep a tight hold on all background elements. Zeppelin Field in Nuremberg, for instance, was ringed by forest, and the stadium in the city was a closed set. By contrast, in Chicago, there was no way to hide the periphery of Riverview Park. The rally grounds themselves were usually reserved for a golfers' driving range and midget auto races, and so—all too visible beyond Johnson's massive Keck-built platform—dark netting was strung twenty feet high to keep errant tee shots from bouncing onto nearby streets. Also visible were telephone wires strung from pole to pole, and a few unprepossessing water tanks and smokestacks. In the immediate foreground stood a tall brick workaday building, an auditorium that looked like a site for high school basketball games and school plays.

Big as it was, Johnson's forty-foot-high drywall podium ended up dwarfed by the competing urban landscape. When Coughlin ascended into his floating pulpit, instead of looking massive, monolithic, inspiring, he looked like an insect, a nondescript, ineffectual speck floating alone, his little hands impotently cutting the air as he spoke. The visual impact of Philip Johnson's very first fascist building project was meh.

The people in the crowd also appeared, well, exceedingly ordinary. The women wore light-colored summer dresses and wide-brimmed hats to ward off the afternoon sun; the men wore felt hats or straw boaters with colored bands. Almost all the men had stripped down to their shirtsleeves, many swiveling their sharp features on necks thinned by Depression-era rations, with a little too much room in the collars. Nobody in the crowd was in uniform, or arrayed in tight, geometrically pleasing rows and columns; no cathedral of lights was projected onto the clouds overhead; no band blared patriotic songs; no squadron of fighter planes appeared on the horizon in perfect swastika formation. Chicago looked like cheap theater, even at fifty cents a ticket. "All those blond boys in black leather" this was not.

The ostensible point of this rally was for Father Coughlin to speak on behalf of his presidential candidate of choice, William "Liberty Bill" Lemke. After Huey Long's assassination, Coughlin, along with Long lieutenant and eulogist Gerald L. K. Smith and a couple of leaders from other ultra-right political sects, had personally selected Lemke, a congressman from North Dakota, as the candidate for president on the ticket of something they called the Union Party. Lemke was a no-account pol, with no national following to speak of, no particular powers of persuasion on the stump, and a near-complete lack of charisma up close. His candidacy was mostly a vehicle for Coughlin, who was Canadian-born and thus unable to run himself.

FATHER COUGHLIN'S "voice carried far by the use of a microphone hanging on his chest like the transmitters used by telephone operators," wrote a reporter from *The New York Times* who was in Chicago that day. "The priest assailed President Roosevelt, when, after an introduction alternating in religion, philosophy, and economics, he took up one of his constant topics, the Federal Reserve Bank. He described 'private control and issuance of money' as one of the 'ulcers of modern capitalism.' " Coughlin also took the hide off Roosevelt's best-known political operatives, especially his female secretary of labor, Frances Perkins. "*The* Madam Perkins," Coughlin intoned, "with her three-corner hat—one corner for communism, one for socialism, and one for Americanism."

"Well, we all know for whom we're voting if we vote for Mr. Roosevelt—for the Communists, the Socialists, the Russian lovers, the Mexican lovers, the kick-me-downers," said the radio priest. When Coughlin asked who among this crowd intended to vote for Roosevelt, there was a hushed silence. "Now, all who are going to vote against Roosevelt," Coughlin instructed, "say 'No.' " The "No!" roared across the field and sustained itself out into the Chicago neighborhoods beyond, a prolonged guttural cry that finally dopplered out miles away.

Coughlin could move a crowd, for sure. But that power turned out to be redeemable only by the holder; it was non-transferable, even to Coughlin's handpicked designees. His chosen candidate did not get a lot of traction in his campaign against the sitting president, and as Lemke's abject failure as a candidate went from obvious to embarrassing, Coughlin's rhetoric became more desperate. And increasingly dangerous. If Roosevelt is elected, Coughlin reportedly warned near the end of the election season, there were going to be "more bullet holes in the White House than you could count with an adding machine."

"Democracy is doomed," said Coughlin. "This is our last election. It is Fascism or Communism. We are at a crossroads. . . . I take the road to Fascism."

CHAPTER SEVEN

SILVER SHIRTS

The same week that Lawrence Dennis was melting into the Nazi masses at Nuremberg, and Father Coughlin was crowing to his flock in Chicago from atop his Nazi-lite architectural backdrop, a rookie newspaper reporter was busily trying to herd a hard-won story past skeptical editors and into the typesetting room of *The Minneapolis Journal*. Eric Sevareid would eventually go on to a long and celebrated career at CBS News and become one of the giants in twentieth-century American journalism. In September 1936, though, he was a twenty-three-year-old kid fresh out of the University of Minnesota looking for his first big front-page headline.

He went by his first name back then, so it was Arnold—not Eric—Sevareid who took the tip from some college friends: a strange political organization appeared to be on the rise in their city—a group calling itself the Silver Shirts. Philip Johnson's Gray Shirts in New York never seemed to get much beyond picking a uniform and designing banners, but these Silver Shirts guys in Minneapolis appeared to have numbers, and maybe even momentum. The group was secretive in the extreme, perhaps even a tad paranoid, but there might be a story there—if Sevareid could somehow get inside. He decided to embark on his first undercover investigation, presenting himself to the Silver Shirts as a potential initiate.

Sevareid, turned out, had little trouble winning the Silver

Shirts' confidence. They happily invited him into their middle-class parlors, then pulled their lace curtains tight so they could safely read him into their worldview, and in on their plans. Sevareid appeared to be just the sort of person who would bring credit to their cause: a striking young college graduate, tall and sinewy, an outdoorsman who knew his way around a hunting rifle, with a face already weathered by the fierce winds of the northern plains. Sevareid had grown up in a small town in North Dakota ("no roof to the sky, no border to the land," he said of his native home), where the economy rose and fell with a single crop. "Wheat was the sole source and meaning of our lives," he would say. The rhythms of farming, and the brutal yearly battles against nature—which could visit drought and dust, gully-washing downpours and terrifying cyclones, or ghastly infestations of grasshoppers that could wipe out months of labor in a matter of hours—dictated the daily life of the community and shaped its ethos. The Sevareid family neighbors depended on one another to produce and bring to market enough of the high-quality wheat—"No. 1 Hard," it was aptly named—to tide them over to next planting season. The town was hardworking, inter-dependent, egalitarian, and small-d democratic; its politics ran conservative. Sevareid described his fellow townsfolk as exhibiting limitless charity toward friends and neighbors and a thorough-going wariness of outsiders.

When Sevareid entered the University of Minnesota in 1931 at age eighteen, he still took it on faith "that [President] Herbert Hoover was a great man, that America was superior to all other countries in all possible ways, that labor strikes were caused by unkempt foreigners, that men saved their souls inside wooden or brick Protestant churches, that if men had no jobs it was due to personal laziness and vice—meaning liquor—and that sanity governed the affairs of mankind."

Sevareid's worldview had somewhat broadened by the time he became a full-time staff reporter at *The Minneapolis Journal*, but he was still at ease with the conservative older white Protestants who were filling up the roster of the local chapters of the Silver

Shirts, and they were at ease with him. Which meant a bunch of them were willing to confide in the young man. Or at least willing to confide what they could, given that anonymity and need-to-know compartmentalization of information were standard practice at the Silver Shirts. The group was organized around "councils of safety," each consisting of nine members so that no one person could know the identity of more than eight other Silver Shirts. Sevareid was unable to get specific names off the master list held by the Minnesota state chairman, but he was able to get some ballpark numbers: the Silver Legion had just begun organizing in Minnesota a few months earlier, but there were already almost five hundred enrollees in the Fifth Congressional District alone and around six thousand statewide.

The mission of the organization, as expressed to Sevareid by his Silver Shirt recruiters, was disquieting. This wasn't a do-good service club like the Elks or the Shriners or the Kiwanis; this was a group of vigilantes, gearing up for a quasi-religious, violent crusade. "One of the Silver Shirt leaders, a retired businessman, led me into his kitchen and opened his cupboards to show me the stocks of canned goods he had accumulated against the day of the Communist uprising, when he expected to barricade himself in his upper duplex," Sevareid remembered. "He raised a quivering finger and in a quavering voice informed me: 'If it be God's will that I fall as a martyr to the cause at the hands of these beasts, I shall die here, in my Christian home, defending my dear wife to the end.' They were quite mad."

The fever dream waking these white Christians was fueled in large part by what Sevareid called "secret-society phobia." Admission to the Silver Shirts had put them inside a special circle of knowledge. The veil had been lifted from their eyes; these Twin Cities burghers suddenly found themselves part of the select few to whom the fearsome truth had been revealed. A dastardly conspiracy was at play in the United States. The conspirators had been identified—commies, Reds, pinkos, otherwise known as international Jewry. They had infiltrated the highest levels of the American government. President Roosevelt's real name was Rosenfelt!

The Silver Shirts in good standing were kept abreast of the current threat level thanks to the newsletter mailed to them, weekly, from the national headquarters of the Silver Legion, somewhere in North Carolina.

"Oh, we've known for a long time that the Jews are plotting to seize the United States government," one earnest and inflamed Silver Shirt told Sevareid. "They want to run the whole world and tell us what to do. Just look at Russia—the Jews certainly got Russia, didn't they?"

Sevareid began sketching out what would become a five-part series on the Silver Shirts, running early drafts up the flagpole to his editors. "Hate and fear bind the members together," Sevareid had written. "Anti-Semitism is the outstanding feature of the Silver Shirts. Absurd as it may seem, to them the [first] World war, the present war in Spain (from where the Jews were expelled in 1492) and all the wars of the world were deliberately inspired by Jews. . . . In the minds of [the Silver Shirts] all Jews are Communists and all Communists are Jews. If one points out certain known Communists are definitely Nordic, their answer is—'Well, he must have a Jewish mind.'"

Sevareid had a good look at the "anti-Semitic poison" they were trafficking in and feared it was already spreading well beyond the membership. He knew the Silver Shirts in Minneapolis were passing around something called the *Protocols of the Meetings of the Learned Elders of Zion* and handing out their already-read copies of the weekly newsletter to uninitiated friends and neighbors so they too would learn that the time might soon come when they would need to be courageous enough to treat the Jews "drastically." The Silver Legion newsletter also offered the occasional vocabulary lesson: "*Pogrom*, lest there be any among us unfamiliar with the word, is a wholesale slaughter of Jews merely because they are Jews."

Arnold Sevareid took the Silver Shirts at their word, and he took them seriously. The hard-boiled city editor at *The Minneapolis Journal*, however, wasn't ready to buy the story at first—not from a wet-behind-the-ears cub reporter anyway. So, he too managed to get invited to a meeting of the Silver Shirts to check it out for himself. Sevareid was in the office when his editor returned from that conclave. "Get me a drink, quick!" the editor yelled. "God, I feel I've been through the most fantastic nightmare of my life."

Although he no longer doubted the shocking details in Sevareid's rough drafts, he was still not convinced of the wisdom of publishing the story. A few local rabbis and prominent Jewish civic leaders counseled the editor to drop the entire enterprise. "It would be painful to them, most undignified, and would merely drag out into the open and abet a virulent form of anti-Semitism," Sevareid remembered years later. They thought it "better to ignore the madmen and pretend they didn't exist."

The young reporter held his ground. The Silver Shirts, he insisted to the city editor, were a serious threat. Readers needed

William Dudley Pelley in his Silver Shirt uniform

to understand just how dangerous these wild conspiracy theories were, and just how widespread. Sevareid wasn't looking to embarrass anybody. He wasn't even going to name names, except for one big one—the man who seemed to have seduced all these midwestern bourgeois. "I spent hair-raising evenings in the parlors of middle-class citizens who worshipped a man named William Dudley Pelley," Sevareid wrote. "To his followers—supposedly 6,000 in Minnesota—Pelley is the coming saviour for the nation. They believe he is the man to do what Hitler has done in Germany."

William Dudley Pelley, like a slug, left behind him a visible, mucoid trail by which we can still know him today. The story of his strange life and his prodigiously vicious political legacy are well recorded, both because of his own enthusiastic telling and thanks to the accounts of dozens of witnesses, informants, and documents that make up the 717-page dossier the Federal Bureau of Investigation accumulated on him in a six-year period beginning in 1933. This much is indisputable: where Lawrence Dennis, self-proclaimed intellectual godfather of American-style fascism, was at pains to mask his personal grievance behind a veneer of scholarly theorizing, Pelley was fearless about using his own compulsive resentments as a tool and a weapon. He sharpened them into something dangerous and lethal and then manufactured it for mass consumption (and for profit)—at the very moment when millions of Americans were looking for somebody to blame, and to punish, for the terrifying want and woe that had been visited on them in the Great Depression of the early 1930s.

Pelley, born in 1890, had come of age like most Americans in his time, which is to say, clinging to the bottom rungs of the country's slippery economic ladder. He was raised in a deeply Methodist household in the stony hills of Massachusetts and Vermont, with a wealth of religious fervor and forced piety—and little else. He would later describe himself as "a perpetually hungry, shabbily dressed, and none-too-happy youngster who had to start his life labor at fourteen years of age and stay with it thereafter . . . a wry, lonely, misunderstood childhood, cluttered up psychologically with the worst sort of New England inhibitions, revengeful that I had been denied social and academic advantages for which my hunger was instinctive."

William Dudley Pelley did not cut a particularly remarkable figure in his adulthood. He did exhibit a flair for the dramatic in his clothing and in his close-trimmed Vandyke beard, but that was about all that stood him apart as a physical presence. The description of Pelley in the FBI files is terse and to the point: *5-8, 150 pounds. Dark brown hair turning gray. Sallow complexion. Good teeth. Squint-eyes. Rimless nose glasses, octagon lenses. Tendency to cock his head to one side when talking.*

Pelley did, however, have indisputable talents, which he recognized in himself and cultivated. He had been a voracious reader from childhood, and though by no means a literary stylist, he was a crack storyteller with an instinct for popular taste. Pelley published scores of well-circulated short stories in his twenties and thirties, including one that shared the second annual O. Henry Memorial Award with F. Scott Fitzgerald and a dozen other writers. Beginning in 1917, Pelley threw himself into the emerging American medium—the cinema—adapting his own stories or writing original scenarios and screenplays. He penned vehicles for early movie stars such as Lon Chaney (*The Shock*), Tom Mix (*Ladies to Board*), Hoot Gibson (*The Sawdust Trail*), and Mary Astor (*The Sunset Derby*).

Pelley got big eyes living among what he called the "Flesh Pots" in Hollywood. But his dream of becoming a publishing magnate like Richard Simon or Max Schuster or a movie mogul like Louis B. Mayer or Samuel Goldwyn or Harry Cohn never panned out; he remained a cog in both those industries all through the 1920s, with unfulfilling sidelights in restaurants and real estate. A quarter century into his life labor, Pelley was, by his own admission, a surly young man spoiling for a fight. "It made me a lone wolf at life, getting the least bit mangy as I reached my forties."

The media maven wannabe did finally hit on a promising vein of commerce around 1930: a combination of charismatic Christianity and the occult. On three separate occasions, he claimed, he had received urgent messages from the world beyond. In the first instance, while alone in a cabin in Altadena, California, he had a near-death experience, the highlight of which was a brief interlude in the afterlife. He described the scene in cinematic detail in "Seven Minutes in Eternity," which was published as the lead story in the March 1929 issue of *The American Magazine* (which boasted a readership of 2.2 million): "A sort of marble-tiled-and-furnished portico the place was, lighted by that soft, unseen, opal illumination, with a clear-as-crystal Roman pool diagonally across from my bench. . . . Out beyond the portico everything appeared to exist in a sort of turquoise haze."

Pelley said his second spectral visitation happened while he was at home in California, reading an essay by Ralph Waldo Emerson. "I had a queer moment of confusion, a sort of cerebral vertigo,"

Pelley wrote, "then a strange physical sensation at the very top of my head as though a beam of pure white light had poured down from above and bored a shaft straight into my skull. In that instant a vast weight went out of my whole physical ensemble."

The third and most dramatic visitation came when Pelley was alone in a railroad car, reading Emerson again, somewhere in New Mexico, as his train "clicked monotonously, eastward, eastward," he wrote. "Suddenly as I turned a page, something happened! I seemed to be bathed in a douche of pure white light on that moving Pullman. A great flood of Revelation came to me out of which a Voice spoke such as I had never heard before. What it said, I prefer to keep permanently to myself. But . . . I knew of the reality of that Entity whom the world now designates as Jesus of Nazareth! I knew that He was not a mythical religious ideal. I knew His ministry and career had been a literal actuality and that I had once seen Him when He was thus in His flesh!"

In Pelley's telling, which he retailed to millions of paying readers across America, he emerged from his three otherworldly experiences as a man reborn, in myriad ways. He no longer required alcohol, tobacco, or caffeine to get him through the day; was no longer plagued by nervous indigestion, or any of his other daily physical ailments. His spine straightened, his shoulders broadened, his waist grew thin, while his chest and biceps swelled—all without benefit of exercise. He was lighter, friendlier, easier in his skin, easier in the world, because he was now in possession of the answers to the mystery of life.

"The day is coming in the evolution of the race when spirituality is going to be the whole essence of life instead of the world's present materialism," he explained to those 2.2 million readers of *The American Magazine*. "A wholly different universe that seems filled with naught but love, harmony, good humor and prosperity."

Pelley got letters from readers by the hundreds, a "clean-cut cross-section of Americans and Englishmen," he wrote. "From railroad and bank presidents; from stenographers and street-car conductors; from . . . octogenarians to boys and girls in high schools and colleges—men and women being equally represented, and . . . Protestant ministers, most eager of all to lead their flocks into a clearer understanding of the eternal verities." But Pelley sensed that story needed an even more dramatic twist.

So he cooked one up.

The visitations, he began to insist, had changed him in one other fundamental way that he hadn't previously mentioned: he had become a human radio receiver, able to "tune in on the minds and voices of those in another dimension of being." He would sit for hours, he claimed, three or four times each week, furiously taking dictation from the learned souls of the Fourth Dimension. "I have in some cases taken down ten-thousand-word lectures on abstruse aspects of science, physics, cosmology and metallurgy," Pelley wrote. "I have taken down a 400-page book on Political Economy so advanced in context and knowledge that it has surprised authorities on the subject who have perused portions of it."

Pelley's first big effort to monetize his new-won occult knowledge was in the summer of 1932, when he and a handful of acolytes moved to Asheville, North Carolina, and started Galahad College, where students could buy and read the various textbooks on science, physics, cosmology, metallurgy, and political economy Pelley had dictated from those learned souls of the Fourth Dimension. Galahad appeared at the outset a promising venture, at least to folks in Asheville, which, like every other town in America in the 1930s, needed a jolt to the local economy. Pelley was establishing an institute of higher learning *and* a publishing house, both of which were paying office rent and creating jobs for the locals. An officer in the Asheville Chamber of Commerce invited Pelley to speak to the Kiwanis Club. Pelley's topic was to be the "Foundation for Christian Economics," but he veered off into a discussion of the awesome power of solar rays, and a warning to the weirded-out Kiwanis that an apocalyptic eclipse might be in the offing.

One Asheville businessman got an earful he wouldn't soon forget from Pelley's right-hand man, Robert Summerville. "It seems—and I also recall again from Mr. Summerville—that both he and Mr. Pelley were the reincarnation of souls who had lived thousands, if not millions, of years ago upon the earth," the man later told an FBI investigator. Pelley and Summerville also seemed to think they knew a good deal about the Great Pyramids in Egypt. Summerville, the local man said, "explained to me how the scientists had discovered the interior vaults of the Great Pyramid contained marks which corresponded to what he termed 'great tribulations' or 'crises' in world history. This began with the exodus of Jews from Egypt, and had such dates as the Fall of Babylon, Rome, and the World War. There were marks from the year of 1931, which Mr. Summerville said was the Depression which would end accordingly in the Great Pyramid on September 16, 1936. . . . Mr. Pelley is a very intense personality. . . . He strikes me as having a great deal of the poseur in his make-up."

Galahad College foundered in a flash. The first class was a small cohort, textbook sales didn't cover costs, and half the students bailed before the summer session of 1932 was complete. Pelley's Foundation for Christian Economics and his publishing house both neared bankruptcy, too, and he was soon skipping rent payments to his landlords at the Woman's Club Building in Asheville.

Pelley appeared destined to take his place in America's long line of failed and forgotten pseudo-religious charlatans, until in 1933 he hooked his buy-my-psychic-claptrap scheme onto the most rapidly ascendant and dynamic political movement in the world. William Dudley Pelley was able to do this, he claimed, because he knew it was coming. The start date of this new epoch in history and politics had been revealed to him four years earlier, he said, back in 1929, by his ethereal interlocutors, or the hieroglyphics on the interior wall of the Pyramids, or Jesus of Nazareth himself (Pelley never practiced strict consistency in his storytelling). An anonymous writer for Pelley's new weekly magazine (likely Pelley himself) concocted the story that he had been preparing for this day in secret since 1929, during which time he had "perfected a great national organization drawing people of importance from the highest walks of life, people whose names have never been published, and may never become known. . . . On January 31, 1933, the date that Hitler came into power in Germany, Pelley came out from under cover with his Silver Shirts national organization. Having planted depots throughout the entire United States, enlightened police and vigilante groups, secured the cooperation of outraged Christian citizens. . . . His organization of Silver Shirts is now snowballing exactly as Hitler's Nazis snowballed in Germany when at last the German people were persuaded to the truth."

Pelley believed Hitlerite fascism could be replicated in America for one simple reason. Unlike Pelley's failed spiritual movement, this new political juggernaut was fueled by the most powerful of human emotions. Love and harmony were nice and all, but for pure motive force, hate trumps. His weekly the *Silver Legion Ranger* provided readers with somebody to hate—the Jews, who were busy planning world domination. Their plot, according to the *Ranger,* was vast and ambitious. Per Pelley, the Jews had a unified and secret global plan to "corrupt youth through subversive teaching"; "destroy family life"; "dominate people through their vices"; "abase art and corrupt literature"; "undermine the respect for religion"; "ruin the nervous system through inoculations and various poisons, and germs of disease"; "poison the relations between masters and men through strikes and lock-out"; "let industry exhaust agriculture and gradually transform industry in wild speculation"; "grant universal suffrage, so that the destiny of each country is entrusted to men who lack culture and breeding"; "organize vast Monopolies, in which all private fortunes will be engulfed"; "destroy all financial stability, multiply economic crises"; "stop the wheels of industry, make stocks and shares crash"; "concentrate all gold in the world into certain hands"; and finally, "exhaust humanity through excessive suffering, anguish and deprivations, for HUNGER BREEDS SLAVES."

It sounds insane, because it is. But an equally insane number of Americans in the 1930s signed right up for it. Pelley put out the call for "Christian Soldiers" to fight the Jewish menace—anybody eighteen or older, "of reasonably sound health, and not afraid to risk your life and limb for your country"—and enlisted more than fifteen thousand people posthaste. After taking the official Silver

Shirt "Oath of Consecration" and paying dues, new members got a weekly mailing of the *Silver Legion Ranger* and, as Pelley promised, the "shirt of silver with the great scarlet L emblazoned on your banner and over your heart, standing for love, loyalty and liberation." Duly initiated members were instructed to keep arms and to be ready to bear them.

Pelley, meanwhile, watched with solipsistic interest as Hitler drew all power in Germany to himself in the next few years. "Read Hitler's autobiography," Pelley would tell his closest aides, "and then compare it with my life and note the similarities between us."

PELLEY ANNOUNCED FOR the presidency of the United States in 1936, of course, and his candidacy was predictably muddleheaded. There was a lot of talk about protecting the U.S. Constitution, though basically all his policy proposals were blatant violations of this document: the chief executive would be given dictatorial powers; the United States would become a corporation, and every (white Christian) citizen would be both a common and a preferred stockholder. In place of capitalism, Pelley proposed a new economic system in which both supply and demand would be strictly and perfectly controlled by government officials. The whole of the plan, Pelley said, "is too big and too dynamic to describe." Who wanted to get down in those weeds? What mattered was that Pelley, the savior, was going to be in charge and he was going to rid America of the Jewish Bolshevist communists.

Pelley had a lot of make-believe facts and figures at hand to make his case: by his math, a clear majority of President Roosevelt's brain trust were Jews or Gentile fronts for Jews (whatever that might mean). Roosevelt himself, Pelley said, was also secretly Jewish. Pelley knew this, he said, because the Silver Legion had taken the time to investigate the Roosevelt family tree. They traced it right back to the Jewish Roscampo family, "which was expelled from Spain and settled in Holland." President *Rosenfelt* had already allowed the Jews to secretly take control of the United States. "This is OUR country, founded in certain inalienable rights, and consecrated to the perpetuation of definite Christian ideals and customs of living. We propose without further ado, without equivocation, without any silly sentimentality sometimes known as Tolerance, to emasculate the debauchers within the social body and reestablish America on a basis where spoilation can never again be repeated," Pelley said. "If you are a weakling, or given to compromise, sentimentality, docile acquiescence to intimidation, and nonentity in general, you are not wanted. . . . ARE YOU WITH US? WILL YOU AID IN HELPING ACTUALIZE THE TRUE DEMOCRACY OF JESUS THE CHRIST RIGHT HERE IN THESE TORTURED UNITED STATES?"

Pelley's bizarre campaign must have been quite a thing to witness. The candidate himself was always armed, decked out in a Sam Browne cross-body ammunition belt and military regalia, and surrounded by a squadron of bodyguards that would have made Huey Long blush. Some of his campaign rallies numbered in the thousands, with the members of his Silver Shirts Christian militia standing at attention, flanking the dear leader. The men were uniformed in their namesake silver shirts with the red silk *L* over the left breast, blue four-in-hand neckties with their membership numbers stitched on, blue corduroy trousers, and puttees. (The entire ensemble could be acquired for a $6 payment to the Silver Legion.) If you were looking for a signature Silver Shirt fetish, it was probably hierarchy and rank. Below Pelley himself—who liked to be called Chief—the Silver Shirts had commanders, chamberlains, quartermasters, sheriffs, censors, adjutants, pursers, bailiffs, marshals, advocates, scribes, and almoners. And a partridge in a pear tree.

One hot July night at the Deutsches Haus in Los Angeles a special cadre of Silver Shirts and members of the West Coast German American Bund stood at attention while one of Pelley's lieutenants warmed up the crowd. According to a report in *Pelley's Weekly,* the Silver Shirter screamed, "I have but one criticism to make of Adolf Hitler. In cleaning the Jews out of Germany, he sent too many of them over here!"

Pelley thus took the stage at Deutsches Haus and "for fully two minutes," one of the attendees reported, "he strutted around [in silence] like a vain peacock." When Pelley finally did speak, he bashed "the Moscow-controlled and the Jew-infested Rozenvelt Administration," as well as the Republican nominee for president. "It doesn't matter who you vote for in 1936—because both candidates are controlled by Jews. But, by the Grace of God, I am going to stop that. . . . By the Grace of God, I will march up the steps at Washington and show them that this is still a Christian nation!" The Deutsches Haus audience, according to the witness on the scene, "stamped the floor and just about took the roof down."

"YOU PROBABLY WON'T believe this story" was the lede on Arnold Sevareid's Silver Shirts series, which debuted in *The Minneapolis Journal*—front page, above the fold—on September 11, 1936. The young reporter couldn't have asked for better placement, but the articles were edited in such a way that they didn't land the punch he had hoped, "not as I wanted them written, as a cry of alarm," he would later say, "but as a semihumorous exposé of ridiculous crackpots." "Ridiculous," "ludicrous," "preposterous"—the editors had peppered these signifiers of Silver Shirt fecklessness and absurdity throughout Sevareid's six-part series. The third-day story had a corker, drawn right from the pages of *Pelley's Weekly:* "The Pyramids of Gizah have forecast dark events for September 16. In the walls of the 'pyramid' are graven the symbols which foretell the epochal doings of that day. It can mean nothing else than the seizure of the world by the Jews, a seizure that has been planned since Solomon's time."

This world takeover would not pass by Minneapolis, not according to Pelley's acolytes. The Jews "are going to start through Kenwood and sweep eastward around the lakes and thence across the city," one of the Silver Shirts had explained to Sevareid. "Yes, sir. September 16 is the day. You want to watch out. We've all got orders to stay home and away from windows."

September 16, which happened to be the day Sevareid's series ended, passed without incident, but the letdown did not diminish the apocalyptic ardor of Pelley's followers in Minneapolis or else-where. They still had their canned goods tucked in their pantries and their small arms near at hand. Neither did it diminish fear and hatred among the Twin Cities Silver Shirts—much of which was now turned against young Arnold Sevareid. The really dishearten-ing thing, to Sevareid, was that his series seemed to *increase* the number of locals who sympathized with Pelley's adherents.

"Odd characters, fuming and bridling, would march to my desk in the city room and demand to know whether I was a Chris-tian or a Bolshevik," he wrote of the aftermath. " 'Lifelong sub-scribers' would lecture me over the telephone, and, when I lost patience and lectured them back, they would call the publisher and I, to my disgust and amazement, would then be lectured by my bosses for being rude to a client. I sat in the balcony of the biggest Baptist church and listened to the influential pastor denounce me as a 'Red.' "

Sevareid received so many threats of physical violence, by tele-phone and by letter, that his brothers showed up at his apartment, with their guns, and offered to provide protection. Sevareid waved them off, explaining that these blusterers talked a big game but were too chicken-hearted to make a real attack.

Here is the one time when Sevareid might have underestimated the ugly truth of America's committed fascists. His window into the movement was a small one, confined mostly to those middle-class Silver Shirt homes dotting the Twin Cities, where *Pelley's Weekly* and the *Silver Legion Ranger* sat comfortably next to the King James Bible and *Reader's Digest* and the latest catalog from Sears.

Arnold Eric Sevareid did not know, as a Seattle gun dealer ex-plained in an FBI field office report dated September 17, 1936, that the Silver Shirt field marshal Roy Zachary had "called upon him and offered to buy large quantities of ammunition, 30.06, 30-40, .38 super-automatic, .45 automatic and many other kinds. It is al-leged that Zachary wanted 15,000 rounds of automatic ammuni-tion. He also desired to buy high caliber rifles in large quantities, claiming he has permits from the local police department for all the side arms which he can buy. . . . Zachary wanted [the gun dealer] to go to Tacoma and appraise and inventory the stock of the Kimble Company, a bankrupt dealer, who has a supply of arms and ammunition, Zachary stating that he had the cash to buy all the arms and ammunition he can get. . . . It is also alleged that Zachary had a permit with the signature of Police Chief William H. Sears and admitted that the guns were to be used by Pelley's private Fascist army in an immense program being planned by the combined forces of the Black Legion, the James True Associates, and the Silver Shirts."

Neither did Sevareid know that this man called James True was telling fellow fascists that the day of pogrom was approaching, that Father Coughlin "will soon let loose on the Jews" and they should all be preparing. Neither did Sevareid know that this James True had recently filed an application at the U.S. Patent Office for a new weapon, ready for mass production—one he called the "kike killer."

CHAPTER EIGHT

TIKKUN OLAM

The "kike killer" was never mass-produced, praise be, but one limited-edition prototype of the weapon did make an outsized mark on history. On Friday, April 22, 1938, it was in its customized leather sheath, hanging on the interior of the driver's side door of a midnight-blue Studebaker Commander that was parked in a lot in downtown San Diego under the watch of a paid attendant. The stately Commander and its contents belonged to Henry Allen, organizer of a new paramilitary squadron called the American White Guard and William Dudley Pelley's keyman in Southern California's expanding legion of Silver Shirts. Allen was a wiry and graying bantamweight who, even nearing age sixty, retained an incandescent temper. He was quick to pick a fight, and quicker to end one. Probably why he liked to keep his "kike killer" close at hand. "Always throw the first punch," he counseled younger men in his charge.

Fascist antisemites were making plenty of noise about punching hard and punching first that spring. Pelley had just released a new pamphlet, "One Million Silver-Shirts by 1939," in which he proposed rounding up all people of "Jewish extraction," along with "the improvident colored people south of the Mason Dixon line," and penning them on reservations. "I propose from this date onward," Pelley wrote, "to direct an aggressive campaign that shall arouse America's Gentile masses to do a wholesale and drastic outing of every radical-minded Jew from the United States soil!"

The latest nationally distributed fascist *News Bulletin* (vol. 1, no. 14) included instructions on how to construct a DIY kit for the "Firy [*sic*] Swastika." "Burned between the hours of nine in the evening and eleven at night," the *Bulletin* explained, it "will have the same effect on the reds and their sympathizers, including Jews, as it had on the Negro and the carpetbagger. . . . A high spot, over-looking the town or city, should be chosen, where it can be easily seen. . . . The press should be tipped off, if possible in advance or immediately after the Swastika is set afire. The idea is to have as many pictures of it as possible broadcast throughout the nation."

Henry Allen, his key aide and confidant Charles Slocombe, and two other confederates had driven down to San Diego from their home in Los Angeles that Friday morning. Allen had parked the Commander in a paid lot, and each of the four men hauled out of its trunk a large box packed with flyers—shouldering as much as they could carry. They were there to "snowstorm" a scheduled speech by a federal judge in the Southern District of California who was also a leading light in Los Angeles's growing and dynamic Jewish community.

"Snowstorming" was a go-to tactic of disruption practiced with increasing relish by the homegrown fascists in Southern California in 1938. Allen and his three cohorts each carried their boxes of antisemitic handbills ("*Jews! Jews! Jews! Jews everywhere!*") to the roofs of four different buildings in downtown San Diego that morning. They planned to drop the leaflets shortly before the judge's talk began. The dump went off right on schedule; thousands of flyers drifted down onto the crowded streets of San Diego. Considering the confusion and upset on the ground and the number of antisemitic "snowflake" flyers that were picked up and passed around, Allen deemed the exploit a success.

But none of the four snowmen made it back to the Studebaker that day, because somebody had dropped the dime on them. Allen and the others were arrested, hauled into the downtown precinct of the San Diego Police Department, and charged with violating the city's anti-handbill ordinance. Slocombe and the two other junior conspirators were released after pleading guilty and paying a

$3 fine. Allen was held on a more serious charge—possession of a deadly weapon.

Turns out the informant had not only given the police advance warning on the date, time, and location of the "snowstorm," he had also fed them specific intelligence about what was hanging in that sheath on the door of Henry Allen's Studebaker. "It is an oak club about 19 inches long with a leather thong to wrap around his wrist," Agent C19 had told the authorities in San Diego. "The club is about an inch thick, and two and a half inches wide. The back of it is rounded and its face is quite sharp. [Allen] calls it a 'kike killer' and showed me how to use it: 'You wrap it around your wrist and poke it in the man's stomach, and when he bends over, come down on top of his head with the flat side.'"

The cops had gone to the parking lot and confiscated the weapon as soon as they arrested Allen. They also impounded the car because Allen was being held over for arraignment, awaiting the judge's decision on bail. He wasn't going anywhere until court was back in session on Monday.

Slocombe raced back to Pasadena to alert Allen's wife, Pearl, who was herself a member in good standing of the Silver Shirts and the American White Guard, an even more militant splinter group founded by her husband. Pearl was uncharacteristically flustered by the news of Henry's arrest, especially when she heard that the cops in San Diego had seized his blue Studebaker. This was bad for the cause. Very bad. "There are papers in that [briefcase] no one is supposed to see," she told Slocombe. Mrs. Allen immediately alerted someone known as "Auntie," who was reputed to be most of the brains and much of the cash propelling the increasingly ambitious fascist movement in Southern California. Auntie told Slocombe to get his ass back to San Diego and do whatever was necessary to secure the briefcase.

Charles Slocombe did just as he was told, after a fashion.

SLOCOMBE WAS BARRELING back down the coast highway first thing the next morning, with the scent of brine drifting in off the Pacific.

His companion on this ride, his real boss, was even more anxious to get to San Diego than Slocombe was, and Leon Lewis was not an excitable man. An accomplished chess player with an unfailing instinct for when to exercise caution and when to take a risk, Lewis was a generation older than Slocombe and a lot more experienced. He had single-handedly stood up and nurtured a secret spy ring operating out of his small legal office in downtown Los Angeles. Lewis had been at it for five straight years, since 1933, when he had made a pledge to "blow the Nazi movement in America to smithereens and to discredit completely all anti-Semitic organizations and American bigots who have any truck with them."

Leon Lewis had been preparing for this mission most of his life. He came of age in small-town Middle America at the turn of the twentieth century, the son of Jewish immigrants from Germany. By the time he finished his law degree at the University of Chicago, he was fluent in English, German, Yiddish, and the Constitution's idealistic promises to each and every American citizen, no matter their race or religious affiliation. Lewis's lifework turned out to be way more than his fair share of helping his country fulfill those elusive promises.

Lewis's journey began at the tiny, cluttered two-desk office of the Anti-Defamation League, which was founded after the wrongful murder conviction of a Jewish American pencil factory executive in Georgia. The thirty-one-year-old businessman was taken from prison and lynched in the summer of 1915, the day after his death sentence was commuted by the Georgia governor. Leon Lewis signed on that year as the ADL's first national executive secretary. Steven Ross, who along with his fellow historian Laura Rosenzweig pried loose Leon Lewis's remarkable and largely untold story from a California university archive less than a decade ago, writes that Lewis was "devoted to the Jewish concept of *tikkun olam*, world repair."

Lewis did take a brief sabbatical to join the military when the United States entered World War I, but not before the ADL persuaded President Woodrow Wilson to order the destruction of all U.S. Army training manuals that included the assertion that Jews are "more apt to malinger than the native born." Lewis shipped off to Europe near the end of November 1917 and spent the next eighteen months both behind the lines and, at times, in battlefield trenches. Some of his work, he later confided to a friend, had been in counterintelligence. Lewis's overseas duty extended for six months after the German surrender, and he spent much of that time helping wounded soldiers and the families of the dead in making their claims for the recompense due them.

Not long after his return from overseas, Leon Lewis presented the Central Conference of American Rabbis with an official ADL report detailing the increasing antisemitism in Europe and in America. For the "in America" part of that thesis, there was an unmistakable Exhibit A in 1920: a man who also happened to be one of the most successful and celebrated industrialists on the planet.

Henry Ford's antisemitism was rank, and it was unchecked. He spewed it freely in private tirades among friends, family, close business cohorts, newspaper reporters, or pretty much anybody within earshot. He lectured his sometimes-weary auditors in the Ford Motor Company offices, in private chats, in interviews, at dinners, even on camping trips. Ford "attributes all evil to Jews or to the Jewish capitalists," a close friend wrote in his diary after witnessing a late-night, round-the-campfire diatribe. Ford whined about "New York Jews" and railed about "Wall Street Kikes." He even ordered his engineers to forgo the use of any brass in his Model T automobile, calling it "Jew metal."

"Wherever there's anything wrong with a country, you'll find the Jews on the job there," Ford said. He blamed a vast and inchoate Jewish conspiracy for inciting his workers and his stockholders to demand that he share a sliver more of the expansive Ford Motor Company profits with them; for the gold standard and the advent of the Federal Reserve Bank; for ruining motion pictures in America, popular music, even baseball; for the military conflagration that nearly destroyed Europe (and the European market for his automobiles). "I know who caused this war—the German-Jewish bankers!" he declared on board his Peace Ship, a publicity-stunt transatlantic voyage he organized in 1915 to try to bring an end to the fighting in World War I. He patted his jacket pocket as he confided this to a fellow traveler: "I have the evidence here." He had no evidence, of course, but that didn't stop him from belching up a constant spew of gory anti-Jewish fantasy.

Ford was hardly the only radical antisemite in the United States circa 1920, but in addition to his fortune, his famous name, and his iconic automobile company, he had a megaphone your average crazy-uncle theorizer lacked: a newspaper, the *Dearborn Independent,* which he had purchased for a song in 1918. The paper was a big money loser in the beginning, with poor to middling circulation, and Ford's editorial harangues did little to draw new readers. How many attacks on the man who bested Ford in the most recent Michigan Senate race (Truman H. Newberry had stolen that election!) did the public really want? One of the *Independent*'s editorial staffers, a veteran of New York newspaper wars, had an idea. "Find an evil to attack," he wrote to Ford's right-hand man, Ernest G. Liebold. "LET'S FIND SOME SENSATIONALISM."

And lo, the answer landed unbidden on Liebold's desk not long after: a newly translated English edition titled the *Protocols of the Meetings of the Learned Elders of Zion.* The pamphlet was the work of rabidly antisemitic Russian fabulists furious at the Bolsheviks' toppling of the old tsarist aristocracy. The tsarists portrayed the Russian Revolution as not merely a local affair; it was the early innings of a plot by a cabal of all-powerful Jewish schemers to take over the world. The *Protocols* was billed as the product of a surreptitious note taker at a top-secret meeting wherein these Jewish puppet masters had drawn up their strategy and tactics in detail. There was no secret meeting, obviously, and no secret plot: the whole thing was a work of fiction—a very considered, very deliberate lie, and a very, very dangerous piece of propaganda.

The copy of the *Protocols* that landed in the Ford camp came from Madame Paquita de Shishmareff, sometimes known as Leslie Fry, a thirty-eight-year-old Paris-born daughter of American expatriates with a very sharp ax to grind. She said her husband, a colonel in the Russian Imperial Army, had been killed by the Bolsheviks in the Russian Revolution a few years earlier. And perhaps he had! Either way, great story. As for the *Protocols,* now that was a *truly* great story. Liebold and Ford were too het up—"I have the evidence here!"—to investigate the provenance or the accuracy of this tract. They merely thanked Leslie Fry for the new material and bore down on a new weekly series in the *Dearborn Independent* based on the *Protocols.* It would end up being a ninety-two-part series.

Every week for nearly two years, headlines such as "The International Jew: The World's Problem" and "Jewish Jazz—Moron Music—Becomes Our National Music" and "The Perils of Baseball—Too Much Jew" were splashed onto the pages of Ford's newspaper, which was distributed in Ford Motor dealerships across the country. Ford also saw to the publication of his foul series in book form, titled *The International Jew.* It ran to four volumes. It included stand-alone essays like "The Jew in Character and Business," "How the Jews in the U.S. Conceal Their Strength," "How Jewish International Finance Functions," "Jewish Idea Molded Federal Reserve Plan," and "Jewish Supremacy in the Motion Picture World."

Never mind that the *Protocols* was exposed as total make-believe in 1921, somewhere in the middle of Henry Ford's anti-semitic screed of a newspaper series. Ford's weekly "International Jew" essays continued without pause, and Ford Motor dealers kept tossing the latest issue of the *Dearborn Independent* onto the front seat of newly purchased Model Ts. Ford saw to it that the four volumes of *The International Jew* were translated and published worldwide, in twelve international editions, including one in Germany, where fresh volumes were still being published even years after the *Protocols* was debunked. Of all the contributions Henry Ford made to this world, one of them was this oeuvre, the most prolific, most sustained published attack on Jews the world had ever known.

Lewis and friends of the Anti-Defamation League fought back. They issued pamphlets deriding the *Dearborn Independent*'s articles as "so naïve in their incredible fantasy that they read like the work of a lunatic" and organized an anti-antisemitic publicity campaign of notable and notably Gentile Americans. Prominent public figures such as Woodrow Wilson, Clarence Darrow, W. E. B. Du Bois, and William Jennings Bryan joined the fight, calling Ford's vile utterings "un-American" and "un-Christian." The former president William Howard Taft, soon to be named chief justice of the United States, accepted a speaking engagement at an ADL meeting in Chicago two days before Christmas 1920 and lambasted Ford and his loony assertion of a powerful Jewish conspiracy surreptitiously stripping power from Christians around the world. "There is not the slightest ground for antisemitism among us," Taft said. "It has no place in free America."

Ford eventually did make a public apology in 1927, but only to settle a libel suit he was about to lose. And then only halfheartedly. The evil genie was well out of the bottle by then, anyway. "Although Jews at various conventions have repudiated the protocols as forgery," Father Coughlin later told his followers, "nevertheless a correspondence between the prophecy contained in this book and its fulfillment is too glaring to be set aside or obscured."

The German edition of Ford's book had landed in the hands of one particularly gifted propagandist. When Adolf Hitler's political-treatise-wrapped-in-an-autobiography, *Mein Kampf*, was published in 1925, the author appeared to lift not just ideas but entire passages from Ford's own publications. The *Mein Kampf* first edition extolled Ford by name, singling out the American automobile baron for his steadfast courage in the face of ongoing assault by strikers, or commies, or bankers, or media moguls, or some combination thereof. Jews all, no doubt. "It is Jews who govern the stock exchange forces of the American Union," Hitler wrote. "Every year makes them more and more the controlling masters of the producers in a nation of one hundred and twenty millions; only a single great man, Ford, to their fury, still maintains full independence." Hitler had already mulled sending some of his "shock troops" to major American cities to aid in Ford's possible run for president in 1924.

When a reporter from *The Detroit News* showed up at Nazi

Party headquarters in Munich in December 1931 to interview Hitler for her "Five Minutes with Men in Public Eye" series, she was surprised to find, hanging on the wall behind Hitler's desk, a large, framed portrait of America's most famous antisemite. "I regard Henry Ford as my inspiration," Hitler explained to the newspaperwoman.

The reporter asked Hitler that day, point-blank, why he was antisemitic.

"Somebody has to be blamed for our troubles," he said without hesitation.

LEON LEWIS RECEIVED news of Hitler's ascension to the head of the German government in January 1933 with a sense of foreboding shared by few other Angelenos—not even in the Boyle Heights section, where much of the Jewish community had settled after having been redlined out of Gentile-controlled L.A. neighborhoods.

Lewis recognized the danger as soon as it arrived. "In the spring of 1933, Hitler sends out one of his captains from World War I, Robert Pape, to organize Nazi groups all along the Pacific coast," Steven Ross says. "He organizes something called the Friends of New Germany in the spring of 1933. In July 1933 the Nazis hold their first open meeting at the Alt Heidelberg Inn, just outside downtown L.A. And the crowd listens to their 'minister of propaganda' lecturing on the new Germany and the wonderful things that Hitler is doing and how Germany would rise again because Hitler would save it. They announced that the Friends of New Germany would also save America by defeating the country's two greatest enemies: Jews and communists."

The story of the meeting was on the front page of one of the Los Angeles city newspapers the next day, with a picture of five men, dressed up as Nazis, in Brownshirt uniforms with swastikas on their red, white, and blue armbands, giving the "Heil Hitler" salute. Lewis read the entire story, right down to the last paragraph, which described how the Friends of New Germany was providing housing, food, and clothing to any World War I veteran in need, at no charge. In 1933, especially after the Depression-depleted federal government had slashed their benefits, there were a lot of veterans in need.

"Leon Lewis knew this was not a humanitarian gesture," says Ross. "This was, in fact, Hitler's attempt to follow the blueprint he had used in Germany as he was building up his Brownshirt army. Here were all these disgruntled World War I vets in Germany, who had no future, no hope, and Hitler offers them hope and offers them a future. He gives them housing. And he starts training them. Lewis reads this article and he says, 'Oh my God, I know what they're doing. They're trying to raise an army here in Los Angeles because Southern California has the largest collection of World War I veterans in the United States.' And German Americans were the largest ethnic group in Southern California. Lewis realizes that the Friends of Germany are going to start training men for their army, for what they refer to as *Der Tag* (The Day), the day that the Germans will take over America. And the way they'll take it over is they will announce that there's a communist plot and that they will save America from the communist Jews.

Leon Lewis

"Lewis decides, well, I need to do something."

What Leon Lewis decided to do was something incredible. And incredibly dangerous. He went out and recruited a small group of men, picked from the exact same pool the Nazis were after—disgruntled non-Jewish American veterans of the recent war. That had been Lewis's war too, and he was a trusted member of the local chapter of the Disabled American Veterans of America. Lewis had spent a lot of hours, pro bono, working to help former military men in bad straits. There were a handful of men willing to return a favor for Leon

Lewis. Many of them German American and many of them combat wounded, they (and in some cases, their wives) agreed to become spies for Leon Lewis, to infiltrate the Friends of New Germany clubhouse and report back on the doings within.

Most of the men willing to help in this dangerous endeavor had already been through harrowing times, but this was risky work, even for the most experienced and able of men. Lewis's first recruit, John Schmidt, was a forty-six-year-old retired infantry officer who had seen combat in Mexico and then France. Schmidt, whom Lewis code-named Agent 11, was on permanent disability for what we now call post-traumatic stress; he suffered acute nervous breakdowns. Even so, Schmidt bravely insinuated himself into the Friends of New Germany clubhouse. He found the FNG officials and their Nazi German minders so troubling that after just one month undercover Schmidt went out and bought himself a revolver. He kept it strapped to his hip, loaded, at all times.

Schmidt and the others in Lewis's first group of spies were surprisingly deft at getting themselves invited into the social life of the Friends of New Germany. They made themselves welcome regulars at Alt Heidelberg, which served as the first hub of Nazi activity in Los Angeles. The building, festooned with swastikas, housed a bustling German-style beer garden, a series of small private dining rooms, a restaurant—schnitzel by the yard!—and the newly established Aryan Book Store. The bookstore was a gathering place for Nazis and would-be Nazis and native fascists. The clientele could buy *Mein Kampf,* or the latest German pamphlets and magazines, or a growing assortment of American-produced antisemitic literature. Chatter on the floor of the bookstore usually ran toward contemporary politics. "The favorite subject of conversation," Schmidt reported: "President Roosevelt was a tool of the International Jew . . . and must be replaced by someone whom the veterans and the Nazis would select." The second floor of Alt Heidelberg—off limits to all but a small inner circle—housed the executive offices of the FNG, where the real business transpired. Lewis's best spies gained entry to the second-floor lair.

The surveillance operation made very quick work in its first year; Lewis's spies filed their reports weekly, identifying all the key active players in the Nazi/fascist movement in Southern California, including hundreds of William Dudley Pelley's Silver Shirts. They also gathered evidence of direct support and guidance for the American groups from the German government, including checks from the German consulate in Los Angeles and eyewitness accounts of the German government illegally smuggling propaganda through the port of Los Angeles, right onto the shelves of the Aryan Book Store.

But the Lewis operation did more than simply investigate and report. Before long, Lewis and his team scuttled a plot by U.S. Marines to sell guns and ammunition to the American fascists. Lewis and his undercover team could not be credited in public for their part in this operation, but it did earn them the enduring and crucial admiration of high-ranking naval intelligence officers. They also exposed an elaborate inside-job scheme to take control of U.S. military armories on the West Coast. That plan was run by Dietrich Gefken, a German national who had been one of the early organizers of Hitler's Brownshirts in Munich. After joining the California National Guard and inventorying the cache of rifles, machine guns, and coastal artillery pieces on hand at the San Francisco armory, Gefken had drawn up "the Armory plans, floor plans, location of ammunition and lockers and rifles, the list of addresses of the officers and all that was needed to take over the Armory on a given notice." Lewis's spies handed over their evidence of Gefken's plot to military intelligence officials, who shut it down.

ALL THIS, LEWIS and his friends had done by themselves, as a private enterprise, with scant help from law enforcement authorities. Not that Lewis hadn't tried to engage the cops. He understood that a private spy ring could do only so much; that he and his team had limited resources and no police powers; that the investigation into a dangerous German-backed political and military movement in America needed to be taken up by local law enforcement, the Department of Justice, and maybe even Congress. Lewis made it his standard practice to alert authorities as soon as he felt his team had collected actionable information. He had, for example, presented evidence of the armory plot, including sworn affidavits from his private spy network and secret recordings of Nazi planning sessions, to Chief James "Two Gun" Davis, the flamboyant leader of the Los Angeles Police Department. (Davis liked to have his picture taken while he posed in a crouch, both guns drawn, ready for trouble.)

Steven Ross found Lewis's memorialization of his meeting with Chief Davis when he was doing the research for his book *Hitler in Los Angeles: How Jews Foiled Nazi Plots Against Hollywood and America*. "When I opened the box, it was like I could feel the heat of the memo coming out eighty years later," Ross remembers. "Leon Lewis says, 'I'm writing this memo just after leaving the chief's office. I told them my background in the service, that I had also done some intelligence work, my background with the ADL and that here's what my spies had uncovered. Before I could proceed, two minutes into it, [Chief Davis] stops me and he says, "You don't get it. Hitler's only trying to save Germany from the Jewish problem. And that the real threat is not from the Nazis and fascists, but it's from all those Communists in Boyle Heights."'

"[Davis] basically says to [Lewis], 'I know every Jew is a commie and every commie is a Jew.' And he throws [Leon Lewis] out of his office. Says, 'There's nothing I can do for you.'"

When Lewis took this same evidence to the sheriff of Los Angeles County, the sheriff agreed with Chief Davis: the Jewish communists, not the German fascists, were Public Enemy No. 1. The head of the local division of the U.S. Secret Service was friendlier but told Lewis he couldn't do anything "without the commission of some overt act" (like, say, after the Nazis had already swiped the machine guns and coast artillery).

The plain truth is that the FBI was missing in action as fascism and Nazism took root and grew in the United States in the mid-1930s. America's much-heralded G-men were famously up to date on all the latest lab analysis techniques like fingerprinting, ballistics, and typewriter identification. They also made a point to scan the daily newspapers for nefarious doings, but they were basically untrained in countersurveillance, counterintelligence, or counter-espionage. They weren't prepared to counter anything. And in Los Angeles, the few resources the bureau did have locally were other-wise engaged, because the FBI chief, J. Edgar Hoover, was obses-sively focused, instead, on the communist threat. (Hoover had been hunting communists for almost twenty years already, and would be for decades to come.) Hoover's crew had, for instance, gathered a nearly two-thousand-page dossier on the left-wing actor and movie producer Charlie Chaplin. Chaplin's weapons of choice—a motion picture camera, a couple dinner rolls on forks, slapstick comedy—were very worrisome, apparently.

When Lewis invested in a cross-country trip from California to Washington to try to instigate a congressional investigation into homegrown American fascists and their enablers from Nazi Ger-many, he came away empty-handed. He did, however, get to sam-ple firsthand some of the prevailing rhetoric on the floor of the U.S. House of Representatives, like from the Republican congress-man Louis T. McFadden of Pennsylvania: "Do you not see the 'Protocols of Zion' manifested in the appointment of Henry Mor-genthau as Secretary of the Treasury? . . . It is not by accident, is it, that a representative and a relative of the money Jews on Wall Street and foreign parts have been so elevated. . . . It is well to re-member the boring-from-within tactics pursued by these alien usurpers who pursued tactics in Soviet Russia which caused the downfall of their government and set up the present Communist-Jewish control government which is now in operation."

Congress did get around to investigating the possible Nazi-fascist threat on the West Coast in 1934, but they conducted their inquiry behind closed doors. Very little of the evidence that Lew-is's spies had developed—which included possible laundering of illegal Nazi funds through one of the country's biggest banks and collusion between the San Diego chapter of the Silver Shirts and law officers in that city—ever got a public airing. And probably never would, according to the committee chairman. "It is of such a poisonous nature," the chairman told reporters, "it might cause serious international complications." Wouldn't want to ruffle feathers in Berlin.

The first year of spying on the Nazis in Southern California was all risk and little reward for Leon Lewis and his operatives. "My [law] practice has been completely shot to hell and I have just lost the best client I had," the spymaster admitted, "because of the way I have neglected their work during the past few months." Lewis was so exhausted and overworked at one point that doctors forced him to take a few weeks away.

His crew was also having a tough slog of it.

When Lewis's first loyal spy, John Schmidt, agreed in 1934 to testify in a civil case that Lewis had orchestrated to try to pit German-backed American fascist groups against one another, it went badly. "We'll kill you, you son of a bitch," one of the local fascists whispered to Schmidt as he prepared to take the witness stand. The German agents and their American allies also menaced Schmidt's wife and made threats against the couple's children. The Schmidt children were put under police guard, but this was cold comfort for their father. "The entire Los Angeles Police Department, Sheriff's Office, Federal Office, including the Department of Justice," one of the Silver Shirts had once bragged to Schmidt, had "taken the oath of the Silver Legion." Schmidt knew this was a wild exaggeration, but he also knew the local cops were generally sympathetic to the local fascists. By the spring of 1934, the pressure had all but cracked brave John Schmidt; he was living full-time at the VA hospital in Palo Alto, having suffered a debilitating nervous breakdown.

One of Schmidt's successor agents, Charles Slocombe, was still in his twenties when he signed on to Lewis's crew of spies. Slocombe's day job was running a water taxi between Long Beach and Catalina Island, but he had also had a brief career as a police informant inside the California chapter of the Ku Klux Klan, which counted more than twenty-six thousand members, hundreds of them policemen. Slocombe hated bigots. He loved adventure. He also turned out to be a very good mole. By 1938, Slocombe had burrowed higher and deeper into the Nazi-fascist operation in Southern California than anybody before or after.

Slocombe ended up helping to check some of the nastiest plots those particular fascists ever cooked up. The first was organized by an impatient Angeleno named Ingram Hughes, who was then running the American Nationalist Party. Hughes had grown weary of waiting for *Der Tag* and meant to hasten its arrival. He drew up a list of around a dozen or so distinguished Jewish men in Los Angeles and marked them for hanging. The list included judges, prominent attorneys, studio bosses, and a celebrated Hollywood choreographer. "Busby Berkeley will look good dangling on a rope's end," Hughes told his co-conspirator Henry Allen and Allen's trusted aide-de-camp, Charles Slocombe.

Hughes tasked Slocombe with buying the rope, then instructed him to go to several different stores to get the many fifty-foot lengths they would need (so as not to raise unwanted suspicion). Slocombe recorded all this and more in his weekly reports to Leon Lewis in the beginning and the middle of 1936. Hughes had selected for the mass hanging a secluded grove in Hindenburg Park, Slocombe reported, where the German American Bund threw parties to celebrate German Day, or Hitler's birthday, or the führer's annexation of Austria. Huzzah! The Bund also planned to run a Hitler Youth summer camp at the park for future Nazis. "There are lots of nice oak trees [in the grove]," Hughes told Slocombe. "It is an ideal spot for almost any occasion. No homes near there or anything."

After the "necktie party" was complete and the scene preserved for newspaper photographers to snap pictures to send across America, Hughes's men would drive through Boyle Heights firing automatic weapons into Jewish homes. This was sure to spark *Der Tag*, Hughes explained: "The custom will be taken up all over the country and will take action like wildfire."

Hughes kept revising and updating the operation, then postponing it—*We should wait until just after the election of 1936, when millions of Americans will be furious at the outcome*—then revising it again. They could set themselves up in a licensed pest control business, Hughes suggested, buy cyanide for fumigation, and pipe it into the homes of Jewish families.

This particular mastermind turned out to be mostly talk. Problem was, he did a lot of talking to Henry Allen, and Henry Allen had an in with some true psychopaths. One of them was Leopold McLaglen, a six-and-a-half-foot-tall former world jiu-jitsu champion, sometime Hollywood actor, and sometime military trainer who could be accurately billed as the originator of the "McLaglen System of Bayonet Fighting." This "death-dealing science," which included the newfangled "neck and trip" and "cross buttock" maneuvers, had been the preferred system for British forces in World War I. Which is to say Leopold McLaglen had already devised new ways to kill and taught others how to do it. He was also a wild-eyed antisemite and, according to Steven Ross, "intelligent, dangerous, and delusional."

Allen and McLaglen took Hughes's plan and put it on steroids. To get "worldwide publicity we are going to have to do a wholesale slaughtering here in the city of plenty of the leading Jews," McLaglen confided to Slocombe. "I can get the Nazi boys and the White Russians who would do this for us."

The number of planned victims expanded. As written out in Henry Allen's hand, the list now included Jack Benny, James Cagney, Eddie Cantor, Charlie Chaplin, Samuel Goldwyn, and Louis B. Mayer. McLaglen told Slocombe, Allen, and the local tsar of the anticommunist White Russians, George Doombadze, that perhaps synchronized firebombings would be more dramatic. McLaglen was sure he could get whatever dynamite they needed from his friends inside local police departments. He also made plans to dynamite any steamships leaving Long Beach with Jews fleeing his pogrom. Slocombe ran fast boats out of Long Beach, right? Perfect.

Lewis and Slocombe started to get seriously worried around then. Hughes had proven a blowhard, but in the hands of McLaglen and these others it felt like this idea was now becoming operational. McLaglen also appeared to have the backing of the Friends of New Germany, and apparently even the German consul in San Francisco—the unfortunately named Manfred von Killinger.

Lewis and Slocombe decided at the tail end of 1937 that watching and reporting on the development of this plan wasn't enough; they would have to find a proactive way to sabotage it, or at least neutralize McLaglen. They did it, too, with the help of Lewis's friends in naval intelligence and the otherwise generally unhelpful L.A. sheriff's office, which would end up taking all the credit in the press.

BY THAT SATURDAY in April 1938 when Lewis and Slocombe were barreling down the coast highway toward San Diego, Leopold McLaglen had been arrested, convicted on lesser charges, and deported to Britain. Henry Allen, thanks to Agent C19 (Charles Slocombe), was at that moment sitting in the San Diego city jail awaiting arraignment for possession of a deadly weapon, the "kike killer." There was good reason to think another conviction could take Allen off the field of battle altogether, because he already had a long rap sheet in California. Allen had done prison stints at San Quentin (Guest No. 25835) and Folsom (Guest No. 9542) for "uttering fictitious checks" and then trying to flee prosecution.

But when Lewis and Slocombe got to San Diego that day, they were clear on their priority mission: get hold of Henry Allen's briefcase.

Neither man could know where exactly the briefcase was at the time, or what exactly it contained. But they both knew it held a potential bonanza of new evidence. They even suspected its contents might reveal the roles being played by Henry Allen and "Auntie"—which they believed to be another alias used by Leslie Fry, the woman who had sent the *Protocols* to Henry Ford nearly two decades earlier—in a much wider fascist conspiracy.

When Leon Lewis and Charles Slocombe walked into the district attorney's office in San Diego, they did not have high hopes about getting what they wanted from the police and prosecutors. Long experience had taught them to temper their expectations where the local police were concerned. Then, too, Slocombe had already recounted for Lewis the reaction of rank-and-file San Diego cops who had arrested Allen and the other snowstormers a day earlier. "This is a hell of a note that we have to pinch a guy that's fightin' the Communists," one police officer had told Slocombe, whom the cops assumed to be one of Henry Allen's men. "I wish I had read that before I brought you to the station. This is good and I am going to put one of those in my pocket." The cop passed flyers around to the jailer and a few other policemen. "Hell," he said, "they ought to give him a medal."

Lewis had every reason to expect the worst from San Diego's law enforcement powers-that-be. But it turns out the district attorney and the San Diego County sheriff did have the briefcase that Allen had stashed in his Studebaker. And remarkably, Lewis was able to persuade them to open it up so he and Slocombe could have a look. The two men were aghast at what they found inside. There sat, as Lewis wrote at the time, "a mass of correspondence and other data covering the past six months, exposing widespread fascist conspiracies, numerous representatives and agents throughout the country and close affiliation with Nazi leaders and Nazi organizations."

Lewis figured he had to act fast, because the briefcase would have to be returned to Henry Allen on Monday, after his arraignment and release. The spymaster begged the DA to make photostatic copies of every scrap of paper in the briefcase. The DA demurred, saying his office didn't have a photostat machine, or access to one. When Lewis asked if he could take the materials and make the photostats himself, offering to pay out of his own pocket, the DA and the sheriff refused. Lewis and his spy network were not officers of the court, they reminded them. They had no legal standing to rifle through somebody's personal property.

Lewis had to find a way. He had been working with naval intelligence officers in San Diego, he told the DA and the sheriff, and naval intelligence would surely want to see the contents of the briefcase. This, he argued, was no longer merely a local issue. This was a matter of national security. From the DA's office, Leon Lewis placed a call to the head of naval intelligence in San Diego, who had already used Lewis's intel to stop fascist ops inside the navy. "Leon Lewis was sending information constantly to the FBI, to army military intelligence, and to naval intelligence," says Steven Ross. "The only group that is listening to him is naval intelligence."

The navy commander ordered the local lawmen, "in pretty plain language," to turn over the briefcase to Lewis and his assistant so they could make a proper inventory. The two men grabbed the briefcase and drove straightaway to the naval base in San Diego, where they could make photocopies of the entirety of its contents.

Lewis was in a real state as they drove down to the base. This might just prove the most consequential bit of spycraft he and his agents had pulled off in five years, and from what he had already seen in his first quick glance inside the briefcase, it was just in time. Lewis was already running through some of the names he recognized: the German consul Manfred von Killinger, Leslie Fry, James "Kike Killer" True. "If your friends want some pea shooters [rifles]," True had written to Allen just two months earlier, "I have connections now for any quantity at any price. They are U.S. standard surplus. . . . [B]e very careful about controlling the information, and destroy this letter." Lewis saw references to Clayton Fricke Ingalls, an outspoken Nazi sympathizer in the San Francisco area; General George Van Horn Moseley, who was still on active duty in the U.S. Army, but maybe not for long. Also: George Deatherage, who along with Ms. Fry had recently instructed Henry Allen to make an offer to the Grand Wizard of the Ku Klux Klan to purchase the organization lock, stock, barrel, crosses, and sheets. For $75,000.

The Klan, if Allen closed the deal, was to be a constituent unit of the American Nationalist Confederation, a political and paramilitary organization founded by George Deatherage and Leslie Fry the previous summer at a posh new high-rise hotel in downtown Kansas City. "The American Nationalist Confederation has been created as a matter of national emergency," read the organization's Constitution, Aims, and Objectives, "in order to provide a political, as well as a defense medium, for the mass of the Christian American people who refuse to subscribe to the Jewish-

Communist domination now in force in the existing Federal Government—and throughout the Nation as a whole."

The Confederation, which claimed offices in Boston, New York, Washington, D.C., Chicago, Houston, Miami, Savannah, Los Angeles, and San Francisco, had adopted as its symbol the Nazi swastika.

CHAPTER NINE

"PROBABLY TEN TIMES MORE"

George Deatherage's heart might have skipped a beat when he sighted the flag flapping high atop Embassy Row, in northwest Washington, D.C., on a cool day in February 1939. The flag had been adopted officially less than four years earlier but was already among the most recognized national symbols in the world. The banner sported a bold red background as a field, with a white circle at its center, and inside that circle, in black, a swastika. "As it brought Germany out of the depths of despair," Deatherage had recently exclaimed to a small, rabid audience of Americans, "so it will bring the United States."

As Deatherage neared the ostentatiously turreted, redbrick German embassy, he entered a Nazi safe space, owing more to American diplomatic imperatives than to German security precautions. The U.S. Congress had recently, by legislation, cordoned off discrete protest-free zones—each with a radius of five hundred feet—where it was unlawful to wave signs or placards or the like "designed or adapted to intimidate, coerce, bring into public odium any foreign government, party, or organization, or to bring into public disrepute its political, social, or economic acts or views, or to intimidate, coerce, harass, or bring into public disrepute any diplomatic or consular representatives, or to congregate . . . and refuse to disperse after being ordered to do so." The new law, inserted into the municipal codes of the District of Columbia, protected every foreign embassy and consulate in Washington. But it's not like Americans were frequently enraged enough to go protest on the diplomatic doorstep of the Swiss or the Ecuadorians. The impetus for the law had plainly been the simmering American feelings about the Nazis who were now in charge of the German delegation. In the late 1930s, though, those feelings were still at only a low boil in the United States.

The Nazi annexation of Austria drew twenty-five thousand demonstrators in London in March 1938 but did not spawn major protests in Washington; neither did Hitler's annexation of the Sudetenland in Czechoslovakia six months later. The true test came several weeks later, in November 1938, when a Polish teenager, Herschel Grynszpan—"an anemic-looking boy with brooding black eyes"—decided enough was enough. "Herschel read the newspapers and all that he could read filled him with dark anxiety and wild despair," explained Dorothy Thompson, the famous American reporter, who had been closely following the German threat in Europe. "He read how men, women and children . . . had been forced to cross the border into Czechoslovakia on their hands and knees and then ordered out of that dismembered country, that, shorn of her richest lands and factories, did not know how to feed the mouths that were left. He read that Jewish children had been stood on platforms in front of a class of German children and had had their features pointed to and described by the teacher as marks of a criminal race." The teenager walked into the German embassy in Paris and shot dead the third secretary.

Young Herschel was thrown into jail to await trial. A postcard he had written to his parents was confiscated. "May God forgive me," it said. "I must protest so that the whole world hears." The Nazis used Herschel Grynszpan's crime in Paris as justification to put the match to a fuse they had been very eager to light. On the night that German diplomat expired in Paris, November 9, 1938, mobs of marauders in Germany, Austria, and the German-occupied Sudetenland—some official police and military, some not—laid waste to families, communities, businesses, and institutions simply because they were Jewish.

News of *Kristallnacht* (the Night of the Broken Glass) flashed around the globe: the German gangs had burned or dynamited synagogues by the dozens, looted or destroyed Jewish businesses, confiscated millions of dollars' worth of assets—cash, securities, personal property, art, even furniture and toys. Germans murdered hundreds of Jews that night, beat and raped others. "Extensive demonstrations," Goebbels called the vicious attacks; he refused to ask for calm for twelve long hours, by which time the mobs had exhausted themselves. Goebbels blamed the Jews for inciting this atrocity against themselves, then announced that he would levy a fine against the German Jewish community at large—an astounding $400 million—to cover the damages.

Even after news of that harrowing night made front-page headlines in the United States, the area around the German embassy in Scott Circle in Washington, D.C., remained relatively calm. Fewer than a hundred members of the League for Peace and Democracy showed up to raise their placards and their voices at the embassy the next day, and the entirety of their sixty-minute demonstration unfolded at a safe distance, behind chalk-marked lines five hundred feet from the four-story building proudly displaying its swastika flag.

The protesters abandoned their plan to fly kites with anti-Nazi slogans when the local police explained that that, too, was illegal within the District of Columbia and would cost them $10 for every offending kite they flew. The earthbound placards noted by local reporters seemed both deeply correct and also feeble in the face of the terror and devastation the Nazis had visited on hundreds of thousands of innocent human beings in a single night: "Resist Fascist Terror," "Boycott German Goods," "Lift the Arms Embargo," "Appease Fascism? Why Not Tickle Tigers?"

ON A QUIET day three months later, George Deatherage stepped over those faded chalky markings five hundred feet from the German embassy and into the safe zone. The forty-five-year-old sometime construction engineer and full-time political activist was six feet, four inches tall and a solid 205 pounds, impressive girth for an

American man in the days before high-fructose corn syrup. Deatherage was combative by nature and girded by a thoroughgoing certainty in his cause, a faith in both the correctness of his views and
the urgency of his mission. He saw himself a red-blooded, real-
American patriot, a dedicated Christian, a fierce protector of
(white) Western civilization. He had looked around, studied and
researched the situation for himself, and here's how it looked in his
benighted view: the commies were on the march everywhere, not
least in his own country; they had already begun to pollute all that
was great and good about the United States. And the Jews were
behind all of it.

Something had to be done, now, was how Deatherage saw it.
Before it was too late. That's why he showed no hesitation in
waltzing up to the German embassy without appointment or letter
of introduction, but with the expectation that he would get an
audience. "We are all brothers in race and culture, devoting our
lives to a common cause," Deatherage had recently written in a
Nazi-owned international news service, "a cause which ultimately
must mean the salvation of the world for Christian and Aryan
people."

Deatherage's arrival—he proudly announced himself as the
person "raising all this hell around the United States"—presented
a bit of a problem at the embassy, a problem that struck at a philosophical and ideological conflict that split its staff right down the
middle in 1939. German officials in the United States knew all
about George Deatherage; just as they'd been tracking fascist public intellectuals like Lawrence Dennis, the Nazis had been tracking
ultra-right American activists like Deatherage for years. When a
political agent of the Third Reich in the United States submitted a
report to Hitler himself in the summer of 1937—"Achieving Collaboration of Germans with the National Men of America on Behalf of Both Countries"—he singled out James True, the wildly
antisemitic Pennsylvania Republican congressman Louis T. McFadden, Father Charles Coughlin, William Dudley Pelley, and George
Deatherage. The fascist publications this group spewed every week
("You can help save America, yourself and your family from the

folly of other nations by making the truth known to your friends")
were seen by the Nazis as helpful to their cause. There was already
an effort afoot in Berlin to help widen their distribution. The author of the "Achieving Collaboration" report even boasted of having introduced Deatherage to Manfred von Killinger, the very
aggressive German consul in San Francisco. (Von Killinger had
been in the loop on the planned mass murder of prominent Jews
contemplated by Henry Allen and his cohort in Los Angeles.)

But many in the German embassy in Washington wanted to
steer clear of the rogue Americans altogether. These were long-
serving professionals of their country's Foreign Office, schooled
in diplomatic subtleties. They did not necessarily share in the enthusiasm for the führer's full program, but it was their sworn duty
to give Adolf Hitler the chance to realize whatever destiny he had
dreamed up for himself and the fatherland. This meant, on a
practical level in early 1939, doing all they could to keep the
United States out of the growing conflict in Europe. The führer
was setting in motion the war machine he had been building for
almost a decade and was confident the German military could
roll over shoddily armed western Europe and Britain without
much trouble—at least as long as the Americans remained on the
sidelines.

And—helpfully for the Germans—lots of Americans wanted
to remain on the sidelines. Memories of World War I were still
fresh. Both the Democratic and the Republican party platforms in
1940 pledged determination to keep America off the battlefields in
Europe. Roosevelt ran for reelection that year insisting that neither
our aid to our allies nor our preparations in case of war should be
seen as any indication that we planned to jump in, unless we were
truly forced to.

In Congress, too, there were the mainstream isolationists, but
also senators like North Carolina's Robert Rice Reynolds, who
had just that week granted an interview to Hitler's mouthpiece
newspaper, *Völkischer Beobachter,* headlined "Advice to Roosevelt: Stick to Your Knitting." A sample of Reynolds's reasoning: "I
can see no reason why the youth of this country should be uni-

formed to save the so-called democracies of Europe—imperialistic Britain and communistic France. . . . I am glad to be able to state that I am absolutely against the United States waging war for the purpose of protecting the Jews anywhere in the world."

Among the most outspoken isolationists was the powerful New York congressman Hamilton Fish, who was already heading up the National Committee to Keep America Out of Foreign Wars. Just a few days after the Nazis strong-armed the rest of Europe into the give-us-Sudetenland-for-peace pact, for instance, Fish kept his date as the main speaker at the German Day celebration in New York City, where a few stray swastikas dotted the room and plenty of people in the crowd of seven thousand gave the Nazi salute. Fish, the ranking Republican on the House Foreign Affairs Committee, had avoided any criticism of Hitler in his speech, using the platform instead to ridicule President Franklin Delano Roosevelt.

For the all-important 1940 U.S. election, the German Foreign Office would certainly not be remaining neutral. Its agents were working within the halls of Congress and beyond to help install a more pliable man than Roosevelt in the office of the American presidency. But this kind of work required delicacy, the German diplomatic professionals knew. That's why the old hands in the Foreign Office, heeding the counsel of American advisers like Lawrence Dennis, had little use for loud, militant, and unapologetic antisemites like George Deatherage. He seemed a cinch to antagonize the very people the Germans most needed to convince of the blessings of neutrality: the middle-of-the-road Americans who were skeptical of expending blood and treasure on a war an ocean away.

There was another faction within the German embassy, however, much more sanguine about Deatherage and scores of other vocal proto-fascists raising hell in America. These younger, more radical players at the German embassy were all in on Hitler's messianic vision. This embassy faction was made up of men and women who were not foreign service experts but enthusiastic Nazis who had risen through the ranks of the Nazi Party's in-house Propaganda Ministry on the basis of zealotry. Their god-head, Joseph Goebbels, had begun sprinkling consulates and embassies around the globe with this new cohort.

These *Volk* read the führer's book-length political treatise, *Mein Kampf,* not as bombast, bile, and political humbug but as Holy Scripture—commandments from a modern prophet. By their lights, Adolf Hitler's ambit could not be restricted by national boundaries and formal international legalities, especially not where the United States was concerned, considering that the United States was filled with so much Aryan blood. More than twenty million U.S. citizens identified as German Americans in 1940, courtesy of a century of immigration. The notion of an iso-lated America living its own national life, separate from an all-powerful German empire in Europe and beyond, simply didn't make sense to the true believers.

"The German race does not cease at the frontiers of the Reich," read an editorial in *Völkischer Beobachter,* in 1939. "It is for us the happy certainty that millions of Germans outside the Reich bor-ders feel more strongly than ever the inner law of the German race, the law of blood, kinship and language. State borders have sepa-rated us Germans long enough; today, however, we surmount all borders to become a spiritual union of the whole nation of the Germans."

This merely answered in the affirmative the question Hitler had asked five years earlier: "So shall we today, as the true chosen peo-ple of God, become in our dispersal the omnipresent power, the masters of the earth?"

Baron Ulrich von Gienanth, the new attaché in the propaganda unit of the German embassy in Washington, was one of those avowed Nazi acolytes of Goebbels. Von Gienanth understood that the first steps to "omnipresent power" and mastery of the planet required regional shock troops to wreak a little havoc and sow a little chaos in their native lands. Soften things up a little bit, for what was coming. Von Gienanth had happily welcomed the "intel-lectual Godfather of American fascism," Lawrence Dennis, into his home in Nuremberg in 1936. And when George Deatherage showed up unannounced at the German embassy in Washington in February 1939, however uncomfortable Deatherage might have made the embassy's career foreign service professionals, von Gienanth welcomed him as an ally; the two men sat down for a long and searching colloquy.

Deatherage wasted no time in bringing von Gienanth up to speed on the current state of the Nazi-friendly movement in the United States. After five years of fits and starts, the train was finally starting to couple up boxcars from Boston and New York and Asheville and Wichita and Seattle and Los Angeles. The membership of the Militant Christian Patriots, the American League of Christian Women, the Christian Constitutionalists, the Defenders of Christian Civilization, the Christian Mobilizers, the Silver Shirts, the German American Bund, and Deatherage's own Knights of the White Camelia, a brother organization of the Ku Klux Klan, were falling in line under the colors—and the swastika emblem—of the American Nationalist Confederation. The plan was for a centralized fascist confederation with a national headquarters and well-armed, well-trained paramilitary cells in crucial port cities like Boston, New York, Washington, Miami, Savannah, Los Angeles, and San Francisco.

All this fascist freight train lacked, Deatherage explained, was an engine capable of political propulsion—a leader who could move the masses. An American Hitler. Deatherage realized early that he himself lacked the requisite measure of charisma (or pretty much any charisma for that matter), and his first and obvious choice, Charles Lindbergh, who was still trying to present himself as a mainstream voice, had declined all entreaties.

But God had recently tapped George Deatherage on the shoulder—according to Deatherage anyhow—and pointed him to the solution: Major General George Van Horn Moseley. Forcibly retired from the U.S. Army at the end of September 1938, General Moseley had gone on a tear against Roosevelt administration policies. "Not since the days of the secession has the future of America hung by so narrow a thread," he claimed in his retirement statement, which was printed in its entirety in newspapers across the country. The peril, Moseley asserted, came from within. He was a tad obscure about what exactly this existential threat to America comprised, but the increasing power of labor unions was implicated, as was the influx of undesirable immigrants (as opposed to immigrants he described as "of the right sort"). FDR's New Deal with its novel attempts to "raise the standard of living by redistributing the wealth" was the fatal tell for Moseley. It reeked of communism.

The genius of the radical-right general was one of the few things William Dudley Pelley, James True, Henry Allen, and George Deatherage agreed on at their occasional meetings in the American fascist clubhouse the Silver Shirts had rented in downtown Washington, D.C. Moseley "made several inflammatory speeches tending toward antisemitism and favoring a form of government other than that which the U.S. has now," one member of the fascist club explained. "This gave rise to considerable excitement at the council meetings and all persons concerned decided that it would be quite possible to consolidate their interests behind a man such as Moseley."

Deatherage had already made a pilgrimage to Moseley's home base in Atlanta, to feel out the general on his interest in leading their charge. The two men first met on Armistice Day, November 11, 1938, just after *Kristallnacht*. Deatherage was optimistic going in, because Moseley was not only an enthusiastic orator but a man of real military command experience. He was the recipient of the Distinguished Service Medal for his "large grasp of supply problems" and "tireless energy" in equipping American troops fighting in France during World War I, and had served at the War Department as deputy chief of staff to Douglas MacArthur.

The general—an unsmiling, beady-eyed man who looked a little bit like Ross Perot without the wing-nut ears—had also earned his reputation as a ruthless, hard-right belligerent. In the early days of the Depression, Moseley had played a key role in launching the U.S. Army's violent attack against American World War I veterans protesting in Washington for bonus payments they had been promised but never paid. Moseley proudly took credit for the part of that operation that resulted in the veterans' possessions being set on fire, burning out their wives and children who were encamped with them. General Moseley also maintained close ties to right-wing active-duty officers and soldiers, National Guardsmen, and the Reserve Officers Association, which made him particularly attractive to a man like Deatherage. "The [American Nationalist Confederation] must be built around a propaganda organization now that can in a few hours be turned into a militant fighting force," Deatherage wrote to a fellow fascist. "That is the idea of [Moseley] also, but it must be kept on the Q.T."

A few weeks later Moseley wrote to a member of the Reserve Officers Association: "It was difficult for me to do much while I was on the active list, for our instructions from Washington were very definite in keeping us away from all inquiries into subversive activities. Now I am perfectly free to tackle this problem. I am deeply impressed with the seriousness of it all, but at the same time I am greatly encouraged by the reaction throughout patriotic America. I have the feeling that a movement is now beginning which will result in driving all our enemies into the Atlantic and the Pacific." The still-robust-at-age-sixty-four (he was married to an heiress twenty years his junior) Moseley had already put a toe in the political waters. He embarked on a speaking tour that winter, with an eye toward announcing for the presidency in 1940. Fascist-friendly publications across the country were beginning to toll the bell for the general.

Still and all, Deatherage confided to von Gienanth at the embassy that day in February 1939, he was having trouble keeping the faith. The time "was now," Deatherage had been saying, but the movement lacked resources. Homegrown fascists in America couldn't compete with the Democratic and Republican parties without a lot more cold hard cash. Deatherage was essentially at the German embassy to beg for financial support, but he was sophisticated enough not make an outright and obvious plea for money. He couched the ask as if he were a man just looking for advice. How did the Nazi faithful keep their new party alive in the mid- to late 1920s, before they gained national power? Deatherage wanted to know. And when might the American fascist movement expect more financial help from industrialists and bankers who plainly despised Roosevelt here in the United States?

Here's how the rest of that chat went, according to Deatherage's sworn testimony and to investigators from the U.S. Department of Justice who later interrogated both men about the meeting at the German embassy in February 1939: Von Gienanth explained to him how the Nazis "originally started out with headquarters at an old brewery, just a few of them, and they pooled most of their money. Then they had some left and they took that money and they got themselves out a little [propaganda] sheet, the same as many of these sheets which you have here. They would peddle them by hand, and they got a little money that way, and they got a little money through party meetings, and they went on literally starving to death. . . . Industry and business as a whole hadn't done anything until they saw what was going to happen, and then they did it."

At one point in the meeting Deatherage asked von Gienanth, "This anti-Jewish feeling, what was the extent of that in Germany before Hitler's rise to power?"

And here was where von Gienanth was able to provide the American fascist a little encouragement. "It looks to me from what I read in the papers and the information I have," said the German attaché, "that probably there is ten times more [antisemitism] now in the United States than there was in Germany before Hitler's rise to power."

There is no direct evidence that George Deatherage relayed the German embassy's advice—and von Gienanth's judgment about the power of American antisemitism—to the man Deatherage was recruiting to lead his movement, General George Van Horn Moseley. But it also doesn't seem like the general needed much prodding along those lines. Out on the hustings, after his retirement from the military, he liked to warm up his crowds with a hearty defense of the Second Amendment—at least for the righteous. "Remember, today the right to carry arms must not be abridged," he told a luncheon group in Indianapolis, to loud applause. "In taking the

George Deatherage testifying at
a hearing of the Dies Committee

rifle or weapon from the Communists, from the [union members who belonged to the Congress of Industrial Organizations], and the murderers, we must not abridge that right of the patriotic Americans to bear arms. Remember that, in all history, before an internal enemy attempts to destroy his victim, he first disarms him by the operation of law."

With the audience sufficiently riled and their minds on their guns, Moseley would then usher them into the home stretch of his oration, which was always antisemitic, featuring the Big Lie first popularized by Henry Ford: that an all-powerful international Jewish cabal was bent on achieving communist rule in America. Ninety of every hundred commies in America were Jewish, Moseley would shout. Moseley often followed that up with admonitions about why America should not give in to "fear and hysteria" and make the foolish attempt to challenge Hitler's powerful army in Europe. General Moseley used as an analogy an observation he had made at a "combat royal" cockfight years earlier, where "all the cocks were put in the pit together and there was a terrible melee as they fought each other. But there was one wise old rooster who stayed on the sidelines and watched the battle. . . . That is what I want to see Uncle Sam do today. Let the foreign nations . . . expend their strength on each other—as they surely will if we will but leave them alone—and then, let us come in at the end and decide the fate of this funny old world."

Again, maybe it was just coincidence, but in the aftermath of Deatherage's sit-down with von Gienanth, Moseley's rhetoric became even sharper. Nazi Germany, he claimed in a speech to the Women's National Defense Committee in Philadelphia at the end of March 1939, had a right to be angry at their ill-treatment in the aftermath of World War I: "Why is the world so surprised at Hitler's action? His plans to reshape middle Europe have been stated openly and repeatedly. Not so very long ago . . . the German Ambassador in Washington was at my home. He stated frankly how Hitler desired peace, but Germany must have 'elbow room' in Europe for her development, and that the powers must not interfere with Hitler as he reshaped middle Europe to the advantage of the German people."

The effort to stop Hitler, Moseley averred, was just part of the conspiracy "for the purpose of establishing Jewish hegemony throughout the world. . . . History will have to repeat itself, and we will have to re-establish the Jew in power, and borrow the money from him. A partner of Kuhn, Loeb & Co., it must be remembered, financed the Russian Revolution, and he was mighty proud of his achievement. Trotsky, under whose orders 3,000,000 Christian Russians were murdered, is now our neighbor in Mexico. . . . What a beautiful picture it will be. Your sons and mine (I have three) fighting shoulder to shoulder with the Communists of Russia and being paid with money borrowed, probably from the Jews."

"Hail Moseley!" read a pamphlet published the next day by a very excited American fascist from nearby Stoddartsville, Pennsylvania. "U.S. Army Major-General Brands Jews as World War-Mongers Working to Have America Force Germany to Reinstate Refu-Jew Communists." Moseley later admitted this pamphlet was something of an embarrassment but explained that he didn't "go around kicking people that are trying to be friendly, in the pants."

A month later, General Moseley took his ugly talk to a whole new level in Springfield, Illinois. He was particularly riled because a major radio network had refused to broadcast his speech that day across the nation, citing Moseley's religious bigotry. The general's reaction to this mid-twentieth-century version of being canceled was unhinged. "Probably all our names will be taken down and listed for liquidation," he told his "Christian" audience in Springfield. "But no, the tide is turning definitely in America from coast to coast, and if there is going to be any liquidation, it may be of a very different order."

He thought America should start things off with a new, very Moseley immigration policy. "Over 2,000 years of recorded history shows very clearly that those traits which have made the Jew unwelcome every place he has been domiciled cannot be bred out," he said. He called for a program of "selective breeding" that included sterilization of Jewish immigrants in America. "If we do not adopt such a course," he told the good Christians in Springfield, "we can know definitely today that in due time we will be licked by some nation or group of nations that have looked to their manpower and bred it up."

To which Deatherage and the other American fascists hurrahed. "Hail Moseley!"

Moseley was back home in Atlanta in early May 1939, considering the possibility of making the city national headquarters of the American Nationalist Confederation and planning to take his political road show to the West Coast. He was prepared to do battle. "If the Jews bump me off," Moseley wrote to a friend of his in the Reserve Officers Association, "be sure to see they get the credit for it from coast to coast. It will help our cause."

CHAPTER TEN

BOUND AND OBLIGATED

Even the biggest, splashiest congressional hearings in the late
1930s were nothing like the televised scenes Americans have
now grown accustomed to—dozens of our elected solons arrayed
in a horseshoe, banked high above and well away from witnesses,
each participant with his or her own dedicated microphone, with
rows of press tables and onlookers arranged in neat geometric
rows of seats. The hearing rooms back around 1938 and 1939 were
neither august nor handsomely appointed, nor were they anything
that you might call well ordered.

Congressmen took up chairs on one side of a large oblong conference table, often with just a single microphone to pass among
themselves. The witnesses took their spots at a small wooden rect-
angular table pushed flush against the committee's table so that
they were on the same level, eye to eye, only about a dozen or so
feet from their questioners. Reporters, staff, and the interested
general public tightly ringed the little question-and-answer pit:
some at desks, some in stiff-backed wooden chairs, some standing
in the corners or leaning against the walls under large sconces
holding inadequate lighting fixtures. Uniformed Capitol policemen stood with arms folded, eight or ten feet behind the witness
table.

At the time, the House Committee on Un-American Activities,
commonly called the Dies Committee after its chairman, the Texas
representative Martin Dies, was about as well funded as it ap-

peared. Which is to say not too well, especially given the size and scope of its mandate: "To investigate (1) the extent, character, and objects of un-American propaganda activities in the United States, (2) the diffusion within the United States of subversive and un-American propaganda that is instigated from foreign countries or of a domestic origin and attacks the principle of the form of government as guaranteed by our Constitution, and (3) all other questions in relation thereto that would aid Congress in any necessary remedial legislation."

THE DIES COMMITTEE was constituted in the spring of 1938, when George Van Horn Moseley was still commanding the U.S. Army Fourth Corps in Georgia, and it was a welcome and friendly development for American anticommunists in and out of government. The initial seven-man roster of the Dies Committee consisted of Republicans and conservative Democrats. They opposed strikes and strikers and collective bargaining; they opposed federal legislation setting minimum wages or maximum hours for most working people; they also suspected that Roosevelt's New Deal had mostly been cooked up by socialist or even communist sympathizers in his cabinet. Key "targets" of the Dies Committee, according to a reporter on the case for *The Atlantic,* included the Department of Labor, the Works Progress Administration, the National Labor Relations Board, the Wages and Hours Division, the Congress of Industrial Organizations, the Civil Liberties Union, the Workers Alliance of America, the International Labor Defense, and the National Negro Congress. But the bull's-eye at the center of the committee target was the Communist Party of the United States of America.

These communists were, by the Dies Committee's reckoning, an increasingly threatening force. Not because the commies had become more revolutionary or more militant. But because they had become more palatable to the mainstream. The Communist Party of the United States of America had changed drastically since its founding in 1919, in solidarity with Vladimir Lenin's peasant-led Bolshevik revolution, which was then driving tsarist Russia to its aristocratic, feudal knees. Party membership in America numbered a scant ten thousand or so through most of the 1920s. These dedicated few had pledged fealty to the Communist International (Comintern) in Moscow and its goal of a worldwide workers' revolution. "If the Comintern finds itself criss-cross with my opinions there is only one thing to do," said one high-ranking American communist in 1925, "and that is to change my opinions to fit the policy of the Comintern." The CPUSA remained a small and toothless adjunct to Moscow throughout the 1920s. Most of its members were immigrants from eastern Europe, many of them garment workers in New York or factory hands in Chicago. Almost two-thirds of the CPUSA membership spoke a language other than English.

Not so by the late 1930s. Stalin in 1935 had proclaimed a "popular front" policy for communist parties around the world that allowed them to take up domestic causes and coalitions that broadly advanced leftist aims. In other words, it was time to operate within the system. The leaders of CPUSA were still quick to accept financial support from Moscow, but they were no longer bound tightly and solely to Moscow's dictates. The American Communist Party changed its new constitution to renounce the notion of the Comintern as the "supreme authority." CPUSA leadership also renounced one of its founding declarations: namely that party members should prepare for "armed insurrection as the only means of overthrowing the capitalist state."

The CPUSA's president went further, promising to protect the United States from any group "which conspires or acts to subvert, undermine, weaken or overthrow, any or all institutions of American democracy." So long as "this majority will is to maintain the present system," he pledged, "we submit ourselves to that decision." The party had gone to work to elect mainstream (but decidedly leftist) candidates to national, state, and local offices. By 1938, CPUSA officials were publicly calling FDR "the symbol which unites the broadest masses of the progressive majority."

The party was also laying down markers that put it inside the cultural mainstream. The Young Communist League celebrated the 162nd anniversary of Paul Revere's famous ride by sending one of its members galloping down Broadway, on horseback, dressed in the tricorne regalia of 1775. The party's national newspaper, *The Daily Worker*, began covering the sporting scene. "When you run the news of a strike alongside news of a baseball game, you are making American workers feel at home," an editor at the newspaper explained. "It gives them the feeling that Communism is nothing strange and foreign, but as real [and as American] as baseball."

The party's public alignment with America's democratic and cultural institutions had effect. CPUSA membership increased from around thirty thousand in 1935 to almost seventy thousand just three years later. These were hardly big numbers, but they were numbers that were still growing at a good clip in 1938. The demographics of the membership were also shifting. Nearly two-thirds of the members were native-born, English-speaking, American-schooled U.S. citizens. Who believed in the power of American institutions. Who could vote. And did.

The communists in America were not dangerous because they were readying some sort of armed insurrection to overthrow capitalism; they were dangerous because they were persuasive. Dies and his fellow conservative committee members were all over it. That was the threat they were hot to investigate in August 1938 as their hearings kicked off.

But a funny thing had happened on the way to the Dies Committee's hearing room; while the committee members were all eyes left, a lot of information on un-American activities of the far right was bleeding into public view. At the same moment the conservatives would have preferred to focus on the Reds, these damn proliferating fascists in America were making themselves difficult to ignore. Dies and his committee (and its successors) would of course go down in history as the legislative vanguard of the mid-twentieth-century communist-hunting Red Scare, but in the late

1930s their one wobbly, short punch at the ultra-right revealed a gathering swirl of hurt and hate that was about to come into direct, potentially violent confrontation with the U.S. government.

ON AUGUST 12, 1938, the first witness called before the committee to testify on fascist organizing in America was a former reporter who had told his personal story in the Chicago tabloid the *Daily Times* the previous year. John C. Metcalfe was a thirty-four-year-old German-born naturalized American citizen whose parents had changed his name from Hellmut Oberwinder when the family arrived in the United States back in 1914. His birth name had come in handy, as had his fluency in the language, when he joined the German American Bund so he could report on its activities for the *Daily Times*.

Metcalfe, whose family said he had "a mad bent for danger," ended up a right-hand man to the national president of the organization, the *Bundesführer* Fritz Kuhn. The young investigator was in the room when Kuhn bragged about his sway in Berlin, like when he had told the German Foreign Office to recall its ambassador to the United States for being too slow to support the Bund's growing mission. Metcalfe was also around when Kuhn boasted of his personal relationship with Adolf Hitler. The two men had met in Berlin in 1936, and Kuhn said Hitler had implored him to "go back and carry on your fight." There was proof of that meeting—a photograph framed by swastikas and splashed across the Bund yearbook of 1937. The caption underneath read "Bound to Germany, Obligated to America." Metcalfe brought a copy of the snapshot of Hitler and Kuhn to the Dies Committee hearing that morning and introduced it into evidence—Exhibit No. 31.

Metcalfe ended up putting into the record in that first session more than three dozen photos. A few came from the files of the German American Bund; most of them he took himself, he advised the committee, with a German-manufactured camera. They were hair-raising shots of Nazis at work and play, often in their somewhat surreal summer outposts: Camp Siegfried on Long Island, Camp Nordland in New Jersey, Camp Deutschhorst in Penn-sylvania, Harms Park in Chicago, and that quiet stand of oaks in Hindenburg Park in Los Angeles. There was a photograph of a biplane dropping swastika leaflets onto a cheering crowd of American Nazis in Camp Nordland. The same had happened in Philadelphia and Detroit, Metcalfe explained.

Metcalfe turned over a snapshot of the rifle range at the Bund camp on Long Island and one of storm troopers being led through military drills in Los Angeles. The pictures were black-and-white, so the witness stopped at one point to describe the American storm trooper uniforms in Technicolor detail: black trousers, silver-gray shirt, silver cap with a black band around it, black tie, an armband with a swastika stitched in, and a brown belt.

Metcalfe introduced and narrated photographs of Bund storm troopers and Italian American fascist "Blackshirts" goose-stepping together past a reviewing stand with *Bundesführer* Kuhn and the Blackshirts commander Joseph Santi. That was on Long Island, on the Fourth of July 1937. Then a photograph of the White Russian fascists throwing the "Heil Hitler" salute alongside their Nazi compatriots. Another photograph showed a flaming swastika in the night. The fiery swastika ritual "was an affair held throughout the country," Metcalfe told the committee.

Among the most unlikely photographs was a shot of an Italian fascist military commander speaking to *ten thousand* people gathered at a German American Bund celebration in northern New Jersey. The most chilling were the candid photographs of the attendees of the Hitler Youth camps; copies of these photographs were being sold as souvenirs in the German American neighborhood Yorkville in New York City: boys and girls at Harms Park and Camp Deutschhorst and Camp Siegfried. The uniformed young *Mädchen* might have been taken for Camp Fire Girls, but for the Hitler salutes and the swastikas in the background. Metcalfe's photos of the boys also showed "Heil Hitlers" and the swastikas, along with some even more disturbing images. Some boys were wearing steel German helmets reminiscent of World War I, and some posed with spears in their hands. "I took that picture of this boy on sentry duty at youth camp," Metcalfe explained to the committee.

The banners the boys flew and the insignia they wore were not entirely uniform. They always included the swastika, but there was also room for local flair, Metcalfe noted, pointing out one Hitler Youth flag sporting a skull in the middle.

Chairman Dies slowed Metcalfe down for a minute to take a measure of these Bund-run youth camps. "What size children do they have in it?" he asked.

"From very tiny tots, six or seven years old, all the way up to about eighteen years of age."

"Do they train them?"

"They train them and drill them and rather thoroughly Hitlerize them in their ideals."

"Do they bring books from Germany over for them to read?"

"They give them literature. . . . They have motion pictures imported from Germany which are frequently brought over by the German Tourist Information Bureau in New York."

"What do they teach them?" asked a second committee member.

"They teach the principles, basically, of National Socialism. They glorify Hitler and all that he stands for; the Hitler youth movement and all that it stands for. They glorify Germany in general."

Metcalfe testified that based on his work inside the German American Bund and his investigation of it from the outside, he had discovered "the real aims and purposes of the Nazi Germans in the United States." They were all tied to the war that Hitler was gearing up to conduct in Europe. "First, the establishment of a vast spy network; second, a powerful sabotage machine; and, third, a German minority with the present group as a nucleus [ready] to encompass as many German-Americans as possible. In this connection, it must be borne in mind that in 1916, prior to the entrance of the United States into the World War, Germany had practically no espionage organization or sabotage machine in this country. It is to avoid a duplication of this mistake that the Bund has become active."

Hitler Youth at a summer camp in New Jersey

Metcalfe returned to the committee three months later to name specific individuals and organizations who had been colluding with the German government in Berlin and its agents in the United States to distribute and amplify Nazi propaganda and to prepare for armed battle if necessary. He called out, with supporting documents, George Deatherage and his American Nationalist Confederation, William Dudley Pelley and his Silver Shirts, James True, Charles B. Hudson of *America in Danger!* (a weekly newsletter claiming "Jewry's UNITED FRONT is one of the Hidden Hand's chief weapons for destroying and enslaving Christendom"), the American Gentile Protective Association (in Chicago), and Henry Allen and his American White Guard. Metcalfe provided the Dies Committee with a July 31, 1937, letter signed by Allen: "Let those who dare attempt to betray America, and there will be more Jew corpses cluttering up American gutters than ever were found in the most ambitious of European pogroms."

Metcalfe identified more than 130 organizations in his testimony and noted an interesting similarity in their brand names.

"There is a common practice of misusing the words 'American,' 'Patriotic,' 'Christian,' 'Defenders,'" he explained. "That is to mislead the public as to the true principles of those organizations."

Metcalfe had done a lot of the work, but he was not alone. *Ken* magazine ran a remarkable journalistic exposé in September 1938, just after the Dies Committee began its congressional investigation. The *Ken* story uncovered a national scheme apparently dreamed up by George Deatherage, with help from friends including Henry Allen, William Dudley Pelley, Leslie Fry (aka Auntie), James True, and Clayton Ingalls. Beyond Deatherage's plan to form an umbrella organization, under the swastika banner, for all U.S. fascist groups, he had also started plotting their ascendance to power. Deatherage had designed a full-on blueprint for overthrowing the American government and installing a fascist regime run by a strongman in waiting; its operational details were designed to ensure absolute secrecy. Sounded a lot like a Silver Shirt operation, only much more ambitious.

"According to the plan that they have, they're going to divide the country into a whole series of cells," says Steven Ross. "And each cell will have thirteen members. No one else knows necessarily who else is in the cell and they certainly don't know who's in any of the other cells. And the leaders of each cell don't know who the leaders are of any other cell." Deatherage's kickoff for the plan was for these thirteen-man cells to begin quietly procuring necessary weapons. (Ingalls reminded his co-conspirators how easy it was to buy mail-order guns through the National Rifle Association.) Then after the election of 1940, when a large part of the country would be upset or even enraged at the outcome, the cells would be instructed to make strikes all over the country, all at once—a burst of armed, targeted violence, widespread and simultaneous. Even small fires, if enough of them were lit throughout the country, were sure to throw the United States into chaos. Then Deatherage's organized cells would take advantage of that chaos to seize power, to discard the election results, and to install their preferred leader. An American Hitler. This story in *Ken*, "Exposing Native United States Plotters," caught the eye of the Dies Committee. The magazine's editor, Arnold Gingrich, was called to testify.

Gingrich proved an enthusiastic, informed, and articulate interlocutor. He handed the committee a copy of a pamphlet containing instructions from "Department 25," the Hitler government's newly formed propaganda wing in the United States. The sheet had been passed out to a set of "reliable agents" in America numbering around five hundred. "The fundamental aim must always be to discredit conditions in the United States and thus make life in Germany seem enviable by contrast," the pamphlet read. "It will therefore be to the best interests of the Reich to cooperate secretly with all persons or groups who criticize the American system, regardless on what ground. The line to be taken in all such cases is to exaggerate the strength of Germany and to contrast it with the weakness of democracies."

What the committee really wanted to know from Gingrich were the sources for his magazine's reporting about German-supported sabotage afoot in America, including Deatherage's plot to overthrow the U.S. government. "Support for this charge is contained in a series of confidential letters that were exchanged by various individuals involved in this plot and signed only with pseudo names," Gingrich said when asked. "These letters were intended to be destroyed. They were, however, turned over to the Navy intelligence in San Diego, California. Those letters are now in the possession of Navy intelligence in San Diego."

So, there was a Jewish cabal, a great Hidden Hand, after all. Of the best possible kind. A superhero still in the shadows: Leon Lewis. Those explosive and incriminating documents that the journalists from *Ken* got hold of were in the hands of naval intelligence because of Lewis and Charles Slocombe, Agent C19. They came right out of Henry Allen's briefcase.

Leon Lewis himself was not altogether pleased that this intelligence had been leaked to the press without his approval. He was wary of anything that could blow his cover; there was still work to be done, and he still had agents undercover, in dangerous and potentially compromised positions. His chief concern remained in protecting what we now know as "sources and methods." But this much was hard to dismiss about Leon Lewis and his secret agents, even if nobody yet knew their names: after many difficult days of dangerous surveillance work, after years of providing intelligence to military and civilian law enforcement, sotto voce and without much effect, Lewis had provided a treasure trove, otherwise known as Henry Allen's briefcase, which felt like the game changer.

AS CIVIC DUTY goes, it was above and beyond the call; maybe one of the greatest acts of citizenship in twentieth-century America. Leon Lewis and his courageous agents had laid the bread crumbs right up to the barn door of fascist seditionists in the United States who were pulling in yoke with Nazi Germany; the trail would have been just as easy for law enforcement and government officials to follow, had they wanted to. But nobody had. Certainly not J. Edgar Hoover's underprepared and overdressed fingerprinters and ballistics experts at the Federal Bureau of Investigation.

Assistant Attorney General Brien McMahon did try to light a little fire under Hoover in January 1939, suggesting a long list of ultra-right plots and connections and potential crimes that the bureau might fruitfully chase down. He even offered to send over to Hoover relevant photostats of the Dies Committee's transcripts and findings. But the director of the FBI just kept, in his own words, "recapitulating" McMahon's memos back to him, eliding most of his requests, even the rather urgent one about this well-armed Deatherage plot. Did Assistant Attorney General McMahon really want the G-men to look into the Silver Shirts connection with the German American Bund, Hoover asked, on top of its work looking into the possibility of communist influence in the Federal Writers' Project? They were supposed to do both?

Other maddening little ditties from the bureau's files from that time include a memo to a thirty-two-year-old assistant director at bureau headquarters dated March 16, 1939, which indicated that nobody at the Chicago field office of the FBI had yet bothered to get a copy of the *Ken* magazine story. Worse, according to that memo, the FBI had been in possession of the actual Henry Allen briefcase file from naval intelligence for almost a year. And done nothing with it at all. "I am wondering whether, in light of the above reference to Allen, we are to be expected to make any additional investigation concerning him," wrote the FBI agent K. R. McIntire. He wondered.

The FBI did start to add to its long-dormant dossier on William Dudley Pelley and his Silver Shirts headquarters in North Carolina. To wit, Pelley "travels by night" and will not answer the doorbell during the day, even for his laundry. His wife has not been home in several months. He is of a "moody, surly temperament" (though probably not because his wife was gone, because he had a couple of local girlfriends), and the checks he draws on his business accounts are often cashed at a local jewelry store, "which is operated by one Ralanski, a Jew." Oh, and Pelley drives a Buick, donated to him by a fan. FBI sources also connected Pelley with Henry Allen, James True, George Deatherage, and something they called "George Van Horn Moseley's vigilante organization in the United States Army." (Moseley had a vigilante organization inside the U.S. Army? Apparently, the FBI both believed that to be true and doesn't seem to have ever looked into it.)

FBI agents from the Charlotte, North Carolina, office finally interviewed Pelley on Tuesday, March 14, 1939. They reported that they found him "in good humor" and "cooperative" even if he did whine a bit excessively about the difficulties of the previous six years. The chief of the Silver Shirts seemed ready to stand aside. "He can't see what it has got him but 'a damned big headache and a lot of gray hairs,'" the G-man reported. "He stated that the word 'Silvershirt' has become a national by-word and that . . . the hard work of organizing and building up this organization is done and is now behind him and that the American people will take care of the rest."

Pelley told the agents he did know Henry Allen, whom he described as a "blabber-mouth." But he didn't want to give up any other names, except maybe to Director Hoover personally. Maybe in a private conference. He trusted his fellow commie-hater J. Edgar Hoover, he explained, but was wary of the "liberal tendencies" of the current attorney general. Pelley was going to have his secretary draw up a history of the Silver Shirts for the FBI files. Pelley's field marshal, Roy Zachary, was on hand for the interview too. The fifty-one-year-old general store operator turned armed political activist thought the FBI agents would want to know that at a recent Silver Shirts meeting in Los Angeles, eight hundred attendees adopted, almost unanimously, a motion to impeach President Roosevelt. Zachary, agents reported, drives a brand-new blue Ford with Washington plates and "is apparently the type of individual who seems to pride himself on the number of difficult situations he has got himself into and out of, wherein he had nothing to lose but his life."

Agents spent another pleasant day with Pelley the following Monday, when the chief proudly informed them that the Silver Shirts had a post with headquarters in the principal city of each state in the union. He was unwilling, however, to provide a list of the post commanders. The agents did not press. Judging from the reports, the issue just didn't seem particularly urgent. The FBI had asserted back in 1934, without looking into it, that the Silver Shirts had no relationship to the Nazi government in Germany or any of its operatives in the United States. Five years later, they still didn't seem interested in finding out whether that was actually true.

There was also a bit of FBI activity concerning George Deatherage, but only after a local citizen contacted the Huntington, West Virginia, field office, essentially waving the article from *Ken*. The informant was an amateur printer in Charleston, West Virginia, who had worked with Deatherage at Carbide and Carbon Chemicals Corporation (later Union Carbide) and had been churning out publications for the Knights of the White Camelia since 1934. The printer wanted the FBI to understand right up front that he was a member in good standing of the local Elks Club and had never been arrested, but after reading the story in *Ken*, the informant "realized that there was a great deal more behind the whole thing than appeared on the surface." He said he could now see how the material he had printed for Deatherage might be used in ways "that were certainly not in the best interests of the United States and its existing government."

In their follow-up report to headquarters, FBI agents in Huntington dutifully cataloged the swastika-rich pamphlets, envelopes, and letterhead stationery the informant handed over; they also quoted liberally from the *Ken* magazine story, four full pages' worth. Their report included notes from talks with a county law enforcement officer and a lieutenant colonel in the U.S. Army Reserve. Each man had already done a cursory investigation into Deatherage, who was not shy about his beliefs or his activities. "I do not have time to make a complete investigation," the army reserve officer had written in his report, "but suggest a check be made to determine whether Deatherage is a. Nut; b. Agent of some Government or organization; c. A legitimate operative."

The local G-men decided not to spend a lot of time and resources in making any of those determinations. "No further investigation is being conducted at this point until instructions are received from the Bureau," read the memo to FBI headquarters in December 1938. The investigation was marked "PENDING." The next report from the FBI field office in Huntington, made five months later, in May 1939, was a brief review of the history of Deatherage's Knights of the White Camelia, his American Nationalist Confederation, and his relationship to the German American Bund and actual Nazis in Germany. The report was nothing more than a rehash of quotations from the literature provided by the amateur printer in Charleston and the facts developed by *Ken*. The team had developed no further evidence in the matter, and apparently asked no further questions.

The agent who wrote up that last review noted for headquarters that George Deatherage was "well poised, self-confident and apparently very well read. . . . [He] is opposed to the New Deal Administration, inasmuch as he considers it Socialistic and Communistic in objective and controlled by the Jews. . . . It is Deatherage's belief that such individuals as the Retired General Van Horn

Moseley and Father Coughlin are allying themselves with the growing feeling against the Jews."

J. Edgar Hoover and his brain trust chose not to spend many of the FBI's dear resources investigating the fascist, Nazified alliance growing in America in 1939. So the Dies Committee—under-resourced and usually looking in the wrong direction—remained the sole and therefore best government investigation into what was quickly becoming a real and violent fascist insurgency. *Oy vey.*

CHAPTER ELEVEN

"THE HANDWRITING ON THE WALL IS CLEAR AS A BELL"

In the third week of May 1939, the Dies Committee heard from a strange duo peddling a story about New York's Harmonie Club, whose membership included some of the most prominent Jewish businessmen, lawyers, and politicians in the country. The two witnesses said they had been getting reports from a member of the Harmonie Club waitstaff who had stumbled on a conspiracy of epic proportions, a conspiracy, the witnesses claimed, that might just involve Secretary of the Treasury Henry Morgenthau, the newly appointed Supreme Court justice Felix Frankfurter, and Undersecretary of State Sumner Welles. The waiter (using the alias "George Rice") had started listening in and then taking notes, and then he provided those notes to a New York real estate man named Dudley Pierrepont Gilbert, who in turn passed them on to a reserve army officer from Kentucky named James Campbell. According to this James Campbell, who heard it from Dudley Pierrepont Gilbert, who heard it from someone not named "George Rice" but who wanted to be called by that name, who heard it from the guys at table three in the corner, these household-name Democrats and liberals and Jewish power brokers at the Harmonie Club were all stuck deep into an elaborate and interlocking plan to overthrow the U.S. government and install a Bolshevik regime. *We have the evidence right here,* as old Henry Ford might say.

The Jewish conspirators, according to the witnesses, were

going to either upheave business conditions on Wall Street or push the United States into a draining foreign war or simply run a Marxist-Leninist proletarian uprising or maybe engage in some combination thereof. Gilbert and Campbell had more or less invited themselves as "expert" witnesses for the Dies Committee, and the story they had to tell was basically the "Protocols of the Elders of the Harmonie Club." Their story was also about as credible as the original. The reports Gilbert and Campbell were passing around—which they code-named "music scores"—were all written in Gilbert's hand; Gilbert had transcribed "George Rice's" handwritten reports, see, and then burned the originals. For safety's sake. Neither Gilbert nor Campbell was able to provide a real name for the elusive Mr. Rice, nor—at the time of their testimony—were they able to locate him to help provide corroboration of their claims, which, after all, they said were *his* claims. Pressed about Rice's "disappearance," Gilbert told the committee darkly, *You'd be running scared, too.*

Gilbert, who kept a town house in Manhattan and a home in the summer resort of Newport, Rhode Island, did not exactly wreath his brow with laurels during his time in the witness seat. When asked who was financing his investigations, Gilbert replied, "I should say *I* have, but to be more truthful, my wife, because I am pretty hard up financially, and she didn't get cleaned out as I did in 1932. Her father died and left her some money." (The first Mrs. Gilbert sued for divorce not long after, successfully, on the grounds of "neglect to provide.")

Gilbert presented himself as merely a disinterested citizen and not the antisemitic fascist he actually was. But he was badly undercut by the photographic evidence of him Sieg Heiling and by his correspondence with his fellow witness. "Remember those who are finally successful always suffer much before victory," he had written to Campbell, in a letter entered into the Dies Committee records. "Mussolini was insulted, stoned, driven from town to town. He and his family suffered much for lack of money. Hitler was jailed and persecuted for years. . . . It is that very suffering that has welded together the strong type of men that have led nazi-ism to victory in other countries. That same will be here. We must win."

Campbell didn't fare much better as a witness. When the Dies Committee counsel asked why Campbell made it a habit to tear off all the return addresses of his correspondence before he tossed the envelopes into the wastebasket, Campbell said it was "because we have a very inquisitive n——r janitor." The committee nonetheless turned up a letter to Campbell from a Republican state party official in Indiana who had helped Campbell set up a speech in Indianapolis by General George Van Horn Moseley; Moseley's audience for the Indiana speech included more than 300 businessmen from across the state, 72 newly elected mayors, 283 newspaper editors and publishers, and 67 legislators. In his letter to Campbell, the Indiana GOP official had asked Campbell to check three questions for him: "Is it true that [Secretary of State Cordell] Hull's wife is part or full-blood Semite? What do you know of [recent Republican presidential nominee Alf] Landon's Semitic connections? What do you know of [journalist] William Allen White's Semitic connections?"

Campbell apparently didn't have the answers, but he dutifully passed the questions along to a man who had an expertise in this kind of "research"—George Deatherage.

Deatherage's return letter, written December 14, 1938, and entered into the record by Chairman Dies on May 18, 1939, was kind of remarkable. "Our time is coming," Deatherage had written. "You may rest assured that the general will take care of that." (The general in question, Campbell explained, was George Van Horn Moseley.) "I believe as you do that it will take military action to get this gang out. . . . [General Moseley] will decide on his return just what procedure he will follow and the plan now, as he sees it, is to start a little [headquarters] in Atlanta where we will map the enemy. . . . Now, we must have State and county leaders all over the Nation that we know without a shadow of a doubt are men that will stick under any kind of fire. . . . I would much prefer, and

I think that you will agree, that the leadership should be officers who have seen active service. . . . I feel sure that if these men, many of whom you and I know, were appraised [*sic*] of the situation, they would resign their commissions and enlist with us for this American-Jewish war."

It was a Thursday when Deatherage's letter to Moseley was entered into the record. By noon on Friday, Chairman Dies had sent subpoenas to both Deatherage and General Moseley.

Moseley hemmed and hawed and explained that it might take him some time to get to Washington. He was traveling, he said, at Imperial Valley, California, a place filled with "pure, loyal, American air," he noted, and "vigilantes"—but lawful ones. Whatever that meant. But he said yes, eventually he would show up in the Old House Office Building.

Deatherage had a very different response. He told Chairman Dies he was heading for the Capitol *tout de suite*. He demanded a public hearing. How about Monday?

THEY SETTLED ON Tuesday, and Deatherage had to wait until afternoon, while that Indiana state GOP official testified. But Deatherage came out swinging, even before he was sworn in. He wanted to be assured that the oath he was taking was a "Christian oath." Then he refused to agree to keep his answers strictly responsive to the questions posed and not wander off into any great anticommunist, antisemitic screeds. "Now listen," Deatherage exclaimed, rising from his chair.

Chairman Dies told him to sit down.

"You come here and make me sit down," he said. Two Capitol policemen unfolded their arms and did just that. And that was just for openers.

When Dies threatened to move the hearing into a closed executive session, with no press allowed, Deatherage settled down. He then proceeded to slalom through an account of his life, his politics, his organizations, including the provenance of his beloved

Knights of the White Camelia, which he had personally resurrected five years earlier. "In 1867, during the Reconstruction Days, the old carpetbagger days, there were several organizations started: the Klan and the Knights of the White Camellia," Deatherage explained, even after the committee said it was not interested in a history of the Klan. "Now you are familiar with what their purpose was. The Knights of the White Camellia were composed mostly of ex-officers of the Confederate Army. The Klan was composed mostly of the men who were in the enlisted division. Naturally they formed buddies and grouped together." When the Klan had exploded back onto the scene in 1915, Deatherage explained, they had borrowed some rituals from the Knights. "The Knights of the White Camellia lay dormant all the time until this Marxist crisis arose and we reorganized it again."

Deatherage refused to divulge any names of the members of his organizations. He had sworn an oath of secrecy. It was a matter of honor. But he did explain his personal biography, including his family connection to the famous feuding Hatfields of West Virginia. In fact, he told the committee, he had just sought out the advice of his cousin, former U.S. senator Henry D. Hatfield, the night before. He'd also had a brief conference that evening with his friend James True. "I have known James True probably for five years," he said. "Anything I can do for Jim True I would do it."

Chairman Dies asked if this was the same James True who had invented the "kike killer."

"I can tell you about that," Deatherage answered. "He patented it."

"A weapon?" Dies asked.

"A piece of wood about that long, a baton, a square piece of wood with notches cut in it. This was a legitimate patent, which he hoped to sell. . . . [H]e had ladies' and gentlemen's sizes."

This comment, unfortunately, drew laughter from the room.

Deatherage confirmed his friendship as well with James Campbell and his working relationship with General Moseley, but said he'd leave it to the general to explain himself. He also spoke of his own political agenda, his methods, and his attempts to reach the

American working man to make him understand the Jewish threat to the country. "You have only one recourse," Deatherage explained to Representative Dies, "and as you know enough about psychology of peoples, you have got to appeal to their emotions, not their reason. The avenues to reason are closed to us."

"That is what Hitler said in *Mein Kampf,*" Dies noted.

"I don't know whether he said it or not, but that is what I said. If he agrees with me, that is all right with me," Deatherage answered, inspiring another slightly nauseous wave of laughter.

Deatherage insisted he was a Christian, an American patriot, a defender of the Constitution, which led Chairman Dies to a spirited defense of national ideals: "You are bound to concede that each individual, whether he is a Jew or a Gentile or a Catholic or a Protestant or what not, must be, if he is an American citizen, protected in the enjoyment of his fundamental rights, the same as everyone else, isn't that right?"

"That is right," Deatherage conceded, "except I am bigoted enough to believe in white supremacy in the South."

Dies and everybody else on the committee allowed that remark to pass without admonition or objection.

All in all, Deatherage seemed pleased with his performance. But he was unmistakably perturbed that the committee did not give him a chance to identify and name all the communists working in the Roosevelt administration. He had a list of them, he explained, alphabetized. He had also cataloged and sorted the vast interlocking international Jewish communist web at work in America. With charts. These documents were in a secret hiding place, in the hills of West Virginia, and Deatherage was eager to be allowed to provide them to Chairman Dies and his cohorts.

There was so much that Deatherage thought the committee should know, and he was excited to come back. "I have been assured that I will be offered an opportunity to offer my evidence of this situation before the committee," he said toward the end of his testimony. "I don't want to make statements that I can't support with documentation. The documentation which will be necessary to support my evidence—I have got about two tons of it in boxes, and I have got it where I can have a truck into it in five minutes on a telephone call and spread out here, and I could take you step by step and show you the whole situation, names of individuals, organizations, methods of financing, documentation, photostats of this and that and the other thing, which support it all."

Deatherage figured he could get through all of it with them in about two days.

Chairman Dies told Deatherage it might be best if they sent the committee's investigators down to West Virginia, where they could look at all this "documentation" and see how much of the two tons of "this and that and the other thing" was reliable. Deatherage thought maybe it would require a little extra time to prepare for such a visit.

"I might add that I am of a very studious nature, and I have tried to be exact," Deatherage told Dies. "I think I am in touch with sources of information all over the United States where I can get anything you want."

At the very end of two days of testimony, the committee offered to give Deatherage a month to compile all his supporting evidence and then haul it up to the Capitol for inspection.

"That satisfies you?" Dies asked.

"Yes; the only thing is, if the committee can give me any assistance regarding typing or help or anything of that sort."

THE PRESS CAUGHT up to General Moseley at the Biltmore Hotel in Atlanta, after he had apparently stopped off in his hometown to collect and review some papers on his way to respond to the committee's subpoena in Washington. He was the victim of a "smearing campaign," the general told reporters, and the committee was derelict in not acting on the "secret report" about the Harmonie Club provided to them by his friends in New York, Gilbert and Campbell. The congressional committee was ignoring evidence of a Jewish plot to deliver America to the communists. "Why don't they investigate these Jews? What powerful government interests are shielding them? . . . [T]he whole thing smells too much like

Russia," Moseley said. The general did finally wend his way to Washington, for what was by then pretty hotly anticipated testimony before Dies and his committee.

Among the handful of amenities the U.S. House of Representatives provided in its committee hearing back in 1939 was a spittoon, which ended up being a very useful stage prop for Moseley and the small team of counselors who accompanied him to his testimony the week after Deatherage. The Dies Committee was still coming to order in the lead-up to the general's second day of testimony, when Moseley pointed at his

Charles B. Hudson carries water for General George Van Horn Moseley.

already-filled drinking glass and, for effect and attention, asked the committee counsel, Mr. Rhea Whitley, if he could "guarantee" the water supply.

Whitley hesitated, wondering what the hell that was supposed to mean. Before Whitley could respond, one of Moseley's factotums, described by various reporters on hand as "stocky," "bespectacled," "short," and "baldish," said to the general, loud enough for all to hear, "Don't touch it. I'll get you paper cups." Having called the room's attention to himself, the aide-de-camp then grabbed the glass and dumped its contents with dramatic flourish into the waiting spittoon. He shortly returned from a nearby cooler with a fresh cup of water, unsullied by committee members or their staff.

"Were you seriously afraid that water had been contaminated?" one reporter asked the man.

"Absolutely," he replied, and then refused to identify himself. Why wouldn't he identify himself? "Unnecessary," he said.

Moseley later explained the reason for his team's acute uneasiness in an exchange with a committee member. "I have been warned [by friends and allies] not to go into certain places, and so forth," he said. "They have heard reports about people unfriendly to me, who have plans to get me out of the way, you know. A lot of people have dropped out of the way in the last few years, very quietly."

"What kind of places do they warn you not to go to?"

"Especially restaurants; that is the reason I asked if this water was all right. I don't trust this committee too far, you know."

There was laughter in the stuffy, standing-room-only hearing room, but Moseley was in dead earnest. Here he sat, after serving with distinction in the U.S. Army for more than forty years, having been summoned under power of subpoena to testify. Under oath. As a hostile witness. To answer for his recent political activities. "All I am trying to do," he wanted it understood, "is save America from herself."

When asked to state for the record a concise résumé of his military career, Moseley sniffed, "Is that necessary? You can find it in Who's Who."

The general asked to be allowed to read his prepared two-hour-long opening statement into the record, but the committee members had good reason to believe Moseley was about to make unfounded accusations against otherwise decent people, as he had been doing to Secretary Morgenthau, Justice Frankfurter, and the president. Dies knew Moseley was a proponent of the farcical Harmonie Club conspiracy theory; he had been sending the Gilbert-Campbell "music score" reports to his friends in the army. The committee asked Moseley to hold off on the statement. "You are not here for the purpose of making speeches, General."

"The American people want to hear this," Moseley insisted. "I have a lot of good evidence. Aren't you interested in un-American activities?"

The general and the committee sparred for a while, but Moseley finally conceded. He turned and pointed to one of his small retinue behind him. "My friend who accompanies me here [Republican representative Jacob Thorkelson of Montana] will bring this all out, I hope on the floor of the House, and I am sure I will bring it out before the American people coast to coast."

The general admitted, under examination, his relationship

with army reserve officer J. E. Campbell, one of the Harmonie Club conspiracy witnesses. Campbell had assisted Moseley in his quest to eradicate venereal disease, the general explained, which had felled many a serviceman. "We have something like twelve million syphilitics in the United States, and if you will investigate my record you will find that I have been interested in that for many years. . . . What we were trying to find was something in the Army that would take the place of silver salts and would not get old. If you are familiar with the silver-salts solution, it is all right for about two weeks, and then it is no good."

But getting to the point, did Moseley know that Campbell had been closely associated with George Deatherage for more than a year?

"I was aware of the fact that they knew each other," he said, and went on to describe his meetings with Deatherage soon after his own retirement. Deatherage "stayed in Atlanta some time, and I saw him practically every day," Moseley testified. "He struck me as just a two-fisted, honest patriot." He later admitted that Deatherage had wanted him "to take leadership of his group," but the general had never agreed to the proposition. Moseley said he made a point never to sign onto any organization, much as he approved of its aims. He certainly wasn't going to bad-mouth them.

"Those organizations on the right are going to continue in some form or another, and whatever you call them, just so long as there is the disease of communism in America," Moseley explained. "If you have got the disease here, you have got the antitoxin there. . . . The disease started on the left—the antitoxin is on the right."

"In other words," asked Congressman Jerry Voorhis, "you feel that the organizations at the extreme right, the Nazi and fascist organizations, are really a good and necessary thing under present circumstances?"

"They are trying to sustain our democracy and the other fellows are trying to destroy it," Moseley asserted, "that is the only difference."

Moseley's frustration was apparent. "The handwriting on the

wall is clear as a bell," he sputtered. He was frustrated with the committee, with Congress, with the White House, which was hamstringing the fight against the Reds. "The first thing I would do if I was in the White House, gentlemen," Moseley testified, "I would issue an order immediately discharging every Communist now in the Government of the United States, and everybody who is giving aid and comfort to a Communist. I would then release the United States Army from the present position which it is in."

"What is that position?" a committeeman wondered.

"It can make plans to take Germany and South America and Japan, but they can't do a damn thing to protect themselves from the enemy within our gates. They have been told not to investigate anything."

"By whom?"

"I guess it comes right from the White House, he is Commander in Chief of the Army."

"Are you going to guess, or do you know?"

"I don't know."

"But you are guessing it comes from the Commander in Chief of the Army?"

"It comes from right at the top," Moseley insisted. "I don't know from whom. But that is a fact, if you will investigate it. We can't, in the Army, investigate a soul in reference to the enemies within our gates, not a soul."

The committee ran through some of the most bigoted passages in Moseley's speeches, which the general confirmed as an accurate reflection of his thinking. "I believe in watching our breed in America very carefully," he told the committee. "I believe the Jew is an internationalist first; he is a patriot at home second." He made wildly inaccurate claims that the communists in America counted more than six million members, nine of ten Jewish. "I have an idea this is still a Christian country, don't you see," Moseley said. "I was brought up to feel that we were and are."

"Do you have any reason to believe," asked the committee counsel, "that we are not, at the present time?"

"There is an objection to the use of the word 'Christian,'" Moseley answered. "They want to take out of my mouth the word 'Christ' and 'Christian,' and they can't do it." Moseley was vague on who exactly this "they" was.

At one point, the committee questioned Moseley about correspondence suggesting the general's admiration for Hitler and his problem-solving skills: "What problem do you think he solved that they had in Germany, General?"

"He has solved, Mr. Congressman, the difficulty of international finance entirely independent of the rest of the world."

"Now," a committee member asked, "there is no other problem that he solved that you had in mind?"

"He has solved the racial problem."

"How?"

"In his own way," the general said. "I am not saying before this committee I approve of his methods."

"Do you disapprove of them?"

"I approve of his taking back and placing in the hands of the German people the control of that nation."

"Do you look upon a Jew, born in Germany, as an alien to that

General George Van Horn Moseley during his testimony at a Dies Committee hearing

country, people whose ancestors have been there for hundreds of years?"

"No."

"Do you think [Hitler] should have taken their property to give to other German people; is that solving it along your ideas?"

"I don't know—you can't expect me to place myself in Hitler's position and solve those problems. I don't know what confronted him. . . . You are asking me to state my opinion on a great question, and I don't want to do that."

CHAPTER TWELVE

HOLLYWOOD!

On the evening of April 27, 1939, studio mogul Louis B. Mayer threw a party and broadcast it live on MGM's own *Good News of 1939* prime-time radio program, which aired coast-to-coast, 6:00 Pacific standard time, 9:00 eastern standard time, on the NBC Red Network. "Friends, tonight there's a very special celebration going on over at the MGM lot," one of the studio's top players, Robert Young, offered by way of introduction. "An elaborate banquet is being held . . . toasting one of the greatest, most beloved American actors. A famous member of a great acting family, Lionel Barrymore, on the eve of his sixty-first birthday."

The occasion itself was not exactly a ready-for-prime-time event. Lionel was indeed part of the nation's most celebrated thespian families—"the name Barrymore is money at any box office," Hollywood's head cheerleader, Louella Parsons, had noted in her column just a few weeks earlier. But even ardent fans would acknowledge that by the spring of 1939, Barrymore's star power was waning. To be blunt about it, the studio had a dozen or more luminaries whose birthdays would seem to warrant greater attention, at least from a business standpoint. And also just from a human standpoint; is sixty-one years really that much of a landmark? Let alone the "eve of" sixty-one? No matter. MGM's head man had decided Lionel Barrymore's sixty-first birthday needed to be marked. Or at least the "eve of his birthday" needed to be marked. Who was gonna question Louis B. Mayer?

In that moment, Mayer was arguably the single most powerful man in one of the most far-reaching and lucrative industries in America. The motion picture business was a juggernaut in 1939. Hollywood releases, according to best estimates, drew more than 80 million paying customers a week in the United States (out of a total population of 130 million) and another 50 million or so worldwide. A handful of movie studios, including Paramount, 20th Century Fox, RKO, Warner Bros., and MGM, dominated the market. And a handful of men dominated those studios. At the top was MGM's Mr. Mayer, who was taking home $1.3 million per year ($28 million in 2023 dollars), making him the highest-salaried man in America at the time. He also decided—personally—how much everyone else in the company received; he set the salary and wage scale from top to bottom at MGM. So, when Mr. Mayer declared that attendance would be mandatory at Mr. Barrymore's birthday for every marquee name and featured player, every major executive, every senior producer and director on the studio payroll, the entire "MGM family" toed the line.

The megastars William Powell, Myrna Loy, Mickey Rooney, Jean Harlow, Norma Shearer, Rosalind Russell, Robert Montgomery, Hedy Lamarr, James Stewart, Joan Crawford, and Clark Gable were all present at the "elaborate banquet" set up on an MGM soundstage. "A thrilling spectacle of red, white and blue decorations," the *Good News of 1939* announcer narrated for the radio audience listening in. Old Lionel received "personal tributes" from a few of the bigger stars there that night, which really just amounted to the recitation of a few lines each from a single execrable poem. "This party's terrific, a genuine sensation," intoned the eighteen-year-old boy wonder Mickey Rooney. "They're all joining in from all over the nation."

Mayer gave the keynote address. He extolled the personal virtues of his long-standing contract player, but mainly used his talk as an opportunity to plug Mr. Barrymore's latest film, the second in the Dr. Kildare series, whose release had been held back until the next day, "to time it with your birthday." The Kildare movies "will grow more popular as we continue," Mayer explained, because just like Mickey Rooney's Andy Hardy teen movies "they have the philosophy, the answer to the hopes and prayers of all fathers, mothers, sons, and daughters. . . . You have been an inspiration to all who have enjoyed the pleasure of knowing you and working with you. And for every man and woman over the world who belongs to our family, and on behalf of the great Maxwell House coffee organization [sponsor of the *Good News of 1939* radio hour] I wish and offer a prayer that you will have many, many more birthdays."

Lionel was permitted a tad less than two minutes of airtime to address the gathering in the room and the nation at large. "I am proud to be a member of a great motion picture industry which brings a troubled world entertainment," Barrymore offered, "through which escape from cares may be found."

The "troubled world" and the American motion picture industry's place in it were exactly what was behind Louis B. Mayer's decision to gather up the jewels of the MGM crown and make sure they were all under his watchful eye on the eve of Lionel Barrymore's sixty-first. The purported cause for celebration was less important than the date. Because on that same spring evening, just a few miles north, a rival studio was premiering a film that Mayer feared would do much harm to both the reputation and the commercial health of the industry he bestrode. And maybe even to the physical safety of its stars and execs. Louis Mayer had not gone so far as to explicitly forbid members of the MGM family to attend that night's premiere at the Warner Bros. Beverly Hills Theatre; he had just made sure they were otherwise engaged. All of them. Mr. Mayer was protecting the brand.

When film historians and pop culture mavens speak of 1939 as the greatest year of Hollywood cinema, they are sure to offer as evidence a roster of films Americans still know, and even watch, more than eighty years later. There was *Mr. Smith Goes to Washington, Stagecoach, Gunga Din, Gone with the Wind,* and *The Wizard of Oz.* Walt Disney took home a special achievement statuette at the Academy Awards ceremony for the groundbreaking animated film *Snow White and the Seven Dwarfs.* But the production that roiled the industry like no other that year, the one that so worried Louis B. Mayer, and the one that might have had the most profound effects in its own time of any film, was one very few living Americans could name today: *Confessions of a Nazi Spy.*

When the movie premiered on April 27, 1939, Warner Bros. had prepared for outrage, protests, and even violence. Studio bosses took the precaution of hiring hundreds of plainclothes security guards to ring the Beverly Hills Theatre that night, all of them on the lookout for saboteurs. The LAPD was concerned enough that up on the roof of the white, gleaming art-deco-meets-mission-style cinema, above the sign that read "The Pride of Beverly Hills," they had posted a team of police snipers. Louis B. Mayer wanted none of his employees anywhere near this *mishegas.* The Warners, as far as Mayer and most of his fellow studio execs were concerned, were playing a dangerous game.

Confessions of a Nazi Spy was a ripped-from-the-headlines story of international espionage that was only barely in the past tense. In late 1938, when four German Americans were charged with spying on U.S. military installations and defense contractors, Warner Bros. had bought the rights to the story even as the prosecution of the alleged spies was still transpiring. The studio sent screenwriter Milton Krims to New York to observe the trial. There was little doubt of the guilt of the accused, but the drama of it all was still stunning: this espionage plot went all the way to the top of the Nazi-led government in Germany, implicating Göring, Goebbels, and even Adolf Hitler himself.

Krims emerged from his courtroom experience with the script in his teeth, just a month after the four defendants had been convicted and sentenced to prison. When the Warners got the pages, they knew they were in for a fight—on multiple fronts. But they were kinda spoiling for it. Jack and Harry Warner were Jewish Americans, from Poland by way of Canada, and they already knew plenty about the Nazis and their network in the United States. The Warners, along with Louis B. Mayer and Mayer's protégé Irving Thalberg, had been financial backers of Leon Lewis's investigative work infiltrating fascist and Hitlerite groups in Southern California. Harry Warner had also spent a lot of time checking on the brothers' business interests in Europe in the previous few years, and he had seen what was happening to his fellow Jews in Germany as the Nazis took power. Warner Bros. had closed all their offices in Germany by the summer of 1934, right around the time they started funding Leon Lewis back home.

At the time, like Mayer, Jack and Harry Warner preferred to do their part behind the scenes. They didn't put their personal politics—which is to say their disdain for Hitler and the fascists—into their films. Movies were supposed to be entertainment first and foremost, as far as the Warners were concerned, with a dollop of "art" and maybe, on rare occasions, education. "If I want to send a message, I'll use Western Union" is a famous Hollywood quip sometimes attributed to Jack Warner.

But by the beginning of 1939, the brothers Warner found themselves on a different path.

When Krims finished his early draft script on the busted Nazi spy ring, Warner Bros. dutifully sent it over to the offices of the Production Code Administration, the industry-invented clearinghouse that served as a censor for material that might offend the delicate sensibilities of moviegoers. Beyond specific sore nerves on swearing, drugs, nudity, sex, gore, religion, and racial controversy, the PCA also enforced a subjective, amorphous sort of ban on political proselytizing.

With the Nazi spy ring story, the Warner team expected plenty of pushback from the PCA. Maybe insurmountable pushback. Since Hitler had come to power, the German consulate in Los Angeles had aggressively lobbied the PCA to be on the lookout for anti-Nazi sentiment in American movies. Hitler himself had promised to meet any anti-Nazi films coming out of Hollywood with equally anti-Jewish films from Germany. And the PCA was itself run by a notorious antisemite, Joseph Breen, who had said that Hollywood was controlled by "lousy Jews . . . a rotten bunch of vile people with no respect for anything beyond the making of money."

So, it was no surprise when the PCA's reader took one look at the script for *Confessions of a Nazi Spy* and recommended halting the film. He said if Hollywood produced such a film, it would be "one of the most memorable, one of the most lamentable mistakes ever made by the industry." The script was an unwelcome departure from "the pleasant and profitable course of entertainment to engage in propaganda," the censor said in his report for the PCA, and it was unduly harsh on one particular real-world political leader. "To represent Hitler only as a screaming madman and a bloodthirsty persecutor, and nothing else, is manifestly unfair, considering his phenomenal public career, his unchallenged political and social achievements, and his position as head of the most important continental European power." Stop for just a second and let that sink in.

The Warners decided to dig in and fight. To placate the hostile PCA, they did make a few minor alterations, and one big one, but they otherwise stuck to their guns. Ultimately, it worked; they managed to get the film made. "Our fathers came to America to avoid just the sort of persecution that is taking place in Germany today," Jack Warner said in a press interview just a few days before principal photography on the movie began. "If we wish to keep the United States as the land of the free and the home of the brave, we must all do everything we can to destroy the deadly Nazi germs of bigotry and persecution."

When a fellow studio head reminded Warner that Germany, Nazi or no, was too big a moviegoing market to risk losing, Warner lost his cool. "The Silver Shirts and the Bundists and all the rest of these hoods are marching in Los Angeles right now," he answered. "There are high school kids with swastikas on their sleeves a few crummy blocks from our studio. Is that what you want in exchange for some crummy film royalties out of Germany?"

The two months of preproduction and filming for *Confessions of a Nazi Spy* were fraught. The German government kept up constant pressure on the PCA to shut down the film. Some actors turned down parts, fearing reprisals against their family members in Germany or attacks by pro-Nazis in the United States. Main players were offered personal bodyguards. The producers gave up on casting a Hitler—nobody was willing to take the role, no matter the pay—and simply wrote the führer out of the film except for newsreel footage. There were reportedly only six copies made of the full script, and actors received only a few pages each night, to prep for the next day's scenes. "The German-American Bund, the German Consul and all such forces are desperately trying to get a copy of it," one Warner Bros. executive explained.

On set, the sense of threat was even more palpable. During filming, a sixty-pound piece of equipment fell from a sound boom and barely missed the film's biggest name, Edward G. Robinson. An investigator pronounced the incident sabotage, pointing out that the boom had been sawed through.

Before the film could be released to the public, the studio was obliged to screen the edited film for the PCA, for final approval. Warner Bros. had made a series of emendations at the behest of the censors, like changing real names to pseudonyms and soft-pedaling the role of the German steamship service that was hauling Nazi agents and propaganda into American ports. Not to mention cutting out most of the Hitler stuff. Reluctantly and begrudgingly, Breen signed off on it for the PCA.

The $1.5 million production ran the rapids and finished shooting two days early, and Warner Bros. premiered it that April night—the eve of Lionel Barrymore's sixty-first birthday—in their own flagship theater. "The evening," wrote the *Hollywood Spectator*, "marked the first time in the annals of screen entertainment that a picture ever really said something definite about current events, really took a side, and argued for the side with which it sympathized." The head of production at Warner Bros. called the premiere a Bar Mitzvah for the entire industry: "Motion picture . . . came of age. It said, 'Today I am a man.'"

After the sniper-protected Hollywood premiere, *Confessions of a Nazi Spy* had a monthlong rolling open across the country. The impact was proof of the power of Hollywood. More than news coverage, more than law enforcement investigations, more than congressional hearings, the film industry could have a huge

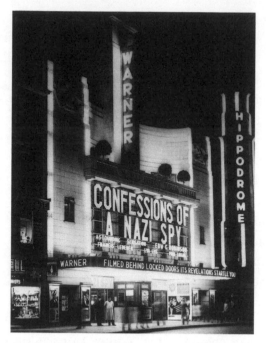

Confessions of a Nazi Spy movie marquee

effect on public awareness. "It marked the moment when millions of moviegoers began to realize the full enormity of what was happening in Europe and what that might mean for the United States," Rhodri Jeffreys-Jones writes in *The Nazi Spy Ring in America*, his 2020 book about the espionage case on which the movie was based.

Much of the Warner Bros. film was Dies Committee investigator John C. Metcalfe's photo album come to life: Nazi propaganda material being off-loaded at U.S. ports by the ton and distributed across the country. Swastika-branded pamphlets dropping from biplanes. City streets "snowstormed" with Nazi leaflets. Attendees of German American Bund rallies swearing loyalty to Nazi Germany and throwing "Heil Hitler" salutes. Armed and uniformed American boys and girls in Hitler Youth camps. "What are the ideals of German Womanhood?" a leading Bad Guy asks one of the Hitler Youth troops. "To be of service to our führer," the little American girl answers, "to be the custodian of our children until he should call them to arms." Swastika-bedecked soldiers-to-be drilling with live weapons, inside U.S. borders. "It looks as if the storm troopers are training to finish off what the propaganda starts," the hero federal investigator explains to his boss. "It's a new kind of war. But it's still a war."

The newsreels incorporated into the film pulled no punches about Hitler's military on the march: "Resorting to its favorite device of stirring up racial prejudices and national hatred, fomenting riots and disorder, the Nazi juggernaut sets the stage for Hitler's invasion, again on the pretext of restoring order. The Democratic republic of Czechoslovakia, modeled on the Constitution of the United States, starts its tragic journey into oblivion by falling into the hands of the new master of Europe, Adolf Hitler, a man whose cry is 'We Germans throughout the world.'"

The main thread of the action was the pilfering of military readiness reports, blueprints, and specs for the latest U.S. bombers and anti-aircraft weapons. "We have spies stationed in all of the navy yards—in Brooklyn, in Philadelphia, in Newport News," says the leader of the Nazi spy ring in America. "There are German agents in the aeroplane and munitions factories."

Confessions of a Nazi Spy rang loud—even melodramatic— alarms about Hitler and his machinations inside the United States, but it was all a true story. The former G-man who led the real-life investigation of the spy ring said as much in the publicity tour that kicked off the movie's release. "The facts in this picture are something the American people ought to know," he said. His message was stark: the Nazi spies are among us, and the nation needs to up its game on counterespionage before it is too late. "We have only scratched the surface," he warned.

But while Warner Bros. was able to get *Confessions* onto the big screen, depicting the real-life spy ring, and the cops-and-robbers hunt to expose and prosecute them, and the Nazi propaganda effort in the United States, and the newsreels, too, in the end there was one striking omission the Production Code Administration insisted on, and on which it would not back down: the words "Jew" and "Jewish" were never uttered. There were Nazified screeds about "subversive elements" and an "insidious international conspiracy of desperate subhuman criminals," but the Nazis' signature Big Lie—that Jewish people were to blame for all ills in the world—was missing. Hitler and company were still the bad guys, but the censors had scrubbed antisemitism from the story.

Nevertheless, the German government registered its anger with Secretary of State Cordell Hull, and demanded that the film be banned from circulation. The leader of the German American Bund, Fritz Kuhn, sued Warner Bros. on behalf of himself and his entire organization, demanding damages of $5 million. The PCA announced it would not sign off on any other anti-Nazi films. A theater owner in Pasadena, hometown of American White Guard founder Henry Allen, said he received hundreds of threatening letters and phone calls when he decided to show *Confessions*. Pro-Nazi Americans—and there were plenty in the United States in 1939—picketed some theaters showing the film and vandalized others.

Still, most theater owners were undeterred. One small-town operator in Hagerstown, Maryland, added *extra* showings, opening his doors at ten o'clock on a Friday morning and running the film continuously through the weekend. The owner did so, according to the local paper, because he "felt that his theater would not only render a patriotic service in showing a film of this kind, but also because he felt it would make Americans more cognizant of the unbelievable spy menace which exists in our democracy."

Confessions of a Nazi Spy did not make its way to the nation's capital until the end of May, but when it did, it happened to premiere in the brief interval between George Deatherage's testimony before the Dies Committee ("You come here and make me sit down!") and General George Van Horn Moseley's ("I believe in watching our breed in America very carefully"). The movie doubtless got a lot more eyeballs at the Earle Theatre in downtown Washington than did the live testimony in the cramped little hearing room in the Old House Office Building on Capitol Hill. Whatever the Dies Committee (and reporters and columnists and activists and politicians) had been trying to convey to the American people about the Nazi threat on the home front, *Confessions* did it better, and with more panache. Local movie critics gave it a thumbs-up. "I found it almost continuously engrossing," Nelson B. Bell wrote in *The Washington Post*. "Not always as drama, but at least as a vivid commentary upon what is going on in these United States under sinister foreign auspices."

The *Post*'s film critic also shouted a hurrah that should have (but didn't) cheer up local Washington boy-made-good and current head of the Federal Bureau of Investigation, J. Edgar Hoover. "It is, furthermore, at times a tense and exciting exposition of the Federal agencies intrusted with the task of stamping out foreign spying, espionage and sabotage in this country—a business that takes on all the color and suspense of the most melodramatic detective fiction."

In truth, the "color and suspense" of the FBI's role in *Confessions of a Nazi Spy* was, if anything, underplayed on the silver screen—not least because of a battle within the FBI over the question of how and whether the story would get out to the public. Star FBI agent Leon Turrou, a Belarusian Jewish immigrant who spoke seven languages, had been the man who cracked open the spy ring case, figuring out the connections between suspicious requests for blank U.S. passports, a known Nazi agent mail drop in Scotland, and a host of other previously inscrutable clues. Turrou already had a high public profile thanks to his quick thinking that assured the conviction of Bruno Hauptmann in the Lindbergh baby kidnapping case in 1935. Once he had broken the Nazi spy ring case in 1938, Turrou wanted to leverage his public profile to inform the public about how much energy and money and manpower the Nazis were devoting not just to propagandizing the American public but to serious sabotage and espionage efforts as well.

On the day when the indictments were handed down in the spy ring case, Turrou announced his retirement from the bureau. When, just two days later, the *New York Post* started running advertisements for a multipart exclusive series by Turrou about his final blockbuster investigation—"Ace G-Man Bares German Conspiracy to Paralyze the United States"—the bureau's director,

J. Edgar Hoover, flipped his wig. He demanded the *Post* hold the story, which it did. Turrou countered that Hoover was acting out because he was "jealous"—literally, that was the headline in *The New York Times:* "Hoover Jealous, Turrou Declares"—because the director himself had been selling the bureau's stories for profit. Turrou's allegation had the benefit of being just as true as it was catty: Hoover had been feeding magazines material from the FBI files for years, for a price, and had already authored a book based on the bureau's cases (which had quickly become a hot property among Hollywood movie studios).

Hoover escalated the personal conflict with Turrou by retroactively dismissing him—*you can't quit, you're fired!*—so that on paper it would look like Turrou had been axed before he resigned. Making sure that the backdated termination was recorded "with prejudice," Hoover ensured that Leon Turrou would lose his entire pension and be blackballed from any other law enforcement job, for life. "Turrou can never get back into any Government Department as long as he lives," Hoover crowed to his most trusted assistant.

But for all that, Hoover couldn't stop the movie.

Confessions of a Nazi Spy threw a spotlight on Hitler's methods and his intentions in America. And it broke the seal on Hollywood doing more of the same. The PCA might not have wanted to see any further anti-Nazi movies after *Confessions,* but times changed. And fast. By the time *Confessions* had completed its first run in theaters, Warner Bros. was already at work on another anti-Nazi movie (*Espionage Agent*) and the down-with-Hitler bandwagon was picking up steam. "Virtually every studio in town has one or more pictures, insulting to the Nazis, on the fire," the United Press's correspondent in Hollywood reported, "with a total of two dozen scripts on the subject at the [Production Code Administration]."

The country was acutely interested in this subject, it turned out, and despite bureau chief Hoover's envious snit about it, the FBI would benefit in the eyes of the public—thanks to Leon Turrou and the new public perception of how central the FBI was to this fight. For an agency that had been studiously ignoring so many fascist and pro-Nazi groups operating in America, including those organizing inside the U.S. military, casing state and federal armories, harassing U.S. Jews, and plotting armed, coordinated actions with help from the German government, the credit the bureau received from the public for its perceived leadership on the problem was something of a windfall.

IN THE LATE summer of 1939, just after the national run of *Confessions of a Nazi Spy* had wound down, a full-time railroad clerk and part-time machine gun specialist for a local National Guard unit walked into the FBI's New York field office with a new story to tell. The railroad man, Denis Healy, explained to the special agent in charge that he had been invited to join a group of fascist militants who were talking big about insurrection. They had approached Healy hoping he might be able to steal machine guns from the guard armory and maybe some dynamite from the New York Central Railroad. One of the key players in the group, which called itself the Christian Front, claimed to be an agent of Adolf Hitler's.

The whole thing seemed a little far-fetched to the New York G-men, but, hey, Leon Turrou was a rich man today. And famous. Celebrated for "smashing" a nest of Nazi operatives in America. According to the gossip pages, their former colleague in the New York field office had just been in Paris doing publicity for the French premiere of *Confessions of a Nazi Spy*. The new special agent in charge in New York decided to play it out, see what this guy Healy could turn up as an undercover informant for the bureau.

A few days later, two FBI agents trailed Denis Healy and one of his new "buddies" to Prospect Hall in Brooklyn, to an open meeting of the organization Healy had come to the FBI about. Healy wasn't bullshitting, the agents quickly determined. He was introduced to the assembly as a new member and as "a future machine gunner for the Christian Front." Moments later, amid a roar of wild applause, a young local Brooklyn man who had just been appointed the head of the organization strutted to the platform. It was apparent from the moment he started talking that John Cassidy and his group were worth watching.

CHAPTER THIRTEEN

COUNTRY GENTLEMEN

John F. Cassidy was not entirely unknown to the Federal Bureau of Investigation. He had walked into the bureau's New York field office back in January 1935, at a time when work in the private sector was hard to come by, and applied for a job as a special agent. Cassidy looked fine on paper: a twenty-four-year-old Brooklyn native with a handful of prizes won in public speaking contests and a fresh law degree from St. John's Law School in Queens. He had failed the bar exam twice already, but that wasn't unusual in New York, nor was it a disqualifier. He was enthusiastic, even eager, his interviewer at the FBI noted, but he "made an unfavorable impression." Cassidy was five feet, seven inches tall and sported a silly-looking mustache, made sillier because he had waxed it for the occasion. The bureau's official report on Cassidy was not kind: "insipid personality . . . limited ability, lacking in initiative," also lacking any "qualifications that might be useful."

Like beauty, however, a man's qualifications and his potential usefulness are often in the eye of the beholder. When John F. Cassidy presented himself, a little more than three years later, to Father Charles Coughlin at the Shrine of the Little Flower church in Royal Oak, Michigan, America's most famous clergyman happily arranged a leadership role for the young man. Cassidy was Coughlin's kind of guy: a devout Catholic, demonstrably committed to God and country.

In 1938, Coughlin was ever more convinced that a sinister plot was afoot in the federal government, and every Sunday on his weekly radio broadcast he spelled it out in increasingly gruesome, alarming detail. The America that the priest and his thirty million faithful listeners loved was being destroyed by a Jewish-commie-Bolshevist conspiracy. Real America needed to wake up! Time was getting short. The time for action—real action by real Christians—was near. Cassidy, too, believed. He also had a lot of free time, because by then he had failed three additional attempts at the bar exam and, more than three years out of law school, was still unable to practice his chosen profession.

Father Coughlin's crusade had given Cassidy a new sense of purpose, as it had Coughlin himself. In the aftermath of his 1936 foray into presidential politicking, Coughlin's star had dimmed a bit. Boisterous rallies of tens of thousands and Philip Johnson's Nazi-inspired architectural platform notwithstanding, Coughlin's 1936 campaign had flopped. He had promised to deliver nine million votes for his third-party candidate, but he came up more than eight million votes short of that goal. His chief target in that campaign, President Franklin Delano Roosevelt, romped to a landslide victory, winning forty-six of the forty-eight states and 523 of 531 possible electoral votes. Coughlin's accusations that "internationalist bankers" and the Federal Reserve Bank and activist New Deal bureaucrats had deliberately caused and then prolonged the Depression in pursuit of Satanic world domination just didn't get the traction he desired. Maybe he wasn't being specific enough?

After that election year, Coughlin made the mean political calculation to call out a more readily identifiable, more precisely defined, more "alien" villain. From that point forward, "the grievance claims that he manufactures are going to be more and more about Jews," says historian Charles R. Gallagher, whose decades of relentless digging only recently uncovered the full story of the Christian Front.

By the summer of 1938, Father Coughlin was all in on explicit antisemitism as the engine of his political crusade, going so far as to follow Henry Ford's example by serializing the hoary and despicable *Protocols of the Elders of Zion* in his weekly magazine, which was called, of all things, *Social Justice*. Coughlin led his editorial introducing the *Protocols* with a quotation from Henry Ford, circa 1921. "The only statement I care to make about the *Protocols* is that they fit in with what is going on. . . . They have fitted the world situation up to this time. They fit it now." Coughlin apparently thought 1938 was an excellent time to assess again just how the *Protocols* fit the new times. "Everyone who mentions the Protocols is listed immediately as a Jew-baiter," Coughlin wrote in the July 18, 1938, edition of *Social Justice*. "That is very poor logic."

Father Coughlin's reach in the 1930s was as astonishing as his radicalism. His weekly audience represented nearly a quarter of the U.S. population. Huge chunks of the aggrieved, Depression-weary, hope-starved American polity kept coming back for more of his political sermonizing. Week after week, Father Coughlin pointed out exactly whom to blame for their troubles. "When he talked about Judaism, he was combining it with communism," says Gallagher. "There was this kind of symbiotic construction that he felt deeply was true. He told his audience that both Marx and Lenin were Jews [neither was] and that Jews created commu-

Father Charles Coughlin with Senator Rush Holt, an ally of Viereck

nism as a secular religion which would advance globally, and that the ideology of communism was going to attempt to both subdue and eradicate Christianity itself. So, for Coughlin, by the late 1930s, this global conflict between communism and Christianity was not just one of an ideological distinction, but one of an existential threat to Christianity itself. And he taints his listenership with those kinds of false premises."

The unsparing particularities of Coughlin's brand of poison became apparent in the days after the Nazis ran their nationwide night of terror against Jews in November 1938. Ten days after news of *Kristallnacht* (and of Joseph Goebbels's decision to charge the Jewish population $400 million for the damages done *to them*) shocked decent people across the world, Father Coughlin gave a weekly radio sermon titled "Persecution—Jewish and Christian."

His sermon conveyed that the Jews of Germany had brought this paroxysm of violence upon themselves by their "aggressiveness and initiative which, despite all obstacles, has carried their sons to the pinnacle of success in journalism, in radio, in finance, in all the sciences and arts." He claimed that Jewish bankers were the force behind communism and that there was a lot more to worry about in the commies killing Christians than there was in the Germans (or anyone) killing Jews. "Nazism is only a defense mechanism against Communism," Coughlin told his tens of millions of listeners. *Kristallnacht* was an understandable outcome, he said, after the "last straw which has broken the back of this generation's patience."

Speaking of last straws, the bosses at WMCA, Coughlin's local radio affiliate in New York, were not Jewish, but they were nonetheless horrified. (They might have been even more horrified if they'd known that Father Coughlin's ministry likely received financial support from Hitler's government through Germany's consulate in Detroit.) The station announced within days that it would no longer broadcast Coughlin's Sunday lectures unless he submitted the text of his sermons in advance for the station to review.

Coughlin's followers heard about this immediately. The radio priest made sure. Their opening salvo against WMCA was a letter from "duly appointed representatives of the Christian Front" charging that the station was violating Father Coughlin's constitutionally protected right to free speech. Never mind that no one has a constitutional right to force anyone else to give them a live radio broadcast. But the letter was just the start. The next Sunday, two thousand Christian Fronters picketed outside the radio station; they continued the demonstration for the next thirty-eight straight Sundays.

The "attacks" on Father Coughlin's rights appeared to confirm his wildest claims, at least for his true believers. John F. Cassidy, who had joined the pickets outside WMCA, was among them. "Communism in America has formerly been a battle of words," he said, "but now has become a battle of militant action."

Cassidy began angling for a leadership job in the Christian Front just as Coughlin was breathing real fire into the organization that had come to his defense. "More than at any other time we need a strong, virilant [sic], sanctified group of Christian Americans," Coughlin wrote in a letter to his followers in New York City. "The time has arrived when defensive policies mean giving way to an offensive plan; for the best method of defense is always of offense." Coughlin started to talk about a Christian Front that could "forefend," and the movement grew. "The Christian Front," he exclaimed in one 1938 broadcast, "grows stronger, more courageous, and more determined. The Christian way is the peaceful way until all arguments have failed, all civil authority having failed, there is left no other way but the way of defending ourselves against the invaders of our spiritual and national rights—Franco's way." Generalissimo Francisco Franco's way, as evidenced in his recent fascist military victory in Spain, was the way of the gun. The death toll of "Franco's way" was in the hundreds of thousands and climbing by 1938, at which point the murderous "White Terror" against the generalissimo's enemies was only just beginning.

Father Coughlin was calling for a Franco-style armed revolt from his followers, with the paramilitary Christian Front in the vanguard. He believed he had the teachings of the Roman Catholic Church on his side. "It's not like he's conjuring this up out of nothing," says Gallagher, who is himself a Jesuit priest. "He uses the theology of Saint Thomas Aquinas, who . . . in the eleventh and twelfth centuries is talking about when it is permissible to use violence in order to overthrow a leader. There is a theology about this, where if the leader is deemed tyrannical, then physical activity can be taken to remove that tyrant. . . . [Coughlin] insinuates that President Roosevelt is Jewish. In [Coughlin's] equation that means he's also a communist. And if you look at his language, he now starts to call President Roosevelt a tyrant. It's not just kind of a metaphor. It's got theological grounding. If he can convince his followers that Roosevelt and his cabinet and the Jews in the administration are tyrants, then there's moral permissibility, theologically, for them to be removed. Through force. We can take up guns against tyrants."

John F. Cassidy was a believer, theologically, politically, militantly, when the twenty-eight-year-old made bold to travel to Detroit to ask Father Coughlin to anoint him into the leadership of the Christian Front. Coughlin did so, on a special shortwave radio hookup to about six thousand of his select followers. He also made the announcement of Cassidy's exalted new status in the July 31, 1939, issue of *Social Justice,* suggesting that Cassidy would help grow the Front up and down the Eastern Seaboard. "I do not think there is a man in the entire movement who does not see eye to eye with you on the pronouncements you have long been making and there are none who would not fight to defend the principles for which you stand," Cassidy wrote to Coughlin shortly after receiving the priestly benediction. "All I am waiting for is the signal to go and when and if I get it I shall never let up until the enemy quits or is beaten."

THE REVOLUTIONARY TEMPERATURE was rising in pockets of every borough of New York City by the summer of 1939, set to boil in no small part by Father Coughlin's inflammatory antisemitism. The leader of one Christian Front splinter group, Joe McWilliams, claimed to be assembling "the meanest, the toughest, the most ornery bunch of German soldiers, Italian veterans and Irish I.R.A. men in the country. I'm going to have the greatest collection of strong-arm men in the city." A two-thousand-strong "Buy Christian" (boycott Jewish businesses) rally that McWilliams organized in the Bronx in mid-August devolved into a street brawl that ended with one cop in the hospital and five Coughlinites in jail. Jewish passersby and businesses were regularly menaced and attacked by crowds and thugs riled up by McWilliams's street-side oratory.

The group's private meetings at McWilliams's Guard Unit clubhouse, lined with ax handles, brass knuckles, and lead pipes, ranged from boisterous to menacing. "Long live our Savior, Father Coughlin," one acolyte yelled. "When we get in power, guys with my type of mind will go to work on them Jews with a vengeance," said another. "There won't be enough lamp-posts to hang them on." McWilliams did most of the talking. "We are going to run this country with an iron hand, the way Hitler runs Germany," he told his boyos. "We want strong men. Men to fight for America's destiny and link it with the destiny of Adolf Hitler, the greatest philosopher since the time of Christ."

"You're right, Joe," came the cry from the clubhouse. "You're Goddam right."

As with Coughlin's media influence, the combination of the radicalism and the reach proved to be a volatile mix. One hot summer night at the end of August 1939, a rally led by McWilliams at Innisfail Park in the Bronx reportedly drew fifteen thousand people. "For size and sheer dramatic color," an undercover reporter wrote, the rally "was unprecedented in the annals of New York." There were uniformed members of the German American Bund, and McWilliams's Christian Mobilizers, along with Christian Fronters and swastika-festooned soldiers of the American Nationalist Confederation, who all took their assigned spots near the stage, under red, white, and blue banners and arc lighting and the crackle of electrified megaphones. The attendees were disappointed that their featured speaker was a no-show. (General George Van Horn Moseley had been taken off the proverbial battlefield, at least temporarily, after his appearance at the Dies Committee hearings had prompted an official investigation by the U.S. military into his activities. The army made clear that Moseley was free to pursue the office of American dictator, but if so, he would be doing it without the benefit of his $6,000-a-year army pension. He elected to keep his pension.)

George Deatherage subbed for the absent general that night in the Bronx and delivered a stem-winder. "I am not content to walk in the footsteps of Christ," he said. "I will walk ahead of Him with a club." He also let the crowd in on the little secret that his German embassy pal, von Gienanth, had confided to him. "Through the nation today [antisemitism] is a smoldering fire, sullen, deadly, and ten times more powerful than existed in pre-Hitler Germany."

THE ENTIRETY OF the Coughlin-led proto-fascist American movement—from what one observer called McWilliams's "prize collection of cut-throats, convicts, rapists, pimps, burglars and goon squad bruisers" to John F. Cassidy's Christian Fronters to the dedicated listeners of the *Golden Hour of the Shrine of the Little Flower* to the *Social Justice* subscribers—woke to a huge jolt on September 1, 1939. Among the first in Coughlin's circle to apprehend the remarkable way the world was about to shake on its axis was a young man on assignment in Europe as a temporary correspondent for *Social Justice*. Philip Johnson was enjoying a warm summer breeze at an outdoor café in Munich when he got the stunning news. "This is the first day of war," Johnson kept repeating to himself, as if it were too good to be true. "This is the first day of war!" Headlines flashed across the world within hours. "German Army Attacks Poland"; "Cities Bombed, Port Blockaded"; "Danzig Is Accepted into Reich."

The invasion was massive in scale, led by two thousand tanks, nine hundred bombers, four hundred fighter planes, and more than a million foot soldiers. Hitler, of course, asserted that this alarming opening act of the full-scale war in Europe was somehow an act of self-defense, that Poland was the real aggressor. Hitler released an official statement to the world in the first hours of the invasion, saying the Poles had "appealed to weapons. Germans in Poland are persecuted with a bloody terror and are driven from their homes. The series of border violations, which are unbearable to a great power, prove that the Poles no longer are willing to respect the German frontier. In order to put an end to this frantic activity no other means is left to me now than to meet force with force. The German defense forces will carry on the battle for the honor of the living rights to the re-awakened German people with firm determination."

Mussolini's fascist government in Italy was totally down with Hitler's farcical explanation for why he just had to invade. As was the communist government in Moscow, where the Supreme Soviet had hastily ratified a nonaggression pact with Germany the day before the Polish invasion. The rest of Europe saw Hitler's aggression for what it was: an illegal and unprovoked attack on a sovereign nation. Unprepared as their militaries were, Britain and France immediately declared war on Germany.

And while a great many Americans were also ready to jump in with both feet, a great many others took a good look at Hitler's war machine—"blitzkrieg" was suddenly part of the American vocabulary—and thought better of joining the coming bloodbath on the other side of the Atlantic. Many months later, one U.S. ambassador would still be telling President Roosevelt, "If we had to fight to protect our lives, we would do better fighting in our own backyard."

The isolationists in America were in the majority in 1939, they were vocal, and they were enterprising. Just four weeks after the Polish invasion, on the day Germany and Russia finished carving Poland in two and devouring every bit, a lone biplane appeared in the skies above downtown Washington, D.C. The pilot was Laura Ingalls, the most famous American aviatrix still alive. She was the first woman to fly solo from North America to South America; she held the record for the fastest ever coast-to-coast round-trip flight by a female pilot; and she held the record for the most barrel rolls on a single flight—714 of them. But on that day in Washington in September 1939, she pulled off a stunt of a different kind; she circled over the national capital for more than an hour and then snowstormed the District with thousands of leaflets printed up by the Women's National Committee to Keep U.S. Out of War. "Never before in history have American women been so aroused and determined to keep their children out of war," the leaflets read. "American women do not intend to have their men again sent to die on foreign soil." The papers fluttered down onto Capitol Hill, the Washington Monument, downtown Washington, and the White House grounds.

A flier even more famous than Ingalls, the hero Charles Lindbergh, was at that moment at work on an article for *Reader's Digest* titled "Aviation, Geography, and Race." Lindbergh had publicly stated his opposition to America going to war against Hitler. In private, he had offered his frank assessment about what a disastrous mistake it would be for the U.S. Army Air Corps to attempt to take on the powerful *Luftwaffe*, which Lindbergh had seen in operation, up close, at the invitation of his friends in Germany. Lindbergh was going to go a step further in *Reader's Digest*, by explaining how airpower was not a point of competition between the United States and the Third Reich, but rather a shared bond between our two countries. On the basis of race. Widely believed to be ghostwritten by none other than America's brainiest fascist, Lawrence Dennis, the article was a paean to the white man and his genius in perfecting the science of flight. "Aviation seems almost a gift from heaven to those Western nations who were already the leaders of their era, strengthening their leadership, their confidence, their dominance over other peoples. It is a tool specially shaped for Western hands, a scientific art which others only copy in mediocre fashion, another barrier between the teeming millions of Asia and the Grecian inheritance of Europe—one of the priceless possessions which permit the White race to live at all in a pressing sea of Yellow, Black, and Brown."

Westerners (including Hitler's Germany) needed to protect "intangible qualities of character, such as courage, faith, and skill," in their own lands, he wrote, and they needed to stick together and avoid at all costs "a war within our own family of nations, a war which will reduce the strength and destroy the treasures of the White race, a war which may even lead to the end of our civilization. . . . It is time to turn from our quarrels and to build our White ramparts again. This alliance with foreign races means nothing but death to us. It is our turn to guard our heritage from Mongol and Persian and Moor, before we become engulfed in a limitless foreign sea."

Subtle guy, that Lawrence Dennis.

Men like Father Coughlin and Cassidy, no surprise, were electrified by Hitler's aggression. Coughlin's correspondent in Europe, Philip Johnson, was escorted into Poland by his Nazi minders so he could report back on the contented new citizens of the Third Reich. "He was fêted by the German authorities in charge of the press correspondents and they were quite solicitous about his welfare," a fellow American reporter noted. Johnson didn't dwell on the death and destruction the *Wehrmacht* left in its wake. He made no mention of the 100,000 dead or wounded Polish soldiers, the untold civilian casualties, the obliteration of large sections of cities and towns. Readers of Johnson's reports in *Social Justice* were told that Hitler's seizure of Poland (or at least the part of Poland that he hadn't gifted to his new friends in Moscow) was met with flowers and felicitations by the Poles, and there was certainly no reason for Americans to get their knickers in a twist about it. That confusing nonaggression pact with the Russians notwithstanding, *Social Justice* readers were assured by their man in the field that Adolf Hitler looked like he would make a damn fine ally in Father Coughlin's existential fight between the Christians and the communists.

THIS WAS THE precise moment that the full-time New York Central Railroad man and part-time National Guard machine gunner, Denis Healy, began his journey into the inner circle of the Christian Front, with the Federal Bureau of Investigation looking over his shoulder. The bureau wired Healy's house in Queens with a detectaphone surveillance device and told Healy to invite his

Christian Front recruiter, Claus Gunther Ernecke, to dinner one mid-September evening. Two agents planted themselves in the overheated attic to listen in on the conversation. Ernecke was a thirty-six-year-old salesman and a corporal in Healy's unit of the New York National Guard. A native of Germany, he had recently applied for American citizenship. Traveling up through the wires from the microphone in Healy's basement to the listening station in the attic, Ernecke's heavily accented voice came through loud and clear as he told Healy that his knowledge of machine guns and his ability to train other recruits would make him a valuable man in the Christian Front. Agent Peter Wacks took meticulous notes, mainly because he was not convinced the detectaphone would successfully record the audio onto tape.

Ernecke told Healy that he would be part of a special faction of the Front called the "Sports Club" or the "Country Gentlemen." These clubs were divided into cells, as Father Coughlin had suggested, with each group limited to fifteen or twenty men. They were preparing themselves for action, to be ready to fight when the inevitable revolution began on the streets of America. Ernecke told Healy he knew of ten such groups already active in New York, and there were plans to activate new clubs across the nation. The Country Gentlemen had just begun accumulating weapons and ammunition. Ernecke had heard rumors that they had already secured a pair of machine guns, which were hidden near Times Square.

Ernecke was in absolute earnest about their mission. The Christian Front was going to "eradicate" the Jews from American life, he said. "It's this way," he told Healy that evening. "We lose—we're dead. We win—we control the country."

A week later, Healy and Ernecke reported to the supervisor of the military wing of the Christian Front, William Gerald Bishop. Bishop was a tough man to pin down. By his own account, he had bounced around from Massachusetts to Toronto to Austria, Belgium, the Netherlands; had been a translator for an international commission on disarmament; had met Lawrence of Arabia "in the desert"; and finally ended up in the Spanish Foreign Legion, where he fought alongside Francisco Franco. He'd been "shot up" so badly in his service to the legion, and in so many separate battles, he claimed, "that he wasn't a pretty sight in a bathing suit."

Sometimes Bishop told his fellow Country Gentlemen he was a reserve officer in the U.S. Army on a secret mission to suppress communism; other times that he was an agent for Hitler. Bishop also liked to preside at the group's "study periods," where he would expound on the Talmud. He "represented that Jews were called upon to violate Christian women, and Jewish doctors to kill or harm Christian patients—but not be caught at it," Healy later explained. "I checked on this. And I found it to be lies."

Healy's cell of the Country Gentlemen tried to meet every Tuesday, with Coughlin's handpicked Christian Front leader, John F. Cassidy, often in attendance. The presence of "the Little Führer," as he was sometimes known, lent the meetings an aura of seriousness, a devout Christian purpose. The Pledge of Allegiance, the oath to the Christian Front, and Catholic prayers were mainstays at those meetings. Healy was soon issued his own rifle, but he balked when Bishop pressed him to steal dynamite from the New York Central Railroad. On October 21, 1939, the Country Gentlemen took a field trip to a small town along the Delaware River, on the New York–Pennsylvania border. Healy's incognito FBI handlers followed the Gentlemen to their destination and were in the public breakfast room of the local inn where they were all staying to watch eight men click their heels together and greet John F. Cassidy with a Nazi salute.

The agents then trailed the cadre to their firing range, camouflaged themselves in the woods nearby, and used a telephoto lens to film the group's maneuvers. The trainees used military-grade rifles to fire at targets set at a distance of a hundred yards. The FBI film doesn't capture this, but Healy later explained they were shooting at effigies of President Roosevelt. "One or two members," Healy told lawmen, "suggested it would be nice to have a Jewish nose on the President's head for a target." After the standing target practice, the men made a series of orchestrated sprints at the Roosevelt dummies, rushing ahead fifteen or twenty yards, then dropping flat into a prone position and firing, reloading, then hopping back up to rush ahead again before diving into a prone position again to fire at President Roosevelt's face.

The Country Gentlemen were feeling their oats when they stopped in at the Peggy Runway Lodge that night for a nightcap. A young editor from the local newspaper was already at the lodge, having a beer with her boyfriend, when the Christian Front crew walked in. They made a spectacle of themselves as soon as they arrived. One of the men, Frank Malone, called President Roosevelt a boob and performed a burlesque of a fireside chat. Clearly unaware the young woman was a journalist, William Gerald Bishop had a very candid chat with her. He explained that the government and the press were both controlled by Jews and that "the government of the United States is going to be overthrown and when it is it will be run by men of my caliber."

Malone interrupted Bishop's impromptu "study period" to exclaim, "You exterminate rats; therefore you exterminate Jews." When the newspaperwoman protested their ugly remarks as unfit talk for decent Americans, Bishop waved her away.

JUST A FEW weeks later, the U.S. Congress, at the request of President Roosevelt, repealed the Neutrality Act of 1937, giving license to the U.S. government and private military contractors to provide cash-and-carry weaponry to Great Britain and France. The United States had finally started to take a side in the accelerating conflict in Europe against Adolf Hitler and Germany. The interventionists harrumphed that it wasn't enough. The isolationists grumbled that it was way too much. The leader of the Christian Front, John F. Cassidy, almost lost his mind, and while the FBI was listening in. The offending congressmen "better reverse themselves," Cassidy told his fellow Fronters, "or there was going to be a revolution." At one point, the incensed Little Führer said it might be time to "knock off" a dozen congressmen "just to show them that the Christian Front means business."

Bishop, as coordinator of the Front's armed Country Gentle-

The Country Gentlemen training near Narrowsburg, New York

men unit, said he concurred with Cassidy, and started to get to work on a plan. At that point, things started moving at a disorienting speed for Healy, who believed both that the Christian Front was entering much more dangerous territory and that he was at increased danger of being found out as a spy. But he stayed on, attending the more and more detailed planning sessions, hearing Bishop boast that he was about to receive two Browning light machine guns stolen from an armory in Boston and that he had a friendly captain in the 165th Infantry Regiment of the New York National Guard who was delivering him ammunition. Members of the 165th began showing up at meetings and dinners with the Country Gentlemen. Among them was Captain John T. Prout Jr., the officer who was acting as Bishop's main supplier of stolen military matériel.

A week later, shortly before Christmas 1939, Bishop showed Healy a cache of seven thousand rounds of .30-06 and "several fully loaded machine gun belts." Bishop later explained the ease of the transaction with Captain Prout. He made three separate trips to the 165th Infantry headquarters to pick up the ammunition. Prout instructed several sergeants and privates on duty at the armory to help pack the rifle bullets and the loaded machine gun belts into Bishop's zippered bag. On one trip, on the way out of Prout's office, Bishop's bag broke, the ammo spilled out onto the floor, and five or six National Guardsmen watched unperturbed as the civilian gathered up his machine gun belts and left the building. Bishop had also been given 166 rings of cordite used to fire mortar shells and a quantity of an explosive compound used in hand grenades.

Denis Healy was among the Fronters called in for instruction on how to construct cordite bombs using soup cans, beer cans, steel plates, and metal piping. The plan was for the Country Gentlemen to hurl these explosives through the windows of the Cameo Theater and the *Jewish Daily Forward* and *Daily Worker* newspapers. They had already dispatched the youngest Fronter—a chubby, baby-faced high school senior—to diagram the exterior and the interior of the *Daily Worker* offices. This act was to be more than just a one-off bit of terrorism; it was the first move in a multistep plan. Cassidy, Bishop, and the other Country Gentlemen were done preparing for the communists to launch their own revolution; they were ready to kick things off themselves.

The bombings were designed to provoke a response not only from the authorities but from the left. "Instead of waiting for the Communists to revolt and then quelling them," one of the Christian Fronters later explained, the bombings would "incite the Jews and Communists to riot and then [the Fronters and their allies would] step in and take over the government." By then, the Country Gentlemen were sure, the governor would have called in the National Guard and the mayor would have unleashed the city police. That's when the Christian Fronters would join the fight en masse, wearing their trademark military caps with "CF" stitched on one side and the sign of the cross on the other, so the police and the guardsmen could recognize them as brothers-in-arms. Bishop figured there were at least 175 men in the NYPD who had already themselves taken the Christian Front oath.

It was what we'd call today an "accelerationist" strategy. Much as white supremacists hope terroristic, spectacular, cruel acts toward racial minorities will provoke retaliation and reprisal to touch off a wholesale race war that they are sure they will win, the Christian Fronters believed America could easily be tipped into a war against Jews and communists in which they themselves not only would end up on the winning side, but would be hailed as a heroic vanguard.

George Van Horn Moseley's name kept coming up in planning meetings for the attack, because they were still counting on the general to take the reins as America's new military dictator after the coup was complete. Moseley had bravely decided that he did not want to risk his army pension by publicly getting out front, but he was not entirely disinterested. At least not according to a letter he sent to Lawrence Dennis that same winter. "My dear Friend," Moseley wrote. "When America finally reacts against the Jews, the severity of that reaction will, in my opinion, surpass anything now recorded in the annals of history—unless we have the character to face the problem now and solve it. But again, that is almost impossible under this form of government, unless we should become involved in an emergency and during the emergency solve the same problem. . . . I ask that you destroy this letter after you have read it."

HISTORIANS HAVE GENERALLY assessed this Christian Front episode as an insignificant blip. That has been driven in part by the framing established in contemporaneous reporting. The press of the day, says Charles Gallagher, "seemed to disregard these folks as being kind of 'crackpots'—that was the main term used—who didn't have any real intent or lethality for any kind of systematic overthrow of the U.S. government. It was, as one journalist put it, 'a playful plot.'"

Gallagher discovered something entirely different when he became the first person to obtain the FBI's case file on the Christian Front, after a years-long effort beginning in 2010. Not only were these religious crusaders determined to carry out their mission, they also had real support inside the National Guard and the

New York City Police Department. In fact, in response to a questionnaire *after* the plot was revealed in 1940, more than four hundred New York City cops voluntarily admitted that they had been members of the Christian Front. God knows how many of the seventeen thousand men in blue were also members but chose not to reveal it.

Gallagher, who was a cadet-policeman training on semiautomatic weapons the first summer he started studying the Christian Front, was shocked by what he saw in the FBI photographs of the armed men at their firing range in Narrowsburg, New York. "The journalists at the time didn't see it, but I knew what they were holding," he says. "They looked like weapons of war to me. . . . Like I knew that the .30-06 shell is about a three-inch-long bullet, full-metal jacket, and one of those bullets can go through a brick wall. These folks were armed for war."

There was also good evidence in the files that Bishop might indeed have successfully obtained two Browning light machine guns stolen from an armory in Waltham, Massachusetts. "The Browning automatic rifle was one of the most lethal weapons of World War II," according to Gallagher. "It was one of the most brilliantly engineered automatic weapons of all time. It shot .30-06 rounds at twenty rounds on full automatic and could actually blast through a building. You could rapid-fire walk with it, and it would just obliterate anything in its path.

CHAPTER FOURTEEN

SMALL WORLD

The role of Christian martyr fit John F. Cassidy like a pontifical glove. Late in life, looking back more than fifty years after the fact, the anointed leader of the Christian Front would insist that he had never truly felt in jeopardy. He put his faith in God and in American patriots and appeared to relish his place in the very public political drama that opened with his arrest on the second Saturday of the year of our Lord 1940. Cassidy got the full glow of the spotlight one day later, when he and sixteen co-defendants were rousted from their holding tanks at the Federal House of Detention at the far end of West Eleventh Street in Manhattan and taken to Brooklyn to be arraigned.

"[FBI director J. Edgar] Hoover came to New York City to hold a news conference," Cassidy told a sympathetic reporter from *The New York Times* in 1995. "You wouldn't believe the show he staged! One by one, we were led out of the Federal detention headquarters into a car. There were three agents in each car and a motorcycle in front. Multiply that by seventeen defendants! The whole motorcade screaming through downtown Manhattan. And above us, on the West Side Highway, they had a full truck of special agents with machine guns pointing at us. What a lot of nonsense."

The defendants did not cut particularly dashing figures when they stood to face Judge Grover Moscowitz in the federal courthouse in Brooklyn that day. The lede in *The New York Times* described the men as "more frightened than revolutionary." The lineup of alleged criminals, according to the brief bios lawmen had already passed out to the media, included a chauffeur, a tailor, a postal telegraph clerk, two Brooklyn Edison clerks (one of them John Cassidy), a telephone lineman, a dogsbody for a local department store and another for a local hotel, a baker, a tailor, a high school honor student, an elevator mechanic, and a washing machine salesman.

The *New York Times* reporter counted about forty G-men in the standing-room-only courtroom that day, and Director Hoover insisted he had a damn good reason to put those defendants under heavy guard, in spite of appearances. The suspects had in their possession at the time of their arrest, according to an itemized list the FBI distributed, fifteen "partly completed" bombs, a significant quantity of cordite and similar explosives, detonators, fuses for dynamite, more than a dozen military-grade rifles (one with a fixed bayonet), a .32 automatic pistol, a 20-gauge shotgun, 4,000 rounds of rifle ammunition and an additional 750 rounds packed into ammo belts to be fed into machine guns, and a long sword. The FBI was still searching other known addresses and safe houses and expected to find more of what Hoover called "a small arsenal."

The G-men had disrupted only one of the Christian Front's paramilitary cells as of that moment, and it was hard to know how many more were out there. The FBI was already hunting similar groups in Philadelphia and Boston. "We expect more arrests," U.S. Attorney Harold M. Kennedy said. "We have merely scratched the surface." The FBI believed the number of New Yorkers who had sworn allegiance to the Christian Front was in the thousands, if not the tens of thousands; it was hard to know how many were active in the group's armed paramilitary wing, but the investigators had reason to believe that number was growing. The numbers, though, were not the most important part of the story. Hoover made sure of that. Remember, he told reporters, "it took only twenty-three men to overthrow Russia."

This particular group of New Yorkers had been conducting

weapons and tactical training for months, Hoover explained. They had been building bombs with their own hands and stockpiling guns and ammunition. And they were set for imminent action, intent on putting in motion an escalating and cascading armed revolt that would end with the seizure of federal armories and arsenals and then the reins of government itself. "The club planned among its early acts of terror, beginning sometime after the training period of January 20th, to bring about a complete eradication of all Jews, seize all public utilities, including power, water, railroads, and all forms of communication and transportation," Hoover said. "The government they proposed setting up, they referred to as 'a dictatorship similar to Hitler's.'"

In case anybody doubted the seriousness of this case, or what was at stake, Hoover pointed to the raw language of the indictment. The men were being charged with "conspiring to overthrow, put down and destroy by force the Government of the United States, and oppose by force the authority thereof." In a word, sedition. They were also being charged with a conspiracy "to seize, take and possess property of the United States." The property in question comprised the explosives, rifles, and bullets the Christian Fronters had already relieved from military armories. Hoover named William Gerald Bishop and John F. Cassidy as the ringleaders of the plot and hinted at the close ties between Cassidy, the Christian Front, and Father Charles Coughlin, the most powerful right-wing media figure in the country.

Father Coughlin's first instinct was to cover his own Christian rear end, which he did in a public statement as soon as news of the arrests flashed across the nation. He was very quick to deflect evidence of the support, financial and otherwise, that flowed between his ministry and "this so-called" Christian Front. "For some time they have been praising me, holding meetings in my name, and pretending to collect money for my support," Coughlin said. "I have roundly disavowed them. Moreover, following Oct. 25 of last year, they sent me a check of some $1,000 which I returned to them in a public manner, telling them that I would not accept any such kind of money and advocating my followers to have nothing to do with such organizations." (This was a lie, as far as anybody could tell, from the man who had in fact been telling his entire listening flock that it was time to organize themselves into Christian Front militia units and that the time was coming to go "Franco's way.")

Coughlin's strenuous disavowal did not last out the week, however, once it became clear that initial public reaction to the dramatic criminal allegations tended toward dismissive. New York City's mayor, Fiorello La Guardia, reportedly laughed at hearing the news. "I don't think the United States government is in much danger from eighteen guys like these," he told reporters. The Christian Fronters' plan to bomb the Russophile Cameo Theater was, snarked one wag in *The New York Times*, "a classic example of the indirect, or super-subtle, approach to overthrowing a government." Even one stridently antifascist New York congressman called the Christian Front's coup plan a "crackpot conspiracy" dreamed up by "political lunatics." Reporters scared up civilians who had witnessed the Christian Front target practice and described their marksmanship as "awful."

"The great plot to seize America," wrote Coughlin's hometown newspaper, the *Detroit Free Press*, "will go down in the funny books of history to be written about the New Deal long after the headaches of it are over." One national wire service reported that "public opinion was inclined to dismiss as fantastic the alleged plot."

The folks who did take the plot seriously often seemed sympathetic to the alleged perpetrators. The defendants played to that audience. Bishop told reporters he was wearing "a crucifix blessed by Father Coughlin" and a medal honoring the patron saint of impossible causes at the time of his arrest. Cassidy was passing time in the holding tank, his defense attorney explained, saying the rosary. The snapshot of would-be American Hitler, William Dudley Pelley, that the G-men had found in his wallet went unmentioned, but Cassidy was not shy about showing off the "symbolic" rifle bullet he carried in his pocket. "I am not guilty of anything but Christian-American self-defense," he told reporters at the arraignment hearing. "All I can say is—Long live Christ the King! Down with Communism! That's my message. And get it right."

"We are defending ourselves against the encroachments of communism," the doughy, dull-eyed defendant Macklin Boettger added that day. "No one pays attention to communism—not even the FBI. Look around and see: the Communists are loose and here we are in the pen."

Coughlin could feel the winds turning in a direction favorable to his now most famous followers, and in his first Sunday radio sermon after the arrest he tacked his vessel to take advantage. "I appear before you today to record the fact that while I do not belong to any unit of the Christian Front, nevertheless, I do not disassociate myself from that movement," he told nearly thirty million faithful listeners across America. "I reaffirm every word which I have said in advocating its formation; I re-encourage the Christians of America to carry on in the crisis for the preservation of Christianity and Americanism more vigorously than ever, despite this thinly veiled campaign launched by certain publicists and their controllers to vilify both the name and the principles of this pro-American, pro-Christian, anti-Communism and anti-Nazi group." (This last bit might have been a bit stinging to the actual Nazis who were helping to support Coughlin's media ministry.)

Coughlin's decision, he said, was to "stand by" John F. Cassidy and the others through their trials. "Real Christians of this nation will not beat a retreat," Coughlin insisted. "And why will we not retreat? Because the Christians of America are asking themselves this question: 'Why did Attorney-General Murphy and Mr. Hoover fail to apprehend the 2,000 or more Communists working in the public buildings at Washington almost under their very eyes— members of an organization foresworn to overturn this Government; foresworn to drag Christ down from His cross, expel Him from our churches, ostracize Him from our schools and public institutions and, according to the pattern of the Spanish loyalists, crucify Him again in the hearts of our citizens? . . . In our days we have seen Christ scourged from our schools, His principles mocked in our courts. . . . Despite the garbled statements contained in some newspapers last Monday relative to my position, I take my stand, not retracting one word which I have said either today or on previous occasions relative to the matter of a Christian Front and to the principles which should characterize its membership. Long live Christ the King! God save the Constitution. For those of us who believe in the principles of Christianity there is no retreat; for us there is no white flag of surrender! Long live Christ the King! God save the Constitution!"

An entire flotilla of isolationists, anticommunists, and/or anti-semites fell into Coughlin's rhetorical wake. The Republican governor of Vermont suggested the prosecution of the Christian Fronters was a cynical ploy by the Roosevelt administration to push the country toward war with Germany and "to teach a lesson to other citizens who feel like criticizing the government." Representative Jacob Thorkelson, the antisemitic Montana Republican who had acted as cornerman for George Van Horn Moseley during the general's congressional testimony, and had briefly been endorsed for president by William Dudley Pelley, released a statement on February 2, 1940. The Christian Front had done nothing more than take some target practice, the congressman wrote, and the entire case was a "childish attempt to shield the Communists."

Two days later, the defense lawyer hired by Cassidy and eight other defendants headlined a rally for the "Brooklyn Boys" in a local arena. "This is a fight for Christ!" the attorney hollered. "I don't have to apologize to anyone for being a Christian!"

THE ROOSEVELT ADMINISTRATION was making no apologies either. When Robert Jackson took over as U.S. attorney general three days after the arraignment of the Christian Front, he found a memo from President Franklin Delano Roosevelt waiting on his desk. The swift and successful investigation and prosecution of "Cassidy & Co" was to be among the Department of Justice's priorities. Jackson scrambled the newly appointed head of the DOJ's criminal division, O. John Rogge, to Brooklyn to oversee the high-profile but knotty case.

A conviction on seditious conspiracy was a tall order, and everybody knew that. Hoover had said as much to his closest assistant—even before he went in front of any cameras to point a finger at the Christian Front plotters. The director could not shake the memory of a case from a generation earlier, when he was a twenty-five-year-old kid lawyer doing his first tour of duty in the attorney general's office. After a bunch of anarchists had been charged with sedition in Buffalo, New York, in 1920, a federal court had tossed out their case and lectured DOJ that the seditious conspiracy statute applied only when there was "an overt act." So Hoover understood that evidence of conspirators taking target practice at Roosevelt dummies and bragging about "overthrowing the government" in the bar of a rustic lodge on the Delaware River was probably not going to cut it, no matter what else they were planning.

A conviction was much more likely on the charge of theft of government property, considering the amount of firepower the Fronters had purloined from U.S. stocks. And on that one, the evidence gathered at the time of the arrest and in the days after seemed unassailable. In the house shared by the National Guardsman Claus Gunther Ernecke and Macklin Boettger, the FBI seized 1,070 rounds of rifle ammunition, seven cans of cordite, and detonating fuses. Bishop's house held more than 400 rounds of machine gun ammunition packed for rapid fire.

The biggest cache was at a house in the Stuyvesant Heights section of Brooklyn, where the Christian Fronter John Albert Viebrock lived with his parents. There was one rifle standing by the coat tree at the entrance of the attached three-story dwelling, but the basement was the mother lode. The G-men found a loaded-up machine gun belt hidden away in one cabinet, and eleven containers, each holding twelve silk rings of cordite in a fireless cooker. "Next, the fireless cooker yielded a coffee can that held thirty-four more rings of cordite and then came four green shells," according to news reports of the testimony of an FBI special agent who cataloged the ammunition and appurtenances. "A container that had held these shells was on a workbench nearby. . . . On the workbench was a piece of paper that Viebrock admitted was a sketch of a bomb drawn by Bishop for his guidance. There was also an envelope containing specifications of three different types of bombs that Viebrock said he was making. . . . The agent identified one after another, twelve soup cans and eight beer cans that he said were being made into bombs. He explained that a smaller can was soldered into a larger can, a tin tube was inserted into a larger can, a tin tube was inserted into the inner can to permit introduction of an explosive charge and a fuse, and then the space between the two cans were filled with plaster of paris."

The G-man, one reporter continued, "found a section of pipe about eighteen inches long upright in a vise at the workbench and that Viebrock had said he was making a bomb out of it. He also identified five sections of brass pipe which Viebrock told him were destined for the same purpose."

The FBI found very little of the Christian Front's stockpiled arsenal in John F. Cassidy's own house, but they did take possession of private jottings and correspondence from the desk of the Little Führer. One of Cassidy's notes to self spoke of plans for a vast expansion of their ammo cache—"30,000 rounds Camp Dix." More worrying was the telegram suggesting that Bishop had got his hands on U.S. Army machine guns. "It's raining today, but the Browning Light Machine guns are rattling on the range," Bishop had written to Cassidy from a training session in the mountains of West Virginia. "A few of the boys, group commanders, asked me to send you and your men greetings from them for Christ and country."

Nevertheless, even the weapons charge soon got wobbly. If the Fronters had gained possession of U.S. military machine guns, that was illegal—no question. FBI investigators thought they had a line on the real story when they learned that two Browning Automatic Rifles—machine guns—had in fact been stolen from a National Guard armory in Waltham, Massachusetts, the previous September, right around the time the Christian Front was recruiting Denis Healy as their "future machine gunner."

When FBI agents showed up in Waltham to trace the stolen

guns, though, the trail ran cold. "There was a cover-up in the National Guard because the sergeant at arms who should have been responsible for these weapons refused to talk to the FBI about their final disposition," says Charles Gallagher, the first person to see the FBI files on the case, seven decades after the fact. "His superior officer also declined to talk to the FBI about this case. And because the commanding officer [of the local National Guard in Waltham] didn't want to have his sergeant prosecuted, they just shut up. Everybody clammed up." If the U.S. military did not want to admit that its weapons had in fact been stolen, then as a criminal matter it was going to be hard to prosecute the theft.

John Cassidy (left) with William Bishop (right) at the Christian Front trial in Brooklyn

By the time the Christian Front trial commenced at the beginning of April 1940, the U.S. marshal in Brooklyn knew to keep backup deputies on alert near the courtroom. Even preliminary bail hearings had drawn as many as five hundred New Yorkers, many of whom had a hard time holding their tongues. A few yelled insults at the defendants, but most were there to show their support. "This is a hell of a country!" they shouted. "Down with the Reds! . . . Long Live Christ the King!" The marshals had to rush in to hold back the crowd, which at one point, according to one newspaper reporter, "surged toward the defendants." The national headline the next day was "Christian Front Men Deny Guilt amid Uproar."

The judge understood emotions were running high, and he meant to limit the opportunity for mayhem. So, for the entire trial, no visitor was permitted into the courtroom without a special pass issued by the marshal; in fact, nobody was even permitted on the same floor of the courtroom while trial was in session unless they could prove they had business there. This did not fully calm the circus atmosphere in the opening days—the deputies still had physical scrapes with would-be spectators trying to force their way in—but it did shunt most of the madness outside. One newspaper reporter who ambled out of the courthouse during the first noon recess witnessed a heated argument about the trial turn into a bare-knuckle boxing match. Meanwhile, four enterprising Cough-linites were selling the latest issue of *Social Justice* on the court-house grounds (a target-rich environment), and a young woman was screaming, on a constant loop, "The same gang that crucified Christ are at it again, trying to convict these seventeen innocent Christian boys." One mounted policeman, the reporter wrote of the scene, "cautioned her not to start trouble, but after he disappeared she continued her cries."

Even the normally placid process of voir dire devolved into a "blistering examination" of the would-be jurors. It was two full days of prodding them about their reading habits, their political affiliations, and their feelings toward Jews, antisemites, Catholics, Irishmen, and communists. One defense attorney claimed to the judge—and every reporter and every potential juror—that prosecutors were trying to stack the deck with an all-Protestant jury. This was not true, but it was a nice way to imply (falsely) that prosecutors were prejudiced against Catholics and needed to be watched. The defense, meanwhile, proved enthusiastic and adept at knocking off the jury anybody who had a whiff of commie to them, even tossing a Works Progress Administration employee be-cause his paycheck came from the federal government—which, after all, was the party bringing the case. The woman finally selected to be foreperson of the jury was a middle-aged Brooklyn housewife who told the attorneys this was her first time ever in a courtroom. The prosecutors, alas, had failed to ascertain that she was related by marriage to the lead defense attorney in the case.

The Brooklyn U.S. Attorney, Harold M. Kennedy, argued the case at trial, but every day in court O. John Rogge, the chief of the criminal division from Main Justice in Washington, was there at the request of his boss, Attorney General Robert Jackson, who in turn had been prodded by his boss, President Roosevelt. "He is kind of tasked with being the executive chess player behind how the government's case is going to be argued," says Gallagher. "Many in the government are critical of Rogge's choice because they feel he does not understand the cultural position on the ground." Rogge "doesn't understand Brooklyn Catholic culture. And he doesn't understand the jury, which is going to be composed of Brooklynites. Rogge is from southern Indiana, and he went to Harvard Law School, and he has no perception that the jury pool is going to lean in certain directions. His legal team was composed of lawyers who were equally deficient in understanding the culture that they were moving in. Brooklyn in the 1930s was deeply . . . informed by Roman Catholicism in their anticommunism and . . . kind of an endemic style of antisemitism."

THE FBI INFORMANT Denis Healy was the crucial witness for the prosecution. At the top of the trial, he spent more than six full days on the stand as the U.S. Attorney led him through his brief career as a mole inside the Christian Front. Healy had at hand a tattered, five-cent, mauve-colored notebook he had used to memorialize conversations from the various dinners and meetings he attended with his fellow Fronters and National Guardsmen. Thanks to the detectaphone system they had installed, FBI special agents had been able to listen in and make contemporaneous notes on any meetings held at Healy's dinner table or in his basement. But it was up to Healy himself to record the minutes of the many secret gatherings held elsewhere. Healy, who had little formal schooling and had largely taught himself to read and write, would spend hours after each meeting painstakingly scratching out his notes on the secret conversations.

In the witness box, referring to his notes, Healy spelled out the recipe of the Christian Front's increasingly violent concoction. He detailed the fanatical antisemitism that united the group; the structure of the paramilitary Sports Club/Country Gentlemen; the stolen weapons and ammunition they stockpiled with the help of National Guard officers and NCOs at a local armory; the classes in bomb making; the discussion about and selection of targets, including the intent to "knock off" twelve congressmen who had voted to permit the United States to help arm the Brits and the French in their new war with Germany. He had it all, right there in those notebooks.

The cross-examination was withering. The defense attorneys painted the FBI informant as a fabulist, a liar, and an agent provocateur who loosened the tongues of these good Catholic boys with government-provided liquor and pheasant dinners. And then, they said, he enticed them into antisemitic rants and an increasingly militant commie-killing plot that was actually dreamed up by Healy himself and the FBI to entrap the Country Gentlemen. Denis Healy, the defense attorneys asserted, was more than disloyal to his friends. He was a snitch. Which was the worst thing you could be in the prevailing working-class, Irish Catholic culture in Brooklyn. He was *worse* than the worst, the defense attorneys claimed. He was a *paid* snitch, having accepted a weekly stipend from the FBI.

Five days into his testimony, with the defense's inquisitors hammering at him, Healy collapsed and had to be taken to the hospital, delaying the testimony until the next day. The trial was delayed again the next day by the disappearance of the defendant Claus Ernecke, the man who had invited Healy into the Christian Front in the first place. Ernecke's defense attorney insisted in court that his client had not skipped bail but had likely been kidnapped and murdered. Probably by commies. Ernecke was indeed found dead in the cellar of a Brooklyn apartment the following day, but not murdered. He hanged himself. Christian Front partisans blamed Ernecke's demise on government-led persecution.

When Denis Healy returned to the witness stand after a brief stay in the hospital, things got no easier. He admitted that he had provided booze to his fellow Fronters; he had not actually *seen* the thousands of rounds of ammo Bishop had bragged about; and yes, he had accepted money from the government for his undercover work. Healy was also badly impeached by the mystery of his own personal history. Which seemed to be a mystery to even Healy himself. He couldn't keep straight the dates of his marriage, or what he had written in his voter registration form. He didn't know exactly where he was born. "Somewhere in the British Empire," he finally said. He was unsure whether his father's legal name was Donald Thomas Healy or Thomas Donald Healy, but he was pretty sure his father had been a spy for the British government. And had infiltrated militant Irish Catholic revolutionary groups. (It was going to be fun going home to the old Irish Catholic Brooklyn neighborhood after testifying to that.) There was a Denis Healy who was also a former member of the British armed forces and wanted by the police overseas, but that was definitely a different Denis Healy, Healy explained, since he was pretty sure the guy wanted by the police was a Denis Healy who had only one eye. And he, Denis Healy, happily had two.

As the Healy testimony went south, special agents of the FBI appeared to save the day for the prosecution. However lax they had been in investigating Hitlerite fascist organizations in America to that point, the leadership at the FBI and its agents on the ground had built an impressive case against the Christian Front defendants. A parade of FBI men testified in open court over the next few weeks. Peter Wacks, described by one newspaper reporter as "a clean-cut, youthful-looking special agent," was the first in the witness box. The reporter was also impressed with "the crisp, concise fashion [with which] he corroborated large sections of the story that had been told by Denis Healy." Wacks had spent many hours in Healy's sometimes-overheated and sometimes-frigid attic, frantically taking notes of the conversations he eavesdropped

on. He was also among the agents hiding in the woods in Narrowsburg, New York, filming Cassidy, Bishop, and six other defendants performing target practice and military exercises. The FBI
entered that footage into evidence, over the screaming objection of
the defense.

Wacks was able to provide verbatim quotations from his notes,
to be entered into the trial record. William Bishop had instructed
his men to "contact all gripers and growlers in the National Guard"
to recruit them for the Christian Front's mission, Wacks testified.
Macklin Boettger bragged that he could blow up a communist-run
newspaper and get away with it. Boettger also told Healy and others that he was on the lookout for a rifle with telescopic sights so
he could "shoot a few of the key men of the Communist Party."

The agents traced much of the ammunition they discovered
right back to the 165th Infantry Regiment armory in New York
City, where a Captain John T. Prout Jr. had instructed his supply
sergeant to provide Bishop with ammo for bolt-action rifles and
machine guns, as well as rings of cordite. Special agent Arthur M.
Thurston dumped onto the desk of the court clerk cartons full of
machine gun ammunition, bombs jerry-rigged out of soup cans,
beer cans, and brass pipes, silks of cordite, miners' fuses, and
sheets of paper filled with bomb-making instructions. These were
all entered into evidence while Thurston, "a husky, dark-haired
man who testified with ready self-assurance," narrated his experience at John Viebrock's basement workbench. Everybody with an
official U.S. marshal courtroom pass was then treated to a screen-
ing of FBI film footage taken in that basement following the initial
arrests. The scenes, wrote a slightly stunned reporter from *The
New York Times,* "showed Viebrock smilingly pointing at bombs
he had been constructing, while in the background an FBI agent
was carrying on the search of the cellar."

Viebrock, who clearly felt he had little to fear, had been exceedingly loquacious in the days after his arrest, bragging that he was
capable of constructing bombs that would be much more lethal
than those found in his basement. He also explained to Agent
Wacks that right up until their arrests the Fronters were discussing

new ways "to incite the Jews and Communists to riot" so good Christians could "then step in and take over the government."

"I asked [Viebrock] what he thought of the whole situation," Wacks testified, "and he replied, 'I'd do the same thing again.'"

This was about the time a Christian Front partisan and local priest in Queens made a not-so-subtle comparison, during one of his Sunday homilies, between the crucifixion of Christ and the prosecution (read persecution) of the Brooklyn Boys. "During the entire legal process" of Jesus Christ's civil trial and execution, Father Edward Brophy claimed, "every detail was in complete and continuous control of the Jews."

THE TRIAL WENT on for ten uninterrupted weeks. The other concurrent happening in those ten weeks was Adolf Hitler's military blitz across western Europe. On April 9, five days after the Christian Front sedition trial opened, Hitler's army invaded Denmark and Norway. Denmark fell in a day; Norway held out a little longer, but fell just as hard. Four weeks later, German paratroopers, tankers, infantrymen, and airmen roared into Belgium, Luxembourg, and the Netherlands. Americans woke every day for the next three weeks to a map of Europe being rewritten by the sheer pitiless force of Hitler's *Wehrmacht*, which appeared unstoppable.

By the last week in May, 200,000 British troops and 140,000 French, Dutch, and Belgian troops were bravely clinging to the last little bit of safe soil, on the far northwest coast of France. "The British Expeditionary Force means to die where it stands rather than let the Germans occupy the coast where they could base an attack on the British Isles," wrote an American correspondent for the Associated Press. "Still they were saying today, as I left, 'let's have a crack at that goddamned Hitler.'"

Five days later, the British were beating a hasty retreat across the English Channel. The evacuation of the French port of Dunkirk would go down in history as the military operation that saved the British Expeditionary Force to fight another day. But not much glory attached itself to the proceedings at the time. The Allied forces abandoned almost all their artillery, tanks, and ammo caches to the approaching German army. By the first days of June, Denmark, Norway, Belgium, Luxembourg, the Netherlands, and much of France had surrendered to German rule. Hitler's army was beginning its final push into Paris. Germany's control of the recently surrendered channel ports along the French coast left England more vulnerable than ever. On May 29, the headline in *The Washington Post* read "Is Invasion of Great Britain Hitler's Present Objective?" Well, yeah.

The fight to save democracy in the world was on. But by huge margins, most Americans were still hoping someone else would handle it. "Sentiment for going to war with Germany has increased since the Nazi invasion," Dr. George Gallup, the nation's best-known pollster, wrote while British warships were still ferrying retreating Allied troops off the Continent, "but the increase has been less than four percent. A nation-wide survey just completed finds the country still more than 13 to 1 against American entrance into the conflict."

Macklin Boettger, defendant in the ongoing Christian Front sedition trial, agreed. While testifying in his own defense, Boettger explained that he would be taking a pass on fighting the Germans in Europe even if the United States entered the war. He had no beef with the German government, just as long as it kept its army out of America. When asked by prosecutors if he had ever expressed sympathy for Hitler, Boettger refused to answer. He testified that he was not antisemitic but that he "might have" said that Father Coughlin's *Social Justice* was "the only [media outlet] in the country not controlled by Jews."

The defense made a rousing final argument for the acquittal of John F. Cassidy and his co-defendants. Unlike Rogge and the rest of the DOJ prosecution team, the defense knew their audience, and they tailored their closing plea to that audience, even stipulating some of the ugliest charges. Sure, defense counsel admitted, Macklin Boettger had some antisemitic literature in his home, but he also had copies of the U.S. Constitution. Which he was trying to protect! From communists! "Macklin Boettger says, 'I'd like to have a rifle with a telescope sight and go out and shoot a few Communists,' " the lead defense lawyer explained to the jury. "So would I, and so would a lot of other Americans. I'd like to see them all strung up by the neck.

"But because you'd like to do something doesn't mean that you're going to do it. I'd like to see [the Brooklyn Dodger outfielder] Joe Medwick hit a home run tomorrow night, but that doesn't mean he's going to do it."

The jury hung. They were unable to reach a verdict on Macklin Boettger, John Viebrock, William Bishop, or Captain Prout. The bloodied DOJ decided not to get back in the ring and pursue another trial against them, so those four walked. The other defendants, including John F. Cassidy, were then flat-out acquitted.

When the verdict was announced on June 24, 1940—not a single guilty verdict against any one of the defendants—three hundred people who had pushed into the courthouse corridors erupted in cheers. Cassidy walked right up to the judge and demanded the return of all the guns.

Father Coughlin released a statement that next day. "The so-called conspiracy," he said, "turned out to be a hoax." He called the prosecution "ridiculous from the outset, insofar as the government agents seized Gettysburg rifles, heirloom bayonets, and soup tin cans." He neglected to mention bombs, cordite explosives, or thousands of rounds ready to be fed into stolen military machine guns. And after his followers were swung at and missed, Coughlin explained, we shouldn't be surprised if the Jews were really gonna get it now. "Regretfully," Father Coughlin said, "the resentment on the part of the victims is liable to increase the wave of antisemitism throughout the country, particularly now that the jury has found them not guilty."

Coughlin's closest ally in Brooklyn, Father Edward Lodge Curran, wrote to Attorney General Robert Jackson to demand that he investigate the investigators. At bottom, Curran was sure, there was a communist plot inside the Justice Department to destroy these Brooklyn Boys, these good and decent Christian patriots who were just trying to uphold constitutional principles.

A few days after the acquittal Curran's colleague Father Edward Brophy—sometimes called the philosopher of the Christian Front—spoke at a rally of two thousand people in honor of the defendants. Brophy did not return that day to his favorite Jews-killed-Jesus harangue, but he did use some of his time at the lectern to celebrate what you might call Brooklyn's community spirit. "There is one matter connected to the jury in this case that hasn't been disclosed up to this moment, but I think it's safe to tell you now. I refer to Mrs. Helen Titus, foreman of the jury." Did he divulge that Mrs. Titus was related to the defendants' lead defense counsel? No. "You may be interested to know," he said, "that she is my first cousin." Huh. Small world.

Brophy went on to shower encomiums on the exonerated suspects. America was founded as a Christian country and remained a Christian country to this day, the priest said, because of "genuine, patriotic citizens" like these men.

The audience roared its approval when John F. Cassidy and seven other defendants were called up by name. Macklin Boettger was invited to say a few words, and he let the audience in on another little courtroom secret. "At least ten members of our jury," Boettger told the cheering crowd, "are going to apply for membership in the Christian Front."

CHAPTER FIFTEEN

TRIP 19

The sun peeked in and out of the clouds for most of the morning of August 31, 1940, dappling the alfalfa and corn fields outside Lovettsville, Virginia, a tiny rural hamlet in the Blue Ridge Mountains, just forty miles northwest of Washington, D.C. This was Saturday morning and a pleasing start to the long Labor Day weekend. By mid-afternoon, though, the sky had begun to turn angry. When Dorothy Everhart stepped out of her farmhouse, just south of town, around 2:30 that day, it smelled like a storm was brewing. There was a great swath of blue sky to the south, but from the front of her house she could see a ceiling of gray clouds dropping overhead and off in the distance, to her west, heavy black clouds clinging to Short Hill, obscuring the mountain ridge that had been visible a few hours earlier. She could also discern a line of rain in the distance, already on her side of Short Hill. The front appeared to be moving in her direction in a hurry.

Suddenly a brilliant spark of lightning flashed across the sky, so close it shook Everhart's house. She went back inside to turn off the electricity, just to be safe, until the storm passed. Then Mrs. Everhart went out onto the back porch to get a different view and caught sight of a bright silver airplane flying just below the cloud ceiling. Lovettsville was in the flight path heading northwest out of the Washington-Hoover Airport, so there was nothing unusual about the sight. The airship was traveling at the standard speed, maybe at a slightly lower altitude than normal, but unwavering in its path—right into the line of approaching rainfall. Then came a second bolt of lightning, which seemed to split the sky out ahead of the plane. This flash was so brilliant and so expansive that she was momentarily blinded, as she would later explain, and lost sight of the plane. Then she heard a "low rumble" of thunder and, maybe five seconds later, an "awful roaring" that she was sure was a sound from the airplane.

Viola and Richard Thompson were standing in their kitchen watching one of the hardest rains they'd seen in years, when they first heard the roar of the plane. "An awful racket," Richard said, like a sudden and frightened acceleration of the engines. "The motor running just about as fast as I thought it could run."

Farther west and practically in the shadow of the Short Hill ridge, Lydia Jacobs heard what sounded like the long, sharp wail of a siren and then an explosion that almost knocked her off her feet. H. O. Vincell, who had lost his view of the falling plane when it "disappeared into a fog," also heard "a devil of a noise," which he was sure must have been a crash. "The pilot seemed to have given her the gun and then—bango," another witness remembered. After the explosion, there was an eerie silence. The sky turned darker, and a torrent of rain swept down from Short Hill and across the town.

Over the next ten to twenty minutes, strange pieces of airborne flotsam settled down over a half-mile area between Short Hill and Dorothy Everhart's house. A threshing crew waiting out the rainstorm in a nearby barn watched one piece of paper detritus float down and alight on the ground near them: a manila envelope, singed at the edges, with a Pennsylvania Central Airlines logo printed on it. A cardboard flight calculator dropped into a nearby stubble field, as did a thin, letter-sized cardboard sign, also with a Pennsylvania Central Airlines logo. "Sorry," it read. "This seat is occupied." Four separate passenger manifests, each of them singed at the edges, also wafted down from above.

The question was, did any of those passengers survive?

The first to the scene of the crash that stormy Saturday afternoon were locals, anxious to help. But it was immediately apparent there would be no need for triage, and nobody to nurse. The 24,372 pounds' worth of Douglas DC-3 airplane and contents (counting fuel, cargo, mail pouches, and passengers) had struck ground at the edge of Clarence Bishop's alfalfa field, at an estimated speed of more than three hundred miles per hour and at a decidedly inconvenient angle—almost straight down. The nose of the fuselage and the two engines had plowed six feet deep into the rain-softened ground. Those manifests and manila envelopes and papers had shot high into the air on impact and caught wind currents strong enough to carry them as much as seven-eighths of a mile behind the crash site.

The rest of the wreckage hurtled forward into Bishop's field and beyond. The landing gear had been thrown ahead 50 feet. One of the tires was set afire by the friction of impact but was merely smoldering in the rain by the time would-be rescuers arrived. The stabilizers, fins, rudders, and aft portion of the fuselage were about 150 feet ahead. The tail number of the aircraft, 21789, was still discernible. Pistons and cylinders from the engine were tossed 300 feet forward; the wings were beyond that; then the largest part of the passenger cabin, and then fuel tanks and flaps and ailerons. One lone blade from the left propeller had pinwheeled to a resting spot 1,800 feet beyond the site of impact.

The vast field of smoldering machine debris was shocking enough for the few folks who raced to the crash site, but it was nothing compared to the sight of human debris. There were twenty-one passengers and four crew members on the plane, according to the manifest, and definitely no survivors. The Loudoun County coroner later assured reporters and anybody else who asked that all the passengers and crew had unquestionably—and mercifully—been killed on impact. The bodies had all been pitched ahead as if shot out of a cannon, some cut in half by their still-fastened seat belts. The nearest remains were 350 feet beyond the crash site; the farthest more than 1,000 feet ahead. "The bodies of the passengers and crew," wrote one reporter, were "mangled beyond immediate identifications."

Nobody who saw that scene would easily shake the memory.

"We walked through this cornfield and parts of bodies were strung along the cornstalks," said Renace Painter, who was interviewed decades later by John Flannery, a current resident of Lovettsville and former federal prosecutor who has made it his mission to unravel the mystery of the crash. Painter was twelve years old at the time of the crash. "I ran across this one, walking around, and it was just from the middle of her stomach, her head and everything, and that was it. I said, 'I gotta get out of here. I can't take this anymore.'"

"Shoes neatly tied sat in the field with feet still in them, separated from the bodies of the people on the plane," says Flannery. "The dive into the ground was so dramatic that there were pieces of people—pardon the description—all over the area."

The violent rainstorm that kicked up after the crash had swollen creeks, temporarily flooded nearby bridges, and washed out roads, so traveling to the crash field became a more treacherous endeavor as the afternoon and evening wore on. It was around 7:30 that night, nearly five hours after the plane went down, when the bosses from the Civil Aeronautics Board arrived from Washington to take control of the crash site and the investigation. All the debris—human remains included—remained in situ overnight so the investigators could draw up detailed schematics of the impact site and debris field. Virginia state troopers and Loudoun County sheriff's deputies dutifully stayed on the scene to dissuade souvenir seekers.

The next morning the bodies were trucked to a chapel one town over, where the difficult process of making identifications commenced. The FBI brought in its fingerprint gurus, who had to inject glycerin into the rain-soaked and shriveled fingertips to get useful prints from the crash victims. Pocketbooks, watches, jewelry, and dental plates helped friends and family identify their loved ones, but there were a few uncomfortable moments when two separate families claimed the same set of remains.

The press already had the names of the dead, even while the identification process was happening. Newspapers across the country had printed the list of the presumed victims from the passenger manifest for Pennsylvania Central Airlines Trip 19. The papers in Pittsburgh, where the flight was headed, had a local angle: "Among the Pittsburgh passengers who died in the plane crash was Joseph James Pesci, former Duquesne University track star, who had just completed a course of FBI training in Washington. He was on his way home to Blairsville to visit his father, who is reported ill."

Most of the passengers on the manifest had lived and worked in Washington, where the flight originated. This included one senior attorney in the Justice Department's Criminal Division and one FBI stenographer; a clerk in the Adjutant General's Office at the War Department; an administrator at the Interstate Commerce Commission; four Internal Revenue Service employees; a draftsman in the Navy Department; and a clerk who had started his job at Pennsylvania Central Airlines five days earlier. But what made this disaster especially big news—beyond the fact that until that date this was the single deadliest airline crash in the United States,

Aftermath of the crash of Pennsylvania Central Airlines Trip 19

ever—was the presence on the manifest, and in that human debris field, of the U.S. senator Ernest Lundeen of Minnesota.

The senator's remains got preferred treatment. His body was the first identified, using a match with a fingerprint on file from his service as an infantry private during the Spanish-American War. Lundeen's remains were also first to be transported back to Washington. There was a silver-colored casket awaiting, in which the politician would make his final train ride home, aboard the Liberty Limited, from Union Station in Washington to St. Paul. "It is a fitting name for this funeral train," said his fellow senator from Minnesota. "It is symbolic of Senator Lundeen's spirited defense of American freedom throughout his public career."

FLAGS WERE SET at half-mast in the nation's capital to honor the fallen senator. To be honest, though, the tributes for Ernest Lundeen were more a trickle than a flood, which was perhaps suggestive of the degree to which he inspired fellow feeling among those who had to work with him on a daily basis. The few Senate colleagues who offered statements were succinct and somewhat vague. "A fine and able man . . . a powerful voice . . . he worked day and night for the cause of peace." Lundeen was a former college football player and a renowned horseshoe pitcher, according to the first-day story in a Washington newspaper, with a "rugged build and marked physical vitality." That at least was a nice thing to point out about a man. One of his home-state newspapers, the *Askov American,* more delicately noted Lundeen's legendary contrariness. "He dared to do the unpopular thing," the paper editorialized.

The sixty-two-year-old senator had spent his career staking out strange positions and then standing his ground against all attacks. As founder and national chairman of the Islands for War Debts Committee, Lundeen demanded the Roosevelt administration seize Bermuda and other British territories in the West Indies as payment for the unpaid bills Britain owed the United States from World War I. Fair enough, maybe, but that war had ended in 1918, and Lundeen didn't get around to founding this committee until 1939. The point of the committee, such as it was—the whole concept behind even creating such an absurd entity—was to remind Americans that Britain still owed us for the first war, and so how on earth could they expect us to support them further in a second one? At least the Islands committee sang the praises of their chairman when they got the news of the plane crash. "The shocking death of Senator Lundeen removes from American life an outstanding champion of non-intervention and a consistent fighter for all things pro-American," said Prescott Dennett, national secretary of the organization. "None will doubt that his contribution to the cause of democracy will remain a distinguished permanent chapter in the history of the Nation." Dennett vowed that the Islands committee would fight on, in memory of Ernest Lundeen.

As a first-term congressman way back in 1917, Lundeen had been a paid contributor to that controversial pro-German, anti-interventionist magazine that started off being called *The Fatherland* but got rechristened *Viereck's American Weekly* when it was revealed that it was secretly funded by the German government. Lundeen made a show of voting against sending U.S. troops overseas in World War I, and he remained a vocal critic of the mobilization even while Americans were dying at the Somme and Belleau Wood and the Marne. "The country is deeply divided over whether the U.S. should go into World War I. But when Wilson makes the call, most members of Congress unite around this. And then certainly when American troops are actually in combat, virtually every member of Congress, every politician, sort of makes a show of supporting the troops and even goes over to visit the trenches of the western front," says historian Bradley Hart, author of the 2018 book *Hitler's American Friends*. "Lundeen doesn't do any of these things. He refuses to support the war effort. At one point he does try to visit the troops and is turned away by the military because he's seen as an almost unpatriotic figure."

Not only was Lundeen voted out of office after one term, but the enraged citizens of Ortonville, Minnesota, once carried him off a speech platform as soon as he started his remarks on foreign policy; they force marched him to the rail yards and locked him in a refrigerated car of a departing train. They literally rode him out of their town on the rails.

Nevertheless, Lundeen managed to fight his way back to the House in 1933 and then into the U.S. Senate in 1937, without softening his isolationist rhetoric.

The summer of 1940 had started with great promise for hard-liners like Lundeen; Adolf Hitler had given them a banner to rally beneath. "America for Americans; Europe for Europeans," Hitler announced in an interview that got play across the United States in June 1940, just as his army was sweeping into Paris and his *Luftwaffe* was preparing for the aerial bombardment of London. U.S. embassies in Nazi-occupied Norway, Belgium, Luxembourg, and the Netherlands were being shuttered; the American ambassador to France was on the run from France's capital city.

At home, both the Republican and Democratic parties had adopted planks in their respective 1940 platforms pledging that America would not involve itself in any foreign war. Nazi agents had energetically promoted that outcome, while also ramping up the German government's secret effort to try to defeat the sitting American president in the upcoming election.

"Roosevelt's foreign policy has during the last few days suffered severe setbacks through Italy's entry into the war and the collapse of France," the secretary of state in the German Foreign Office wrote to his charges in America. "From reports in the USA, I understand that the error of this policy is being more and more realized there. I recommend that you continue to have the above views spread over there by prominent Americans in a manner you considerable suitable."

Lundeen, a member of Minnesota's thriving independent Farmer-Labor Party, had spent the month of August 1940 throwing himself like a monkey wrench into President Roosevelt's preparations for a possible war against Hitler's Germany, in particular one of the president's key legislative priorities: a bill requiring all twelve million American men between the ages of twenty-one and thirty-one to register for a military draft. The conscription bill was "the last crossroad before plunging into war," Lundeen announced at the beginning of August. "The time is here and now when all good Americans who believe in absolute neutrality and America first should rally in great national convention." He was one of three legislators to insert Charles Lindbergh's latest lay-off-Germany speech into the *Congressional Record,* and one of only seven senators to vote against granting President Roosevelt the authority to call out the National Guard and the reserves.

Lundeen's arguments in opposition to Roosevelt's expanding war preparations had national reach; in an August 10 speech on the NBC radio network, Lundeen had called the proposed draft registration bill a proposal "to conscript Americans from the cradle to the grave 18 to 65. Serfs and peons, that is your destiny. . . . We are being urged on by insane hysteria. Reason, we seem to be bereft of reason. . . . I have never heard of German, or a German born American, with a goal to ask that we help Germany, but red, yellow, brown, black, and white races all are expected to die for the British Empire. I warn the American people that we cannot defend America by defending old, decayed and dying empires. . . . Our Wall Street plutocracy will not listen. They seem bent on their own and the nation's destruction."

Lundeen's pronouncements had become even more shrill in the last weeks of August. He called the draft bill "nothing short of slavery." He gave the keynote address to the national congress of one of Father Coughlin's pet groups, the Mothers of the United States of America, whose delegates had come to Washington from fourteen states to sit in the actual Congress, in funeral veils, to protest the Senate as "a den of murderers, planning to murder the sons of every mother in this room." Conscription, Lundeen told the cheering women, is "un-American and disloyal to the Constitution. . . . Anyone who wants to fight Europe's battles [should be] sent back to where they came from. Britain declared this war. Let them finish it themselves."

German pilots, flying off the coast of France, had started raids into England by then. Their campaign would include fifty-two straight days of bombing sorties over the city of London. The German air force destroyed the homes of one in every six Londoners in the Battle of Britain and killed forty-three thousand civilians. But Lundeen said he could "see no difference between the democracy of the British Empire and the German Empire. Both are aggressors."

On the last Friday in August, when Congress rushed through Roosevelt's $5 billion "Total Defense" package to fund the building of a navy capable of defending two oceans, and the production of tanks, guns, artillery, and ammunition for a two-million-man army, Lundeen rose in anger on the floor of the Senate. "Such figures are fantastic and astronomical," he bellowed, on the day before he stepped onto that ill-fated flight. "It means panic and depression. It means bankruptcy. I am against this hysteria going any further because we are bankrupting America."

It was only the next evening when a reporter from *The Washington Post* showed up at Lundeen's Capitol office, to get a comment on the Minnesota senator's demise. The gist of the message from the office was this: his death was a tragic loss of one of America's most capable and dedicated anti-interventionists. The senator had been on that flight because he was going home to make another "plea for strict neutrality" at a Labor Day picnic in Minneapolis. An old family friend who had also stopped by the office let the reporter in on a bit of Lundeen's private thinking. "The words he used so often," she said, "were that the United States 'must not try to become the arbiter of European real estate disputes.' That's what he would have talked about on Monday, if he had given his speech."

Two weeks after the crash of Trip 19, the Civil Aeronautics Board investigators were still at a loss as to the probable cause of the crash. They had trucked the engines, propellers, and radio parts from the ravaged DC-3 to the Pennsylvania Central Airlines maintenance shops in Pittsburgh to pull apart what was left of them for inspection. Some key pieces of the plane were then hauled to the National Bureau of Standards in Washington for further review. The board then held a weeklong hearing, open to the public, in which it examined 134 exhibits and heard testimony from

Senator Ernest Lundeen (at right) giving a radio address

eighty-five separate witnesses, including the Lovettsville locals, and a series of experts—fellow pilots, engineers, meteorologists, and a specialist in electricity from GE. The bottom line of all the testimony was this: there was no obvious reason why Trip 19 went down.

The Douglas DC-3 was one of the safest planes in the air, and Pennsylvania Central Airlines had one of the best safety records in the industry. The airline had flown more than 113 million miles without a fatality, including 71,200 consecutive flights between Washington and Pittsburgh without incident. The pilot and his first officer were experienced fliers with hundreds of hours at the controls of a DC-3 and no physical impairments. All routine maintenance and preflight checks had been done. The plane was carrying an acceptable amount of weight, and its load was properly distributed. There was no evidence of an engine malfunction or a fire inside the cabin.

Everybody agreed that the thunderstorm around Lovettsville had been frightful that day, and the board even managed to track the probable path of the lightning bolt the witnesses had seen flash across the sky, just in front of the plane, moments before the crash. "The terminal of the stroke was a .22 caliber rifle that hung on a wall in the garage of I. F. Baker, Morrisonville, VA., farm supervisor, whose home is three and one-half miles from the crash scene," wrote a Washington-based reporter covering the hearing. Mr. Baker had even driven to the hearing to show the Civil Aeronautics Board his rifle's splintered wooden stock.

And yet all the experts agreed that it was unlikely, given their examination of the exterior of the plane and the susceptible parts of its radio system, that lightning had struck the DC-3. Even if it had, they told the board, a DC-3 was built to withstand any such strike. Planes like that flew through storms like that all the time.

The weeklong investigation produced no definite answer as to the cause of the crash . . . and tantalizing questions. The Civil Aeronautics Board got a little esoteric in its wonderings. "We are obliged to look for the extraordinary, and to examine into the possibility and probability of occurrences that are so rare in practical operating experience as to be highly obscure, if not virtually unknown," the board wrote. Among these "highly obscure" possibilities was a theory that the newly hired Pennsylvania Central Airlines clerk had somehow been flung out of the jump seat, hurtled into the cockpit, and knocked the pilot and his first mate away from the controls.

There was also the question of outright sabotage. A Pennsylvania Central Airlines employee at Washington-Hoover Airport testified that he had seen one man enter the DC-3 before boarding began, while he was still trying to clean the plane. But the cleaner didn't recall whether the crew had already been on board, or whether the mystery man had stayed on the plane for the flight. There also was one alarm clock found in the Trip 19 debris field outside Lovettsville—briefly raising the prospect of some kind of time bomb—but its alarm was set not for the time of the crash, 2:40 P.M., but rather for 9:15. Also, um, there was no detonating device attached.

But still, there was the undeniable fact that the DC-3's two engines were wide-open full throttle when the plane slammed into the ground. The plane's airspeed was in excess of three hundred miles per hour, nearly double its planned cruising speed. "It is possible that for some reason the pilot and co-pilot were prevented from effectively operating the controls," the board concluded.

The question remained: Prevented by what?

DREW PEARSON, THE renowned political columnist and inveterate digger into the capital's vault of secrets, thought he might be onto something, thanks largely to the staff inside Senator Ernest Lundeen's decidedly unhappy office. In the aftermath of Lundeen's death, the senator's aides were ready to spill. For one thing, the loyalty Lundeen's young staffers might otherwise have felt for their senator boss was sorely tested by his petty corruption and greed. Lundeen was a man who cultivated a political reputation for caring for the little guy and looking out for the poor, when in fact he took a good portion of his own living out of the financial hides of his least paid underlings. Lundeen had instituted a "kickback" program in his office reminiscent of Huey Long's rip-off of state employees in Louisiana. As a matter of public record in the federal government payroll, for instance, Miss Harriet Johnson's salary was $150 a month. But when her check came, she had to hand back $15 in cash to Lundeen. When her reported government salary rose to $325, she had to "kick back" $180 to the senator. The same was true of Lundeen's most senior aide, Edward Corneaby, as well as Phyllis Posivio, as well as everybody else on his official payroll. "We handed the money directly to the senator and no receipt was given," Posivio said. "There was no alternative except to lose our jobs if we didn't pay the senator what he asked."

Johnson and Posivio were both disillusioned by the time of their boss's death. There was talk in town that Harriet Johnson had gone to the FBI to tell what she knew, including how Lundeen appeared distraught, was even in tears, on the morning of his fatal flight. "I've gone too far to turn back," the senator had cryptically confided to her. Johnson had also told G-men, according to later accounts, that when she had taken her boss to the airport for the flight, she had noticed through the open doorway of the plane some sort of scuffle inside. "Some of the passengers were locked in a struggle" of some kind. It looked to her like her boss, Senator Lundeen, might even have been among the people involved in that struggle. But she couldn't be entirely sure.

Phyllis Posivio was keeping notes, too, in the aftermath of Lundeen's death. She received a memorable visit from the senator's widow just after the plane crash. Mrs. Norma Lundeen, having flown across the country in a rush (at a time when that was not an easy thing to do), appeared more anxious than distraught two days after her husband was killed. Striding into the senator's Capitol office, she made an odd but not altogether unexpected request; she told Posivio that she wanted her to pull together every piece of correspondence between her husband and George Sylvester Viereck, that long-ago author of gay vampire fiction, editor of *Fatherland* magazine, and cheerleader for all things German. Among the debris found near the wreckage of Trip 19 was a slightly charred draft of a speech Viereck had ghostwritten for Lundeen: "The German Element in America." Viereck was well known to Posivio and to the rest of the staff; he had been a mainstay in their workday lives, basically using Lundeen's Capitol Hill office as his base of operations to lobby Congress.

"Mrs. Lundeen directed us to put everything relating to Mr. Viereck in one file and give it to her," Posivio later testified in a Washington courtroom.

"Did she take charge of all the senator's files after his death?" an attorney asked.

"No, just the Viereck matter," Posivio explained. "She wanted that in her possession, and she took it."

Drew Pearson's best source inside the office was Edward Corneaby, until recently Lundeen's top aide, who had left the senator five months earlier to go home to Minnesota to run for Congress. Corneaby told Pearson that his own political ambitions were not the only reason for his departure from Lundeen's employ. Corneaby had been warning Lundeen for months about his involvement with this character Viereck, but Lundeen refused to listen. After the plane crash, Corneaby filled Pearson in on what Viereck and Lundeen had been up to.

Pearson published his exclusive scoop on September 13, 1940, two weeks after Lundeen's death, and the day the Civil Aeronautics Board wound up its public hearings into the Trip 19 air disaster. "If federal authorities probe deep enough into the crash of the Pennsylvania Central Airlines plane which carried Senator Lundeen to his death in Virginia, they may find some highly interesting facts regarding Nazi activities in the United States," was the lede on Pearson's nationally syndicated column. Pearson reported that the FBI already had an open investigation on the matter and that at least one of the Justice Department employees on board the plane was, as Pearson put it, "definitely" tailing the senator. "Suspicion had been directed in Senator Lundeen's direction after many mysterious visits to his office on the part of George Sylvester Viereck, famous German propagandist and reputedly a cousin of the Kaiser. . . . Viereck frequently came to the office to inquire if certain speeches had been inserted in the Congressional Record. . . . Viereck bought frequent gifts of candy to the Lundeen stenographers, but eventually they got suspicious and reported the mysterious goings and comings of Nazi sympathizers to the Lundeen office."

Norma's race across the country to remove the Viereck file from her husband's Senate office suddenly took on a new cast. "I had my eyes open," said Phyllis Posivio.

CHAPTER SIXTEEN

"PROMISCUOUS USE OF HIS FRANK"

The Dies Committee was in session the last week of August 1940, just a few days before Senator Ernest Lundeen's plane went down, and its investigators were not sure what to make of one of its witnesses. He was a rather bland-looking milquetoast of a middle-aged man. Tall and thin, with an indoor complexion, the forty-six-year-old New Yorker was dressed in conservative businessman's attire, with a softening, about-to-double chin above his expertly knotted tie; he wore wire-rimmed spectacles and a slightly out-of-date haircut, cropped tight at the sides and swept back off his high forehead.

Henry Hoke cut an entirely unalarming figure. His testimony, however, belied his looks. A dangerous tide was surging into America from Europe, Hoke insisted, and the country seemed both insensate to the unfolding peril and powerless to stanch it.

Dies Committee investigators, who had spent most of their working hours in the previous two years on the trail of what they were sure was communist infiltration of American labor unions and New Deal work programs, cast a wary eye on Hoke. The witness was a respected advertising man, a leader in a fast-growing and lucrative sector of the industry, with a successful consulting business and his own nationally distributed trade magazine, *The Reporter of Direct Mail Advertising*. But Henry Hoke, as a private citizen, had also been inundating the Dies Committee, the U.S. Postal Service, and the FBI with reams of evidence of German agents operating inside the U.S. government. The adman seems to have made a second full-time job of this crusade.

"Do you receive any compensation," the committee's lead investigator asked the witness, "from any Jewish organization?"

"No," Hoke answered, unperturbed by the question.

"Are there any Jews furnishing you with any money?" the investigator pressed.

"No," Hoke said. "Except possibly a normal number of subscribers. . . . I should say they are in a minority."

"You do not receive any money from the Nonsectarian Anti-Nazi League?"

"No."

"Or any other organizations?"

"No," Hoke replied. "I became first interested last September [1939], when I was sending my boy to his freshman class at the University of Pennsylvania, and some three weeks after he had started there I got a note from him to the effect that he was being annoyed and very much worried and didn't want to stay. He told me that each morning he found some kind of a slip underneath his door and that it was propaganda."

Henry Reed Hoke is a name mostly lost to American history, except within a narrow band of the advertising profession. Even into the twenty-first century, the trade association of direct mail and marketing professionals was still bestowing the annual Henry Hoke Award, which recognizes "the campaign with the most courageous solution of a difficult sales marketing problem." His name also still pops up occasionally in academic papers or trade publications, with tried-and-true copywriting formulas he invented back in the 1930s, like Picture—Promise—Prove—Push: "You start by painting a word picture of what the product or service will do for the reader. Then promise that the picture will come true if the product is purchased. Offer proof of what the product has done for others. Finally, end with a push for immediate action."

Henry Hoke's most impressive push for immediate action began with that plea from his son Pete. Hoke knew hard-sell propaganda when he saw it. All these mimeographed sheets shoved under his son's dormitory room door or passed out at the student union had a simple and direct theme: Keep America out of Europe's war. Leave Hitler alone. "Urgent pleas," Hoke explained, to even "resist efforts to protect the country by building defenses or developing training programs."

Hoke, a Penn graduate himself, checked in with a few faculty members on campus; they told him they were aware of the antiwar pamphlets but "didn't think it was serious." Back home in New York, Hoke chatted up other fathers with college-age sons and learned that Pete's experience at the University of Pennsylvania was hardly unique; similar pamphlets were appearing at institutions of higher learning all over New England and the mid-Atlantic and the Midwest. A few of the fathers put Hoke in touch with professors at different universities, and two of those faculty members told him that the flurry of propaganda sheets was not confined to campus. Local clergymen, for instance, were receiving a mailing called *Facts in Review* from something called the German Library of Information.

Hoke kept digging. Over the next six months, he collected a vast amount of pro-Nazi, isolationist literature that was being mailed to American citizens across the country. These weren't just coarse pamphlets thrown off tall buildings or fanatic broadsheets sold on street corners; this was slick and state of the art. The expert adman was shaken by the increasing sophistication of the obviously well-financed German propaganda campaign. He at first hesitated to publicize what he had learned, but in May 1940, over the objections of friends and colleagues who warned Hoke not to get caught up in politics (could be bad for business), he published a long exposé in *The Reporter of Direct Mail Advertising*. This was a major departure for Hoke's trade publication, which tended toward advice on running in-house corporate publications or the latest techniques in trick folds, die cuts, and pop-ups for 3¼-by-5-inch advertising postcards. Hoke's feature article, "War in the Mails," was a stunner. It laid out the evidence and credibly asserted that a fairly massive pro-German propaganda campaign, funded from Berlin, was flooding the United States, reaching millions of Americans at school, at work, and at home.

The story also identified the front organizations pulling it off. By name. And output. The German Library of Information was mailing nearly 100,000 copies of its weekly news digest, *Facts in Review,* to the 1940 version of American "influencers"—ministers, priests, teachers, editors, elected officials. The way *Facts in Review* digested the news for its audience, readers were given to understand that Germany had been victimized and threatened beyond patience; Hitler was justified in tearing up the Munich Pact, annexing Czechoslovakia, taking over Poland, Norway, Sweden, the Netherlands, and Belgium, attacking France and England, and terrorizing the Jewish population in Germany and every other place his storm troopers took control. The German Railroads Information Office was sending a similar weekly bulletin to 40,000 U.S. bankers, stockbrokers, and small businessmen. The German American Board of Trade produced its version of the same message in a slick, expensively printed monthly journal that it sent to CEOs, finance industry leaders, and elected officials.

Beyond the expensive, extensive mailing campaign, the German-funded American Fellowship Forum was sponsoring all-expenses-paid speaking tours by pro-fascist, isolationist Americans. The debut issue of the Forum's new magazine, *Today's Challenge,* featured articles by Lawrence Dennis, Senator Ernest Lundeen, Congressman Hamilton Fish, George Sylvester Viereck, and Philip Johnson. Johnson's "Are We a Dying People?" was a thinly veiled call to cleanse America of Blacks, Irish, eastern Europeans, and of course Jews.

Lawrence Dennis—by 1940, firmly established as America's foremost fascist intellectual—was busy with his own weekly newsletter, also financially supported by the Hitler government, which incorporated plenty of news from *Facts in Review*. But he still had time to send new submissions for the coming editions of *Today's Challenge*. "The third piece on the cures of the crisis will link the New Deal, Nazism, and Fascism," Dennis wrote to the head of the

Forum, Dr. Friedrich Ernst Auhagen. "This, I think, is a swell attack on the problem for your purpose. It completely blanks the fire of the Government and Liberal crowd and it will even amuse and please the reactionaries more than it annoys them—to have the New Deal linked to Nazism."

When Dennis wrote to Auhagen again, this time requesting yet more financial assistance for himself from the Nazi government in Berlin, he touted his growing relationship with America's most famous isolationist. "Dear Fritz," Dennis wrote, "I saw Lindbergh last week and will see him often from now on. He is optimistic about keeping us out of the war." The German Foreign Office, meanwhile, was consulting directly with Dennis and with Philip Johnson about starting yet another new magazine to carry the Nazi-fascist banner in America.

Hoke wrote in fulsome detail about the scale, sophistication, and massive price tag of the Germans' ongoing mailed propaganda operation in the United States. He also explained exactly why the Germans had been ramping up their propaganda campaign so aggressively. The Nazis' plain intent was to add stress to the cracks and fissures already visible in American political life, Hoke explained: rich versus poor, foreign born versus native born, nonwhite versus white, Gentiles versus Jews, northerners versus southerners, Democrats versus Republicans, conservatives versus liberals. "Do you remember what Hitler had said?" Hoke wrote. "'America is permanently on the brink of revolution. It will be a simple matter for me to produce unrest and revolts in the U.S., so that these gentry will have their hands full with their own affairs.'"

Hoke sent his May 1940 article to the postmaster general of the United States, along with a cover letter, asking for an official government investigation into mail fraud. "We will be glad to cooperate with you, as usual, in any possible way," Hoke wrote, "and will reveal our sources."

Postmaster James Farley did send a few men to have a look at the evidence Hoke had collected, but the postal inspectors spent most of their time at Hoke's midtown Manhattan office explaining why it didn't much matter. "Interesting," they told him. "But it's not actually against any existing law." Another man might have been discouraged, or at least apt to listen to the fellow advertising man who told Hoke his "efforts will be as ineffective as a pebble dropped into Lake Michigan." But Hoke had got the idea he was onto something big and something worth pursuing, not least because of the peculiar character of the negative response his work was starting to provoke.

Soon after the publication of "War in the Mails," Hoke's wife called his office to tell him he had received some interesting mail from the head of the German Railroads Information Office. The letter from Ernest Schmitz, sent to Hoke's home address, accused the adman of "hysteria," loss of "good judgement," and "slanderous libels." Schmitz deemed this alleged libel actionable in American courts. "You are hereby invited to retract your false and libelous statements with proper apologetic regrets," Schmitz wrote, "and in such language as decency and common courtesy prescribe, and to publish your retraction in the next issue of your magazine, devoting the same space and position to your correction as was given to your libelous statements."

Hoke did not back down, even if both the letter itself and the deci-

Henry Hoke with candidate Emily Taft Douglas, who defeated Representative Stephen Day, another ally of Viereck, in 1944

sion to send it to his home address were meant to shake him. Henry Hoke would make no retraction, he told Herr Schmitz. He would in fact welcome the chance to present evidence in open court. "I refuse to be intimidated by you or by any other German controlled organization," he wrote back. "You, and all the other Nazis who are abusing the privilege and hospitality of this free nation, are trying to dupe and dope the American Press and Public. . . . Americans resent your campaign to create fear and awe of German Might, a campaign which hides behind the protective skirts of our generous laws."

Hoke kept up his private, personally funded investigation, only now he was starting to get some help in amassing evidence. After the publication of "War in the Mails," other private citizens around the country started sending him samples of the Nazi propaganda they were receiving. One concerned German American sent Hoke twenty-five separate pieces of mail he had received, originating in different locations in Germany, in a single month. One thing that struck Hoke about the German propaganda campaign was the technical competence of Nazi copywriters. Each mailing was a simple, straightforward attack on a single subject: President Roosevelt's war preparations, or the Jews, or the Catholics, or America's licentious freedoms, or the British. Sometimes the mailings included messages from the newly formed isolationist group the America First Committee. Sometimes they included reprints of quotations by famous America Firsters, like Charles Lindbergh, who had just told a rally of forty thousand people at Chicago's Soldier Field that it was time to make a deal with the new master of Europe, Adolf Hitler: "An agreement between us could maintain civilization and peace throughout the world as far into the future as we can see."

Hoke kept going, publishing a series of stories throughout the summer of 1940 on the vast and growing propaganda campaign the German government was waging in America. He was still gathering receipts, and those receipts were starting to turn up links between the German government's disinformation operation and powerful Americans who really ought to know better. Who maybe did know better. Congressman Jacob Thorkelson of Montana, Hoke found, and Senator Robert Rice Reynolds, honorary chair of the late Ernest Lundeen's Islands for War Debts Committee, had both made isolationist speeches lifted straight from the German-authored *Facts in Review.*

Hoke's appearance as a witness at the Dies Committee in the last week of August 1940 gave the direct mail expert a chance to present Congress with the evidence he'd gathered about the German propaganda campaign in America and to explain to legislators why they were going to have to come up with some kind of strategy to contend with it. Congress should perhaps reconsider the international Postal Union treaty, which obligated the United States to deliver anything sent from another country—including Germany—free of charge. "Only the country in which the mail is stamped receives any recompense for the delivery," Hoke explained to the committee, which meant U.S. taxpayers were unwillingly subsidizing the part of the German operation that sent Americans propaganda direct from overseas.

"Our theory of freedom of press and speech is a sacred heritage," Hoke offered to the committee that late August day in 1940. "But the misuse of that 'freedom' is more dangerous now than hordes of bombers. We do not ask for a law which would prevent a foreign country, in peaceful pursuit of business, from advertising the advantages of travel (for example). But we sincerely believe that if America is to be kept free, freedom of speech and press in America must be an exclusively American right. That is, let American citizens say or write what they wish but bar foreign disrupters."

Henry Hoke, a private American citizen, had been thoughtful, intrepid, and outright courageous in his one-man campaign to unveil the Nazi propaganda operation in the United States. But, as Leon Lewis had already learned with his anti-Nazi spying operation in California, that and a nickel bought him a cup of coffee in the nation's capital. Congress was tied in its usual partisan knots, and with an election only a few months away they were unwilling or unable to act in response to what Hoke had exposed. The postmaster and his inspectors said they were powerless to do anything ("it's not actually against any existing law"), and the FBI and the federal prosecutors at DOJ—with the Christian Front embarrassment still fresh—were not looking for another fight with the far right.

The country did catch a small break when the head of one of the main German government front groups, the American Fellowship Forum, was apprehended in Los Angeles while running from a subpoena issued by the Dies Committee. Federal prosecutors believed they had no big case to make against Dr. Friedrich Ernst Auhagen on the propaganda front, but it so happened that the German immigrant and former Columbia University philosophy professor had in his possession a series of obscene photographs of children when he was arrested. Auhagen insisted to the agents who apprehended him that these shots were merely "art studies," but a prosecutor in Los Angeles described them as "so shocking that only the least repulsive would be shown to the jury."

Dorothy Thompson, the celebrated and influential American journalist, further outed Herr Auhagen in her syndicated column of October 23, 1940. In the column, Thompson identified as Auhagen's "leading brain-trusters" in America the Tweedledee and Tweedledum of American fascism, master Lawrence Dennis and protégé Philip Johnson. "Seldom directly, but by consciously directed indirection," Thompson wrote, "their business is . . . to penetrate high places—centers of political influence and economic power—reach the so-called realists and convert them to the idea that democracy needs considerable streamlining, discipline and authority [read: fascism], and that the economic interests of the United States, its welfare and its peace can best be served by collaboration with the Germans, who are going to win the World War anyhow and who represent in a general pattern, the future form of civilization."

About a month later, the Dies Committee made a public report on the German government targeting the American public with propaganda through the mails and the media. They made a rough estimate of the size of the operation and named some of the Nazi propaganda agents working inside the German embassy in Washington and its U.S. consulates around the country. The report named Auhagen as "the guiding light" of the Nazi effort in the United States. He was convicted for operating as a foreign agent and later deported back to Germany.

Henry Hoke, meanwhile, continued to be the one-man Little Engine That Could. He ignored the hate mail he received at his home in Garden City, Long Island. "We have good reason to believe that you will be placed in a concentration camp before another two years will have passed," wrote one foe. "You have the nerve to complain about German propaganda, when half our radio commentators spew out volumes in praise of the British," wrote another. "I expect to be in Garden City [soon] and will drop in for a little chat." Hoke kept on, gathering string on the Nazis' disinformation operation in America, which he then passed on to the Dies Committee investigators, to FBI agents, to the attorney general, and even to the White House.

Hoke was reading everything he could; and his antennae were always up for language and phrases being used by both German propagandists and American isolationists, like Senator Burton K. Wheeler of Montana, who went on the *American Forum of the Air* radio program in January 1941 and claimed that President Roosevelt's proposed Lend-Lease program to supply our allies would ensure American entry into the war and would "plow under every fourth American boy." (The head of the press department of the German Foreign Office in Berlin would later take credit for inventing this earthy phrase and for pushing it out into America.) Six weeks later, Senator Wheeler banged the gong a little harder, blaming America's "international bankers joining with . . . the Sassoons of the Orient and the Rothschilds and the Warburgs of Europe" for hurrying the country into a war against Hitler that would benefit nobody but the Jews.

Hoke was paying particular attention to Wheeler because the senator's name kept showing up in the rafts of Nazi-friendly mailings that concerned citizens were sending on to his offices. The senator's name ended up laying one of the trails of clues that Hoke followed to find the origin of the Nazis' propaganda sheets,

and their path through the United States. When Hoke ran forensics on envelopes that bore Senator Wheeler as the sender's
address, he learned something intriguing. Wheeler's signature
had been stamped onto the envelopes "with a peculiar style of
duplicating machine," Hoke later explained. "The lettering and
impression did not look like the product of an American manu-
facturer. We thought it might be a German-made addressing machine. But with the help of some of the equipment manufacturers,
we found that the addressing had been done by an old-fashioned
Elliott Addressing Machine which had been out of general use
for more than twenty years."

In a move straight out of a detective story, Hoke and his team
managed to get hold of the Elliott corporation's old supply order
records and tracked one of their three extant addressing machines
to the offices of the Steuben Society in New York City. The society,
founded in the aftermath of World War I to "bring about a complete rehabilitation" of the reputation and the status of the Germanic element in the United States, had morphed into a Nazi
apologist organization. With quiet support from the German Foreign Office, the leadership of the Steuben Society was working
hard to keep the United States out of the fight in Europe. The
group had, for instance, engaged the U.S. Senate's most vehement
antiwar spokesman, Senator Ernest Lundeen, to give the keynote
address at its annual dinner on September 14, 1940. When Lundeen died in the plane crash two weeks before the appointed date,
the society's national chairman called instead on his good friend
Congressman Hamilton Fish, who graciously agreed to take Lundeen's spot in the speakers' lineup. Ahead of Fish's remarks, the
national chairman let 'er rip. "Insolent agents and propagandists
infest our shores, seeking to drag us into the final horrors of war,"
he said. "So-called 'Americans' dare suggest that we again become
a colony of Great Britain."

"We obtained samples of confidential bulletins issued by the
Steuben Society," Hoke said of his office's investigation into the
Wheeler-stamped envelopes. "In these bulletins, the [society's]
Secretary urged members to attend specified meetings with em-

phasis on the assurance that reprints of speeches by Senator Wheeler and Senator Nye would be available *in franked envelopes* to be mailed to friends. 'No postage required.' The peculiar addressing style used by the Steuben Society matched the addressing on the Wheeler franked envelopes. The old-fashioned blue ink was the same. A code on the addressee plate was identical."

So, there it was, finally. By late spring 1941, after nearly eighteen months of investigation—which had drained the finances of his own consulting business—Hoke had obtained real evidence of the scheme he had long suspected. "That gave us definite proof," Hoke wrote, "that Senator Wheeler was allowing a German organization to make promiscuous use of his frank."

The frank Hoke was referring to is a special privilege first extended to America's elected officials during the Continental Congress in 1775; it continues to this day. Every member of Congress is given an allowance to cover the costs of sending communications to his or her constituents, over his or her own signature (or frank), free of postage costs. This privilege was judged by the Founders as a necessity for transparent democratic government and governance: Members of Congress should be able to easily communicate with their voters back home about what they're doing in Washington. It should literally be free to send their constituents mail about any government business, including anything that appeared in the *Congressional Record,* whether it was actually spoken on the floor of the House or Senate or simply inserted therein by an interested member. The concept is certainly sound; the foundation of a strong and functioning democracy, after all, is an informed citizenry. And for most of the life of the nation, before Instagram and Twitter, before Facebook and texting and emailing, before television news and even radio news, the mail was the best way to circulate information, the lifeblood of democracy. That was certainly still true in 1940.

But here was the problem, as Hoke judged it: with the right allies in Congress, the German government and its agents in America could shove pro-Nazi propaganda by the truckful through one particular loophole in the law. It's one thing for a member of

Congress or a senator to send stuff home—or even around the country—to keep Americans apprised of the goings-on in Washington. It's another thing altogether for them to give that free-mail privilege away to groups funded by hostile foreign governments, to use Americans' tax dollars to pump into the United States propaganda authored by that foreign government. If a president was given free national airtime to make an Oval Office address to the American public, but then at the start of it he instead handed over the mic to a foreign dictator, the country would be at first confused and then upset and then before too long probably up in arms. But that's effectively what these senators and congressmen were doing with the free-mail franking privilege. How many of them were doing it? And why?

Hoke was hot to determine just how successful the Hitler regime had been in making friends in Washington to help with this scheme, but he was at a decided disadvantage as a private investigator. Citizen Hoke had no subpoena power; no means to compel sources to talk to him; no money except what came out of his own pocket or what he raised from private sources. Even more difficult, he was working from the outside in. His starting points were the *Facts in Review* pamphlets, direct mail letters, copies of pro-Nazi speeches, and articles that other concerned Americans were sending to his office. What was happening before that matter landed in mailboxes across the country—the precise origin of the material—was not always easy to discern.

But Hoke was good at following the clues. Unaddressed franked envelopes under the signatures of Senator Wheeler, Representative Thorkelson, and other isolationist elected officials had been given to the America First Committee, the German American Bund, and clubs and organizations run by raging antisemite fascists like the Christian Fronter Joe "We're going to run this country the way Hitler runs Germany" McWilliams in New York, Gerald Winrod in Wichita (called "the Jayhawk Hitler" when he made his surprisingly credible run for the Republican U.S. Senate nomination in Kansas), and Omaha's Charles Hudson, the quite insane helpmeet who had saved General Moseley from that dangerous water glass proffered him at the Dies Committee hearings. Franked mail was also given to the office of Elizabeth Dilling, who had made a career of alleging without proof the communist proclivities of thousands of American officials and regular citizens (Mrs. Dilling's work was funded by Henry Ford). The spiders in this web would receive the franked (so, no postage required) but unaddressed envelopes, then stuff them with pro-German propaganda of various stripes, then fill in the addresses and send the envelopes to folks on any mailing list they could get their hands on. All free of charge, postage paid by the taxpayer.

Hoke was feeling some urgency in the spring and summer of 1941, and with good reason. "We learned from a girl who worked in a locked and guarded room on the top floor of the Ford Building at No. 1710 Broadway in New York City," Hoke later wrote, "that Ford Motor Car Company employees were compiling a master list of appeasers, anti-Semites, pro-Nazis and Fascists from fan mail" addressed to the most high-profile isolationist members of Congress, like Senator Rush Holt and Representative Hamilton Fish, and also to the most high-profile isolationist of them all: Charles Lindbergh, who had in late April 1941 formally attached his name to the America First Committee. By then the America First Committee was the biggest and most influential voluntary political organization in the United States. And growing fast.

When America First called a rally in New York City on May 23, 1941, the crowd could not be contained by the capacious Madison Square Garden. Three hours before curtain time, twenty-two thousand New Yorkers were jammed into the arena, waving small American flags handed out by the ushers, while fifteen thousand more people who couldn't get in formed a horseshoe that extended from the sidewalks onto Forty-Ninth Street, Fiftieth Street, and Eighth Avenue. The organizers set up a loudspeaker so the overflow street crowd could hear speeches given by the event's headliners: Charles Lindbergh and Senator Burton K. Wheeler.

"If we go to war to preserve democracy abroad, we are likely to end by losing it at home," Lindbergh crowed. "We have been led toward war against the opposition of four-fifths of our people."

The loss of American lives in a war against the Nazis, Lindbergh asserted, was "likely to run into the millions . . . and victory itself is doubtful."

Senator Burton K. Wheeler (at left) and Charles Lindbergh (center) at an America First rally in New York City

The eight hundred New York City policemen assigned to the event had no problem cordoning off the small number of anti-Nazi picketers outside the Garden, but the speech still ran longer than Lindbergh expected because he had to pause so often to let the applause and hurrahs of the appreciative crowd die down. When Lindbergh finally worked his way to the end of his talk, he received a standing ovation that lasted nearly five full minutes. Senator Wheeler followed, dressed in his trademark suit of white duck, similar to the ones favored by Huey Long. Wheeler had been visiting with Americans all over this country, he said, and he knew their hearts. "The American farmer and his wife are no Judas Iscariot," he said. "They will not sell their sons into war for thirty pieces of silver." They understood, as the senator understood, that "a cold dispassionate analysis of the facts explodes the fanciful theory of a military invasion of the Western Hemisphere, which your Secretary [of War Henry] Stimson talked about only a short time ago. We are safe now and we are safe for years to come. . . . I am afraid that if the President accepts the advice of that little coterie who surround him, most of whom have never faced an electorate or met a payroll, or tried a lawsuit and many of whom are impractical dreamers, he will wage an undeclared war. And then Constitutional government in the United States will be at an end."

The anti-Roosevelt polemic was fair enough, a natural part of American politics whenever momentous questions of war and peace arose. But the threads of isolationism, antisemitism, and fascism were becoming an ominously tight weave. The recently founded antifascist New York City Coordinating Committee for Democratic Action sent a hair-on-fire memorandum to the FBI about what they were seeing that summer. "Today, street rioters have merged with big-time [Hitler] appeasers and an air of respectability cloaks the Fascist front," the coordinating committee reported. "Unanimously Lindbergh is acclaimed the leader." The coordinating committee also passed on newspaper reports about an attack by Joe McWilliams's street fighters and friends on a group advocating U.S. intervention into the war: "Pro-Nazi hoodlums, German Bundists, Christian Mobilizers and Christian Frontists attacked an orderly street meeting of Fight for Freedom at 59th St. and Lexington Ave. These Storm Troopers tried to push two women off the platform. . . . In a disciplined formation, they charged the crowd shouting 'We Want Hitler' and 'We want Lindbergh.'"

In the final days of that summer, Lindbergh himself began to slough off any ambiguity or coyness about his real views. And it came with a none-too-subtle threat. "When this war started in Europe, it was clear that the American people were solidly opposed to entering it. Why shouldn't we be? . . . Why are we on the verge of war? . . . Who is responsible for changing our national policy from one of neutrality and independence to one of entanglement in European affairs? . . . The three most important groups who have been pressing this country toward war are the British, the Jewish, and the Roosevelt administration."

The Jews, he said, "for reasons which are as understandable from their viewpoint as they are inadvisable from ours, for reasons which are not American, wish to involve us in the war. . . . Instead of agitating for war, the Jewish groups in this country should be opposing it in every possible way for they will be among the first to feel its consequences. Tolerance is a virtue that depends upon peace and strength. History shows that it cannot survive war and devastation. A few far-sighted Jewish people realize this and stand opposed to intervention. But the majority still do not." His threat that America's "tolerance" for Jews would end if war began was only barely tacit. To Lindbergh, the Jews were not only alien to America, they ought to be afraid about it.

Lindbergh was not alone. His speech in Des Moines about "the Jewish" came at the same time that General Moseley was making his public case to sterilize any Jewish person immigrating to the United States. It was also when Senator Robert Rice Reynolds, a North Carolina Democrat, was calling for federal legislation to close our borders to European Jews, despite the widespread knowledge by then that they were being rounded up—men, women, and children—and murdered by the Nazis. They were going to be "seeping into this country by the thousands every single month," Reynolds said, "to take the jobs which rightly belong" to Americans. "I wish to say—and I say it without the slightest hesitation—that if I had my way about it at this hour, I would build a wall about the United States so high and so secure that not a single alien or foreign refugee from any country upon the face of the earth could possibly scale or ascend it."

WITH THE STAKES rising by the day, Henry Hoke stayed in the game. He identified twenty representatives and senators who were inserting German propaganda into the *Congressional Record* and letting pro-Nazi groups use their franking privileges. This included Congressman Hamilton Fish and Senator Burton K. Wheeler, who both had pearl-twisting cases of the vapors when the news got out. "We cannot and do not intend to require an affidavit from every person who asks for copies of my speeches regarding their personal qualifications to distribute them," Wheeler announced in a huff. "This is still a free country and so long as American citizens request copies of my addresses for the purposes of aiding in their distribution, they shall have them."

Hoke kept hammering away, and other important voices were finally starting to join in. Secretary of War Henry Stimson was appalled when he learned that Wheeler's pro-Nazi "anti-war cards" were sent not just to American civilian homes and businesses but to active-duty American soldiers on U.S. military bases. Wheeler "comes very near the line of subversive activities against the United States," Stimson told reporters on July 24, 1941, "if not treason."

Wheeler punched back. *The New York Times* dutifully reported Wheeler's rejoinder that "he paid for the printing of the cards with his own check, but that the money came from funds of the America First Committee," whatever the hell that meant. The senator also unleashed a nasty personal attack on his seventy-three-year-old accuser: "One can probably excuse Secretary Stimson on the ground of his age and incapacity. Everyone in Washington knows that the old gentleman is unable to carry on the duties of his office, and some go so far as to say that he has reached the point where—to use the expression of a Britisher—he is gaga. . . . Before [President Roosevelt and Secretary Stimson] are through they will be doing what I said at first. They will be plowing under every fourth American boy."

Hoke himself was still working from the outside in, so proving his hunch that there had to be some central figure, or figures, coordinating the campaign was going to be a challenge. "The insertions in the *Congressional Record* did not happen by accident," Hoke posited. "The facts showed there must be a plan to get the material inserted into the *Record* and there must be a guiding control office which arranged for the reprints . . . and for the distribution in various sized lots to the scattered propaganda bases which handled final distribution, addressing and mailing. The job was . . . to find one master headquarters."

Hoke understood he was never going to have the resources or

the investigative tools to get to the bottom of the story by himself, to find out who exactly inside Congress was coordinating this Nazi op, but he never wavered in his conviction that this was all worth the effort. His feeling was never stronger than at the end of the summer of 1941, when a federal government official told Hoke about a strange happening at a recent cocktail party in Washington. One of the guests, an aide in a congressional office, was in his cups that evening and blurted out that there was a hell of a lot more to the franking scandal than anyone really knew. "If I ever told my story," the congressional aide had confided, "it would blow the Dome off the Capitol."

CHAPTER SEVENTEEN

"I'M NOT SUPPOSED TO BE DOING THIS KIND OF WORK"

D illard Stokes had good sources close to the U.S. Department of Justice's newly formed "propaganda squad" investigation. On one unseasonably cool end-of-summer morning in September 1941, the thirty-three-year-old *Washington Post* reporter was pursuing a very hot tip he'd received from one of those sources about an address worth watching in a nondescript residential neighborhood near downtown Washington, D.C. When his taxicab arrived in front of the modest apartment building at 1430 Rhode Island Avenue, NW, a little after 9:00 A.M., Stokes was worried he was already late to the proceedings. The anxious newsman directed the driver to nose in catty-corner to the building and keep the meter running. Stokes stayed in the backseat and watched, undetected, as two obviously unhappy young men finished hauling a bunch of unwieldy and overstuffed canvas bags down the steps of the apartment building and into an official government mail truck.

When they finally finished the loading and one of the young men edged the truck out into traffic, Stokes thought the driver might be headed to the federal courthouse. A recently impaneled grand jury, under the guidance of Special Prosecutor William Power Maloney, was weighing evidence suggesting that German agents were working in concert with members of Congress to paper America with carefully scripted Nazi propaganda, funded and directed by the Hitler government in Berlin. Since grand jury subpoenas often came with requests for documents, maybe these heavy bags full of paper that were being hauled out of the apartment in question were going to be part of the grand jury presentation. In fact, the jurors were expecting to hear testimony that morning from a resident of that very address: 1430 Rhode Island.

The main aim of the Germans' massive U.S. propaganda effort was to keep American public opinion firmly positioned against our armed forces joining the Allies in the war in Europe, which—the Nazis knew—was the most important thing that could be done anywhere in the world to clear the way for Hitler's conquest of all of Europe, and perhaps beyond. Germany trying to run this kind of massive information operation on American soil, targeting the American public, was one level of threat; elected members of the U.S. Congress helping them do it—that was something else. And that was the plot that William Power Maloney's newly created DOJ propaganda squad was onto, thanks in no small part to the work Henry Hoke had started more than a year earlier. Hoke's exposés—and Drew Pearson's columns, and reporting by newspapers like the left-wing tabloid *PM* in New York—had alerted the public, and upped the pressure on DOJ to get to the bottom of it.

Maloney had been handpicked for this propaganda investigation by the attorney general of the United States, and for good reason. Just thirty-seven years old at the time of his appointment, the exuberant, bantamweight government attorney had already won a reputation as a fearless prosecutor (the "Little Napoleon of the courtroom," one defendant called him). He had spent six years as the assistant U.S. Attorney for the Southern District of New York, where he prosecuted rich and powerful businessmen, made himself an expert in mail fraud and stockjobbing, and ran up an eye-popping 400–0 trial record. The Fordham Law School graduate seemed to live for the hard challenge; he preferred a swim in the rough ocean surf of Long Island to the placid chlorinated water of the lap pool. The choppier things got, the more he liked it. He was known around DOJ as bright, pugnacious, and fond of the spotlight, pushing high-profile, high-risk cases. "Hustling young William Power Maloney," *Time* magazine noted back in 1935, "obtained a $4,500,000 mail fraud indictment against three young

Yalemen, 49 other individuals and 20 corporations—biggest mail fraud indictment in U.S. history." This new investigation he was heading, Maloney figured, could be even bigger. Dillard Stokes, already hot on the trail of that same story, agreed with the prosecutor's assessment.

WHEN THE TRUCK took off from 1430 Rhode Island Avenue that Friday morning, Stokes bade his taxi driver to follow. And at first, as Stokes suspected it would, the truck appeared to be hurrying toward the courthouse at Judiciary Square, where Maloney and his propaganda squad awaited. But the truck blew past the court facility and continued southeast, before turning in to an alley behind some low-key Capitol Hill offices. There, the driver stopped just long enough to drop off what looked like about a dozen of the stuffed mailbags he had removed from the apartment. He then hopped back into the truck and headed to the other side of Capitol Hill, where he got help hauling the remaining bags inside a building that housed official government offices for members of Congress.

That morning, Dillard Stokes was unable to determine the ultimate destination of those big canvas bags that had been removed from the apartment of the man who had just been subpoenaed to testify to the propaganda squad's grand jury. And he didn't know what was in the bags, either, other than that it was clearly printed material. But he knew that material didn't get delivered to the courthouse, and he had a sense he might have finally found a lever to crack open this story that he very eagerly wanted to tell.

By that Friday morning, September 19, 1941, Dillard Stokes had been on the trail of Nazi propagandists on Capitol Hill for nearly as long as Henry Hoke. His managing editor at *The Washington Post* had got the scent in his nose first; something about all this pro-German, isolationist propaganda flooding the country just smelled wrong. So, the graying leader of the *Post* newsroom put Dillard Stokes on the story. Stokes was one of the newspaper's best legmen and a licensed attorney to boot. He knew his way around the law. "Take your time, be sure of your facts," *Post* editor Casey Jones told Stokes.

Once he had witnessed the curious route of those official congressional mailbags, it didn't take long for Dillard Stokes—or the prosecutors—to start to unravel the mystery. Within the span of a week, the grand jury was hearing testimony from the superintendent at the House Post Office, which had dispatched its mail truck to and from the apartment on Rhode Island Avenue. They heard from the truck driver, too. The panel also heard from Isabel French, a secretary who worked at the D.C. headquarters of the America First Committee, which was the first location where the truck dropped off some of the mailbags from the Rhode Island Avenue apartment.

The day after Mrs. French's less than candid grand jury appearance, propaganda squad investigators dragged ten mailbags out of the America First office for further inspection. They found them filled with unaddressed envelopes, adorned with the franks of a host of members of Congress, and stuffed with copies of German-friendly treatises, each of them ready to be addressed for (free) shipment. Mrs. French told the jurors she had no earthly idea why anybody would want to send those bags full of free-postage envelopes to her office. The chair of the America First Committee's Washington chapter promptly issued a statement exclaiming that this was exactly the sort of persecution she had come to expect from the warmongering Roosevelt administration. "The smear of the America First Committee undertaken by the Department of Justice will fade into nothing but a cheap trick on the part of the department itself," Mrs. Bennett Champ Clark, wife of a sitting U.S. senator, told the press. "The committee has always been on the 'up and up' and always will be."

Dillard Stokes, meanwhile, was naming names in the *Post*. The headliner was the powerful Republican congressman Hamilton Fish of New York, who counted among his least favorite constituents President Franklin Delano Roosevelt of Hyde Park. The German Foreign Office had been assiduously cultivating Fish over the years, counting him friendly to the Reich in spite of his occasionally professed unease with its Jewish policies. There was hard evidence that the truck from the House Post Office had been sent to the Rhode Island Avenue apartment on orders from Fish's congressional office, which Stokes reported in the *Post*.

Congressman Fish was in no position to make a flat denial, but he did have an explanation at the ready: the whole mailbag escapade was the doing of the fellow living and working at 1430 Rhode Island Avenue, one Prescott Dennett. (Dennett was the press agent for the Islands for War Debts Committee who had so mournfully lamented the committee founder, Ernest Lundeen. He had also started a small "Fish for President" boomlet in 1940, at Fish's request, and for a small fee.) Dennett—whom Fish claimed not to have laid eyes on for a year or more—had casually called up an aide in Fish's office and asked if he wanted five hundred reprints of Hamilton Fish's recent antiwar speech, at least according to the congressman. Fish's aide said, Why sure, there was a great and growing demand for that particular speech, and promptly sent a House of Representatives mail truck to Dennett's apartment. When questioned directly by Stokes, Fish had insisted he was not personally involved in, or even aware of, the transaction; said he didn't know a thing about any mailbags taken to his office.

Too bad for Fish, Dillard Stokes found out two days after that interview with the congressman that some of the unaccounted-for mailbags were now residing on an upper floor of the New House Office Building, where Fish's office had an official storage space. Stokes dutifully called the Fish office for comment on this odd happenstance. "They are not ours," Fish's first secretary, Walter Reynolds, told Stokes. "We don't care what happens to them. Mr. Fish said the Department of Justice can have them if it wants them. You can come and get them yourself if you want to." Reynolds even offered to have somebody escort Stokes to the location of the bags.

When Stokes showed up at Fish's office fifteen minutes later, Reynolds was nowhere to be found. But Dillard Stokes didn't need a guide. He'd been aggressively reporting the story for long enough, and he had a pretty good idea where to look. Stokes raced up to the sixth floor, to storeroom 30, and—sure enough—found eight full-sized mailbags, sitting just outside Representative Fish's designated area. At first glance, this appeared a mighty large number of mighty large bags for just five hundred reprints of a single speech. Either that was a monstrously long speech, or something else was going on. Stokes settled in to examine the contents of the bags, but not before he called in a photographer from the *Post*.

"Eight mailbags crammed with anti-Roosevelt speeches by many members of Congress, in franked envelops [*sic*], which ten days ago were spirited away from grand jurors investigating German agents 'turned up' yesterday," Stokes wrote in his splashy story in the *Post,* which included a photograph of Stokes in the storeroom examining the contents of the open bags. On the front page. Above the fold. After the jump, there were reproductions of the printed speeches and franked envelopes signed in the names of at least a dozen members of Congress. Among the franking signatures was Ernest Lundeen, who had been unable to sign anything for the past year, on account of being dead.

William Power Maloney and his team of prosecutors, according to Dillard Stokes, were going to be "anxious to unravel" the meaning of all this. Happily, Stokes himself had already handed them another important clue. "One of the bags," he had written, "had a tag with this address on it: Cong. Fish. Attention Mr. Hill."

Hamilton Fish, beetle-browed, lantern-jawed, entitled by a storied family history in politics, and pugnacious to a fault, went to the floor of the House to defend his wounded honor. He attacked the *Post* and called its recent reporting "contemptible, dastardly, and lying."

Stokes answered the next day with a deliciously detailed account of how the mailbag plot unfolded: Prescott Dennett—residing with his mother at 1430 Rhode Island Avenue—had been served with the grand jury subpoena on the night of September 18, directing him to turn up to the grand jury room to testify the very next day. Dennett had immediately called George Hill, secretary to Congressman Hamilton Fish. Hill went to the House Post Office, demanding a truck be sent to Dennett's home to "pick up some things." The foreman assigned the driver Charlie Wilson to the task; he piloted the mail truck over to Prescott Dennett's apartment, and with the help of Dennett himself he trundled twenty or so mailbags into the truck. This required multiple trips up and down the interior stairs of the building. When a neighbor complained about the noise, young Charlie was clearly rankled but also somewhat apologetic. "I'm not supposed to be doing this kind of work, anyway," he said.

THAT SAME WEEKEND that Dillard Stokes was exposing the involvement of members of Congress in the Nazi propaganda operation, Senator Burton Wheeler arrived in Los Angeles for a week of anti-Roosevelt, isolationist rallies, replete with broadsides against what the senator and his supporters were calling the warmongering, anti-German U.S. movie industry. Wheeler was promising an investigation aimed at bringing to heel the Hollywood studios (a lot of them run by Jews, you know). "Some claim," Wheeler said, "the silver screen will become known in the future as the modern Benedict Arnold."

Wheeler's activities were well covered that week, thanks to Leon Lewis and his undercover team of antifascist spies. Lewis and his double agents had been hunting and cataloging Nazi-friendly and fascist Angelenos for eight years by then. They had been feeding reports to Congress, military intelligence, and the FBI for nearly that long. They had also started publishing their own weekly broadsheet, *News Letter,* which made Wheeler's visit to Southern California the anchor for its next issue.

The Montana senator was met at his train in Los Angeles by a crowd of cheering fans "liberally sprinkled with well-known Nazi agitators," the *News Letter* reported on its front page. Its reporters followed Wheeler closely all week. One of the ushers at the senator's biggest event that week, it was noted, was "the swastika-braceleted" woman who doubled as a waitress at downtown L.A.'s Deutsches Haus. Lewis's *News Letter* identified dozens of German agents and leading antisemites in attendance at Wheeler's speeches and symposia. "Among the Senator's Heilers were Hermann Schwinn, West Coast leader of the German-American Bund until his citizenship was revoked; Hans Diebel, proprietor of the Aryan Book Store, whose application for U.S. citizenship was denied by Federal Court . . . Charles Cobb, chairman of the Pasadena chapter of America First, whose rantings against the Washington Administration were such that the school board withdrew the use of the hall until Cobb promised to 'tone down.' "

Leaflets from the Los Angeles headquarters of the National Peace Crusade papered some of the events: "AWAKE, CHRISTIAN AMERICA AND CLAIM YOUR BIRTHRIGHT . . . Let's Be Frantically American. LET'S SAVE U.S. FOR US." Attendees received instructions about boycotting a local dentist and other businesses who advertised in the *Los Angeles Daily News,* a newspaper that had voiced support for Roosevelt's tough stance on Hitler. A leaflet defending Charles Lindbergh against a "peevish power-mad Roosevelt" offered reprints of the famous flier's recent Des Moines speech (about "the Jewish") at ten cents a dozen.

BY THE FIRST day of October 1941, Prescott Dennett, resident at 1430 Rhode Island Avenue, had been on the witness stand in front of the grand jury for seven days, mostly filibustering. But Congressman Hamilton Fish was clearly getting anxious. He made a twenty-two-minute speech on the floor of the House in which he accused the *Post* reporter Dillard Stokes of illegally obtaining the contents—and publishing photographs of same—from the mailbags left outside storeroom 30. He wanted Congress to call Stokes "before the bar of the House and try him for violation of the law." Moreover, Fish charged, somebody was likely giving information to Stokes. "There is some leak on the part of some of the witnesses, or on the part of the grand jurors, or the officials," Fish said in his floor speech, "and it may be necessary for the House to call this reporter before it and ask him how he got this information from the grand jury."

Things started moving apace after that, and not in Fish's favor. Prosecutor William Power Maloney summoned to the witness box, for the first time, a known German agent: George Sylvester Viereck. Viereck first appeared on the grand jury witness stand on October 3, exactly two weeks after the day Stokes had seen the mail truck at Dennett's home. Five days later Viereck was charged with falsifying statements he had filed with the U.S. State Department about his role as an agent for the German government.

The indictment charged Viereck with "aiding, abetting and assisting Prescott Dennett and divers other persons in organizing and setting up a certain committee known as the Make Europe Pay War Debts Committee." This was the group first chaired by Ernest Lundeen, which had morphed into the Islands for War Debts Committee by the time of his death. In the indictment, prosecutors spelled out that Viereck was acting as an agent of Hitler's government when he paid Prescott Dennett to help set up and run the War Debts Committee chaired by Senator Lundeen. No wonder Senator Lundeen's widow had been so eager to collect her husband's correspondence with Viereck before anyone else could get their hands on it.

Viereck was arrested at his home on Riverside Drive in New York. Federal agents reported that the apartment was "adorned with pictures of Hitler and Goebbles [sic], its bookshelves packed with the books and articles [Viereck] has written to depict Kaiser Wilhelm as a wronged statesman and Hitler as a champion of peace." Dillard Stokes was on hand to report on Viereck's arraignment in Washington. "Small, slender, and graying with the quiet dress, heavy spectacles and diffident manner of a 'typical' college professor," Stokes wrote, "the 57-year-old Viereck has been the acknowledged leader of pro-German thought in this country all his adult life."

Prosecutors called Viereck "one of the most serious menaces in this country." The defendant insisted he was tragically misunderstood. "If I had worked for war as I have for peace I would not now stand indicted," Viereck dashed off in a statement for reporters. "My real crime, whatever the accusation against may be, is twofold: I am American of German blood and I oppose this desperate and despicable attempt to catapult our country into Europe's war." The indictment, he said, "is only an incident in the perfidious plot to smother and smear all opposition to the arbitrary forces cunningly at work to destroy the America we know and love." He made bond and went home to prepare his defense.

The day after Viereck's arraignment, congressional staffer George Hill was called before the grand jury to give evidence. He fared no better than Viereck. Hill was a slim, lipless, not particularly attractive figure who was nevertheless known as a man-about-town, with multiple girlfriends and a reputation as someone who always had money to spend. A small part of Hill's problem before the grand jury was his reluctance to produce the eight mailbags that had been stashed at storeroom 30. He said he could not do so without the blessing of his boss, Congressman Fish—a position the judge found understandable. A bigger problem was Hill's refusal to identify the source of the $12,000 that had fallen into his bank accounts in the previous five months. (A pretty good take for a man whose federal salary was around $2,000 per year.) But Hill's biggest problem was falsely swearing under oath that he had nothing to do with the mailbags, that he had not met with George Sylvester Viereck in any congressional office, and that in fact he was not acquainted with Viereck at all, except by reputation.

LATE ONE NIGHT in the third week of October 1941, Dillard Stokes was out on the streets of D.C., keeping a vigil on the America First Committee's headquarters. The reporter really did have good sources, because somebody had put him in place that night to witness an America First employee burning a pile of mail in a trash can in the alley behind the committee offices. Stokes waited until the coast was clear and then rushed over to pull what he could from the can. "The ashes still warm and slightly smoking," he reported. The charred fragments Stokes examined included more franked envelopes from the isolationist wing of Congress. Now that Prescott Dennett had been hauled before the grand jury, and the Viereck indictment was laying out the connection between Dennett and a Nazi agent, here was the America First Committee burning the evidence that had been piled up in Dennett's apartment and then trucked to them once Dennett was subpoenaed. Stokes, aware that he was both reporting on a story and witnessing part of a crime spree that was actively under federal investigation, decided to deliver the warm and smoky remainder of that evidence to the propaganda squad at DOJ, even as he rushed to file with his editor. "Early today," Stokes wrote in his story that ran that very day, "the crumpled but faintly legible ashes were being studied by Special Prosecutors William Power Maloney and Edward J. Hickey."

This turned out to be an especially busy Friday for Maloney and Hickey. That afternoon, they indicted George Hill for his role in the cover-up of the franking operation—for coordinating the effort to hide evidence that was being sought by the grand jury investigating the German government's secret propaganda operation inside Congress. According to the prosecutors, Hill was the person inside Congress Henry Hoke had been looking for—"the keyman of a propaganda machine master-minded by German agents."

Hill pleaded not guilty, and his lawyer, a former congressman, stood up to defend both Hill and Hill's boss. Hill "is an unimportant person in the picture," said the defense attorney, John O'Connor. "This is aiming at the lion and shooting the rabbit, and if I may say, I am here to plead Congressman Fish 'not guilty.' "

"I am not aware that Congressman Fish has been indicted," Prosecutor Maloney countered. "Mr. O'Connor's protestations remind me of Shakespeare in that he 'protesteth too much.' "

When Fish himself was finally summoned to appear before the grand jury a few weeks later, the congressman went on the floor of the House and more or less begged the body to formally instruct him not to comply. He was very anxious to protect them all from *any* grand jury invading "the rights and privileges of the House of Representatives."

By the time the House got around to explaining that Congressman Fish did indeed have the discretion to appear before the grand jury if he so desired, Fish had left town for reserve army training.

He was defiant in his too-tight colonel's uniform when he boarded the train for North Carolina. Fish harrumphed to a reporter on hand that he *did* know the identity of the benefactor who bestowed the $12,000 worth of mysterious payments on his aide George Hill. But he was not at liberty to divulge the source to the reporter or anyone else. "They can't subpoena me while I'm in the army," he said on his way out of town.

CHAPTER EIGHTEEN

TO TELL THE TRUTH

It was unlike Congressman Hamilton Fish to absent himself from the center of the action. An imposing man who had well earned a place in the future College Football Hall of Fame, a bona fide war hero in World War I, where he was one of the white officers who served with the storied African American regiment known as the "Harlem Hellfighters," Ham even had that unforgettable family

Representative Hamilton Fish heads to army reserve training in 1942.

name that marked him as the scion of American political royalty. In a line directly descendant from at least one signer of the Declaration of Independence, previous Ham Fishes had been congressmen, senators, governors, and a U.S. secretary of state. Our Ham had gone to a Swiss boarding school, spoke French, held two law degrees plus his Harvard B.A. (cum laude), and, at a bulky six feet, four inches tall, towered over his contemporaries. His ingrained confidence was unwavering. In 1939, it had borne him on a solo diplomatic errand of his own invention, right to the center of world crisis.

Headlines were full of war talk in Europe that summer: "Hitler Lays Plans to Cut Up Poland"; "Heavy Troop Movements Reported on Border of Silesia"; "Democracies Gird Their Loins." Fish told reporters he was heading to Germany on a personal mission to keep the peace. The Nazi foreign minister hosted Fish at his mountain retreat for a one-on-one conference. "We talked over the general situation and how we could establish better relations with the United States," Joachim von Ribbentrop would say later. "[Fish] was counted on our side as one of the people who would be likely to collaborate with us."

At the meeting with Ribbentrop, Fish decided not to push too hard on the "refugee question," as he put it, which was really the eliminationist persecution of the Jews question. "The European situation is so tense that this might irritate Germany," Fish explained to reporters. Fish also told the press he was hopeful that tensions over Germany's designs on Poland could be resolved peacefully, and that Germany's claims were "just." The American then accepted a ride in Ribbentrop's private plane to a convention of European officials in Oslo where he appeared to be carrying water for the German Foreign Office—basically urging the delegates to accommodate Hitler and not fight him.

At the exact same time—just a few weeks before Hitler started World War II by invading Poland—George Sylvester Viereck was in Germany, too. On his own personal mission to solidify his position with the Nazi Foreign Office as its indispensable man in the United States, Viereck had more success on his German trip than Fish did. He departed Berlin with a couple of fat contracts in hand.

One was with the state-run *Münchner Neueste Nachrichten* newspaper, where he would serve as correspondent reporting on the latest developments in America. The other was with the German Library of Information, another Nazi government front, for which Viereck would produce *Facts in Review,* the digest of world news with a Nazi point of view that would be distributed to influential voices in America who could keep up the pressure to keep the United States out of the war. The contracts were each worth $500 a month to Viereck (about $10,000 in today's dollars), plus a generous stipend for expenses. The big bonus, though, was that the contracts gave Viereck cover. He was able to work directly for, and in the pay of, the Nazi government while registering at the U.S. State Department as an "author and journalist" in the paid employ of these two "privately-owned" German press services.

Viereck's real job, of course, was as a Nazi agent blanketing America with a message sharpened largely by Joseph "Propaganda will help us conquer the world" Goebbels but conceived by Hitler himself. The great masses, he wrote in *Mein Kampf,* "will more easily fall victims to a great lie than to a small one, since they themselves perhaps also lie sometimes in little things, but would certainly still be too much ashamed of too great lies. Thus, such an untruth will not at all enter their heads, and therefore they will be unable to believe in the possibility of the enormous impudence of the most infamous distortion in others."

Hitler's lies spread misinformation that was favorable to Germany and unfavorable to us and our allies, and sowed dissension among the American public not just about the war effort but about our own basic system of government. His very well-funded propaganda mission in the United States was twofold: to try to keep the United States from getting into World War II, and also to soften us up, to mess with us, to make us less effective as a country, by finding and exploiting what the Germans called "kernels of disturbance" in the United States.

The German propaganda operation in America, according to the first U.S. academic study on the topic, identified these kernels of disturbance as "racial controversies, economic inequalities, petty jealousies in public life," and "differences of opinion which divide political parties and minority groups." Even the "frustrated ambitions of discarded politicians." Germany's agents were tasked with finding these fissures in American society and then prying them further apart, exploiting them to make Americans hate and suspect each other, and maybe even wish for a new kind of country altogether. A partisan, bickering, demoralized America, the Nazis believed, would be incapable of mounting a successful war effort in Europe. It might even soften us up for an eventual takeover.

Hitler was counting above all on racism and religious bigotry to carry the day in the United States, and to set the stage for global domination. "The wholesome aversion for the Negroes and the colored races in general, including the Jews, the existence of popular justice [lynching] . . . scholars who have studied immigration and gained an insight, by means of intelligence tests, into the inequality of the races—all these strains are an assurance that the sound elements of the United States will one day awaken as they have awakened in Germany," Hitler said.

His not-so-secret weapon of choice was plain antisemitism. It was the indispensable first step to global, genocidal, total race war. "My Jews are a valuable hostage given to me by the democracies. Antisemitic propaganda in all countries is an almost indispensable medium for the extension of our political campaign. You will see how little time we shall need in order to upset the ideas and the criteria of the whole world simply and purely by attacking Judaism. . . . And, once the principle of race has been established by the exposure of the particular case of the Jews, the rest is easy. It logically follows step-by-step that the existing political and economic order has to be ended and attention paid to the new ideas of biological politics. . . . We cannot set limits here or there as we please. We shall succeed in making the new political and social order the universal basis of life in the world."

EVIDENCE OF HITLER'S propaganda operation in America started to spill into public view as early as 1940 because of intrepid diggers like Henry Hoke and Drew Pearson and Dillard Stokes. But the story was told in full, point by point, at George Sylvester Viereck's criminal trial. Viereck had wasted no time upon his return from Berlin in 1939. His first important stop once back in Washington was at the office of an old friend, Senator Ernest Lundeen. Viereck and Lundeen had a relationship that went back two decades, back to when Viereck was working on behalf of the kaiser to keep America out of World War I and Lundeen was contributing to his German-funded *Fatherland* magazine. Twenty years later, Lundeen was still decidedly antiwar, decidedly pro-German, and, just as important, decidedly greedy. This was a man who was demanding huge cash kickbacks from his entire Senate staff, after all.

Viereck basically offered Lundeen a deal too sweet to refuse. The senator could keep doing what he was doing already—working hard to keep America out of the war in Europe—but Viereck would arrange for him to make some serious cash while doing so. Taking his propaganda directives from the German Foreign Office, Viereck would write speeches and articles for Lundeen. Under the senator's name, he would arrange for them to be printed in major American magazines and newspapers. And then Viereck and Lundeen would get paid for it. Viereck was already rich thanks to his multiple German government contracts and front operations, but for the Minnesota senator this was more than just pocket money; it was a whole new serious stream of income.

The two men did it in broad daylight, from inside Lundeen's Senate office. The Nazi agent, as the senator's ghostwriter, penned warnings that Americans should not believe "atrocity tales" about the Nazis, and that Germany posed no threat to the democracies of England and France. He wrote that America was being "laughed at for our trouble" even as "mysterious influences [were] at work" to maneuver us into paying for Europe's war. One of Viereck's pieces ran in the *New York Journal and American* newspaper over a stoic three-quarter-profile photo of Senator Lundeen and the senator's byline: "Democracy and U.S. Can Be Saved, Asserts Lundeen. But Survival Depends on Minding Our Own Business, Says Senator." Viereck even wrote a "personal" reflection by the senator about his son, Ernest Lundeen Jr., attending a military academy. That one, Viereck explained, was to give the senator cover as an all-American "patriot" while he assailed Roosevelt's measures to shore up the U.S. military in the event of war. Lundeen was paid—and paid well—for all of it. And once the money was coming in, Viereck made sure to keep him on the hook, telling the senator that he shouldn't even consider trying to write his own articles, but instead should let Viereck do all of it for him: "I think in the long run you will find collaboration with me . . . more profitable both politically and financially than anything that you yourself can do, loaded down as you are with work. I am, after all, right here on the spot. I know the editors and I have some journalistic skill in preparing material in a manner suitable to their needs."

In 1939, after his return from Berlin, Viereck brought a whole new energy to the collaboration; his propaganda directives were now coming straight from the German Foreign Office. Lundeen's top Senate staffer, Edward Corneaby, personally witnessed the supercharged Viereck-Lundeen operation in action: He heard and saw Viereck use one of Lundeen's Senate office phones to call up the German embassy and ask somebody there to send over material ASAP. When the messenger soon arrived from the embassy, Corneaby saw that he bore with him a fully written speech attacking the late British ambassador to the United States. Senator Lundeen then delivered that speech in the Senate and made sure it was entered in full into the *Congressional Record*.

The staff member who was charged with typing Lundeen's speeches, Phyllis Posivio, also had a good vantage point on the Viereck-Lundeen scheme. From her desk right across the hall from Lundeen's personal office, she saw Viereck constantly coming in and out, sweet-talking her and bringing her candy, and going over the texts of the speeches. Viereck clearly was the writer and Lundeen just the mouthpiece. "I've tried to phrase this as best I could in the manner in which you speak," Posivio overheard Viereck say to Lundeen.

The reason Lundeen made sure to enter those speeches—even the article about his son at the military academy—into the *Con-*

gressional Record was so the material could be printed in bulk by the U.S. government, at a discount, and then mailed out for free, under Lundeen's frank, to as many of his constituents as possible.

Your tax dollars at work, busy eroding American strength and resolve.

Viereck dreamed up a way to further boost distribution through the congressional franking privilege. Why limit this to Lundeen's Minnesota constitutents? To get his Nazi-approved material spread farther and wider, he knew he would need a justification for using Congress's free postage to send out Lundeen's mailings nationwide. The law forbade a member of Congress to let any outside committee, organization, or association use the franking privilege, but that law had a nice little Sylvester-sized loophole exception: "This provision shall not apply to any committee composed of members of Congress." In other words, if Viereck created a national "committee" of some kind for Senator Lundeen, well, that would be fine. They could use the committee instead of Lundeen's Senate office to send their propaganda anywhere.

So Viereck set up the Make Europe Pay War Debts Committee (it would later be known as the Islands for War Debts Committee) with Lundeen as chairman and Senator Robert Rice Reynolds (the original champion of Build a Wall to keep out refugees) as vice-chairman. Prescott Dennett went on the Viereck payroll, which was really the Hitler government payroll, to run War Debts Committee publicity out of his home office on Rhode Island Avenue. They fitted out the office with three telephones, a separate system for summoning messengers, and plenty of open floor space for mailbags. Dennett lived in the apartment with his widowed mother, who was happy to stuff and address envelopes for her boy. As the committee became a high-volume hub for pro-German isolationist propaganda, Mother Dennett even enjoyed fielding the occasional inquiry from a U.S. congressman about how she liked a speech.

A typical item mailed out in the operation was a Viereck-written speech, "Six Men and War," which charged President Roosevelt and five other administration officials with nefariously and deliberately driving America into a European war for their own self-serving purposes. The speech echoed falsified reports the Nazi government was releasing to the international press in the spring of 1940. Lundeen delivered the speech on the Senate floor, entering it into the *Congressional Record*. Then Viereck used laundered German funds to pay for the U.S. government to print 125,000 copies at a discounted rate. Then the War Debts Committee and other like organizations mailed them all over America, postage free, under Lundeen's frank. The outer envelope included a slogan that grew from the long Hitler-Viereck collaboration: "Europe for Europeans; Asia for the Asiatics; America for Americans."

The "Six Men and War" propaganda operation set off a significant stir here at home. The War Debts Committee honorary chair, Senator Reynolds, called for an immediate investigation into Lundeen's bombshell claims about Roosevelt's secret treachery; after all, they sounded a lot like disturbing reports that were starting to appear in the press around the world. Representative Fish suggested a presidential impeachment.

It was working great, and bonus, it was cheap. The Germans were delighted.

"I think I can report that this propaganda campaign has been carried through with the success we envisaged," wrote Hans Thomsen, chargé d'affaires at the German embassy in Washington, in a top-secret telegram to Berlin. "These speeches, whose aim is to prevent America's entry into the war and to ward off all attacks by interventionist politicians, will be printed each time in the official American parliamentary publication, the Congressional Record, by these Senators and Congressmen, and then an edition of 50,000 to 1 million copies will be sent by them to specially chosen persons. In this manner, German influence is not visible to the outside, and, thanks to the privilege of free postage enjoyed by American Congressmen, the cost of this large-scale propaganda can be kept disproportionately low, since, at the very least, mail expenses amounting to many tens of thousands of dollars would be saved."

Viereck got big eyes once his tiny hive in Mrs. Dennett's apartment on Rhode Island Avenue started buzzing in the spring of

1940; he was ready to scale this operation. Viereck started negotiating to buy a publishing house, the decidedly Anglo-sounding Flanders Hall, so he could pay elected officials in America to write books and pamphlets, or simply put their names on the books and pamphlets written by himself or Goebbels's staff in Germany. He also started putting out feelers to other outspoken isolationists, like North Dakota senator Gerald P. Nye, who by then was making hay attacking Hollywood for "drug[ging] the American people . . . fill[ing] them with fear that Hitler will come over here and capture them." No fan of *Confessions of a Nazi Spy*, that Gerald P. Nye, even without having seen the movie. Viereck approached Senator Nye's top Senate staffer to inquire about buying some reprints of Nye's latest screed to send out in a mass mailing. When he asked the aide, Gerald Movius, for six or seven million reprints, Movius thought he must have heard wrong. "My God, Mr. Viereck, do you realize how much that would cost you?" Movius did the math and said $75,000 (about $1.5 million in today's dollars), even with the steep congressional discount for government printing. "I think perhaps it could be arranged," Viereck told the secretary.

Movius and his senator boss demurred, but Viereck had Lundeen and plenty of other isolationists in both the House and the Senate who were happy to help. In the House, the most important was the reliable congressman Hamilton Fish. Fish and Viereck had been friends and collaborators for years. Fish had reportedly quashed a subpoena the Dies Committee issued to Viereck back in 1938. Two years later, Fish and his office still stood ready to assist Viereck as needed. "Representative Fish," Viereck wrote to Lundeen in July 1940, "told me that the man in his office is absolutely reliable, and that he knows all the tricks of getting work of the type you contemplate done speedily and economically." That same month, Fish introduced the German agent to his trusted longtime staffer, George Hill, telling him, "Mr. Viereck has some speeches to send out—of Senator Lundeen's." The congressman told Hill to send the speeches out to the national mailing list already compiled in their office for Fish's own committee, the National Committee to Keep America Out of Foreign Wars.

When Fish left Hill and Viereck alone to make a plan, Viereck asked how big this mailing list was. Hill said it was about 100,000 names. Viereck, skeptical, asked to see it. Hill handed over not only that list but also another with about 30,000 additional names. Thrilled, Viereck told Hill to call up Lundeen's office to get the ball rolling. There was a lot of material they were going to need to print and mail out.

On his way out of the office, Viereck handed Hill two rolled-up bills. Two *fifty-dollar* bills. Which represented more than two weeks' pay for Hill. And so, George Hill got right to work. In fact, when Trip 19 crashed in the Virginia foothills less than two months later, George Hill had become so efficient at running Viereck's propaganda operation out of Hamilton Fish's congressional office that they barely skipped a beat when they lost Senator Lundeen.

According to a postwar records scrub in Germany by the U.S. Department of Justice, Viereck and his Nazi friends (with help from George Hill) built up mailing lists "containing the names of 650,000 teachers, 157,000 clergymen, 162,000 physicians, 144,000 lawyers, 73,000 dentists, 46,187 of the larger investors, 21,345 newspapers, 15,000 municipal officials, 11,687 millionaires, 11,000 libraries, 7,419 members of state legislatures, 7,000 accountants, 5,500 judges, 4,612 college fraternities and sororities; and . . . more than forty other lists ranging from breweries to chain butchers." That's on top of the 130,000 names Fish's office started them off with, plus another 30,000 names they gleaned from *Who's Who*. All were targets for Viereck's well-oiled Nazi propaganda operation.

It soon emerged in the press that there was more to the German scheme, including a big lift from the biggest name in American industry. A secretary working out of the Ford Motor Company in New York gathered what she called "a mammoth mailing list" from the return addresses on fan mail sent to Charles Lindbergh, Representative Hamilton Fish, Senator Rush Holt, Senator Burton Wheeler, and other famed America Firsters. This list was compiled in Ford Motor Company offices by Ford employees working on company time and shipped to a Nazi-funded publication called

Scribner's Commentator, whose editors were pleased to send out whatever material the German Foreign Office and its agents in America sent them. *Scribner's* was also happy to augment this list, which ended up at more than 300,000 names and addresses. The German Foreign Office clearly appreciated the effort: a Nazi agent handed over to those editors $39,000 in cash—almost all of it in $20 bills—in four separate hand-to-hand transfers.

By then, too, Viereck's Nazi-funded Flanders Hall was publishing anti-interventionist, anti-British books by the hundreds of thousands. The German Foreign Office was advancing him $10,000 per title to cover printing, marketing, and payments to the scribes. Among Flanders Hall's stable of well-paid authors: Senator Rush Holt of West Virginia and Representative Stephen Day of Illinois. Senator Nye of North Dakota also reportedly entertained his own Flanders Hall publishing offer for a book to be called *Aggression,* though it never came to pass.

The War Debts Committee mailing operation out of Dennett's home office, meanwhile, was amping up its rhythm all through the back half of 1940 and first half of 1941. George Hill was like a blur in and out of the Government Printing Office with discounted *Congressional Record* reprint requests from Viereck. And, boy, was he happy to keep up the pace. What German government money didn't land in the government printing account ended up accruing to Hill's personal benefit. While more than $12,000 (about $250,000 in today's funds) passed through Hill's bank accounts over just a few months in 1940 and 1941, we know Hill sent a minimum of 620,000 separate reprints in franked envelopes to Dennett's War Debts Committee office. Likely it was many more. This was mail by the *ton.*

AND SO IT was that Congressman Hamilton Fish was making sure to steer well clear of the jury box in early 1942, when his staffer George Hill finally went on trial in the first week of January. The congressman voiced support for Hill, whom he had known for a quarter century, since the two had served together in World War I.

"George Hill is 100 percent OK," Fish told reporters, "and I'll back George Hill to the limit on anything." Representative Fish made this statement from the safe confines of his office, though; he was not going anywhere near that courthouse, no matter how many times his name came up in Hill's trial and no matter what means the prosecution came up with to try to get him in to testify.

America was a different country by then. The temper of the nation had changed in a flash on December 7, 1941, when Japan attacked Pearl Harbor. Four days later, in solidarity with his Asian ally, Adolf Hitler declared war on the United States.

There was little patience for German-friendly agitation in the country after that. Homegrown purveyors of pro-Axis propaganda who missed that point put themselves in peril. Like Ellis O. Jones and Robert Noble, who, four days after Pearl Harbor, impeached a wax dummy of President Roosevelt at a rally of about two hundred Americans at an auditorium in Los Angeles. "The Japanese have a right to Hawaii," Jones exclaimed. "I would rather be in this war on the side of Germany than on the side of the British." Noble claimed, "Our country has not been attacked. . . . Japan has done a good job in the Pacific." The two were arrested the next day and charged with making "false statements intended to interfere with operations of the United States military and naval forces." Those charges didn't stick, but that arrest marked a change in the weather for men like Jones and Noble.

Any Nazi sympathizers, fascists, and antisemites who were capable of "reading the room" started to do so around that time. Lawrence Dennis, for example, still claimed in private (and would continue to do so until the end of his life) that President Roosevelt had secretly welcomed the attack on Pearl Harbor because he believed a war would consolidate his "dictatorial" power. Yes, Dennis may have been a cynic and a deeply committed fascist, but he was also savvy enough to decide, after Pearl Harbor, that it would be unwise to start that pro-fascist, German-financed magazine he had been working on with Philip Johnson.

Johnson, sufficiently worried about his previous and very public pro-Hitler mania, abandoned his own authoritarian fever dream and cloistered himself as a newly apolitical student in Harvard's architecture program. He quit writing essays and articles for Father Coughlin's *Social Justice,* and he cut off his financial support for Joe McWilliams's violent Christian Mobilizers and similar groups. When the FBI came around to investigate, most of the faculty and fellow students in Cambridge told the agents that Johnson appeared to have turned over a new leaf. One professor who knew Johnson from his undergraduate days a dozen years earlier explained that the young man was simply "a flighty individual with a feeling for adventure." The professor assured the G-men that despite the fervor of Johnson's Nazi years the young man must have since matured, telling them that Johnson "does now see the advantage of democracy."

The vaunted America First Committee did a full U-turn and announced its support for the war against Japan while the U.S. warships in Pearl Harbor were still ablaze. The attack happened on a Sunday. By Thursday, the day Hitler declared war on America, the organization announced it was shuttering for good. "The period of democratic debate on the issue of entering the war is over; the time for military action is here," read the official statement. "Therefore, the America First Committee has determined immediately to cease all functions and to dissolve as soon as that can legally be done. And finally, it urges all those who have followed its lead to give their full support to the war effort, until the peace is attained."

In the middle of all this political undoing and in the rush to a full-scale national mobilization for war, defendant George Hill found himself stuck between a rock and a very hard Fish. Representative Fish kept insisting that he had never had any great feelings for Germany; it's just that he was against *any* foreign war. He frankly could do without any public suggestion to the contrary, now that we were at war with Germany, and in an election year, too. What a terrible time for Hill, Fish's top aide, to feel a new urge to confess everything and tell the truth about the Nazi-run propaganda operation inside Congress. Although Hill had initially pleaded not guilty, he told his defense attorney that he'd had a religiously induced change of heart. "I was at the communion rail at the Epiphany Church one Sunday when I decided to tell the truth," Hill later explained. "I then went to my attorney. I told him I was going to the FBI and tell the truth." Attorney John O'Connor, the former congressman who was essentially working for his friend Hamilton Fish, sized up Hill and said, "You are going nuts." O'Connor told Hill he best keep his trap shut about George Sylvester Viereck and Ernest Lundeen and Hamilton Fish and the rest. "You would not rat on them, would you?"

He eventually would. But not just yet.

Hill sat mum through his trial, sometimes working nervously at his pipe. His appearance belied his womanizing reputation. Reporters described him as reedy, graying, meek, bespectacled, older-looking than his forty-five years, often wearing the same "shabby brown suit." Dillard Stokes, who covered the entire franking affair for *The Washington Post,* wrote that Hill looked "more like a middle-aged professor visiting an angry dean than the German propaganda machine 'key man.'" But whether he looked the part or not, the open-and-shut evidence in Hill's five-day trial told the tale conclusively.

The proceedings would have been even quicker than five days but for continuous objections and interruptions from O'Connor: his perorations about defendant Hill, "a poor, little insignificant clerk to Mr. Fish," and his baseless accusations that the prosecutors William Power Maloney and Edward J. Hickey had planted evidence in the mailbags that Hill had tried to hide from investigators. The entire trial, O'Connor kept reminding the jurors, was an "effort to smear" the great and good representative Hamilton Fish, a patriot and from such a good family, who had worked so hard to keep American boys out of another war. Fish himself, careful to get nowhere near the courtroom, provided backup vocals from the safe zone of his congressional office. "Mr. Hill," Representative Fish said, "had no use for the Nazis. As a disabled combat veteran, he had an obsession against our involvement in the war." But that was *before* Pearl Harbor, of course. Hill and Fish both, naturally, now stood ready to serve.

O'Connor promised to produce a parade of defense witnesses and much exculpatory evidence for his client. He produced exactly none. He offered no defense. Largely because there was none. George Hill, plainly and incontrovertibly, had lied about his acquaintance with George Sylvester Viereck, about trying to hide all those big mailbags from the grand jury, and about his knowledge of the overall congressional Nazi propaganda scheme. Hill was convicted of perjury and sentenced to a minimum of two years in prison. Given a chance to make apologies at his sentencing hearing, Hill simply nodded his head side to side and remained silent.

Still, the prosecutors William Power Maloney and Edward J. Hickey had not given up hope of persuading George Hill to come clean. Maybe his earlier, religiously inspired twinge of conscience had not been enough to get him over the line, but the prosecutors hoped they could still do it; they resolved to keep talking with him. And it worked. Somewhere along the way, Hickey made a comment to Hill that stuck with him. "The main thing I recall was that Mr. Hickey reminded me I was an American citizen," Hill explained. "That worked on my mind. And a couple of days later I decided I would tell the truth." Threats from his own attorney (his boss's friend) notwithstanding, George Hill agreed to testify at Viereck's upcoming trial, as did various staff members of the Islands for War Debts Committee, as did most of the office staff of the late senator Ernest Lundeen.

In just four weeks, prosecutors at Viereck's trial revealed exactly how George Sylvester Viereck wheedled into the heart of American power, into the U.S. Congress, and then persuaded elected officials to sweet-talk their countrymen about all the fine, fine qualities of Nazi Germany that we were overlooking. Viereck's strategy, as Maloney summed it up, "was to put words in the mouths of legislators on Capitol Hill who were duped with his clever talk—we don't know what else—while he laughed at them in secret reports he sent to Berlin."

CHAPTER NINETEEN

"MR. MALONEY WOULD HAVE PULLED NO PUNCHES"

Summer in Washington, D.C., is a season of acute physical depletion. Heat is a daily drain on the most energetic of federal employees and officials; humidity shrink-wraps sweaty shirts and dresses onto just about everybody, regardless of status or standing. Very democratic, the weather in Washington. In July 1942, back before the widespread use of air-conditioning, the nation's capital was slogging through its annual communal torpor. But not William Power Maloney. The "Little Napoleon of the courtroom" had a real bounce in his step. He was on a roll.

Maloney had already won the convictions of both George Hill and George Sylvester Viereck. During the Viereck trial, the widow of Senator Ernest Lundeen had shown up in court to testify in Viereck's defense. When later commanded to produce the Viereck files she had spirited away from her husband's Senate office a few days after the plane crash that killed him, Mrs. Lundeen explained to the court that, sadly, there had been a break-in at her home and that some of the files must have been taken by the burglar. Yes, it must have been a burglar. (Years later, hundreds of pages of correspondence from the "missing" files would turn up—not burgled at all—in the Lundeen family archives.) Up against evidentiary shenanigans like that, Maloney still achieved not only the conviction of Hill and Viereck but also the exposure of the Lundeen-Viereck congressional Nazi propaganda scheme, all in open court.

Maloney had also successfully prosecuted Charles Lindbergh's female doppelgänger: the famous lady flier and America First spokeswoman Laura Ingalls. The same Laura Ingalls who had stunt dropped antiwar leaflets on the White House grounds in 1939. *United States v. Laura Ingalls* was a novel and telling case in the Department of Justice's effort to stem secret Nazi-funded information operations in America. Ingalls was not charged for her political views or for her vocal support of Adolf Hitler—all perfectly legal, constitutionally protected speech. But at trial, Maloney did make sure the jury got the drift of her pro-Nazi sentiments: She often wore a silver swastika bracelet. She had asserted that democracy was a dying form of government ("bunk," she called it) and that the United States "needs somebody like Hitler." The führer, she would say, "is building a country, while America is in chaos." She hurrahed the sinking of a British battle cruiser by the German navy in May 1941. "I could tear the skies apart in triumph," she wrote to a friend at the German embassy, "Sieg heil." She prayed for a "swift German victory" in Europe, which would keep America on the sidelines, and perhaps even leave the United States open for Hitler's taking.

When the question of entering the European war still hung in the balance, Baron Ulrich von Gienanth, the SS officer and Lawrence Dennis pal who oversaw U.S. propaganda operations out of the German embassy in Washington, had counseled Ingalls that "the best thing you can do for our cause" would be to affiliate with the America First Committee. Just like Lindbergh. Problem was, the America First Committee was kind of cheap. Ingalls complained to von Gienanth about the pittance of a travel stipend the committee offered. So, he offered funds from the Nazi coffers to put her on their payroll, which she happily accepted; another German diplomat later explained that von Gienanth "had a special liking" for Ingalls and "thought she would be a good propagandist." Whether she was good at propaganda or not, Ingalls failed to register with the State Department as a paid agent of a foreign government. That's what put her in the dock, indicted by Maloney's special grand jury.

The Ingalls defense team decried the prosecution as a "witch hunt" and portrayed the celebrity aviatrix as a sort of aeronautical Joan of Arc: righteous and inspirational. Also: crafty. Her attorney told the jury that her relationship with the Nazis was all part of an intricate and reasoned double-agent ploy: she was only faking at being pro-Nazi; all along, she had been planning to turn over to the FBI all the inside dope on Germany she could glean by (very convincingly!) pretending to be on their side. This defense did not fly.

Ingalls, Hill, and Viereck were all in custody—and news of the Nazi plot in Congress was still making waves—when, on July 23, 1942, Maloney's federal prosecutors unleashed yet another court filing to shake the nation's capital from its summer doldrums. All at once, they indicted twenty-eight people and charged them with sedition. Viereck and Prescott Dennett from the War Debts Committee were both named, as were William Dudley Pelley of the Silver Shirts; General Moseley's water taster and antisemitic publisher, Charles Hudson; James True (he of the "kike killer" weapon); and Noble and Jones from Los Angeles, whose stand-alone charges just after Pearl Harbor had previously been dropped. Among the organizations named in the court papers were the Silver Shirts, the German American Bund, the Crusader White Shirts, the Protestant Gentile League, and the America First Committee, as well as Viereck-run entities like Flanders Hall, the Make Europe Pay War Debts Committee, and the Islands for War Debts Committee.

Maloney's terse and declarative twenty-eight-page indictment was based on almost seven thousand pages of grand jury testimony from more than 150 different witnesses. It charged the defendants with "intent to interfere with, impair, and influence the loyalty, morale, and discipline of the military and naval forces of the United States." Germany's propaganda scheme targeting the United States went far afield from military bases and installations, of course, but Maloney believed this was the charge that would stick. And also get the word out. Without naming or indicting them, Maloney in his court filings described how members of Congress had helped the Hitler government launder Nazi propaganda and send it, in bulk, to American soldiers, sailors, and marines as well as to the public at large.

Maloney had developed evidence that franked envelopes from Representative Hamilton Fish's office had been used to send out literature from Pelley's armed Silver Shirts, as well as a mail-order form for people to receive copies of the *Protocols of the Elders of Zion,* Henry Ford's go-to anti-Jewish forgery promoted by the Nazi Party and their fellow antisemites across the United States.

Crucial new pieces of evidence in the charging document were provided by that seasoned sleuth from *The Washington Post,* Dillard Stokes. Under the pseudonyms "Jefferson Breem" and "Adam Quigley," Stokes had sent requests for information to various ultra-right publications in the spring of 1942. These publications then happily shipped to Messrs. Breem and Quigley Nazi-produced propaganda, often reprinted by the federal government right from the *Congressional Record* and then tucked into franked envelopes from congressmen. The franked envelopes were supplied by Prescott Dennett or George Hill, who were on the payroll of Nazi agent George Sylvester Viereck. One of these mailings to "Jefferson Breem" at 3917 Pennsylvania Avenue, SE, for instance, showed that writing to an antisemitic extremist newsletter like Charles B. Hudson's *America in Danger!* was enough to put you on the mailing list to receive free, German-funded, congressionally franked propaganda from America First's favorite senator, Burton K. Wheeler.

The senators and congressmen who had participated in Viereck's scheme knew when Viereck was convicted and the sedition indictment was unsealed that DOJ prosecutors were onto them. The investigation had clearly expanded beyond the offices of the late senator Ernest Lundeen and Congressman Hamilton Fish. If prosecutor William Power Maloney was indeed hot on their trail, the implicated members of Congress were going to have to figure out a way to deal with him. As Henry Hoke put it, "When the first special Grand Jury brought in its indictment against 28 persons, Maloney became one of the most hated men in Washington."

But any pained shouts and murmurs from Viereck's congressional co-conspirators were drowned out by the commotion in or near the courtroom. The newspapers couldn't get enough, for instance, of the Henry Ford–financed huntress of American commies, Elizabeth Dilling, and her attorney husband. Dilling had been dumping antisemitic fantasist bilge into America's information waterways for twenty years, but now was her chance to enjoy getting some real ink for herself in the mainstream press. Dilling, for example, would stop on her way into the courthouse to treat reporters and her supporters to performances of her latest songs, like "B-b-baloney," mocking Prosecutor Maloney. (Which was disruptive, but not as vicious as the outlandish rumors she circulated that Eleanor Roosevelt had infected the president with gonorrhea.)

Even after the indictment, Dilling, the "den mother of anti-Semitic conspiracy theories," was still giving interviews praising Germans as "the best-fed, best-housed, most powerful, hopeful in Europe." At her arraignment, where she pleaded "*absolutely* not guilty," Maloney called her a "stooge" of the Nazi Goebbels. Which was kind of true, but perhaps not politic.

At a later hearing, Dilling's attorney husband complained to the judge about the unfairness of it all, claiming he had heard rumors that the Department of Justice was preparing a massive new indictment of *any* Republican *anywhere* who had voted against Roosevelt. Going back to 1932! *People are saying.* "Those rumors have their origin in the fertile mind of Mr. Dilling," Maloney told the judge, who probably already knew as much.

Pretrial hearings and motions dragged on through the end of the year; the judge in the case refused to grant the defendants' pleas and motions to drop the charges. As the 1942 Christmas season approached, Maloney's sedition case was clearly headed for trial, which promised a very public airing of some very dirty laundry on the congressional clothesline. Lawyers for the accused seditionists—wisely—made it a point to keep all the implicated elected officials informed as to the ongoing proceedings at court. Lawyers for Viereck and the other sedition defendants reportedly met in person every weekend in the office of Senator Gerald Nye to plan strategy. Now that Viereck had been exposed at his own trial as a Nazi agent, of course, one option for lawmakers would be to help with the case. Fess up, cooperate, help root out the rest of the Nazi propaganda operation that might still be ongoing.

But apparently that option did not appeal. The congressmen and senators instead chose door number two: try to burn the whole thing down.

ON DECEMBER 8, 1942, Representative Clare Hoffman of Michigan (whose frank had been used by Charles B. Hudson's *America in Danger!* to mail out antisemitic poison) invoked a point of personal privilege on the House floor, shutting down all legislative business in the chamber. He then took a full hour to defend himself and other members who were being investigated and questioned by federal prosecutors. Hoffman's integrity, his patriotism, his exemplary character, had been called into question, he claimed. He was deeply hurt. The way Representative Hoffman saw it, the sedition indictment itself was an act of religious bigotry; the defendants were poor, persecuted Christians.

Hoffman then introduced a resolution calling for a special committee to investigate DOJ for its overreach and demanded that Dillard Stokes and his editor at *The Washington Post* be called before the new committee and compelled to testify. He even wanted to haul in the famous Nazi-bashing newspaper columnist Walter Winchell for questioning. "Is it not true," Hoffman said on the floor that day, "that Walter Winchell, the gossipmonger, Peeping Tom, the digger into garbage cans, and the purveyor of rot; William P. Maloney, pettifogging special attorney for a grand jury; and Dillard Stokes, alias Jefferson Breem, alias Quigley Adams [*sic*], he of the perverted mind, acting together, sought to create, and did create, the false impression that Members of Congress were disloyal and unpatriotic and, by doing so, frightened some Members of Congress into silence?"

However frightened Congressman Hoffman might have felt, he was sufficiently sure of himself to accuse the DOJ's William Power Maloney of gross prosecutorial misconduct.

DOJ prosecutor William Power Maloney

Maloney was undeterred. In fact, he was apparently inspired to swing for the fences. Four days into the new year of 1943, he produced a superseding indictment, adding five new defendants, including George Deatherage, and Deatherage's onetime assistant Frank Clark, a Silver Shirt true believer who had moved to Tacoma, Washington, to found something called the National Liberty Party. Clark's party pledged to stay active "as long as a single Jew remains alive on the North American continent." Also named in the superseding indictment: Leslie Fry, the woman who had first given the *Protocols of the Elders of Zion* to Henry Ford, and later gave succor (and cash) to the Los Angeles crazies who planned the mass lynching of prominent Jews in Hollywood. The updated indictment made the single biggest sedition case in American history even bigger. The new court filing also dated the beginning of the Hitler-run propaganda conspiracy to 1933, back to when Leon Lewis had first stood up his cadre of private spies in Southern California.

What seems to have led to the superseding indictment is that William Maloney's investigators had finally traveled to Leon Lewis's headquarters and hoovered up the files Lewis and his spies had been producing for an entire decade. Those same files that Lewis had been trying to give to local law enforcement, the FBI, the Secret Service, army intelligence, the Department of Treasury. There was so much there. "All of these individuals, all of these groups who Leon Lewis and his team of private undercover agents had been tracking for years while law enforcement couldn't be bothered—they were all now being wrapped up," says historian Steven Ross. "[Lewis and his team] were providing not just witnesses, but they were providing all the paperwork and spy reports dating back to August 1933.

"There's an old expression, 'If you live long enough, you'll win all the awards.' Well, [Leon Lewis] may not have won all the awards, but he earned the admiration or at least the respect of the American government."

WITH THE ADDITION of Lewis's extraordinary mountain of evidence, Maloney and his investigators had discovered the double helix of the violent, Nazi-supporting, and Nazi-supported threat in the United States; it was part foreign and part domestic, part propaganda and part armed paramilitary movement. One of Lewis's agents provided eyewitness evidence that some pro-Nazi groups knew in advance of a raft of explosions at industrial plants in 1940, one of which was manufacturing a million pounds of TNT for Great Britain every month. The biggest explosion was at the Hercules Powder plant in Kenvil, New Jersey, which was operating twenty-four hours a day to stock the arsenal of democracy, to feed the U.S. allies in Europe, and to prepare the American military in the event the country was drawn into the war. At least forty-eight workers died in the blast. Two months later, three explosions within half an hour of each other rocked three separate war plants in New Jersey and Pennsylvania. The damage, according to some estimates, cost the U.S. war preparation effort $1.5 billion in man-hours.

Whether those explosions were accidents, or strictly a Nazi sabotage operation, or sabotage plotted to help the Nazis but carried out by Americans was never conclusively proven by the government. But a spy on the ultra-right providing advance warning of the first blast, and then the choreographed timing of the second round of explosions, was enough to rattle everyone's cage.

This much was certain: Germany had agents at work inside the United States; armed American fascists were being actively supported by the Hitler government; members of Congress were colluding with a German propaganda agent to facilitate an industrial-scale Nazi information operation targeting the American people; critical U.S. munitions plants were blowing up in multiple states. And the Justice Department, at last, was going to act to take it all apart. At least it was going to try to.

Representative Hoffman, Senator Nye, and Senator Wheeler kicked up a second storm after Maloney's superseding indictment. They continued to demand an investigation of the investigators. Hoffman invoked his personal privilege anew and excoriated "the misuse by Maloney, an assistant to the Attorney General of the United States, of his official power, used as it was in furtherance of a conspiracy to destroy the Congress, a coordinate branch of our government." Nye chimed in too but did himself no favors. The defendants, the North Dakota senator claimed, "have seemingly done nothing more than I and others of us here have done time and time again." He said they "are no more guilty than I am." Henry Hoke noted, "In that he may have been right."

Wheeler was the most voluble, as always. The senator accused Attorney General Francis Biddle of overseeing "one of the most disgraceful proceedings ever carried on in this country" and claimed the case was brought solely to smear America First, which was now defunct. He also claimed that one Dillard Stokes report that his frank was being used by a crazy fascist antisemite in Omaha to send out Nazi propaganda was a "plain, unadulterated lie." Which was itself a plain, unadulterated lie, based on the actual evidence. But evidence notwithstanding, Senator Wheeler predicted that Stokes and Maloney and the rest of the prosecutors would rue the day they started this investigation. This was not an idle threat.

Two weeks after Wheeler's ominous philippic, William Power Maloney was named the chief of the criminal trial section of the Justice Department, which, technically, was a promotion. But it was also something else. Senator Burton Wheeler was more than just a blowhard in white ducks; he was a senior member of the Senate Judiciary Committee, which oversaw the Department of Justice. Wheeler had paid a visit to Attorney General Francis Biddle at his office at Main Justice. In what was described as a stormy and violent session, Wheeler reportedly threatened the attorney general that he would make good on his promise to launch an investigation of the *entire* Department of Justice, from the attorney general on down, unless Biddle took Maloney off the case.

In the face of that threat, Attorney General Biddle—remarkably—caved. He gave in to the pressure from Wheeler and other members of Congress. Biddle "promoted" Maloney, and in so doing, removed Maloney from the case he had been building for more than a year. Maloney himself got the news while he was sitting at his desk, working. First he heard of it was when a newspaper reporter called him up to ask his reaction to getting fired. He'd had no idea, he said. They hadn't bothered to tell him.

In this historical era of the Department of Justice, alongside whatever heroics may attend to its prosecutors and investigators, there is also this broken bone, sticking out like a compound fracture. In the middle of this controversial, high-profile case, William Power Maloney was removed as prosecutor because of pressure from members of Congress who themselves were implicated in his investigation. *The Washington Post* published a blistering editorial criticizing Biddle's decision: "In this case the public could have been sure that Mr. Maloney would have pulled no punches, whether the evidence incriminated a conspirator or embarrassed one of his friends in Congress. Maybe that was why Congressional friends of the defendants hated and feared this prosecutor and publicly harassed Mr. Biddle with windy threats of investigation, with boasts of what they would do to the Department of Justice unless they got Mr. Maloney's scalp. Now they have it."

THINGS GOT WORSE for Maloney in the coming weeks. The U.S. Supreme Court, in a 5–2 decision, overturned the conviction he had won in the Viereck case. The majority found that the main fault was in the murkiness of language in the Foreign Agents Registration Act. Viereck, they decided, had possibly complied with the letter of the law by registering himself as an "author and a journalist" in the pay of Germans, even though he didn't mention his voluminous German-funded work in Congress on a propaganda scheme dreamed up and directed by the Nazi high command.

The court's majority opinion basically missed the entire point of Viereck's endeavors and his paymasters, but it didn't stop at the nearest exit, where it could have; the opinion also made a frontal attack on William Power Maloney and his personal exuberance. "In his closing remarks to the jury, [Maloney] indulged in an appeal wholly irrelevant to any facts or issues in the case, the purpose or effect of which could only have been to arouse passion and prejudice," wrote Chief Justice Harlan Fiske Stone. "At a time when passion and prejudice are heightened by emotions stirred by our participation in a great war, we do not doubt that these remarks addressed to the jury were highly prejudicial, and that they were offensive to the dignity and good order with which all proceedings in court should be conducted."

William Power Maloney, in other words, in the opinion of the most powerful jurists in the land, had been way too mean to George Sylvester Viereck, and way too fired up about the stakes of this case.

There were plenty of voices in Congress that agreed; it's easy enough to imagine exactly who. Clare Hoffman, for instance, said it was an "outrage" that Maloney was still drawing a government paycheck; he called for Attorney General Biddle's head on a platter, too.

AFTER THE HIGH court's decision, a remarkable new character entered the stage: North Dakota senator William Langer, an unpredictable, eccentric isolationist known as Wild Bill in his native environs. Langer had been convicted of a bold pocket-lining kickback scheme while serving as governor of his state back in 1934. He was hit with a federal charge, convicted, and sentenced to eighteen months in prison. Governor Langer pronounced his federal criminal conviction illegitimate, rejected the court order removing him from office, declared martial law in the state, attempted to declare North Dakota's independence from the United States, barricaded himself in his office, and refused to leave.

After his supporters filled the streets of Bismarck and called for the shooting of his successor, the lieutenant governor, Langer finally gave up the governorship and then managed to win an appeal of his conviction. He was re-elected governor in 1936, and won a seat in the U.S. Senate in 1940. When he got to Washington, his fellow senators weren't sure whether they should seat him. A special committee made an investigation into his whole corruption, martial-law, secession, armed-revolt thing and found that Langer's path to the Senate was definitely problematic. The phrase "moral turpitude" was used. The investigating committee found that Langer had exhibited "continuous, contemptuous, and shameful disregard for high concepts of public duty" and was therefore unfit to serve. The full U.S. Senate took the findings under advisement, but in the end they decided that a little coup here or there didn't necessarily render a man unfit to serve in the highest legislative body in the nation.

Wild Bill, who believed he knew all about persecution and redemption, had an immediate reaction to the high court overturning Viereck's conviction. His statement was in the evening papers the day the Supreme Court's decision was announced: "Senator Langer, praising the decision, said he would propose that a committee be named to determine the expense Viereck incurred in his defense, with a view to compensating him for his expenditures as well as for the time he has spent in jail. He added that whatever relief Congress may be able to give Viereck will be 'inadequate' to 'wipe out the wrong that has been done.'"

CHAPTER TWENTY

BEDLAM

O. John Rogge was just thirty-nine years old when he was tapped to take over the sedition case in February 1943, only ten days after the attorney general of the United States had caved to Senator Burton Wheeler and cashiered the prosecutor who had been leading the case, William Power Maloney. Rogge was a prodigy, but a complicated one. Born on a farm in rural Illinois, he was the son of recent immigrants from an obscure region in the northwest corner of Germany known as Frisia, which shared a very porous physical and cultural border with the Netherlands. Despite having spoken only Low German before he went off to public school—on horseback, five miles each way—Rogge proved himself a rare intellect. O. (for Oetje) John sped over and around all academic hurdles, graduating from the University of Illinois at the tender age of eighteen and Harvard Law School three years later. He passed the bar exam and was admitted to the practice of law at age twenty-one. After a brief turn in private practice, he was handpicked by Franklin Delano Roosevelt's New Deal brain trust for government service. One of his earliest cases at the Reconstruction Finance Corporation pitted him against three hundred lawyers on the other side; the civil case went to the Supreme Court, and Rogge won. Rogge did a tour at the newly formed Securities and Exchange Commission and also at Treasury, before taking over as the head of the criminal division at the U.S. Department of Justice in the spring of 1939, by which point he had attained the ripe old age of thirty-five.

His sharp intellect and his innovative application of the law had scooted Rogge quickly up the DOJ ladder, but he had also proved himself fearless. In 1939, Attorney General Frank Murphy sent him to Louisiana to investigate the surviving regime of Huey Long, still roaring along four years after the Kingfish's death. Rogge showed up in New Orleans and said he figured he'd be there about a week. He ended up spending eight months in Louisiana investigating what was perhaps the most corrupt statewide political machine America had ever known. The Long operation—with or without him—was not just built for venality; it was built to enforce its prerogatives through all available means. Huey Long had used bribes and threats to take just about anything he wanted, including from the state legislature. He was credibly accused of trying to arrange the murder of a political opponent. When two men came forward before his Senate election to accuse Huey of maintaining a mistress, he didn't stoop to pay the hush money they demanded; he instead simply had the men kidnapped and hidden away until Election Day had passed. He had watched in amusement as his "bodyguards" physically assaulted reporters and news photographers. He had trucked National Guard troops into New Orleans for an honest-to-goodness armed military assault on New Orleans city government.

After his assassination, Long's successors soon found that they weren't as skilled at corruption and intimidation as he had been, but they sure were trying. Rogge got a little taste of their sinister misconduct himself when, early in his investigation, he received a note on cheap white paper, written in black pencil: "You will die before Wednesday if you don't get out of this city. We just paid $18,000 for your death. You must die." Tucked inside the envelope were two .38-caliber bullets. Just by way of emphasis.

Rogge made sure to go out into the street that night to tell the whole story to reporters. "Any threat like this will only make me strive harder to uncover any scandal in this state," he told them. "The United States Department of Justice cannot be threatened."

Rogge then set about collecting hides. Seymour Weiss—the bagman who used to pass Huey Long sackfuls of cash at the Roosevelt Hotel bar in New Orleans—Rogge put him in jail for more than two years. Rogge also put away the recent governor of Louisiana, Long's lieutenant Richard Leche, who admitted on the witness stand that he had pocketed almost $500,000 in his single gubernatorial term (more than $10 million in today's dollars). His annual income had jumped from $14,000 a few years before he became governor to $282,000 by only his second year in office.

Rogge also tied Weiss and Leche to one of the most spectacular instances of graft ever described in the immediate post-Huey era, the "hot oil" scandal. Like every other oil-producing state, Louisiana had a state agency that set production quotas, right down to the individual well. Oil companies, as a matter of federal law, were not permitted to produce and sell oil in excess of those quotas (so-called hot oil) without a special exemption, and only after that state agency undertook careful study. In Louisiana, Weiss and Leche simply ordered the state's oil-regulating agency—the Conservation Commission—to grant them all the special exemptions they asked for. The hot oil was then sold to an understanding millionaire in Texas, who gestured vaguely at disguising its origins by moving it around a bit by pipeline, truck, and train. Some of it was ultimately shipped off, illegally, to Europe, where it was rumored to have ended up in both Nazi Germany and fascist Italy.

For their part in the scheme, Leche and Weiss collected ten cents on every barrel of hot oil, plus a $100,000 payment for the Texas pipeline. In his 1941 book on Huey's legacy in Louisiana, Harnett T. Kane explained how the Texas oilman in the middle of the scheme insisted that the whole allegation was a "trumped-up piece of nonsense. He was only a legitimate businessman; everything had been legal." That said, the oilman did also cop to "sending $48,000 in $1000 bills to Seymour Weiss, wrapped up and by express. ('Just like he was sending a pair of socks,' Rogge fumed.)"

Rogge managed to haul the official in charge of Louisiana's oil quotas before a judge for testimony. Dr. D. A. Shaw (he'd been to dental school with Huey's brother) said he had been forced to sign the illegal "special allowance" orders and that he figured Governor Leche and his friends were making bank on the transaction. "I didn't *know* they were going to get a thing," Shaw told the judge. "But I had an idea. Because they don't do things for nothing."

The judge wanted to be clear: Shaw had signed the order without making the proper and required investigation? "I do what they tell me to," Shaw explained, or he would be out of a job. "I would sign anything they stuck in front of me, except an order to hang me."

The hot oil case never made it to trial. For one thing, star witness Shaw committed suicide. For another, the judge wasn't enormously impressed with the need to punish any functionaries in a system everyone damn well understood. "It is a matter of general and common knowledge that the state of Louisiana was more or less under a dictatorship and had been for ten years," he said.

Rogge didn't seem to sweat it. At the age of thirty-six, he had put away Weiss, Governor Leche, and other key cogs in the zombie Huey Long machine. Even without a trial in the hot oil case, Rogge's indictments still made his evidence about that scheme a

Maloney's successor, O. John Rogge (at right), with his family

matter of public record, out there for everybody to see. The Department of Justice, by Rogge's lights, had an "educational function." Beyond miscreants being put in prison, Justice Department investigations should also result in transparency. Voters need to be informed; he believed democracy depends on it.

The education Rogge provided Louisiana through those indictments and prosecutions, and his bravery and skill in dismantling the violent, entrenched thugocracy there, were big national news. His Louisiana tour of duty was called "sensational" in papers like *The New York Times*. *The Saturday Evening Post* did a whole series on it—portraying Rogge's feat as "especially remarkable as he had never tried a criminal case before he arrived in Louisiana." Here was the man who had brought down the Huey Long machine. This was a career-making triumph for a man who was probably already on the fast track to the top of the Justice Department.

Rogge announced that he was headed to Michigan next, to take on official grifters in that state, too. But before he could get there, he was asked by his bosses to make a little detour to Brooklyn in 1940, to prosecute the Christian Front fascists—the seventeen guys who had stockpiled bombs and ammunition and U.S. military machine guns and then trained for a violent takeover of the federal government.

ROGGE, IN THE END, didn't get any of them. When that case fell apart in the summer of 1940 and the Christian Fronters were all set free and even got their guns back, that was on John Rogge's watch.

The failed prosecution of the Christian Front was not just a high-profile embarrassment for the U.S. Justice Department. For John Rogge, it was a fall from a great proverbial height, a shocking personal failure. Rogge didn't lose. He had never lost. Except this time, he did. Rogge put his tail between his legs and left the criminal division the next year.

By early 1943, he had just finished work on a complicated bankruptcy proceeding involving a utility company. And he was getting bored. In his memoir, he wrote, "Time began to grow heavy on my hands." Happily, an unexpected phone call from Attorney General Francis Biddle plucked Rogge from that slough of despond and set him on a new course. He accepted Biddle's offer to return to government service, to replace William Power Maloney in the mass sedition trial in Washington. Rogge would have his chance at redemption, after all; the failed Christian Front trial would not be his last shot at locking up a band of violent fascists intent on ending American democracy and overthrowing the U.S. government.

As a first step, Rogge and Biddle made the determination to withdraw Maloney's indictments and start fresh. The new prosecutor would "bring to trial only those defendants against whom the Department would have a case that would stand up in court," a Justice Department source told reporters. That ought to have gone without saying, of course, but after a first indictment that named dozens of defendants, and then a second superseding one that added still more, and with the whole matter now under the purview of a high-profile prosecutor whose last case saw every single one of the accused seditionists walk free, that simple statement of prosecutorial intent—to only bring charges against those to whom charges could stick—made for a newsworthy assurance.

Americans were seeing the world with fresh eyes by then; it looked quite different from what it had been in the fall of 1941, back when William Power Maloney had begun his grand jury proceedings. Anne Morrow Lindbergh's pro-fascist book, *The Wave of the Future* (written at least in part by Lawrence Dennis), was still a bestseller in 1941, while her husband, the hero pilot, was out on the hustings leading the isolationist and increasingly antisemitic America First movement. Many if not most Americans agreed with the Lindberghs on one thing in 1941: they did not want to send their husbands, brothers, and sons to fight a new war against Germany.

In 1943, by contrast, few Americans remained neutral and few doubted the evil of fascism as personified by Adolf Hitler's Nazi Party and its look-alikes in this country. The runaway bestseller in

1943 was a deeply reported, 540-page book by Arthur Derounian (pen name: John Roy Carlson), who had infiltrated a number of America's fascist Nazi-colluding groups beginning in the late 1930s. *Under Cover* sold nearly a million copies that year; it was both a page-turner and an eye-opener. For four years Derounian had traveled the country's homegrown fascist web, tracing strands connecting William Dudley Pelley, George Deatherage, James True, Elizabeth Dilling, Laura Ingalls, Father Coughlin, the Christian Front and the Christian Mobilizers; Senators Ernest Lundeen, Robert Rice Reynolds, Gerald P. Nye, and Burton Wheeler; Representatives Hamilton Fish and Jacob Thorkelson; and General George Van Horn Moseley. Derounian's reporting showed how they had all been in league together, either providing cover for Hitler's Nazis or actually doing their bidding inside the United States.

Among the gems in the book was Derounian's long interview with Lawrence Dennis. Ham Fish, Dennis said, "has no brains. His sympathies are all right, but he is dumb." He was slightly more charitable about Senators Nye and Wheeler, who had made successful attacks on the Department of Justice and Prosecutor Maloney. "You can give me credit for that," Dennis told Derounian. "I've been talking to them all along."

Under Cover also introduced some previously unknown fascist characters, like a forty-eight-year-old working-class widow, Lois de Lafayette Washburn. Washburn (who claimed to be a descendant of the famous French marquis and wrote under the pen name TNT) believed the Boy Scouts, the Yellow Cab Company, and every president since Lincoln had been under the control of a great Jewish cabal.

The ultimate takeaway from Derounian's bestseller was the breadth and depth of fascist America. "Most of the saboteurs of democracy looked and acted like ordinary men and women, went quietly about their work of destruction, lived on Park Avenue as well as Yorkville, came from our best families, and the most efficient of them were American-born and boasted of their ancestry," Derounian wrote. These fascist saboteurs "could lurk in the pulpit and cocktail lounge as well as the factory."

While *Under Cover* tore up the charts (first published in June 1943, by the fall of that year it was already in its seventeenth printing), Rogge bore down on his own work. He stripped the case down to the studs. He made a top-to-bottom review of the entire investigation to that point. He pored over volumes of grand jury testimony; brought Maloney's witnesses back in front of his own grand jury; called new witnesses. Rogge did all this behind closed doors; nobody on Capitol Hill knew what he was doing. Nearly a year after Maloney's departure, there had been no news from Justice. Which was good news to Wheeler, Fish, Hoffman, and the rest of Viereck's friends inside the U.S. Congress. When Rogge's review of Maloney's case dragged on for months without any public-facing action on it at all, it must have seemed like maybe they had dodged the bullet entirely.

They had not.

In the first week of January 1944, John Rogge burst back into public view with a brand-new indictment, including some new names and some familiar ones. "George Sylvester Viereck," intoned one radio announcer, "heads the list." But there also was Lawrence Dennis, indicted for the first time. Dennis, characteristically, was dismissive of the indictment and also still name-dropping, pointing out that DOJ did not have the courage to include his friend Charles Lindbergh in the list of defendants with him. "Lindbergh had too much popular appeal," Dennis would say years later, still miffed. "[Rogge] had as good a case against Lindbergh as against me."

Rogge's new charging document, like Maloney's, alleged violations of the Smith Act—an effort to demoralize America's armed forces. But Rogge had sharpened the case, alleging targeted efforts by the defendants to recruit National Guardsmen, reservists, and even active-duty U.S. troops into these ultra-right groups, where they could use their military skills, connections, and access to weapons to help arm and train paramilitary fascists for the overthrow of the U.S. government. Rogge also racked focus on the German side of the equation. The defendants, Rogge's indictment read, "unlawfully, willfully, feloniously, and knowingly conspired with each other and officials of the Government of the German Reich and leaders of the Nazi party." These Nazi leaders and functionaries were thereafter referred to as the "unindicted co-conspirators."

No member of Congress was named as a defendant, but the political threat embodied in the charging document was nevertheless real. The United States had just rounded into its third year of war against Germany. Nobody wanted to be the member of Congress caught even unwittingly working with Nazi sympathizers and Nazi agents, or taking money from the same sources, or using America First/Islands for War Debts/Keep America Out of Foreign Wars mailing lists to help these people and their cause. Rogge was threatening to expose all that. Maybe more.

THE TRIAL OPENED on a cool spring morning in Washington, D.C., April 17, 1944. Rogge was there at the prosecutor's table, raring to go. He figured on a two-month schedule, from jury selection to verdict, maybe three months at the most. What he had not factored into that plan was what would befall him and his case as soon as the curtain rose on his long-awaited trial: preplanned, unmitigated chaos.

There were thirty defendants and twenty-two separate defense attorneys, not counting Lawrence Dennis, who had decided to act as his own counsel. George Deatherage, as a stunt, announced that he chose to retain former Republican presidential nominee Wendell Willkie for his defense. Willkie had nothing to do with Deatherage and nothing to do with the case—"I have never heard of the man and never saw him," Willkie had been forced to explain—but Deatherage enjoyed trolling everyone about it nonetheless. He made sure all the reporters saw his receipt showing that he had sent Willkie a $10 retainer and that they covered his "I want my money back" rejoinder when Willkie told him to pound sand.

As overpopulated as that courtroom felt on opening day, it turned out the defendant cohort was one seditionist short. Edward James Smythe, who had headlined joint rallies between the Ku

Klux Klan and the German American Bund and solicited help from the Hitler government in Berlin in propagandizing the American people and targeting Jews, was a no-show as the trial started. His lawyer said he had no idea as to Mr. Smythe's whereabouts. When law enforcement found Smythe and hauled him into court, he told the judge it was just an unfortunate misunderstanding. He'd got his dates mixed up. Which seemed slightly implausible given that they had caught him about forty miles south of the Canadian border, heading north at a fairly frantic clip. He claimed to the arresting officers that he was on a fishing vacation.

Things did not get any smoother in the early days of the trial. Jury selection was a slog, in part because defense attorneys kept making motions to release the entire jury pool by claiming they had been prejudiced by sensational stories in newspapers and on radio. There were also a slew of even more frivolous and time-consuming motions having nothing to do with jury selection. One defense attorney, James Laughlin—who had been introduced to his defendant client by Senator William "Wild Bill" Langer—asked the judge to seize the records of the Anti-Defamation League and other civic organizations, claiming those files would prove that Jewish organizations were conspiring to blacken the good names of men like Nye, Wheeler, Fish, Hoffman, and even General Douglas MacArthur. He also motioned to compel Henry Ford and Charles Lindbergh to appear as witnesses for the defense.

Judge Edward C. Eicher was required to read and consider these motions, no matter how frivolous or how far out of bounds. The defendants, meanwhile, were playing hard to their own crowd right from the start. Lois de Lafayette Washburn, somewhat famous already thanks to Derounian's hit book *Under Cover,* stopped to make the Nazi Sieg Heil salute on her way into the courtroom on the opening day of the trial. When other defendants followed suit, Mrs. Washburn upped her game by literally thumbing her nose at reporters, Three Stooges style. She once arrived at the courthouse wearing nothing but a blue satin nightgown, claiming the rest of her clothes had been stolen. Defendant James True held up the proceedings for an hour when he made an unannounced and unapproved visit to the dentist, then brought the trial to a halt for another full day when he stayed home because he said he just didn't feel well.

Lois de Lafayette Washburn on the opening day of trial

Judge Eicher insisted over and over on "common courtesy" inside his courtroom, but he certainly didn't get it. Eicher was well regarded by his peers and was considered a seasoned political hand; he had been a three-term congressman and a veteran of the Securities and Exchange Commission. But running a trial of any kind was relatively new to him. The biggest sedition case in American history would have been a challenge for the most experienced jurist, but when the case was assigned to Eicher, he had been a judge for all of thirty months.

Eicher allowed defense counsel to ask prospective jurors if they were Jewish, if they had Jewish relatives, or if they read Jewish publications, and even weirder inquiries along those same lines: "What does Jew mean? ... What does international bankers mean? ... Do you think the Jews are an international people? ... What is meant by Mongolian Jew?"

And those were the questions Eicher allowed to actually be asked. The list of *proposed* voir dire questions to prospective jurors included "Do you believe that in the sight of God Jews only are human and Gentiles are only beasts in human form made by God to serve Jews? . . . Do you accept the Jewish doctrine that Gentiles are all profane beasts? . . . Do you know the distinction between Levantine Jews and what are commonly called Kikes? . . . Considering [Supreme Court justice Felix Frankfurter] is a Jew of Austrian origin, do you believe he can be a bona fide citizen of the United States or psychologically qualified for the position on the bench? . . . If you know a Judge had in him Jewish blood would you consider him qualified to sit in judgment upon Christians? . . . Do you believe a Jew can go to heaven? . . . Do you believe activities directed by Jews can be the bona fide activities of the United States? . . . Do you have definite views on the so-called Jewish question? . . . Do you believe Christ was a Jew?"

It took a month just to seat a jury. That was a long enough slog that one of the defendants, Elmer J. Garner, up and died during the process. On the day the jury was finally seated, defense lawyers moved to delay the trial until the war in Europe was over. Until then, they argued, their clients had no shot at a fair trial.

But finally, in mid-May 1944, more than a month after the trial had limped out of the starting gate, John Rogge got to make his opening statement. At last he would have the opportunity to state his case. At least in theory he would.

Rogge stood to make his argument in the smallish thirty-eight-by-forty-foot courtroom, packed with the twenty-nine surviving defendants, the twenty-two defense lawyers, a small squad of prosecutors, court bailiffs, family, spectators, reporters, and a fistful of U.S. marshals to keep the peace. As soon as Rogge began his presentation, a new round of chaos erupted. "That's a damn lie," a defendant would scream from the wings. Or "What about Roosevelt?" Edward James Smythe yelled, "I'm a Republican, not a Nazi!"

"John Rogge tried to talk through catcalls and comments from the defense tables," a radio correspondent reported at the end of a very exasperating day. "Defense attorneys were popping up all over the place with motion after motion, and the twenty-nine defendants themselves indulged in asides, shouts, stage whispers, and at one point broke into a kind of derisory chant."

During John Rogge's opening statement, the defendants banded together and repeatedly shouted at Rogge to sit down and shut up. At another point, the defendants and their attorneys hurled nonstop objections at Rogge for more than thirty minutes straight. "The din becoming so intense," *The Washington Post* reported, "defense lawyers could not hear their own voices."

Lawrence Dennis rose from his seat in the middle of the proceedings to demand an answer from the judge on his recent motion. He had not been recognized to speak, but he nevertheless insisted upon an immediate response to his petition to force mental health evaluations of Prescott Dennett (Viereck's employee, who was commuting to court each day from the psych unit of Walter Reed Hospital), Lois de Lafayette Washburn (in the nightgown, with the nose-thumbing antics), and Edward Smythe (the AWOL fisherman caught making a beeline for the border). When the marshals, at the judge's annoyed insistence, finally wrestled Dennis back into his seat, Smythe himself jumped up out of his own chair. "I demand a mental examination," he shouted.

The court had slotted a two-hour window for Rogge's opening statement. It took him all day, and nobody could be sure how much of it the jury could hear, or process, over the continual din.

BUT WHEN YOU go back and read those parts of the court transcript from Rogge's statement and strip out all the yelling and screaming and chanting and caterwauling, it's clear what Rogge meant to accomplish. He was trying to explain to the jury what was at stake for us as a country in the sedition trial. The defendants, Rogge said, "intended to impose on us a one-party system, just as the Nazis had done before them in Germany. The evidence will show that they intended to abolish the Republican and Democratic parties. The evidence will show that they intended to abolish freedom of speech, freedom of the press, freedom of assembly, freedom from arrest without cause, and all the other civil liberties guaranteed us by the constitution.

"Thereafter, the evidence will show they intended to run this country not according to our constitution, but according to the so-called 'fuhrer' principle and the Nazi concept of Aryanism.

"The evidence will show that the defendants themselves talked in terms of bloodbaths, or blood flowing in the streets, hanging people from lamp posts, of pogroms. One of the defendants stated that our pogroms in this country would make Hitler's look like a Sunday school picnic.

"The evidence will show that the defendants regarded themselves as enemies of democracy. According to them, democracy was decadent. It was weak, false, rotten, corrupt. It was senseless and dangerous. It was a monstrosity of filth. There was no principle, according to the defendants, that was as wrong as that of democracy. The Nazis, and the defendants, were going to destroy it throughout the world."

A heck of a message if anyone had been able to hear it. No one had. The stories in the next day's newspapers and radio programs were about tumult and disruption. "They probably should have held the sedition trial in Madison Square Garden or in Bedlam," noted one radio reporter. "Probably nothing so daffy has ever been put on in the American courts. . . . Edward James Smythe, one of the defendants, had the time of his life with this sport until a marshal was posted at his side to shush him every time he opened his mouth."

The next day, six separate defense motions to declare a mistrial landed on Judge Eicher's desk, all claiming Rogge's opening statement had been "inflammatory." Lawrence Dennis told the court the entire trial was part of an enormous political "conspiracy . . . to throw the [1944] election" to Roosevelt and the Democrats.

The trial proceeded in fits and starts and shouts and tantrums and delaying motions and nonsensical objections, followed by ever-sterner admonitions from Judge Eicher and then ultimately fines that he levied against defense attorneys. One of the defense lawyers, Judge Eicher said, exhibited "complete loss of self-control, a violent and belligerent manner, a threatening attitude and being utterly contemptuous of the court." The attorney fired right back at the judge. "It don't make no sense," he said. "I come here to work for nothing and get fined. I move that in view of your honor's attitude this afternoon—the way you looked at me and condemned me, you have become so prejudiced against me, it will be impossible for you to sit in fairness in this case, both as arbiter and in judgment—that you disqualify yourself."

Judge Eicher was probably sorely tempted to take him up on that and get himself removed from this madhouse. Various defense lawyers in fact made multiple demands that Judge Eicher recuse himself from the case. When those were denied, defense attorneys filed appeals in higher court, and then lost those appeals, too. But that all took time—which was the point. Even under the best of circumstances, the sheer size of the indictment, the sheer number of defendants, gave defense lawyers an opening to at least try for crippling delay, to sow confusion, to make it as difficult as possible for the prosecution to lay out their case and for the jury to be able to follow along with what was happening. But these were not the best of circumstances. Judge Eicher had lost control of the courtroom atmosphere and the pace of proceedings from the first moment of the trial's first day.

Defense lawyers "resorted to every legal trick at their command to forestall the proceedings and suppress the painstakingly gathered evidence," wrote *The Washington Post*. The defense insisted that if Judge Eicher would not delay the trial until after the war was over, he should at least delay until such time as defense lawyers could call Joseph Paul Goebbels, Rudolf Hess, Adolf Hitler, and Winston Churchill to witness the innocence of their clients. One of the defense counsel's proposed voir dire questions asked potential jurors if they "have heard of or know Adolph Hitler."

They also moved to subpoena the prosecutor himself, to put O. John Rogge on the stand, accusing him in open court of bribing witnesses. They further moved to remove the court reporter from the case because she worked for a company that employed a Jewish executive. Probably no surprise, but that ended up being a big theme for the defense lawyers and their clients beyond just the process of selecting the jury. One attorney railed in court against "Jewish international bankers" and claimed to the jury that Rogge's case was a "Jewish conspiracy." He tried repeatedly to introduce the *Protocols of the Elders of Zion* as evidence of this imaginary conspiracy.

IF IT SOUNDS like a circus, that's because it was a circus. At one point *The New York Times* led its front-page story on the trial with news that the judge himself had been driven out by the crazy. He had left the courtroom in the face of what the *Times* described as "a violent uproarious argument" among the defense lawyers and defendants. The judge just couldn't stand the screaming anymore, so he got up and walked out. Reporters felt the same way, overall; the huge press interest in the early days of the trial quickly waned as each new day's proceedings became more incoherent than the last.

Despite Rogge's expectation that the whole trial—jury selection, the prosecution's case, the defense's case, jury deliberations— would take about two months, maybe three at the outside, just his own presentation of the prosecution's case dragged on through May, June, July, and August. And it was still nowhere near done.

When Judge Eicher adjourned the trial for a much-needed two-week vacation a few weeks before Labor Day, one of *Time* magazine's rewrite men executed a nice little bullet-point summation of proceedings to date. The number of defendants had been reduced to twenty-six, on account of death, medical issues, and "obstreperous conduct." The judge had levied $1,000 in contempt-of-court fines against defense attorneys and defendants. (One lawyer was facing jail time for walking out on the trial back in July.) "Time & again the trial has plowed on while various defendants were excused," the magazine noted: "1) to have teeth fixed; 2) to go apartment-hunting; 3) to sit up with sick relatives; 4) to be treated for poison ivy and carbuncles."

Rogge had been able to present testimony from a scant percentage of the two hundred witnesses he had planned to call to the stand. But he insisted he was going to present them all, along with more than nine thousand supporting documents, "if it takes forever." It might. His initial hope of a two- or three-month trial now seemed laughable. "It's just impossible to estimate the length of this case," Rogge admitted. "All our estimates seem now like fairy tales."

"PARALYZE THE WILL"

On the day the sedition trial resumed, in the first week of September 1944, a surprise visitor arrived in Judge Eicher's courtroom. Eicher needed this like a hole in the head. He had already spent his first day back from his much-needed vacation wading through all the paper that defense lawyers had dumped on his desk in his absence. *The Washington Post* called it "an avalanche of motions of mistrial, severance of some defendants from the case, squashing indictments, and ruling out of evidence." The motions, which varied from nonsensical, to irrelevant, to contemptible, sorely tested Judge Edward Eicher's normally deep reserve of calm and general equanimity. Now, on top of that, into Eicher's already unruly courtroom strutted Senator William "Wild Bill" Langer, whose reputation preceded him and whose own insurrectionist past had quite nearly precluded him from being seated in the Senate. Langer "was not someone who practiced the fine art of reason and compromise," says historian Nancy Beck Young. "His style was aggressive and in your face. And he saw this as a headline-grabbing moment. He saw it as a way to poke a stick in the eye of the [Roosevelt] administration."

Langer had already secretly provided one of the defendants with a lawyer—a lawyer whom Eicher had then tossed off the case for bad behavior back in July. The senator made multiple visits to the D.C. jail to show his solidarity with eight defendants who spent the duration of the trial in custody because they were unable to make bail. He socialized openly with the defendant Elizabeth Dilling, who could afford bail; Langer even hosted her for conferences at his Senate office.

Now, in the courtroom, Wild Bill threw his arm around some of the defendants, whispered unheard confidences with them, laughed with them, made his presence in the courtroom in support of them as ostentatious as he possibly could. He spent a good bit of time in serious conversation with Nazi agent George Sylvester Viereck, mastermind of the Hitler government's propaganda operation in America. As disruptive as Langer was to the already nearly ungovernable proceedings, Eicher couldn't exactly shoo a sitting U.S. senator from his courtroom. Well, theoretically he could, but Eicher would never.

After two days at the trial, Wild Bill was back in the Senate chamber, where he commandeered the floor to call for the dismissal of all charges against all the defendants in the sedition trial. Eicher's court was in recess that day, so among the spectators in the gallery for Langer's speech was the defendant Lawrence Dennis (who might himself have been the author of a good bit of Langer's oration). The senator spoke for more than two hours. He cast the defendants who were being held in the D.C. jail as "political prisoners." The trial was a "legal farce" and a "preversion [sic] of justice." The defendants were all great people, Langer asserted, great Americans. Langer's characterizations elided much. Lawrence Dennis, on the payroll of Hitler's government and America's foremost fascist intellectual, was in Langer's telling just "a man of moderate means . . . defending himself as his own attorney and room[ing] here with his wife and two small daughters." George Deatherage, the former Klansman who was also funded by the Germans and who had set up armed cells around the country to overthrow the U.S. government after the 1940 election, was described blandly by Langer as an "industrial efficiency engineer with a son fighting in the service." Lois de Lafayette Washburn (Sieg Heil!) was a simple woman who made her living doing housework. "The son of the other woman defendant, who is Mrs. Elizabeth Dilling, graduated on March 4 from officer candidate school, but a few hours before graduation his commission was withheld, allegedly . . . because his mother is a defendant in this trial."

The "allegedly" was doing a lot of work in that sentence. Senator Langer did not mention that Kirkpatrick Dilling was reportedly in danger of being stripped of his corporal's stripes because, just the previous day, he had joined his mother in attacking a young member of the U.S. Army Air Corps as a "God-damn Jew" and reminding the serviceman that "the Jews have been driven out of Europe and you'll all be driven out of this country too."

The German-supported antisemitic publisher and General Moseley water taster, Charles B. Hudson, was a man with "a small home-mimeographed bulletin," said Langer. "His wife kept roomers, and for several years he was unable to get his teeth fixed because of lack of money." (Dental health was an unexpected theme running through this trial.) Another defendant wrote hymns and taught Bible classes.

What Langer really wanted etched into the *Congressional Record* was that these defendants simply posed no actual threat to America. They were "small fry . . . little old men and women who have no more influence than a rooster." Langer demanded that Attorney General Biddle call off his dogs, and even offered him a

William "Wild Bill" Langer near the end of his long career in the U.S. Senate

script to do so: "Developments have demonstrated that some of these defendants, if guilty of reprehensible conduct toward the country, are either actually demented or approximately insane—at least to the point of belonging distinctly to the lunatic fringe." Maybe they engaged in some unfortunate activity, Langer conceded, but "the evidence shows, however, that these efforts were impotent and characteristic of a general conduct of these defendants, relatively ineffective."

In the courtroom, Rogge was still trying to beat down motion after motion, objection after objection, disruption after disruption, to make his case to the jury. Press coverage was waning precipitously by the middle of September. Even in Washington, D.C., where Rogge's ordeal was playing out live, the daily coverage felt more like a series of sidebars—details about the color and texture and logistics of the case and not so much about the substance. For variety, stories occasionally ticked off updates on the named but unindicted German co-conspirators. Manfred von Killinger, for instance, who as Nazi consul in San Francisco had provided German support for the plot to lynch powerful figures in Hollywood, shot himself dead in Romania as the Russian army advanced on German positions. One less alleged co-conspirator for the indictment, then.

The Washington *Evening Star* worked up a juicy little feature on the logistics of feeding the eight sedition defendants who were being held in jail. The medical officer at the jail had worked out a strict dietary schedule, which was reportedly a step up from regular inmate fare, on account of the difficulties of the trial schedule. Fruit juice and eggs for breakfast, for staying power. Then a packed sandwich for lunch at the courthouse, where the defendants could also get hot soup and coffee. The alleged seditionists got two portions of beefsteak each week (but small portions). And because the prisoners returned to jail from the courthouse after the evening meal was over, the wardens had arranged to keep their dinner plates warm. Three of the eight had to be put on special diets—no fried chicken, no pork chops—because of tummy issues. The med-

ical officer at the jail would not divulge the identities of the gastri-
cally impaired to the *Star*'s intrepid reporter but did explain that
the trio had been "nervous and jittery" while on the normal prison
diet.

There were reports that the court-appointed defense attorneys,
who were not being paid to provide counsel, had pleaded with
Judge Eicher to shift trial hours to the afternoon and evening. The
attorneys wanted their mornings free to make a living. There was
also much speculation in the press about how long the trial would
drag on. Some reporters figured the prosecution's presentation
might go into 1945. And with twenty-six separate defense cases to
make after that . . . well, there was no telling. The auditor for the
district court was able to knock down outlandish estimates that
the trial was going to cost taxpayers upwards of $1 million; the
actual cost to date, to the penny, was $65,819.73 going back to the
early grand juries in 1941. He expected the final tally to come in
around $85,000.

By the fall, any news of the sedition trial that editors deemed
worthy of the front page was invariably below the fold. The headline stories were about the war in Europe, which had a way of
making everything else seem much less urgent. Allied troops had
taken the beaches of Normandy, on D-day, just a few weeks after
Rogge began to mount his case for the prosecution. The Allied
breakout across France followed in the next few weeks. A few days
after Judge Eicher called the two-week summer recess, the Allies
had liberated Paris from Nazi rule. Victorious Allied troops pa-
raded down the Avenue des Champs-Élysées, through throngs of
cheering liberated French, and just kept going. They chased the
fleeing German military across France, Holland, Belgium, Luxembourg, and right up to the Siegfried line. "A solid front from the
North Sea to the Mediterranean was formed by a junction of General George S. Patton's 3rd Army and the 7th Army of Lt. General
Alexander Patch," the Washington *Evening Star* reported on the
very same day it wrote up the story about the sedition defendants'
sour tummies. The first American columns had already crossed

onto German soil, pointed straight for Berlin, "the first time since Napoleon's day that an invading force from the west had entered Germany in more than patrol strength."

The other big story that fall was the upcoming national election, which was drawing new figures into the campaign. Henry Hoke, the direct mail adman whose intrepid work had spurred the Department of Justice investigation into the illegal Viereck-led congressional franking operation, traveled to Chicago to support a candidate running against Representative Stephen Day, who had been one of Viereck's most prolific and best-paid authors at Flanders Hall. Hoke also published his own book about the scandal in the lead-up to the election, in hopes that it might have a salutary effect on voter behavior. "It is a sizzling document," wrote an early reviewer of Hoke's book, on September 10, 1944. "One can only say that 'Black Mail' should be read—and thoroughly—by every American."

Eight weeks later, on November 7, 1944, the president who had been leading the country in the war against the Nazis, Franklin Delano Roosevelt, won an unprecedented fourth term, with 432 electoral votes to Thomas E. Dewey's 99. Roosevelt's Democrats gained twenty-two seats in the House and protected their whopping nineteen-vote cushion in the Senate. The beauty of that election, though, was in the finer details. Members of Congress who had been in on Viereck's scheme paid the price. Robert Rice "Build a Wall" Reynolds lost his seat in the U.S. Senate and so did Gerald Nye. Stephen Day was shellacked in Illinois. The big get was Hamilton Fish, who suffered his first and only election defeat in twenty-five years. The campaign against him focused almost exclusively on his Nazi ties. The Republican presidential nominee, Dewey, who was also the governor of Fish's home state, had felt the need to publicly repudiate the veteran congressman during the campaign.

Hamilton Fish was about as gracious a loser as you might expect. "I admit, publicly, that my defeat should be largely credited to Communistic and Red Forces from New York City backed by a large slush fund probably exceeding $250,000," he said. He added that he was "fearful that the overwhelming election of President Roosevelt is a step toward setting up a one-man and one-party government in our own country."

IN THE FALL of 1944, the daily reporter contingent in the courtroom had dwindled from forty down to four "regulars," according to *The New York Times*. The press and America in general had simply lost interest after more than six months of watching the prosecutorial wheels spinning in the mud. Washington reporter Carter Brooke Jones, one of the few "regulars," estimated the word count—witness testimony, objections, motions made and denied and made and denied, and all the catcalls and caterwauling that made it into the record—at more than two million. "One at a time, please" was an oft-used phrase by Judge Eicher, though there was no way for the stenographer to convey in words the jurist's depth of exasperation.

The transcript, which surpassed thirteen thousand pages in the middle of October, was overwhelming. It was impossible to parse even for reporters—who were trained and professional observers—let alone, presumably, for the regular-joe jurors. But for anyone willing to slog through it, it emerges in that record that in the weeks before and after the 1944 elections, John Rogge was beginning to uncarth some fascinating artifacts. The trial, in substance, was becoming downright intriguing to anybody who was there to see it.

Rogge had been presenting evidence to make the case that the defendants were part of an analog worldwide web, operating in America, on a very specific mission. In mid-October, Rogge put Dr. Hermann Rauschning on the witness stand to expound on the man who created that web: unindicted co-conspirator No. 1 in Rogge's indictment, Adolf Hitler.

Rauschning, a German national, had been an early acolyte of Hitler's, drawn to National Socialism as a means to restore Germany to its former honor. He had been an occasional personal interlocutor of the führer's during Hitler's rise to power and his early days in office. But he lost his faith in Hitler's vision. Rauschning left Hitler's side and fled Germany in 1936, just as the Nazis were constructing their heinous anti-Jewish legal regime.

From his unique and unsettling perspective as a high-placed former Nazi, Rauschning had tried to tell the world about Hitler's mad plans starting even before Germany began invading other sovereign nations. "Warning to the West" was the subtitle of his first book to reach a wide American audience, published in 1938. Rauschning had been met with plenty of wariness and criticism in 1938, before Hitler began his headlong run at world domination. But by the time of his appearance at the sedition trial, at the end of 1944, his warnings—viewed in hindsight—had clearly been prescient. With so many of his darkest prophecies about Hitler having come to pass, Rauschning made a very compelling and very expert witness.

In his testimony, Dr. Hermann Rauschning invited the jury into private dining rooms and Nazi leadership conferences circa 1933, when Hitler was gaming out the strategy and tactics he was already setting in motion to target America. Hitler had by then started sending special Nazi agents into major cities all over the United States. In fact, this was the moment Leon Lewis, in Los Angeles, first realized what Hitler was up to and began recruiting undercover agents to document it. Hitler had already sent a man to that crucial West Coast city to organize the Friends of New Germany and other civic programs. This included setting up the Aryan Book Store, which accepted and distributed tons of Nazi propaganda shipped in from Germany and secretly off-loaded at the ports of Los Angeles, San Diego, and San Francisco. It also included setting up Hitler Youth camps and training grounds for German American storm troopers all over the United States, as well as funding and encouraging the arming of the American ultra-right, through men like George Deatherage, Clayton Ingalls, Edward James Smythe, Lawrence Dennis, and William Dudley Pelley and his Silver Shirts. But what exactly was Hitler's aim? Rauschning had the answer in his contemporaneous notes from conversations with Hitler himself.

"Adolf Hitler said," Rauschning explained in his testimony, "the United States was threatened with a bloody revolution. He said he would be able to make this revolution come to pass. He explained the methods by which he would be able to paralyze the national unity of the United States and the power of resistance in this country. . . . He said the cleavages in the [American] population could be widened to disunite the country." This was talk Rauschning dated from 1933, but he said Hitler was still expounding on the subject a year later, just after the führer had murdered his political rivals in the Night of the Long Knives. Rauschning was in Hitler's personal lair in Berlin when the führer, Goebbels, and other henchmen made plans to blanket America, Poland, France, and Great Britain with propaganda—"the artillery and trench warfare" of modern warfare, Hitler had called it. "We have to paralyze the will and national unity of [these] and other countries," Hitler said. "The great issue was to liberate the world from the poison of democracy, with its degenerating doctrine of liberty and equality."

Rauschning's testimony, in other words, was that the Nazi game plan aimed to disunite the United States by tearing at the weakest political and cultural seams in American society: the divide between haves and have-nots, fear and hatred of immigrants, white supremacist race hate, and antisemitism. Rogge's job before the jury was to prove that these disparate defendants were part of that plan. The question before the court was whether their actions, in fact, constituted a seditious conspiracy.

Right before Thanksgiving, Rogge called an extraordinary witness to help answer that knotty question: this was Henry Allen, one of William Dudley Pelley's key Silver Shirts, founder of the American White Guard, and confederate of, well, just about every defendant in the sedition trial. This was an incontrovertible fact, and the proof resided in Allen's own briefcase. The briefcase Allen had left behind in his midnight-blue Studebaker Commander, very near his "kike killer" weapon, when he went to San Diego to snowstorm the city's downtown with antisemitic flyers. The briefcase the San Diego police had confiscated after spymaster Leon Lewis and Charles Slocombe (Agent C19) had alerted them to its existence. The briefcase Lewis and Slocombe had rushed to retrieve before Allen was let out of jail. The briefcase Lewis and Slocombe had driven over to the naval base in San Diego, under the good offices of naval intelligence, so they could make photostats of every document it contained. The briefcase whose contents had finally been taken in, along with a decade's worth of files, from Leon Lewis's Los Angeles office, by William Power Maloney and the team at DOJ investigating alleged sedition.

That briefcase, as much as anything, formed the backbone of Rogge's spectacular indictment. The contents connected almost every defendant to the others, all through Henry Allen. Allen, a hostile and very reluctant witness, spent more than a week on the stand as Rogge walked him through photostat after photostat of incriminating evidence. Here was defendant Frank Clark writing to Allen: "Later on we will have baseball bats in our hands or special devised 'Hitler spades.' . . . The Jews will be buried here. . . . These Jews have been holding meetings all over the country for the purpose of gathering-in funds and having them shipped here by the boatload. While some people think there is to be somewhere in the neighborhood of a few thousands, the fact is, they have planned to bring 5,000,000 here—and that means that many more to slaughter."

Here were letters from James True, who had been severed from the case because of his ill health; and from Lois de Lafayette Washburn, who was still on trial, and now famous for her defiant Nazi salute and her blue satin nightie. Mrs. Washburn had written to Allen of "the inevitable day of reckoning, which is now at hand." Thank God Frank Clark was a military man, she said, who "had the foresight to begin organizing military men 10 years in advance of this crisis."

Here was another missive from George Deatherage, head of the swastika-bedecked American Nationalist Confederation (whose members included most of the defendants). Deatherage's documents partitioned the country into specific geographic military divisions, "in a similar manner as was done in Germany," with General George Van Horn Moseley standing by to lead the armed insurrection that would unseat Franklin Delano Roosevelt. Henry Allen had occasionally identified himself as a "regional commander of the Confederation." Deatherage's American Nationalist Confederation contact list included almost all of the defendants, and many, many others: like the Grand Dragon of the Ku Klux Klan; Christian Front leader John "Little Führer" Cassidy; former senator Rush Holt; Hamilton Fish's Keep America Out of Foreign Wars committee; the attorney who ran interference for Fish in the trial of his aide George Hill; Hitler's state-run news service in Erfurt, Germany; and U.S. Fascists Inc.

"The time has arrived for a practical and constructive plan of government to be offered to the Nation," read one Deatherage letter in the Allen photostat files. "That plan is that of a Fascist state. . . . Fascism has proved itself. It saved Italy and Germany when they were faced with complete destruction by Jewish Communism."

Leslie Fry (the woman who had gifted Henry Ford his first copy of the *Protocols of the Elders of Zion*) was on that list too, since she was one of the co-founders of the American Nationalist Confederation. Allen testified before Judge Eicher that Mrs. Fry had once instructed him to toss "a hunk of concrete" through the front window of Leon Lewis's home.

When Henry Allen finished his nine-day run facing direct examination, cross-examination, and re-direct on November 28, 1944, Rogge's legal theory of the conspiracy no longer seemed merely "theoretical." This was a big week of breakthroughs. American troops in Europe had breached a key barrier in Germany when the first armored forces crossed the Rhine. The German military was retreating at speed, under a pounding by Allied bombers, all along the advancing four-hundred-mile front. And John Rogge was maybe starting to break through all the noise and chaos in the courtroom.

FUNNY THING HAPPENED the next day. Something that, even for this absurd proceeding, was almost too much to be believed. A group of the sedition defendants had up and started operating what looked like a clerical assembly line. While the trial was in session. They would take an envelope, stuff it with a document, pass it down, hand address it, pass it down, seal it, pass it down, put it in a pile, and move on through the stack. One of the few "regulars" among the reporters still covering the trial noticed that these weren't any old envelopes the defendants had stacked in front of them. They were congressionally franked envelopes from the office of a Republican U.S. senator: Wild Bill Langer of North Dakota.

Langer had not only provided the defendants with thousands of franked envelopes; he had provided them with thousands of copies of that two-hour speech he had made in defense of the "fine Americans" on the Senate floor a few months earlier. The speech was already in the *Congressional Record;* so he simply made a discount price order from the Government Printing Office, at taxpayer expense, and had them delivered to Judge Eicher's court along with the franked envelopes. Then he enlisted this weird little secretarial team of accused fascists and Nazi operatives to stuff the envelopes in the courtroom so he could mail that speech out around the country, postage paid by the U.S. taxpayer. They were working the Viereck playbook. Still. While literally in federal court.

Eicher was at his wit's end. He reportedly considered a blanket contempt-of-court citation for all the defendants, one that would result in locking up all of them, even the ones who made bail, until the trial was over. The judge also reportedly considered the unprecedented step of holding Senator Langer himself in contempt, which could conceivably have also included jail time for the senator. The judge considered these remedies, but he decided not to act. Not that day anyway. Judge Eicher wasn't looking to invite any further harassment and antagonism from Capitol Hill, where supporters of the sedition defendants had already started serious talk about impeaching him.

THE JUDGE'S EXHAUSTION was understandable. He had already ruled on more than five hundred separate motions for mistrial. He had heard seventy-two thousand objections made by defense law-yers and out-of-order defendants. He had levied contempt fines on seven different defense attorneys and ordered one to jail for ninety days. He had watched for more than seven months as the defen-dants and the lawyers had sung and chanted and screamed their way through such an array of delaying tactics that there were three million words entered in the trial transcript, which was now at 17,879 pages (weighing in at 150 pounds, a super welterweight by fight standards) and growing.

The prosecution had been able to call only thirty-nine wit-nesses to that point, with more than a hundred still on deck. Thereafter, the defense would get its turn to mount a case too, a full and fair defense for each of the remaining twenty-six defen-dants. There really was no end in sight. "For more than seven months," *Time* magazine noted, Judge Eicher "had banged a tire-less, ineffectual gavel at a score of jack-in-the-box defense lawyers bent on turning his courtroom into a vaudeville stage."

That Wednesday, November 29, 1944, the day Langer had de-fendants stuffing envelopes for him in the courtroom, was maybe the toughest day to date. Judge Eicher's law clerk noticed that something seemed a little off about her boss, like he wasn't feeling well. He kept turning his back to the court during proceedings; it looked like maybe he was trying to catch his breath. The clerk sug-gested to Eicher that he call an early end to the day and go home to get some rest. He insisted it was just a little indigestion and pressed on.

He made it to regular quitting time, gaveled the proceedings to a close, went home, had dinner, and went to bed. When his wife went to wake him at six o'clock the next morning, he was dead. Died in his sleep. Sixty-five years old. Heart attack. The widely ac-cepted consensus was that the pressure of the trial had killed Judge Edward Clayton Eicher, and it was hard to argue otherwise. Some of the alleged seditionists had a different take. Charles B. Hudson called the judge's heart attack an "act of God," according to a re-port from *The Washington Post*. One of his co-defendants, ac-cording to that same report, took partial credit. Gerald Winrod said he had seen a vision predicting the judge's death and had "stayed up all night praying" for exactly this kind of deliverance.

Whatever the actual cause, Judge Eicher's death was an unmitigated disaster for John Rogge. The federal court could not simply slot in a new judge and pick up where the trial left off, not unless all the defendants signed off. And they did not. A replacement judge took the bench just long enough to declare a mistrial, leaving the Justice Department with a decision to make: Would they start all over with a new trial, from the beginning? Take it from the top?

Attorney General Francis Biddle decided instead to take a breath, to hold the decision in abeyance. But it seemed obvious where he was headed. Faced with the prospect of starting the whole proceeding all over again from jump, recognizing what a chaotic mess it had been the first go-around, and how much criticism of the Justice Department it stirred up on Capitol Hill among the defendants' allies, Biddle was inclined to take a pass. The attorney general's sentiments were not a secret around the halls of the department, or a surprise, or a cause for much criticism.

John Rogge stood apart.

For Rogge, the idea of abandoning the case was crushing. He had tried and failed to convict members of the Christian Front in New York in the last big sedition trial of the era. He had now tried and failed to convict this band of alleged seditionists as well, many of whom had been working with members of Congress—members of Congress who had injected themselves into this trial. And in this case, he didn't even get the chance to have a jury render a verdict. This was his own side just giving in. The Justice Department seemed to be walking away.

John Rogge was not.

CHAPTER TWENTY-TWO

"WISE CHOICES"

The top political appointees in the U.S. Department of Justice spent an uncomfortable several days at the end of October 1946 tracking one of their own: an assistant attorney general—perhaps the most famous assistant attorney general in the long history of assistant attorneys general—who was then careering across the United States, from Philadelphia to New York to Seattle. O. John Rogge had asked for a two-week leave of absence from the department, but appeared to be embarked on a personal mission, in the form of a nationwide speaking tour.

Unfortunately for his once-promising career, the message he was intent on bringing to the American people was a disconcerting one, which a country just emerging from a long, bloody fight was not eager to receive. The war in Europe and the Pacific was finally over. The country, at last unburdened of the immense responsibility it had chosen to accept, was understandably hungry for normalcy, for freedom from the epic weight the country had shouldered the past five years. Neither was it the sort of message Rogge's political bosses at the Department of Justice wanted splashed across front pages of newspapers. DOJ, too, was ready to move on. But John Rogge did not always show a talent for reading the room. He was determined to deliver the news as he saw fit, to tell the American people the truth, whether they wanted to hear it or not.

Rogge was still the lead prosecutor of record in the largest sedition case in the history of the United States, a case that was just barely alive two years after the shocking, judge-killing mistrial of 1944. By the autumn of 1946, the consensus at DOJ, now led by Attorney General Tom Clark, had hardened into the stance that it was time to let bygones be bygones, that convictions in the sedition case were no longer worth pursuing. Rogge would eventually reluctantly concur on the latter, but he would not concede the former. Bygones be damned. He had been working this investigation for almost three years; he was a constitutionally stubborn man, and he had the bit in his teeth.

Rogge and his investigators had emerged from the mistrial debacle back in 1944 determined to show for the record—at least for national security purposes, and hopefully for criminal convictions—that the Hitler government had been successful in its efforts to set up shop in the United States. And that a surprising number of Americans, including some in surprisingly high places, had colluded with the Nazis against U.S. interests.

The final stage of his investigation, when there was still a sliver of a chance that the attorney general would okay a do-over in the sedition case, landed Rogge in Germany in April 1946, during the International Military Tribunal at Nuremberg, the most important war trial in human history. His German-language fluency had never been more valuable to his legal career than when he and his small team spent eleven weeks interrogating more than sixty captured Nazi officials, including some of the highest rank. Rogge's team also accessed and examined more than thirty thousand documents retrieved from the file cabinets of the German Foreign Office.

Rogge had come back to Washington with that extraordinary cache of evidence, thousands of pages of previously inaccessible data. He had in hand logistical and financial details of the German government's energetic operations inside America long before the two countries were officially at war. Or at least long before the United States understood it was at war. From Germany's perspective, this was and always had been a war operation.

Bottom line, the evidence Rogge gathered in Germany confirmed all they had learned on the American side of DOJ's investigation. The operation went back to 1933, when Hitler first became chancellor and seized full control of the German government. The Nazis had immediately embarked on an intense and multifaceted and well-funded effort to dissuade America from coming to the aid of the besieged democracies in Europe—the democracies Hitler and his Nazis were intent on demoralizing and then destroying—so Germany could incorporate those fallen nations into its world-dominating, planetary Third Reich.

He also returned with more hard proof as to the identities of Americans who had aided and abetted Hitler in his Keep America Out of Foreign Wars campaign, and hard proof of the specific emoluments these agents had received from the German government in exchange for their cooperation. He knew who had been paid (and when, and how much) by Nazi agents in America.

Rogge and his investigators in Germany had also found the field of Nazi fanboy (and fangirl) collaborators in America to be much wider than was previously known. The names on Rogge's list were not confined to the kinds of ultra-right activists and operators who had been on display in the misbegotten Great Sedition Trial of 1944. The updated list included well-known American businessmen, labor leaders, and elected officials. The interviews and files in the German government offices confirmed, yet again and beyond doubt, that members of the U.S. Congress had used the privileges of office to help further the Nazi cause. These were men of standing, and some remained on friendly terms with President Harry Truman, who had assumed office after the untimely death of Franklin Delano Roosevelt in the spring of 1945.

When Attorney General Clark read Rogge's preliminary report of his findings in Germany, he did not particularly like what he saw. Clark suggested the removal of certain of the more boldfaced names, especially the elected officials. Many of these men had exercised poor judgment, true; others had likely been duped by clever German operatives like George Sylvester Viereck. But, big picture, the war was over, after all. The good guys had won. The United States and its allies had wiped fascism and Nazism from the earth. No reason to go rattling through the skeletons in the closets of (otherwise) upstanding, still powerful American public servants. Rogge gritted his teeth and took his boss's suggestion under advisement.

When he submitted the final draft of his report on September 17, 1946, though, much to Attorney General Clark's chagrin, Rogge had not scrubbed the names of all prominent Americans from the document. The attorney general recoiled. His instinct was to stamp *The Official German Report* secret and put it on a shelf for good. President Harry Truman's instinct, turned out, was the same.

World War II had been bloody costly. More than 400,000 Americans had been killed in the fighting; more than a million were wounded, many permanently disabled. But the American people were close to unanimity in believing in the righteousness of the cause, the conviction that the sacrifice had been worth it. The United States and its allies had vanquished Hitler and the Nazis, defeated fascism, struck a blow against racial and religious bigotry. The most despicable and dangerous foreign threat the United States had ever faced was a threat no more.

As steep as the price of that victory had been to America, we were much better off than most. World War II had fully eviscerated the diplomatic, military, and economic capabilities of the exhausted Great Powers of Europe. Truman understood, as did almost everyone else on the planet, that the United States had emerged from the war as the most powerful single force among the world's democracies. As hard a sell as it might be to the put-upon American people, the burden of rebuilding our allies in Western Europe, as well as our vanquished foes Germany and Japan, would likely fall to us.

In that unparalleled moment in American history, Truman did not see much upside in reminding the country of what so recently had divided us. There was a very rational argument to be made that looking backward, scratching at old wounds, just invited unwanted trouble.

. . .

THIS INSTINCT CUTS across historical eras, and it cuts across political parties. It is our long and continuing American tradition to carefully avoid reckoning for the grandest of American sins, especially when they involve alleged (or actual) illegal activity by government officials. Lincoln's "malice toward none" of the Confederate insurrectionists in the aftermath of the Civil War; Ford's full and unconditional pardon of Nixon after Watergate; Obama's reluctance to prosecute anybody for systemized, well-lawyered torture practices during the post-9/11 wars. Truman's 1946 turn in that moral barrel looked like this: "Truman essentially decrees that this report should never see the light of day," says historian Bradley W. Hart, author of *Hitler's American Friends*. "It is simply too explosive. . . . Perhaps the most explosive political report of the twentieth century."

After all the work he had done, all the hard work, including the damning corroboration he had obtained in Germany from the actual Nazis, Rogge's years of painstaking digging seemed to be coming to naught. Rogge had already conceded to the attorney general that the department should not waste more time and resources on a rebooted prosecution of the sedition trial defendants, which meant that he would not be detailing his findings from Germany in any court document. He had taken solace, though, in the fact that those findings could be compiled in an official DOJ report not for the court but for release to the public. This was a consolation prize, admittedly, but a worthy one. Rogge's evidence from Germany might not serve as the basis for criminal convictions, but it could be the basis for a national reckoning with just how far Nazi influence and global fascism had crept toward the heart of American power.

When Rogge determined that his boss, apparently encouraged by the president himself, had reneged on that agreement, the career prosecutor decided to request a brief leave. On his "vacation," Rogge let the attorney general know, he planned to make a handful of speeches to alert Americans to the depths of "the attempted Nazi penetration" in this country.

Attorney General Clark did not say no at that meeting, at least not according to Rogge. But the attorney general did remind his stubborn underling that it would be improper for him to quote from an unreleased government-funded report in a public setting. Rogge recalled that Clark also asked him, facts notwithstanding, to tell his audiences that the Department of Justice "had not attempted to restrain him in any way." They of course had done exactly that. But Rogge nevertheless agreed to Clark's terms. He would later say that he took this agreement with the attorney general as tacit approval for his speaking tour. Maybe so. But truth was, department approval didn't much matter to Rogge. He knew where this was heading.

ROGGE'S FIRST STOP on his tour was a guest lecture for faculty and students at Swarthmore College, a leafy and sheltered liberal arts school swaddled inside an expertly manicured upper-middle-class suburb of Philadelphia. When the event was over, *The Washington Post* couldn't help but wonder why Assistant Attorney General John Rogge "chose the placid Quaker College at Swarthmore, Pa., as the place in which to explode a tremendous quantity of political dynamite."

The New York Times had gotten wind of Rogge's planned appearance and made sure to get a reporter there. The newspaper's resulting lede was this: "A political science class at Swarthmore College tonight heard from O. John Rogge, special Assistant to the Attorney General, a detailed account of efforts which Hermann Goering, Joachim von Ribbentrop and other high Nazi officials say they made to defeat President Roosevelt for re-election in 1936, 1940 and 1944." Rogge had explained that the Nazis' election interference occurred in all three elections, but was most aggressive in 1940. Asked about a $5 million fund the Nazis had set up for surreptitious anti-Roosevelt activities in the 1940 campaign (about $100 million in today's dollars), Hitler's designated successor, Hermann Göring, had told Rogge that he would have gladly spent not just $5 million but $150 million to defeat Roosevelt. Hitler and his brain trust weren't so excited about the Republican nominee,

Wendell Willkie, but he seemed at least marginally more likely to keep America on the sidelines of a war in Europe. And, the Germans were willing to bet Willkie would be a less effective leader if and when America did join the fight in full.

While he had described at Swarthmore the basic outline of the Nazi plot against Roosevelt, Rogge had not, per his boss's instructions, quoted from some of the remarkable top-secret cables a German operative in America sent back to the Foreign Office in Berlin during the 1940 Republican National Convention in Philadelphia. Like the one explaining how a Nazi influence campaign helped secure the anti-interventionist plank of the Republican Party's official platform, vowing to keep America out of foreign wars: "The success of the isolationist Republicans in the field for foreign policy was made possible in part by the promotion campaign authorized by telegraphic instruction No. 666, of June 17. This fact is reflected, for instance, by the circumstance that the . . . principles of the Republican platform on foreign policy were taken almost verbatim from conspicuous full-page advertisements in the American press (e.g., *New York Times*, June 25, p. 19), which were published upon our instigation."

Neither did Rogge note that the full-page advertisement in question, the one that the Germans took credit for "instigating," had ostensibly been paid for by the National Committee to Keep America Out of Foreign Wars, chaired by Hamilton Fish, George Sylvester Viereck's closest ally in the U.S. House of Representatives. (The committee's second vice-chair was John J. O'Connor, the attorney who tried to muzzle George Hill.) The Nazi agent Viereck, through his factotum Prescott Dennett, even deserved credit for conjuring the "Fish for President" media boomlet in the lead-up to the nominating convention. Whether or not they could get Fish onto the Republican ticket (they could not), buzz promoting his prominence and influence in the party could only help bolster what were perceived to be his pet issues at the convention. Like, say, the concerns expressed in that full-page ad in the *Times* attributed to him, but actually cooked up by the Hitler government.

Rogge also told the Swarthmoreans that in the lead-up to the same election, when the Nazis had dumped funds on a sympathetic American oil baron—he sold a lot of oil to the German navy—he then allegedly funded one of the most powerful labor union leaders in America in his public crusade against Roosevelt. The financial sums involved here were as staggering as the standing of the Americans who were involved in these machinations. These were multimillion-dollar campaigns and schemes, conducted illegally and in secret, all targeting the U.S. public and the U.S. government, all with household-name American "leaders" in the mix.

Tom Clark was not well pleased when he read the account of Rogge's lecture in the *Times* the next day. Rogge had not stopped at mentioning the labor leader and the businessman involved in the Nazi election interference efforts: "There were also listed these Americans who, as Mr. Rogge said at Swarthmore, were reported to the [Hitler government] as persons who 'could be organized against United States participation in the war' soon after the Nazi invasion of Poland in 1939," including one particularly problematic person mentioned by name in Rogge's speech, and printed right there in the paper: Senator Burton K. Wheeler of Montana.

Harry Truman (at left), with his friend and onetime U.S. Senate colleague Burton Wheeler

Wheeler was, in 1946, about to be a *former* senator, having lost the Democratic primary in Montana a few months earlier. But at the time of Rogge's Swarthmore speech in October he was finishing the last of his four terms in the U.S. Senate and still had friends in high places. His highest-placed friend was a former Senate colleague who was now president of the United States. A very angry Burton Wheeler marched into the White House at 11:30 on Thursday morning, October 24, 1946, two days after Rogge's Swarthmore event, and got an audience with his old friend Harry Truman. Truman, according to White House logs, did not entertain another guest in the Oval Office for almost four hours. There are no known notes from that meeting, but it's a small leap to guess at the conversation. Wheeler had been insisting all over town that he was the victim of a political "smear campaign" from the left, all because he had been a sincere isolationist who bucked the country's drive to enter another European war. The Montanan, for example, had famously made that nationally broadcast radio speech on the *American Forum of the Air* in January 1941 opposing President Roosevelt's plan for shoring up Britain in its fight against Hitler. The Lend-Lease program to supply military aid to the Brits would lead America directly into a war that would inevitably, as Wheeler put it, "plow under every fourth American boy."

But that 1941 speech was five years ago now, and Wheeler was tired of being hounded for what he claimed had been a reasonable and principled stand; he wanted Truman to *do* something about it. This fellow Rogge was training his fire on decent, God-fearing Americans who had simply exercised their right to try to correct the country's course.

What happened next is hardly surprising, but exactly *who* drove the action is a murky bit of history. There were credible reports at the time that the president had leaned hard on Attorney General Tom Clark, had perhaps even taken time from his plans to escort Mrs. Truman to the theater that evening to call Clark (or even "summon" him to the White House) and give him a talking-to about controlling his staff. There is also a chance that Clark was himself in the long White House meeting with Truman and

Wheeler; the attorney general's handwritten calendar has a notation that he was expected at the Oval Office just ahead of Wheeler. Here's what we do know for certain: Attorney General Clark called a very unusual press conference—unusual in the sense that it was called after midnight—at the Department of Justice that very night after Wheeler had spent the afternoon with Truman. Then (and good thing the department was tracking Rogge on his "vacation" speaking tour around the country) Clark sent an urgent telex to FBI field offices out west. It took a little less than twenty-four hours for that message to catch up to its intended recipient.

O. John Rogge's westbound flight ran into a patch of rough weather on the way to Seattle on the night of October 25, 1946. His airplane had been forced to touch down in Spokane a little after midnight to wait out a thunderstorm. Rogge was stuck in the Spokane airport long enough for an agent from the local FBI office to race over and ask him to confirm his name. When Rogge did so, the agent handed him a missive hot off the DOJ telex machine: O. John Rogge's employment at the U.S. Department of Justice had been terminated. Effective immediately. As in, right there in the airport.

The FBI agent asked the now former special assistant to the attorney general to hand over any official DOJ documents and materials he had on his person. Rogge patted his pockets and said all he had was his (expired) DOJ parking pass. The agent took it, turned on his heel, and that was that.

THIS WAS BURTON K. WHEELER'S second DOJ scalp: William Patrick Maloney back in 1943, before he could bring his sedition indictments to trial; and now Maloney's successor, O. John Rogge, before he could release his DOJ report on sedition to the public. Attorney General Francis Biddle acceded to Wheeler's demands the first time. Now it was Attorney General Tom Clark, as well as President Truman. Whatever else there is to say about Montana's senior senator, the man had pull. Also, it's worth saying, the U.S.

Department of Justice is not supposed to work this way. Even a senator with Olympian influence should not be able to arrange the firing on demand of a prosecutor leading a federal investigation in which the senator himself is adversely implicated. But in this episode in American history, it happened. Twice.

That said, as unseemly and self-serving as it all was, Rogge had also earned that termination. He'd at least invited it. The U.S. Department of Justice speaks only through its court filings, its official statements, and its official reports, for a reason. Rogge had long expected to be able to act within DOJ guidelines, to make public his report on the sedition evidence and its corroboration by captured German officials and files. He expected to do so with the blessing of the attorney general. When that changed, Rogge decided to go public anyway.

A rogue decision. And almost certainly a firing offense.

Once the attorney general had issued his order to quash the report, Rogge—at a basic level—was using the power of the Justice Department's investigative functions for an unauthorized purpose. He was probably going to be fired and he knew it. There was even a chance he would be charged with a crime.

But Rogge had decided to take his chances anyway, and he kept going even after he was fired. He hopped back on that plane in Spokane, flew to Seattle as planned, and kept his scheduled speaking engagement there: "When I was first preparing the report I was under the impression that the Attorney General, for the future security of the United States, was going to make the report public," Rogge told his audience in Seattle. "After all, the study of how one totalitarian government attempted to penetrate our country may help us with another totalitarian country attempting to do the same thing. . . . I think the American people should be told about the fascist threat to democracy."

Rogge went even further a few days later, publishing an exposé in the ardently antifascist ad-free daily newspaper *PM*. (*PM* had been the first paper to report on the Viereck propaganda scheme involving members of Congress.) Rogge's article detailed the toxic stew of authoritarianism, armed militia madness, antisemitism, and collusion with a foreign government bent on destroying American democracy that nearly boiled over before World War II. And might again in the future. His long article was essentially a Cliffs-Notes version of the suppressed three-hundred-plus-page report Rogge had submitted to the attorney general. He started by identifying a handful of the ultra-right American groups and individuals who had been in bed with the Nazis, most of them still free: Lawrence Dennis, William Dudley Pelley, Leslie Fry, Elizabeth Dilling, George Deatherage, James True, and Joe McWilliams, to name a few.

Then Rogge shot right down the halls of Congress, publishing for the first time a full accounting of the two dozen congressmen who had aided and abetted George Sylvester Viereck's campaign to divide and weaken America, to render it not just incapable but unwilling to meet the threat of Hitler and his Nazis. Rogge cataloged, in print, every Nazi-written speech or book or pamphlet those members of Congress had put their names on and reprinted in bulk and sent out under their free-mailing privileges. And often using manpower from the vilest, most fascist, most antisemitic, most antidemocratic organizations America had ever known—organizations and organizers who were themselves receiving support, often cash, from Nazi Germany. Two dozen sitting members of the U.S. Congress! "The list is probably not complete," Rogge admitted.

These congressmen, Rogge now knew, had colluded with Viereck to produce and distribute more than *three million* separate pieces of German propaganda. All of it financed by the German government and unwittingly subsidized by the American taxpayer. The list included Representative Clare Hoffman, Senator Robert "Build a Wall" Reynolds, Senator Gerald Nye. The worst offenders among the elected officials were Minnesota senator Ernest Lundeen, New York congressman Hamilton Fish, and Montana senator Burton Wheeler.

•   •   •

ROGGE'S DISMISSAL AND the suppression of his official report were big news, and drew a lot of criticism. "When I fired Rogge," Tom Clark still remembered a quarter century later, "there were over 26,000 pieces of mail that came in within the next three or four days." President Truman was also inundated with angry letters: *We threw men like Wheeler and [Senator Champ] Clark out of office. Then we see how the President of the U.S.A. knuckles down to them! . . . How do you think the Gold Star mothers feel and us veterans. . . . I suppose the next move will be to give Coughlin or Lindbergh or Gerald [L. K.] Smith a high position in our government. . . . As one artillery man to another, here's a chance to prove yourself not a dud. Replace Tom Clark with John Rogge.* There were also a raft of calls—from private citizens, civic organizations, and elected officials—demanding the release of Rogge's 396-page report in full. But Truman stuck to his guns. He kept that report hidden from the American public. Worse than that: he never took the time to say *why* he had done it. He may well have had a noble motive for this decision, but he didn't ever tell the American public what exactly that might be.

America wasn't quite sure what to make of O. John Rogge at the end of 1946. Reporters and legal analysts noted that the former prosecutor's allegations could best be described as hearsay. This was largely true, because the Justice Department—to protect famous men—had forbidden Rogge to quote directly or otherwise publicly present any of the documentary evidence he had gathered in Germany. Neither could his star witnesses from Nuremberg stand up in court to testify or be cross-examined. A week before Rogge began his five-alarm speaking tour, Hitler's *Reichsmarschall,* Hermann Göring, had killed himself in his jail cell by chewing a potassium cyanide pill. The German foreign minister Joachim von Ribbentrop and nine other Nazi high officials had been hanged for their war crimes.

By going public with what he had learned, Rogge had "stirred up a hornet's nest," according to the host who introduced him on Mutual Broadcasting System's weekly radio program *Meet the*

Press. Six weeks into his one-man antifascist publicity tour, on December 6, 1946, Rogge got an absolute grilling from the four journalists in the close quarters of the *Meet the Press* studio.

"I'd like to ask you this, Mr. Rogge," said Marquis Childs, a Washington-based newsman whose career dated to the Coolidge administration. "If you could have made this report public, what would have been the gain in public opinion? What did you *want to do* with the report?"

"Well," replied Rogge, "I operated on this basis: that if democracy's going to work, if our assumption is correct that people can make wise choices on issues, it can only be if they know the inside story. . . . I thought the American people were entitled to the facts on Nazi penetration."

Childs then asked Rogge if he agreed that presenting evidence suggesting collusion between notable Americans and the German government "had the effect of convicting people in the minds of the public without a trial or without a hearing."

"No. No I don't," Rogge said, growing a little heated. "As a matter of fact, I'd say this to you: we had reached the point where legal remedies were inadequate. . . . You [in the press] are in the field of education. The field of education is bringing these facts to the American people. Now if you are going to say to me that I can't use the facts in an educational way, then you are in effect saying there's no way of meeting the fascist threat." Using a legal term to describe the government's abandonment of the earlier sedition charges, Rogge railed at the civic no-man's-land into which his evidence was falling: "You can't do it legally, and you say to me, 'Ah, but you mustn't talk about these things because the case was *nolle pros.*' And if you put me in that position, there are no remedies against fascism."

Doris Fleeson, a respected syndicated columnist, was in high dudgeon at her studio microphone that day. She did not question Rogge's motives, she told him, but she did suggest that he had abused the extraordinary powers he had been given as a federal prosecutor to "pry and to examine into the affairs" of American citizens.

"Oh, I wouldn't say pry, Miss Fleeson," Rogge answered. "The Department of Justice, when there are complaints, has the right to investigate and investigations were made. Now then, not only did I have this material, but it was my recommendation to the Department of Justice that the documents should be filed in court, explaining what we had found in the way of Nazi penetration. Explaining that the defendants in the sedition case did have connections with the Nazis. Explaining that legal remedies, because of the full measure of Freedom of Speech which our Supreme Court now gives, which is probably broader than at any time in the history of the Supreme Court, after explaining those things and saying the legal remedies are inadequate, nevertheless making those facts public and saying the people should know these facts. The law is powerless, but nevertheless people should know them."

"Mr. Rogge," Fleeson cut in, "you're making excuses on general principles. Philosophical ideas on which everybody agrees. Everybody wants the public to have information."

Mr. Childs piped up again to provide the guest a little flanking cover, but Rogge waved it off. "I can add this to Miss Fleeson's question. I was told . . ."

"Told by whom?"

"By Attorney General Clark, before I went to Germany, that I could make public any evidence of Nazi penetration that I might find. And why did he change his mind? Because twenty-four congressmen are mentioned in this report that I have prepared. Now do you think that's a sufficient basis to keep these facts from the American public? . . . My conscience wouldn't let me do anything else than make those facts public.

"I have studied fascism both here and abroad for almost four years," Rogge reminded the panelists, "and I think I know something about the fascist pattern." Take Burton K. Wheeler's pronouncement that Roosevelt's foreign policy was sure to "plow under every fourth American boy," Rogge explained. That language appears to have been developed in the Nazi propaganda shop in Berlin *before* Wheeler's national radio speech. "In 1940 the Germans devised a slogan about plowing under American boys," he told the national broadcast audience of *Meet the Press.* "We got this from [the] head of the press department of the German Foreign Office," Rogge explained. "Now Wheeler used very similar language in a radio speech which he made on the *American Forum of the Air* in January 1941."

Rogge was careful not to accuse Burton K. Wheeler of outright and intended collaboration with the Nazis in Germany, of being a witting mouthpiece for Hitler. "For all I know," Rogge said, "they both thought of this unique phrasing independently." But the American people, he believed, should be advised.

Which is why, and how, a man who had been on the fast track to the very top of the Justice Department willingly destroyed his career. What good was a career when your country was at risk, and you had crucial information to impart that could help meet that peril?

By Christmastime in 1946, O. John Rogge was reportedly already nearing completion of a book and looking for a publisher. "The present manuscript, telling in detail all the evidence he unearthed about the Nazi links in America, is over one million words long," wrote one nationally syndicated columnist, who was clearly prone to exaggeration on word count. But Rogge was apparently racing to finish the manuscript, to get it all down while it was fresh. He was bursting to tell what he knew.

And then . . . nothing.

For years. Rogge negotiated with DOJ about what it would allow him to publish, and then with publishers about what they were willing to publish. Fifteen years passed. When Rogge did finally see *The Official German Report* into print in 1961, the country had very much moved on. Nobody bought the book. Few media outlets bothered to review it. One of the few reviewers had this to say: "[Rogge's] practice of presenting the names of the conservatives and isolationists in much the same context as the names of disgraceful racists and Nazis is unpleasantly reminiscent of anti-leftist excesses. Widely varying degrees of pro-Nazi activities are lumped together." What exactly was the cutoff for having a name scrubbed from the public wall of shame, what exactly was an acceptable or forgivable degree of "pro-Nazi activities," the reviewer did not say.

IN THE BATTLES that form the moral foundation of America, it is sometimes painful to contend with the stories of Americans who chose the dark side in those fights. But they have histories, too. And legacies.

And we're not alone in finding this all hard to talk about. In postwar France, the size of the French resistance to the Nazi occupation grew a thousandfold after liberation. Everyone wanted it to be known, after the fact, that of course they had been part of the heroic minority who never gave in, who fought the fascists. So, too, in Germany itself, where it didn't take long after the war before no one would admit to having been a National Socialist true believer, an enthusiast, a willing participant.

Here at home, World War II vibrates with such moral intensity for Americans that it's hard to picture, hard to believe, hard to conceive, that there were Americans—let alone lots of them—who thought not just that we should stay out of the war but that if we did decide to fight, then joining the Axis powers would be the better bet. That happened, though, and that, too, is the history of America's fight against fascism.

It is also part of our history that there were Americans of that era who decided to get in the way of America's own fascist movements and agents. To stop them. By any means at hand. They, too, have histories. And legacies.

At this writing, in 2023, Freedom House reports that almost two-thirds of the world is governed under some form of authoritarian rule, with a smaller but steady proportion of that number under full-blown autocracy. Those international winds blow across our borders as well. And in our time, once again, the story of our democracy bracing against those gales is complex. It's at least complex in the sense that we're not all one mass of Americans, all pulling in the same righteous direction. There are plenty of our fellow citizens fighting on each side of our generation's battle for democracy. And that will be true for the next one, too.

If we're willing to take the harder look at our American history with fascism, the truth is that our own story in this wild, uncertain twenty-first century has not an echo in the past but a prequel. For our turn in history—and for the next time this comes around, too—we have the advantage of knowing that which preceded us.

The story of what it took, inside and outside the government, to stop the violent American ultra-right in the run-up to World War II—that's a gift from the smart, brave, determined, resourceful, self-sacrificing Americans who went before us. If we learn it, and we choose it, we can inherit their work.

EPILOGUE

PHILIP JOHNSON

Philip Johnson fully expected to be indicted alongside his friend Lawrence Dennis and so many of his fascist fellow travelers in the early 1940s. Johnson had for years taken meetings with Nazi officials and had personally funded some of the ugliest ultra-right, violent antisemites in the United States. In his bestselling *Berlin Diary* in 1941, journalist William Shirer had described Johnson as not just a fascist and a Nazi sympathizer but likely a Nazi spy. Given the nature and frequency of Johnson's contacts with officials from Hitler's government at the time, that prospect is not impossible; contemporaneous Office of Naval Intelligence files confirm that Johnson was officially suspected of espionage.

Although Johnson was summoned in May 1942 to appear before the federal grand jury investigating U.S. fascist and Nazi plots inside America, friends in high places appear to have intervened to keep Johnson out of the dock; the secretary of the navy and the supervising architect of the federal Public Buildings Administration were among those who met with Attorney General Francis Biddle—at his home—to discuss Johnson's case.

While the story of Johnson's fascist years was never a secret, exactly, it had a way of sinking out of view for long periods as he ascended into the firmament of America's most celebrated architects. In 1957, as the Museum of Modern Art considered electing Johnson to its board of trustees, Blanchette Rockefeller proclaimed him absolved of any past fascist sins. "Every young man should be allowed to make one large mistake," she said.

When Johnson died at age ninety-eight, in 2005, the burning question among the cognoscenti in New York was who might inherit Johnson's regular daily lunch spot at the Four Seasons restaurant (table thirty-two, Grill Room) in the Seagram Building. Johnson had designed both the restaurant and the building. "It was his place," another renowned architect and sometime dining companion explained to a reporter. "He knew everybody there and he always had the best seat in the room." Johnson's history with antisemitic, Nazi-friendly fascism landed in the sixth paragraph of the obituary that ran in *The New York Times,* described blandly as a "bizarre and, he later conceded, deeply mistaken detour into right-wing politics."

LINCOLN KIRSTEIN

Lincoln Kirstein served honorably—and memorably—in World War II as part of the Allies' Monuments, Fine Arts, and Archives unit, which found and retrieved important works of European art looted by the Nazis. (In the 2014 film *The Monuments Men,* Bob Balaban's character, Preston Savitz, is modeled on Kirstein.)

In early 1944, while he was still in the army and his old friend Philip Johnson was facing possible indictment for sedition, Kirstein wrote a letter vouching that Johnson had surely grown out of his fascist phase: "I am a United States Citizen. . . . I am of Jewish origin. . . . In his most rabidly facist [*sic*] days, [Johnson] told me that I was number one on his list for elimination in the coming revolution. Since being in the Army, I have seen Pvt Johnson frequently. . . . I am convinced that he has sincerely repented of his former facist beliefs, that he understands the nature of his mistake and is a loyal American."

That very generous apologia from Kirstein predated by several decades any statement of contrition from Johnson himself.

In New York after the war, Kirstein founded the New York City Ballet with George Balanchine. He was awarded the Presidential Medal of Freedom by President Ronald Reagan in 1984.

JOHN C. METCALFE

After infiltrating U.S.-based Nazi groups for the *Chicago Times,* John C. Metcalfe spent a year in Washington leading investigations of Nazi and fascist groups for the Dies Committee. Returning to journalism during World War II, he served as a war correspondent and foreign correspondent for the *New York Herald Tribune, Time* magazine, and other publications. In 1946, he was named an honorary citizen of Norway in recognition of his coverage of Norwegians' fight against Nazism.

LEON TURROU

Leon Turrou's work on the Warner Bros. blockbuster movie *Confessions of a Nazi Spy* and his bestselling book *Nazi Spies in America* raised his profile to become perhaps America's most widely admired G-man. It also earned him the lifelong enmity of FBI chief J. Edgar Hoover. Despite Hoover's efforts to blackball Turrou from any form of government service, Turrou in 1943 lied about his age to enlist in the army, where he was able to secure a position with the military police. After the war, the famed investigator ended up in charge of the Central Registry of War Criminals and Security Suspects, which hunted down Nazi war criminals worldwide. CROWCASS was headquartered in Paris, and Turrou lived the rest of his life in France, dying there in 1986 at the age of ninety-one.

LAWRENCE DENNIS

After the sedition case ended in mistrial in 1944, Lawrence Dennis remained a quasi-intellectual figure of the American ultra-right, writing contrarian essays on American foreign policy right to the end. The mystery that Anne Morrow Lindbergh had noted—"that curious downward pout of the mouth that is almost like the terrible mouths of the Greek masks for tragedy. He has suffered, this man, been badly hurt"—had by then been solved by a few who knew him best. The answer to that mystery puts a very strange cast on Dennis's advice to his Nazi friends back in Nuremberg in 1936: "Why don't you treat the Jews more or less as we treat the Negroes in America?"

Turns out America's best-known fascist intellectual had been born Lonnie Lawrence Dennis, son of a white man and a Black woman who were not married. He was never acknowledged by his birth father, and his birth mother had given young Lonnie to his aunt and uncle (both Black) to raise. Lonnie Lawrence enjoyed a brief celebrity, before he reached double digits in age, as a boy preacher—first on the circuit of Black churches in America and then in Europe. When Dennis turned twenty, he later said, "I decided I had to go to college, so I sort of broke with my mother and I applied to go to Exeter."

Light-skinned enough to pass, Dennis renounced his family—his mother and his aunt and uncle who had raised him—and never looked back.

When Dennis's first wife divorced him in the 1950s, he lamented to a friend that he couldn't understand her pique; the women he'd had affairs with, he explained, had always quite liked him: "What jolts me is that over sixty-two years in which I had lots of affairs and nearly a dozen women one time or another who seriously wanted to marry, I never had a single one turn on me. . . . This is the first time a woman ever turned on me. The only logical motivation must be spite. But why?" Why, indeed. After his second wife died, Dennis moved in with one of his daughters in New York. His biographer, Gerald Horne, writes, "In a final act of definition, perhaps rebellion, he finally allowed his hair to grow, taking on the newly popular hairdo—an 'Afro.' " Dennis was eighty-three years old when he died in 1977.

FATHER CHARLES COUGHLIN

Father Charles Edward Coughlin remained in the pulpit of the Church of the Little Flower in Michigan until 1966, but his star had dimmed greatly. After the death of the bishop who had acted as his professional heat shield, the Catholic Church finally forced Coughlin to give up his national radio show in the early innings of World War II. The federal government also banned his *Social Justice* magazine from the mails.

By then, however, the yield from all his years of public appeals to support the Coughlin parish, the Coughlin publication, and the Coughlin cause had somehow accrued personally to Coughlin. By 1942, investigators discovered that he had amassed a nice little nest egg (worth more than $15 million today), which he had stuffed in a secret overseas bank account. This nest egg allowed for a second career as an intrepid and successful real estate speculator; he maintained homes in multiple states. When he died in 1979, Father Coughlin was no longer a man of influence. He was no longer even really a public figure. But he did die rich. And unapologetic. The Associated Press described Coughlin in 1962 as a man still "insisting he was right in his caustic denunciation of President Franklin D. Roosevelt in the days during the rise of Hitler." In an interview he granted on his seventy-seventh birthday, in 1968, Coughlin told a reporter that he "couldn't honestly take back much of what I said in the old days when people still listened to me."

JOHN F. CASSIDY

John F. Cassidy, the onetime "Little Führer" of Father Coughlin's Christian Front, popped up in the news at the end of May 1995. Fifty-five years after his national-headline-blaring trial, Cassidy claimed that he and the Country Gentlemen had only been arming themselves back in 1940 for the same reason that every American should have been: to fight off the imminent communist revolution.

The New York Times 1995 profile of Cassidy ("Jack to his friends and followers") ran on the occasion of his finally receiving his law license from the State of New York. After his 1940 acquittal on sedition charges, Cassidy succeeded in getting his guns back from the court, but a state board would not permit him to practice law. He gave up trying for the license after a failed appeal of the ruling in 1947. "Brokenhearted, he retired from political activism," the Times wrote of Cassidy—you could almost hear the sad violin playing in the background. "[He] made a modest career as a field accountant for construction projects, and became involved in his Brooklyn parish."

But in 1995, with the help of friends and followers, Cassidy finally won acceptance to the New York bar. He had no intention of hanging out his legal shingle; he was eighty-four years old, with failing eyesight, the *Times* noted, but "it restores his reputation, he says."

The 1995 profile of Cassidy was published at one of those moments when something other than hope rhymes with history. Timothy McVeigh had just demolished a federal office building in Oklahoma City with a seven-thousand-pound fertilizer bomb, killing 167 people, including 15 children in the second-floor daycare center. There were false conspiracy theories circulating (stoked by the ultra-right) that militant Muslims in America were responsible, even though McVeigh was already in custody and the evidence against him was overwhelming. The twenty-six-year-old former tank gunner in the U.S. Army was a weapons-crazed, white supremacist, neo-Nazi, right-wing militia member who believed this murder of innocents was a righteous attack on the federal government. He hoped it would set off an apocalyptic race war.

Busy "restoring his reputation," John F. Cassidy refused in his *New York Times* interview to condemn McVeigh, or any of the latest generation of right-wing militias. "I don't think they are a threat to the country that the Communists were," he told the *Times* reporter. "You don't know who blew up the Federal building in Oklahoma City yet. I wish I were a defense lawyer."

GEORGE DEATHERAGE

When the Nazis brought George Deatherage to Erfurt, Germany, to attend the "World Conference of Antisemites" in 1938, he became a mentor to Emory Burke, another young American fascist who was also invited to attend. In the immediate postwar period, Deatherage's mentee founded America's earliest neo-Nazi party, the Columbians. The Columbians aimed to deport all Jews and all Black people from the United States; until that could be done, they contented themselves with dynamiting the homes of Black families and beating up Black men in the streets of Atlanta.

Deatherage himself contributed to the early founding discussions for the Liberty Lobby, a far-right, antisemitic Washington-based lobbying group that exercised surprising sway over the elected American right for decades, while also shilling Holocaust denial on the side. Deatherage died in 1965 at age seventy-one.

WILLIAM DUDLEY PELLEY

William Pelley's Silver Shirts organization was packed away by 1941, and he avoided conviction with the other Great Sedition Trial defendants thanks to the mistrial in 1944. Separately, however, Pelley was convicted of sedition and treason on his own, and he faced repeated legal sanctions for a creative fraud scheme in which he sold fake "stock" in his Silver Legion and then pocketed the proceeds. Pelley spent all of World War II behind bars and remained jailed until 1950.

Upon his release from prison, he retreated to his pseudo-spiritual "I've seen heaven" grift, in later years adding new twists involving UFOs and extraterrestrials. In the years since his death in 1965, Pelley's writings—both the fascist, antisemitic ones and the ones about the afterlife and aliens—have enjoyed fairly robust circulation, particularly on the conspiratorial far right.

For a flavor, consider Pelley's florid introduction to a book-length violently antisemitic screed published by his fellow sedition trial defendant Ernest F. Elmhurst: "Jews, murderers and liars—and the sons of murderers and liars . . . no price is too great to pay personally, to see this pestilence of Jewry forever exterminated from a Christian United States!" To this day, you can purchase this publication (and many others by Pelley) at Amazon and other fine retailers.

GEORGE VAN HORN MOSELEY

General George Van Horn Moseley lived out his life in high style in a fancy hotel in downtown Atlanta, thanks to his army pension and his wife's inheritance. After his semi-voluntary retreat from public life, Moseley's name still occasionally found its way back into the news. He made multiple appeals to the Georgia Parole Board on behalf of neo-Nazis, including Emory Burke, the Deatherage mentee who had been convicted for, among other things, illegal possession of dynamite. Moseley supported a convicted Nazi war criminal for the chancellorship of Germany. He chaired the Texas Education Association, an anti-Jewish group that offered monthly grants and endowments to schools that agreed to restrict their enrollees to white Christians. In 1949, the disgraced general continued to warn of the Jewish plot that Bernard Baruch and Justice Felix Frankfurter and their friends at the Harmonie Club were (still?) hatching. Moseley also made the occasional suggestion on fighting crime in America, urging "the horse-whipping of juvenile delinquents at Five Points, Atlanta's busiest intersection."

When Moseley died in November 1960, the day before the election of John F. Kennedy, his passing went largely uncovered by the mainstream press. Although he had served at the very highest levels of the military—he had at one point been a serious contender for army chief of staff—his few obituaries simply referred to him as a white supremacist and an antisemite. His last known publication was an article titled "Let's Rescue Uncle Sam" submitted to a far-right racist newsletter in August 1960. It argued for white racial solidarity against the threat of Black Americans' rising political power.

ELIZABETH DILLING

Elizabeth Dilling resumed her antisemitic organizing while World War II raged and then became a leading voice of the ultra-right's bold new invention—Holocaust denialism. She claimed that President Eisenhower was a secret Jew ("Ike the Kike," she called him) and that his successor, President John F. Kennedy, was pushing the "Jew Frontier." She opposed Barry Goldwater's 1964 run for president because he chose as his running mate a man who had prosecuted Nazi war criminals at Nuremberg.

Bizarrely, at the beginning of the Tea Party movement in 2010, then Fox News host Glenn Beck tried to revive interest in Elizabeth Dilling, enthusiastically promoting her books on his highly rated cable news programs and radio show. Dilling, he said, had been "doing what we're doing now."

NORMA LUNDEEN

In the wake of Senator Ernest Lundeen's death, his widow, Norma, briefly and unsuccessfully ran for Congress herself. If she had expected to ride her dead husband's coattails into that job, there were two fundamental problems with the plan. First, her husband was barely cold before he was exposed for his knowing, well-compensated role in a Nazi propaganda plot. And second, his aggrieved staff—who told federal investigators about the plot—weren't going to let her forget it. At Viereck's trial, Norma testified that she had been warned off by her husband's chief aide, who threatened to "run her out of the state" if she tried to follow her husband into Congress.

Unfazed, Mrs. Lundeen found another way to stay in Washington. She married another U.S. senator, this one from Oregon, a high-ranking Ku Klux Klansman.

Norma went on to give speeches at racist rallies organized by Gerald L. K. Smith, the protégé of Huey Long's who had eulogized Long at his funeral back in 1936. Smith preached something he called Christian Nationalism—a segregationist, white supremacist doctrine—and joined Elizabeth Dilling as a pioneer of American Holocaust denial. Smith ran for president in 1944 on the America First Party ticket, which called for the sterilization and deportation of all American Jews.

WILLIAM LANGER

Among the U.S. Senate's wingmen for the Nazi agent Viereck and the sedition trial defendants, William "Wild Bill" Langer was the only senator to survive the scandal politically. Star journalist Allen Drury used the erratic and cantankerous Langer in his 1963 book, *A Senate Journal,* to illustrate the Senate's unsettling capacity for growing and empowering mean old weirdos. "Langer's filibuster collapsed this afternoon. . . . If his ideas have any value, no one will ever know it, for he presents them at the top of his lungs like a roaring bull in the empty chamber, while such of his colleagues as remain watch him in half-amused, half-fearful silence, as though in the presence of an irresponsible force they can neither control nor understand."

After assailing the sedition trial and championing the idea of paying U.S. government reparations to Viereck, Langer proposed legislation to encourage self-deportation of all Black Americans to Africa. It was taken up as a rallying cry by the National States' Rights Party—another early neo-Nazi group, whose members were put on trial for allegedly bombing an Atlanta synagogue in the 1950s. Senator Langer also assailed the postwar military tribunals in Germany, including those at Nuremberg. He agitated—successfully—for the United States to grant clemency for at least one convicted senior Nazi war criminal. Langer died in office in 1959 at the age of seventy-three.

HAMILTON FISH

Hamilton Fish had a long and contented life after he lost his congressional seat. He liked to boast that the Fish family—whose run in political office proceeded uninterrupted from 1843 to 1995—was as notable as the Adams family, only the Fishes had more money. "We are indeed unique," he said of his family in the late 1970s.

At the time of his death, in 1991, at the age of 102, his progeny were still trying to buff up Ham's marred reputation. He accepted that ride in the Nazi plane back in 1939, Fish's eldest son explained, only because his long discussions with the German foreign minister had put his father so far behind schedule that it would have been impossible for him to get to the Oslo "peace conference" on time any other way.

Although Fish never claimed any regrets about his interactions with the Nazi government and his involvement with Nazi propaganda efforts in America, he did hint in an interview on his hundredth birthday that his Keep America Out of Foreign Wars effort might have been less driven by any particular ideology than by personal animus. Mostly, he suggested, it was his beef with a single, notable constituent in his congressional district, President Franklin Roosevelt. "I know he hated me," Fish said in 1988, "but I really don't believe in hate. So now I don't hate Roosevelt—but frankly I despise him."

In 2023, trustees of the locally beloved Desmond-Fish Public

Library, endowed by Fish and his third wife in Garrison, New York, began considering the possibility of changing its name.

CLARE HOFFMAN

Congressman Clare Hoffman of Michigan, summoned to testify four times before the federal grand jury investigating Nazi propaganda operations in the United States, was also a rare political survivor of the scandal. He gave speeches for Gerald L. K. Smith's America First Party, with its platform to deport and sterilize American Jews, and promoted Elizabeth Dilling's antisemitic literature. He described the precise (and secret) location of the government's bomb shelter for President Roosevelt and White House staff, and had it printed in the *Congressional Record*. In the U.S. House after World War II, Hoffman was vociferously opposed to civil rights legislation of all kinds. Having refused to sign up for Medicare as "socialized medicine," Hoffman died of pneumonia in 1967, at the age of ninety-two.

GEORGE SYLVESTER VIERECK

George Sylvester Viereck—the Nazi agent—was convicted in his retrial, in July 1943, for violating the Foreign Agents Registration Act. The conviction held up on appeal this time, and he was jailed from 1943 until 1947. Viereck's eldest son and namesake, George Sylvester Viereck Jr., did not live to see his father's release; he was killed in battle in Italy in 1944, fighting heroically against the Nazis as a U.S. Army corporal, while his father sat in jail for his service to the Nazi cause.

By the time he got out on parole, Viereck Sr.'s wife had left him and sold all his earthly possessions, donating the proceeds to Jewish and Catholic refugee groups. Viereck moved in with his younger son, Peter, an accomplished professor and poet at Mount Holyoke College in South Hadley, Massachusetts. In declassified FBI files, Viereck was revealed to have been advising the National Renaissance Party, another early neo-Nazi party in the United States, before his death. Viereck died of a cerebral hemorrhage in 1962, at age seventy-seven.

HENRY FORD

With circulation in the hundreds of thousands and the additional unique distribution channel of Ford dealerships around the country, Henry Ford's *Dearborn Independent* amounted to a mechanized, mass-production antisemitic propaganda engine in early twentieth-century America. His real innovative leap, though, came when he chose to not copyright *The International Jew,* the four-volume collection of antisemitic essays and commentary that had first run in his paper. Those volumes have been translated into more than a dozen languages and remain in the public domain and widely available today. As the centennial of his purchase of the *Dearborn Independent* approached in 2019, an article in a municipally supported local history magazine explored the long-standing influence of Ford's antisemitic writings and his continuing status as a validator and inspiration for ultra-right and neo-Nazi movements. Dearborn's mayor responded by ordering the destruction of that issue of the magazine and then the firing of the journalist who wrote it. The fearless alternative news site *Deadline Detroit* published it anyway.

WILLIAM POWER MALONEY

William Power Maloney retired from the federal government in 1946 and went on to a long, colorful career as a criminal defense attorney. He retained his talent for inducing screaming fits from both adversaries and judges. "Still a lawyer and still exuberant," one newspaperman described Maloney in 1964, in a story about the rumor that one of Maloney's clients, the mob boss Joseph "Joe Bananas" Bonanno, had been assassinated: "It was Maloney who had described how two men, presumably gangsters, had wrestled Bonanno into a car outside Mr. Maloney's apartment last Oct. 21. Mr. Maloney, a small wiry man, also ducked a shot fired in his own direction, he said."

O. JOHN ROGGE

John Rogge remained a high-profile figure in the late 1940s; he was considered a potential vice presidential running mate for Henry

Wallace on the Progressive Party ticket in 1948. Rogge helped lead the defense in the notorious "Trenton Six" civil rights case, in which a group of African American men were convicted of murder by an all-white jury. Rogge also pleaded (unsuccessfully) with the U.S. Senate to vote down the Supreme Court nomination of Tom Clark, the attorney general who had fired him upon his return from Germany with evidence of Nazi penetration of the U.S. Congress.

Rogge criticized Red-baiting by the later iterations of the House Un-American Activities Committee, and he railed publicly against the Truman administration's loyalty oath. He was denounced as a communist by his opponents on the political right, and then, for what it's worth, he was denounced *by* the communists with equal fervor.

At the spying trial of Ethel and Julius Rosenberg, Rogge represented Ethel's brother, who dropped the dime on his sister and brother-in-law in exchange for lenience for himself and his wife. In the 1990s, Rogge's client would recant his testimony about his sister Ethel, by which point of course it was far, far too late.

Rogge's book on his findings in Germany, *The Official German Report*, was a bust when it was published in 1961. He disappeared as a public figure by the mid-1960s and died in relative obscurity in 1981. His obituary was headlined "O. John Rogge, Age 77, Anti-Nazi Activist."

DILLARD STOKES

Dillard Stokes, the *Washington Post* reporter who dug and dug and faced down threats, harassment, and lawsuits to get the story of George Sylvester Viereck's Nazi propaganda operation (and his accomplices) inside the U.S. Congress, won one of the most prestigious awards in newspaper journalism for his efforts back in 1942. The rest of his life's work was in the quiet service of American democracy and American institutions. Stokes was the president of the Washington Newspaper Guild and a military intelligence officer in World War II and then won plaudits covering the judiciary (one Supreme Court justice called him "one of the best men covering the court"). He wrote an early book on the Social Security system; served as a lawyer for the AFL-CIO's political action committee; moved to Iowa, where he won more awards for his reporting; and then served as the assistant attorney general of the state. He died in Alexandria, Virginia, in 1980. "An award-winning journalist," was the underwhelming lede in *The Washington Post,* "who covered congressional investigations and the U.S. Supreme Court." He deserved better.

HENRY HOKE

Henry Hoke's 1970 obituary was of the same ilk. He was "a leader in direct mail advertising for many years," was the lede in *The New York Times,* who "founded and published . . . [a] monthly trade magazine." There was no mention of Hoke's remarkable public campaign to uncover the Nazi propaganda operation in America and no mention of the threats to himself and his family that this ordinary citizen was willing to endure to do this important work. The Hoke legacy lives on today, of all places, in the awards programs of a direct-marketing trade organization.

LEON LEWIS

Leon Lewis was also a forgotten man at the time of his death, at age sixty-five, less than ten years after the end of World War II. His passing was not national news, a chance to recall the extraordinary things he had done to safeguard American democracy. Even the death notice in the *Los Angeles Times,* his hometown newspaper, was thin, announcing the cause of death ("a heart attack Thursday night while driving to his home") and the time and place of the funeral services two days hence. The few paragraphs summing up his life neglected to mention his grueling, thankless, and ultimately successful decade-long enterprise to reveal and destroy the most dangerous agents of Hitler-inspired fascism in America. But he did do that, and it's not too late to shout it to the rooftops. Lewis's contemporaneous reports from his spy operation, preserved at California State University, Northridge, now offer historians a window into one man's remarkable, daring, harrowing contribution to the task, and the honor, of repairing the world: *tikkun olam.*

ACKNOWLEDGMENTS

This book would not exist without Mark Zwonitzer, with whom I am always and forever in joyful cahoots. Mr. Mark, you are a prince among men (and also you would never use a cliché like that).

Great thanks to my wonderful colleagues and co-creators, Mike Yarvitz and Kelsey Desiderio, with whom I embarked on the podcast *Rachel Maddow Presents: Ultra;* the research for *Ultra* led me to this book and beyond. Thank you to Janmaris Perez, Will Femia, Laura Conaway, Cory Gnazzo, Bryson Barnes, Tarek Fouda, Holly Klopchin, and Eva Ruth Moravec. Thank you to Rashida Jones, Cesar Conde, and Phil Griffin.

Deep thanks to historians and researchers Steven J. Ross, Bradley W. Hart, Charles R. Gallagher, Nancy Beck Young, and John Flannery.

Thank you to Jack Bohrer for your perfectly timed and very urgent trek west!

Thank you to beloved friend Jill McDonough for turning me on to Woody Guthrie's "Mister Charlie Lindbergh."

Thanks to Laurie Liss, Gillian Blake (and her secret alter ego), and David Drake.

Thank you to the kind, patient, highly skilled staff at the Library of Congress, the National Archives, the University of Iowa, Stanford University, and the Harry S. Truman Presidential Library, and to archivists and librarians everywhere who marshal history for our contemporary benefit by preserving, storing, and indexing the often ephemeral texts and audio recordings that hold these stories.

Librarians and archivists and teachers are the Fort Knox of memory, history, and truth. We must defend them with everything we've got.

NOTES

PROLOGUE

xvii   "Wilde is splendid" David J. Skal, *Something in the Blood: The Untold Story of Bram Stoker, the Man Who Wrote "Dracula"* (New York: Liveright, 2016), 393–94.

xviii   "A tremendous force trembled" George Sylvester Viereck, *The House of the Vampire* (New York: Moffat, Yard, 1912), 183–84.

xviii   "absorbing from life" Ibid., 23.

xviii   "In every age there have been" Skal, *Something in the Blood,* 398.

xviii   "The style of the book" Ibid., 399.

xviii   Viereck had been born in Munich For background on Viereck and his family, see Phyllis Keller, *States of Belonging: German-American Intellectuals and the First World War* (Cambridge, Mass.: Harvard University Press, 1979); Niel M. Johnson, *George Sylvester Viereck: German-American Propagandist* (Urbana: University of Illinois Press, 1972).

xix   "the most widely discussed" Keller, *States of Belonging,* 132.

xx   "The facts absolutely justify" Johnson, *George Sylvester Viereck,* 34.

xxi   how much Roosevelt enjoyed Roosevelt to Viereck, March 15, 1915, Theodore Roosevelt Center Digital Archives.

xxi   "To me the men to whom I have talked" George Sylvester Viereck, *Glimpses of the Great* (London: Duckworth, 1930), 10.

xxii   "In view of your years-long manly struggle" Johnson, *George Sylvester Viereck,* 123.

xxii   Viereck's own son remembered Tom Reiss, *The Orientalist: In Search of a Man Caught Between East and West* (New York: Random House, 2006), 289.

xxii   "We refused in the end" Viereck, *Glimpses of the Great,* 43–44.

xxiii   "80 percent clever" Johnson, *George Sylvester Viereck,* 147.

xxiii   "You have sought, year after year" Viereck, *Glimpses of the Great,* 34.

xxiii **When Viereck met him** George Sylvester Viereck, "Hitler the German Explosive," *American Monthly,* Oct. 1923.

xxiv **Viereck recycled his interview** George Sylvester Viereck, "When I Take Charge," *Liberty,* July 9, 1932.

xxv **"magnetic blue eyes"** O. John Rogge, *The Official German Report* (New York: Thomas Yoseloff, 1961), 150.

xxv **The führer's portrait now held pride of place** Dillard Stokes, "Hill Testifies Fish Ordered Him to Mail Out Nazi Propaganda," *Washington Post,* Feb. 20, 1942.

xxv **"There must be a great crop of oysters"** Rogge, *Official German Report,* 150.

xxv **"Propaganda helped us to power"** Ibid., 42.

xxv **"Our strategy is to destroy"** Ibid., 75.

xxvi **"We were pikers"** George Sylvester Viereck, *Spreading Germs of Hate* (London: Duckworth, 1931), 24.

xxvi **"If the German Government had provided"** Ibid., 72–73.

xxvi **"America for Americans"** Rogge, *Official German Report,* 157.

xxvi **According to records discovered** Ibid., 61.

xxvi **the embassy vault still held** Ibid., 88–89.

xxvi **"The more I study the record"** Ibid., 146–47.

xxvii **Nazi shortwave radio stations** Ibid., 305–6.

xxvii **facilitated by a cadre of American troops** O. John Rogge, "Fight Against Fascism," *PM,* Oct. 29, 1946.

CHAPTER ONE: THE GLASS HOUSE

3 **The young man had been a lonely outsider** The best general background on Johnson is from Mark Lamster, *The Man in the Glass House: Philip Johnson, Architect of the Modern Century* (New York: Little, Brown, 2018); Franz Schulze, *Philip Johnson: Life and Work* (New York: Knopf, 1994); Marc Wortman, *1941: Fighting the Shadow War* (New York: Atlantic Monthly Press, 2016); Philip Johnson FBI file, digital copy accessed at archive.org.

4 **He covered any suspicions** Martin Duberman, *The Worlds of Lincoln Kirstein* (New York: Knopf, 2007), e-book, 85.

4 **"all those blond boys in black leather"** Schulze, *Philip Johnson,* e-book, 90.

4 **Hitler came to the stage** "Hitler Addresses Huge Youth Rally," *New York Times,* Oct. 2, 1932.

4 **"You simply could not fail"** Schulze, *Philip Johnson,* 89.

5 **"pulsating with new ideas"** Calvin Tomkins, "Forms Under Light," *New Yorker,* May 23, 1977.

6 **On warm summer nights** For Johnson and Jimmie Daniels, see Charles Kaiser, *The Gay Metropolis: The Landmark History of Gay Life in Amer-

ica (New York: Grove Press, 2007), e-book, 41. For Miss Merrill's and other descriptions of Johnson, see Johnson FBI file, 118–19; and Duberman, *Worlds of Lincoln Kirstein*, 85, 157.

7 **"[He] just has a lot of money"** Johnson FBI file, 56.

7 **"only real passion"** Duberman, *Worlds of Lincoln Kirstein*, 193.

8 **Frankfurter spent the 1933–34** Brad Snyder, *Democratic Justice: Felix Frankfurter, the Supreme Court, and the Making of the Liberal Establishment* (New York: W. W. Norton, 2022), e-book, 163–64.

8 **a wealthy socialite was in her cups** Duberman, *Worlds of Lincoln Kirstein*, 232–33.

9 **"I ask no sympathy"** Robert Nedelkoff, "Remainder Table: Jack B. Tenney and Lawrence Dennis," *Baffler*, Dec. 1999.

10 **"Smarter than Hitler"** For Dennis quotations on Huey Long, see Gerald Horne, *The Color of Fascism: Lawrence Dennis, Racial Passing, and the Rise of Right-Wing Extremism in the United States* (New York: New York University Press, 2006), e-book, 51, 65.

CHAPTER TWO: "COME TO MY FEAST"

12 **There were only maybe twenty thousand** James M. Gregory, "Communist Party Membership by Districts 1922–1950," Mapping American Social Movements Project, University of Washington, 2015.

14 **"None shall be too rich"** For anybody interested in these and the other quotations from Long's speeches, including his barbecue speech, there are plenty available on YouTube for the searching.

15 **Long's Share Our Wealth Society counted** Robert E. Snyder, "Huey Long and the Presidential Election of 1936," *Louisiana History: The Journal of the Louisiana Historical Association* 16, no. 2 (1975): 123.

16 **twenty-five hundred miles of new paved roads** The historian T. Harry Williams lays out the statistics in his 1964 introduction to later editions of Long's 1933 autobiography. See *Every Man a King: The Autobiography of Huey P. Long* (1933; repr. New York: Da Capo Press, 1996).

17 **"I am the Constitution"** "That Meteor of the South, the Louisiana Kingfish," *New York Times*, April 16, 1933; "Democrats: Incredible Kingfish," *Time*, Oct. 3, 1932.

17 **"It takes a man like Long to lead"** Arthur M. Schlesinger Jr., *The Age of Roosevelt: The Politics of Upheaval* (Boston: Houghton Mifflin, 1960), 77.

17 **"the skull crushers"** Associated Press, "Huge Cash Gifts to Long Charged," *Washington Evening Star*, Feb. 16, 1933.

17 **"A perfect democracy can come close"** T. Harry Williams, *Huey Long: A Biography* (New York: Knopf, 1970), 762.

17 **"Control of a state government"** Horne, *Color of Fascism*, 65–66.

18 **Lincoln Kirstein had started warning** Duberman, *Worlds of Lincoln Kirstein*, 233.

18 "when the revolution comes" Johnson FBI file, 2, 66.

18 "Johnson felt the fate of this country" Ibid., 119.

18 Philip Johnson and Alan Blackburn summoned The entirety of the *New York Herald Tribune* story from Dec. 18, 1934, "Two Quit Modern Art Museum for Sur-Realist Political Venture," is transcribed in the Johnson FBI file, 119–22.

19 Kirstein, for one, was not unhappy Duberman, *Worlds of Lincoln Kirstein,* 272.

20 Johnson's nastiest remark Kaiser, *Gay Metropolis,* 42–43.

CHAPTER THREE: *UMWEGE*

21 "Awful it may be to contemplate" James Q. Whitman, *Hitler's American Model: The United States and the Making of Nazi Race Law* (Princeton, N.J.: Princeton University Press, 2017), e-book, 4–5.

22 "Hitler Learns from America" Sarah Churchwell, "American Fascism: It Has Happened Here," *New York Review of Books,* June 22, 2020.

22 "Fascists is Jim Crow peoples" Langston Hughes, "Love Letter from Spain," quoted in full in *The Daily People's World Magazine,* Jan. 22, 1938, sect. 2, 8.

22 When young Heinrich Krieger was sent Whitman, *Hitler's American Model,* 113; Michael Adkison, "The University of Arkansas's Hidden History of Helping Nazis," *Facing South,* April 30, 2021.

22 "From the United States and Australia" Theodore Roosevelt, review of *National Life and Character, a Forecast,* by Charles M. Pearson, *Sewanee Review,* May 1894.

23 "but a few degrees less meaningless" Theodore Roosevelt, *The Winning of the West* (New York: G. P. Putnam's Sons, 1894), 3:44.

23 "gunned down the millions" Whitman, *Hitler's American Model,* 9.

23 Roosevelt was still in full cry For Roosevelt's "race suicide" and the "war of the cradle," see Nell Painter, *The History of White People* (New York: W. W. Norton, 2010).

23 "The two races, equally free" Extract from Jefferson's draft autobiography, Feb. 8, 1821, accessed at Thomas Jefferson Monticello digital library.

24 "the vicious, the weak of body" Calvin Coolidge, "Whose Country Is This?," *Good Housekeeping,* Feb. 1921.

24 The architect of Coolidge's 1924 immigration Russ Bellant, *Old Nazis, the New Right, and the Republican Party* (Boston: South End Press, 1991), 32.

24 "represents a carefully thought-through" Whitman, *Hitler's American Model,* 51–52.

24 *Umwege* For discussion/explanation of *Umwege,* see ibid., 69–70.

25 "artificial line-drawing" Ibid., 119.

25 "alien races" Text of opinion of *Downes v. Bidwell,* accessed at supreme .justia.com/cases/federal/us/182/244/.

25 **"exceedingly motley, almost confusing"** Whitman, *Hitler's American Model*, 41–42.

27 **"The Jews in Germany represent"** Ibid., 98.

28 **"American race legislation certainly"** Ibid., 104.

28 **"can only be achieved"** Ibid., 98.

30 **A crowd of nearly two thousand** For accounts of the SS *Bremen*, the Nazi flag, the protest, and Judge Brodsky, see Whitman, *Hitler's American Model*; "Reds Rip Flag Off Bremen, Throw It into Hudson; 2,000 Battle the Police," *New York Times*, July 27, 1935; "Berlin Is Angered by Ship Riot Here," *New York Times*, July 28, 1935.

30 **"What a beautiful sight it was"** Knute Berger, "Meet the Woman Who Fought Northwest Nazis," *Crosscut*, June 17, 2022.

30 **U.S. Department of State released** "Nazi Protest," *New York Times*, Aug. 4, 1935.

30 **Brodsky went out of his way** "Brodsky Releases 5 in Bremen Riot," *New York Times*, Sept. 7, 1935.

31 **Nazi commissar of justice railed** "Nazi Tells of Protest," *New York Times*, Sept. 15, 1935.

31 **Hull, somehow felt obliged to apologize** "Overseas," *New York Times*, Sept. 15, 1935.

31 **Goebbels, confided to his diary** Whitman, *Hitler's American Model*, 24.

31 **Hitler took time in his own Nuremberg speech** Ibid., 25.

CHAPTER FOUR: "LOUISIANA WAS NOT QUITE READY"

32 **where Huey Long was at almost any time** Hermann B. Deutsch, *The Huey Long Murder Case* (Garden City, N.Y.: Doubleday, 1963), 64.

33 **Long's guards arrested two newspapermen** "Dictatorial Power Given Long over New Orleans," *Washington Times*, Aug. 18, 1934; "Long Is Granted Dictator Power in Wild Session," *Washington Evening Star*, Aug. 18, 1934; Westbrook Pegler, "Fair Enough: The Damage Huey Wrought," *Washington Post*, Sept. 11, 1935.

34 **Trice got it worse six months later** "Long Grins as Guard Beats News Man," *Washington Times*, Feb. 1, 1935; Associated Press, "Huey's Yeggs Beat Up Man," *Brownsville (Tex.) Herald*, Feb. 1, 1935; "Warrant Out for Long Bodyguard," *Hendersonville (N.C.) Times-News*, Feb. 7, 1935.

34 **"We have a Governor"** "Long Called Liar at Hectic Hearing," *Washington Evening Star*, Feb. 17, 1933.

35 **Senator Long was measured and fitted** See case report on the Long assassination: "Final Investigative Report in re: Senator Huey P. Long," State of Louisiana, Department of Public Safety and Corrections, June 5, 1992, 6, 12, 16.

35 **Weiss was Huey's key bagman** "Huge Cash Gifts to Long Charged," *Washington Evening Star*, Feb. 16, 1933; Thomas L. Stokes, "Huey Long—

'Louisiana—I'm It!,'" *Indianapolis Times,* Dec. 4, 1934; "Long's Financ-ing Will Be Probed," *Washington Sunday Star,* Nov. 19, 1933.

35 **When they found out that Long was decamping** Lamster, *Man in the Glass House,* e-book, 143–44.

36 **having just pocketed $350,000** Associated Press, "Wealth of Huey Long Is Variously Estimated," *New York Times,* Sept. 11, 1935.

36 **When Alan Blackburn leaked a story** Lamster, *Man in the Glass House,* 144; "2 Huey Long 'Tutors' Are Unpaid Admirers," *Washington Post,* April 11, 1935; notes from Blackburn's interview with the FBI, Oct. 2, 1941, in the Johnson FBI file, 35–36.

36 **"One of [Senator Long's] people"** Johnson interview in 1991 on the occa-sion of his receiving the Golden Plate Award from the American Academy of Achievement, accessed at achievement.org.

37 **On the morning of September 8, 1935** "Long Orders State to Jail Federal Aides Defying Rule," *Washington Post,* Sept. 9, 1935.

37 **Bulletins in the next day's newspapers** "Surgeons' Bulletins on Long," *New York Times,* Sept. 9, 1935.

37 **The suspected assailant was identified** See talk by the alleged assassin's son, Carl Weiss Jr., Aug. 28, 2010. Accessed at c-span.org.

38 **"All day men and women"** "100,000 Pay Last Tribute to Sen. Long," *Washington Post,* Sept. 13, 1935.

39 **Smith was characterized as "a viper"** Donald Warren, *Radio Priest: Charles Coughlin, the Father of Hate Radio* (New York: Free Press, 1996), 68.

39 **"The ideals which he planted"** "100,000 Pay Last Tribute to Sen. Long."

39 **He had "a streak of deep sincerity"** "Huey P. Long," *Washington Post,* Sept. 11, 1935.

40 **"That Huey built roads"** Pegler, "Fair Enough."

CHAPTER FIVE: "HE HAD A VERY HIGH OPINION OF ME"

41 **The bells began to ring out** For an account (by Team Hitler) of the Nazi conclave in Nuremberg in 1936, see the translation of the official book published by the Nazi Party. Accessed at Professor Randall Bytwerk's ex-cellent German Propaganda Archive at Calvin University.

41 **The city had swelled** Frederick T. Birchall, "Nazi Parley to See Huge Army Display," *New York Times,* Sept. 7, 1936; Frederick T. Birchall, "1,000,000 Gathering for Nazi Congress," *New York Times,* Sept. 8, 1936; Freder-ick T. Birchall, "Welcomed by Streicher," *New York Times,* Sept. 9, 1936.

42 **A fascist-leaning history professor** Horne, *Color of Fascism,* Preface.

42 **Lawrence Dennis's biographical file** For Dennis's background, see ibid.; "Reminiscences of Lawrence Dennis," interviews conducted by William Keylor in 1967, Oral History Research Office, Columbia University. There is also a biographical sketch in the Lawrence Dennis FBI file, in a report dated Oct. 1940.

43 **"We have founded recent American policy"** William Philipp Simms, "U.S.

Policy in Revolutions Is Held Obsolete," *Indianapolis Times,* Dec. 22, 1930.

44 self-identified as a "maverick" "Reminiscences of Lawrence Dennis," 10, 36.

44 whenever Lawrence Dennis came to Washington Ibid., 46.

44 "Until Mr. Dennis arrived on scene" Karl Schriftgiesser, "Must America Go Fascist?," *Washington Post,* Jan. 12, 1936.

45 "I took my isolationism" "Reminiscences of Lawrence Dennis," 18.

45 "He had a very high opinion of me" Ibid., 32–33.

45 "thought very highly of me" Ibid., 33.

45 "had read my latest book" Horne, *Color of Fascism,* 72.

45 "There were no pro-German French" "Reminiscences of Lawrence Dennis," 54.

45 Dennis was shown around by George Kennan Ibid., 55.

46 "I just wanted to be able to say" Ibid., 48.

46 "Leaving now for Nuremberg" Rogge, *Official German Report,* 179.

46 "When this reaches you" Ibid., 176.

47 "the paramount objectives of public policy" Lawrence Dennis, *The Coming of American Fascism* (New York: Harper & Brothers, 1936), 261–62.

47 "Human nature has not changed" Ibid., 100.

47 "Social order requires" Ibid., 7.

47 "For the masses, the school" Ibid., 227.

47 "I'm not very emotional anyway" "Reminiscences of Lawrence Dennis," 65.

48 "He was rather reserved" Anne Morrow Lindbergh, quoted in Horne, *Color of Fascism,* Preface.

48 "We aren't concerned with moral issues" Associated Press, "U.S. Fascist Head Hits 'New Deal,'" *Washington Sunday Star,* March 4, 1934.

48 "What would our opponents have said" "Chief Points of Chancellor Hitler's Proclamation to Nazi Congress at Nuremberg," *New York Times,* Sept. 10, 1936.

49 The totality of Germany's newfound military power Pierre J. Huss, "Hitler Seeks 'Holy Alliance' for Drive Against Reds," *Washington Times,* Sept. 11, 1936.

49 the display of military maneuvers Account and Hitler quotation from "The Wehrmacht on the Zeppelin Field," in the official Nazi report of the Rally of Honor; Frederick T. Birchall, "Hitler Warns Reds Millions of Nazis Are Ready for War," *New York Times,* Sept. 14, 1936.

50 "No other country, not excluding Russia" Birchall, "Hitler Warns Reds Millions of Nazis Are Ready for War."

50 "Last summer I found" Dr. Ewart Edmund Turner, "Jews in the Reich," *Washington Post,* Aug. 28, 1936.

51 "These young Nazi elite guards" Horne, *Color of Fascism,* 74.

51 **"Hitler was able to exploit"** Lawrence Dennis, *The Dynamics of War and Revolution* (New York: Weekly Foreign Letter, 1940), xxx.

51 **"They didn't try to propagandize"** "Reminiscences of Lawrence Dennis," 59–60.

51 **Dennis suggested that the Nazis' treatment** Rogge, *Official German Report,* 177; also Horne, *Color of Fascism,* 66; and "Reminiscences of Lawrence Dennis," 57.

52 **"The strongest thing they said to me"** "Reminiscences of Lawrence Dennis," 57.

CHAPTER SIX: BULLET HOLES

53 **When Philip Johnson strolled into** For the story of Johnson's visit to the Keck office, see Betty Blum, "Interview with Robert Bruce Tague," Chicago Architects Oral History Project, Art Institute of Chicago, 1995, 14–15.

54 **Coughlin had been one of Long's spurs** Michael Connolly, "Splitting the Vote in Massachusetts: Father Charles E. Coughlin, the Union Party, and Political Divisions in the 1936 Presidential and Senate Elections," *Historical Journal of Massachusetts* 43, no. 2 (Summer 2015).

55 **"discourse on Increased Wealth"** From a 1934 pamphlet titled "Share Our Wealth: Every Man a King," 27.

55 **on the day Long was shot** Warren, *Radio Priest,* 68; "Coughlin Is Guest of the President," *New York Times,* Sept. 12, 1935.

55 **"seemed the most dynamic populist"** Warren, *Radio Priest,* 76.

55 **"betrayer" and a "liar"** F. Raymond Daniel, "Coughlin Wins Townsend and Long Group to Lemke," *New York Times,* July 17, 1936.

55 **"Fred Keck was a good Democrat"** Blum, "Interview with Robert Bruce Tague," 15.

56 **"taken it upon himself"** Interview with Anson Gear, quoted in Johnson FBI file, 44.

56 **"The police were all pro-Coughlin"** Warren, *Radio Priest,* 76.

56 **The paid attendance** "Coughlin Declares Rome Report a Lie," *New York Times,* Sept. 7, 1936.

58 **Father Coughlin's "voice carried"** Ibid.

59 **"more bullet holes"** Warren, *Radio Priest,* 94.

59 **"Democracy is doomed"** Ibid., 105.

CHAPTER SEVEN: SILVER SHIRTS

60 **In September 1936, though** Eric Sevareid, *Not So Wild a Dream* (New York: Diversion Books, 2017), e-book, 104; Sarah Atwood, " 'This List Not Complete': Minnesota's Jewish Resistance to the Silver Shirt Legion of America, 1936–1940," *Minnesota History* 66, no. 4 (Winter 2018–19): 146.

61 **"Wheat was the sole source"** Sevareid, *Not So Wild a Dream,* 20.

61 **"that [President] Herbert Hoover was a great man"** Ibid., 32.

62 "One of the Silver Shirt leaders" Ibid., 105.

63 "Oh, we've known for a long time" Arnold Sevareid, "Silvershirts Hoard Food in Readiness for Siege Foretold by Pyramids," *Minneapolis Journal,* Sept. 13, 1936.

63 "Hate and fear bind the members" Arnold Sevareid, "New Silver Shirt Clan with Incredible Credo Secretly Organized Here," *Minneapolis Journal,* Sept. 11, 1936.

63 "*Pogrom,* lest there be any among us" Ibid.

64 "Get me a drink, quick!" Sevareid, *Not So Wild a Dream,* 105.

64 "better to ignore the madmen" Ibid., 106.

64 "I spent hair-raising evenings" Ibid., 104.

65 the 717-page dossier A digital copy of the two-part FBI file on Pelley can be accessed at vault.fbi.gov.

65 "a perpetually hungry, shabbily dressed" William Dudley Pelley, *Seven Minutes in Eternity, with Their Aftermath* (New York: Robert Collier, 1929), 17–18.

66 "It made me a lone wolf" Ibid., 21.

66 "A sort of marble-tiled and furnished portico" Ibid., 10.

66 "I had a queer moment of confusion" Ibid., 22.

67 "Suddenly as I turned a page" W. D. Pelley, "First Contact with the Elder Brother," *New Liberator,* Oct. 1930.

67 In Pelley's telling Pelley, *Seven Minutes in Eternity,* 27, 31, 32.

67 Pelley got letters from readers Ibid., 37.

68 "I have in some cases taken down" Ibid., 41–42.

68 he veered off into a discussion Pelley FBI file, pt. 1, 189.

68 "It seems—and I also recall" Ibid., 187–89.

69 "perfected a great national organization" A copy of Pelley's *Silver Legion Ranger* newsletter is in the Pelley FBI file, pt. 1, 122–23.

70 Per Pelley, the Jews had a unified Pelley FBI file, pt. 1, 55–56.

70 After taking the official Silver Shirt "Oath of Consecration" Ibid., 122–23.

71 "Read Hitler's autobiography" Ibid., 432.

71 The whole of the plan From Pelley's Official Silver Shirt Dispatch, in Pelley FBI file, pt. 1, 65.

72 "I have but one criticism" Robert Summerville, "Anti-Jewish Feeling Is Ominous," *Pelley's Weekly,* July 29, 1936, in Pelley FBI file, pt. 1, 97.

72 Pelley thus took the stage Laura B. Rosenzweig, *Hollywood's Spies: The Undercover Surveillance of Nazis in Los Angeles* (New York: New York University Press, 2017), 127–28.

73 "not as I wanted them written" Sevareid, *Not So Wild a Dream,* 106.

73 "The Pyramids of Gizah" Sevareid, "Silvershirts Hoard."

74 "Odd characters, fuming and bridling" Sevareid, *Not So Wild a Dream,* 106–7.

74   **as a Seattle gun dealer explained** Pelley FBI file, pt. 1, 125–27.

75   **application at the U.S. Patent Office** For a copy of James True's patent application, see www.nbcnews.com/msnbc/msnbc-podcast/archives -episode-eight-ncsl1300876.

<h2 style="text-align:center">CHAPTER EIGHT: TIKKUN OLAM</h2>

76   **On Friday, April 22, 1938** For details of the "snowstorm" plot and arrest in San Diego, see Steven J. Ross, *Hitler in Los Angeles: How Jews Foiled Nazi Plots Against Hollywood and America* (New York: Bloomsbury, 2017), 228–30; Rosenzweig, *Hollywood's Spies,* 130–31.

76   **"Always throw the first punch"** Ross, *Hitler in Los Angeles,* 158.

76   **Pelley had just released** The Pelley-authored handbook "One Million Silver-Shirts by 1939" (April 2, 1938) was transcribed by FBI agents in a memo to Director Hoover, April 25, 1939, in the Pelley FBI file, pt. 2, 80–84.

77   **The latest nationally distributed** The *News Bulletin* is reproduced in *Joe Kamp: Peddler of Propaganda and Hero of the Pro-fascists: A Report* (Kansas City, Mo.: Friends of Democracy, 1945), 16. Kamp was the executive editor of *The Awakener.* Lawrence Dennis was an associate editor of the publication. The chairman of Friends of Democracy Inc. was Rex Stout, an antifascist crusader who was famous as the author of the Nero Wolfe detective series.

78   **"It is an oak club"** Rosenzweig, *Hollywood's Spies,* 130–31.

78   **"There are papers in that [briefcase]"** Ibid., 131.

78   **"Auntie," who was reputed** Ross, *Hitler in Los Angeles,* 228; Henry Allen testimony in "Hearings Before a Special Committee on Un-American Activities," House of Representatives, 76th Cong., 1st Sess. (Washington, D.C.: U.S. Government Printing Office, 1939), 6:4141.

79   **"blow the Nazi movement in America"** Ross, *Hitler in Los Angeles,* 20.

79   **"devoted to the Jewish concept"** Ibid., 8.

80   **an official ADL report** Ibid., 9.

80   **"attributes all evil to Jews"** "Ford's Anti-Semitism," interview with the historian Hasia Diner on the *American Experience* series website.

80   **"Jew metal"** Steven Watts, *The People's Tycoon: Henry Ford and the American Century* (New York: Vintage Books, 2005), e-book, 419–20.

80   **"Wherever there's anything wrong"** Ibid., 417.

80   **"I know who caused this war"** Ibid., 419.

81   **"Find an evil to attack"** Bill McGraw, "Henry Ford and the International Jew," *Deadline Detroit,* Dec. 31, 2019.

81   **Madame Paquita de Shishmareff** Watts, *People's Tycoon,* 420; Ross, *Hitler in Los Angeles,* 245.

82   **Every week for nearly two years** Editions of the *Dearborn Independent* are in the digital collection of the Library of Congress: chroniclingamerica .loc.gov/lccn/2013218776/issues/1920/; chroniclingamerica.loc.gov/lccn/201 3218776/issues/1921/.

82 **Ford also saw to the publication** *The International Jew,* 4 vols. (Dearborn, Mich.: Dearborn Publishing Co., 1920–22).

82 **Never mind that the *Protocols* was exposed** Philip Graves, "'Jewish World Plot': An Exposure," *Times* (London), Aug. 16, 1921; Philip Graves, "'Jewish Peril' Exposed," *Times* (London), Aug. 17, 1921; Philip Graves, "The Protocol Forgery," *Times* (London), Aug. 18, 1921.

82 **Ford Motor dealers kept tossing** McGraw, "Henry Ford and the International Jew."

82 **Lewis and friends of the Anti-Defamation League** "The International Jew: 1920s Antisemitism Revived Online," Anti-Defamation League, Jan. 30, 2017, adl.org.

83 **"There is not the slightest ground"** "Taft Flays Story of Zion Protocols," *New York Times,* Dec. 24, 1920.

83 **"Although Jews at various conventions"** Father Charles Coughlin, "From the Tower: 'Protocols of the Wise Men of Zion,'" *Social Justice,* Aug. 1, 1938.

83 **"It is Jews who govern"** Ken Silverstein, "Ford and the Führer," *The Nation,* Jan. 24, 2000.

83 **Hitler had already mulled sending some** Raymond Fendrick, "'Heinrich' Ford Idol of Bavaria Fascisti Chief," *Chicago Tribune,* March 8, 1923.

84 **"I regard Henry Ford"** Annetta Halliday Antona, "Five Minutes with Men in Public Eye: Adolf Hitler, the Man Without a Country," *Detroit News,* Dec. 31, 1931.

84 **"In the spring of 1933"** Interview with Ross, 2022.

86 **Schmidt went out and bought** Ross, *Hitler in Los Angeles,* 40.

86 **"The favorite subject of conversation"** Ibid., 22.

87 **That plan was run by Dietrich Gefken** Rosenzweig, *Hollywood's Spies,* 44–45; Ross, *Hitler in Los Angeles,* 35–36.

87 **"the Armory plans, floor plans"** Ross, *Hitler in Los Angeles,* 36.

88 **"When I opened the box"** Interview with Ross, 2022.

88 **"without the commission of some overt act"** Ross, *Hitler in Los Angeles,* 33.

89 **"Do you not see the 'Protocols of Zion'"** Ibid., 49; Lawrence Bush, "The Anti-Semitic Congressman," *Jewish Currents,* May 2, 2017.

89 **"It is of such a poisonous nature"** Ross, *Hitler in Los Angeles,* 104.

90 **"My [law] practice has been"** Ibid., 73.

90 **"The entire Los Angeles Police Department"** Ibid., 62.

90 **living full-time at the VA hospital** Rosenzweig, *Hollywood's Spies,* 83.

91 **"Busby Berkeley will look good"** Ross, *Hitler in Los Angeles,* 160.

91 **"There are lots of nice oak trees"** Rosenzweig, *Hollywood's Spies,* 99–100.

91 **"The custom will be taken up"** Ross, *Hitler in Los Angeles,* 161.

92 **"McLaglen System of Bayonet Fighting"** Captain Leopold McLaglen, *Bayonet Fighting for War* (London: Harrison and Sons, 1915), 3, 11, 12.

92 **"intelligent, dangerous, and delusional"** Ross, *Hitler in Los Angeles,* 201.

92 **Allen and McLaglen took Hughes's plan** Ibid., 205–7; Rosenzweig, *Hollywood's Spies,* 139–41.

93 **Allen had done prison stints** John L. Spivak, *Secret Armies: The New Technique of Nazi Warfare* (New York: Modern Age Books, 1939).

94 **"This is a hell of a note"** Ross, *Hitler in Los Angeles,* 229.

94 **"a mass of correspondence"** Rosenzweig, *Hollywood's Spies,* 131.

95 **"Leon Lewis was sending information"** Interview with Ross, 2022.

95 **"If your friends want some pea shooters"** "Hearings Before a Special Committee on Un-American Activities," 6:4134–37.

95 **Ms. Fry had recently instructed** Ibid., 4090.

95 **"The American Nationalist Confederation"** George Deatherage FBI file, 317, accessed at archive.org.

96 **claimed offices in Boston, New York** Ibid., 51.

CHAPTER NINE: "PROBABLY TEN TIMES MORE"

97 **"As it brought Germany"** Quoted in Charles R. Gallagher, "Adopting the Swastika: George E. Deatherage and the American Nationalist Confederation, 1937–1942," in *Religion, Ethnonationalism, and Antisemitism in the Era of the Two World Wars,* ed. Kevin Spicer and Rebecca Carter-Chand (Montreal: McGill-Queen's University Press, 2021), 38.

97 **The U.S. Congress had recently** For text of the law, see U.S. Court of Appeals for the District of Columbia majority opinion in *Frend et al. v. United States,* decided Oct. 31, 1938. Accessed at law.justia.com.

98 **The Nazi annexation of Austria** "Chamberlain Held Ready to Join France," *Washington Post,* March 14, 1938.

98 **a Polish teenager, Herschel Grynszpan** Dorothy Thompson, "Dorothy Thompson Urges Boy Who Shot Diplomat Be Spared," *Washington Post,* Nov. 15, 1938.

99 **"Extensive demonstrations"** "Goebbels Calls Halt, Pledges Revenge Law," *Washington Post,* Nov. 11, 1938.

99 **an astounding $400 million** "Kristallnacht," accessed at encyclopedia.ushmm.org.

99 **the area around the German embassy** "Nazi Embassy Picketed by Remote Control," *Washington Post,* Nov. 12, 1938.

100 **"We are all brothers in race and culture"** Rogge, *Official German Report,* 201.

100 **report to Hitler himself** Ibid., 187–88.

101 **Von Killinger had been in the loop** Ross, *Hitler in Los Angeles,* 206; Rogge, *Official German Report,* 195–96.

101 **"I can see no reason"** Michael Sayers and Albert E. Kahn, *Sabotage! The Secret War Against America* (New York: Harper & Brothers, 1942), 250.

102 **Fish kept his date as the main speaker** "German Day Rally Splits with Nazis," *New York Times,* Oct. 3, 1938.

103 **"The German race does not cease"** Rogge, *Official German Report*, 34.

103 **"So shall we today"** Ibid.

104 **Deatherage wasted no time** For specifics of the Deatherage–von Gienanth meeting here and throughout the chapter, see "Hearings Before a Special Committee on Un-American Activities," 5:3530–33; Rogge, *Official German Report*, 197; "Deatherage Sought Advice of Nazi Envoy," *Washington Post*, May 25, 1939; "Deatherage Tells of Reich Rebuffs," *New York Times*, May 25, 1939.

104 **Major General George Van Horn Moseley** "Deatherage Tells of Reich Rebuffs."

104 **Moseley had gone on a tear** "Full Text of Gen. Moseley's Statement," *Washington Post*, Oct. 1, 1938; "Gen. Moseley, Retiring, Warns U.S. Faces 'Danger of Decay,'" *Washington Evening Star*, Sept. 30, 1938.

105 **"made several inflammatory speeches"** Pelley FBI file, pt. 1, 377.

106 **"The [American Nationalist Confederation] must be built"** The letter was introduced as evidence in the House Un-American Activities Committee (the Dies Committee) Hearings in May 1939, quoted in the *Washington Evening Star*, May 21, 1939; Sayers and Kahn, *Sabotage!*, 149.

106 **"It was difficult for me to do much"** Moseley to J. E. Campbell, Dec. 7, 1938, in "Hearings Before a Special Committee on Un-American Activities," 5:3614.

107 **Here's how the rest of that chat went** "Hearings Before a Special Committee on Un-American Activities," 5:3530–33; Rogge, *Official German Report*, 197.

107 **"Remember, today the right to carry arms"** The full text of Moseley's speech in Indianapolis on Dec. 29, 1938, was entered into the record of the Dies Committee hearings. See "Hearings Before a Special Committee on Un-American Activities," 5:3628–33.

109 **"Why is the world so surprised"** The full text of Moseley's speech in Philadelphia on March 28, 1939, was entered into the record of the Dies Committee hearings. See ibid., 3634–39.

109 **"Hail Moseley!"** A digital copy of Robert Edmondson's "Hail Moseley!" pamphlet is available at Temple University library digital collection.

109 **"go around kicking people"** "Hearings Before a Special Committee on Un-American Activities," 5:3627.

109 **"Probably all our names"** The full text of Moseley's speech in Springfield, Illinois, on April 26, 1939, was entered into the record of the Dies Committee hearings. See ibid., 3638–42.

110 **"If the Jews bump me off"** "Waiter Sought in Anti-Jewish Campaign Probe," *Washington Evening Star*, May 19, 1939.

CHAPTER TEN: BOUND AND OBLIGATED

112 **Key "targets" of the Dies Committee** Raymond P. Brandt, "The Dies Committee: An Appraisal," *Atlantic*, Feb. 1940.

112 **The Communist Party of the United States of America** For background on

CPUSA, its membership, and its politics, see Fraser M. Ottanelli, *The Communist Party of the United States: From the Depression to World War II* (New Brunswick, N.J.: Rutgers University Press, 1991); Gregory, "Communist Party Membership by Districts 1922–1950." The Library of Congress's 1992 exhibition *Revelations from the Russian Archives: The Soviet Union and the United States* is available in digital form on the LOC website.

115 **John C. Metcalfe was a thirty-four-year-old** Bradley W. Hart, *Hitler's American Friends: The Third Reich's Supporters in the United States* (New York: Thomas Dunne Books, 2018), 24–25; "Hearings Before a Special Committee on Un-American Activities," House of Representatives, 75th Cong., 3rd Sess. (Washington, D.C.: U.S. Government Printing Office, 1938), 1:3–5.

115 **Metcalfe ended up putting into the record** For the photographs entered into the record by Metcalfe and his descriptions, see "Hearings Before a Special Committee on Un-American Activities [1938]," 1:14–25.

117 **"What size children do they have in it?"** Ibid., 17.

117 **"First, the establishment of a vast spy network"** Ibid., 25.

118 **Charles B. Hudson of *America in Danger!*** Ibid., 3:2344.

118 **"Let those who dare attempt"** Ibid., 2357–58.

118 **Metcalfe identified more than 130 organizations** Ibid., 2342–89.

119 **"There is a common practice"** Ibid., 2367.

119 **"According to the plan"** Interview with Ross, 2022.

120 **Gingrich proved an enthusiastic** For Gingrich's testimony and quotations from *Ken* magazine, see "Hearings Before a Special Committee on Un-American Activities [1938]," 2:1221–37.

121 **Brien McMahon did try to light** For correspondence between McMahon and Hoover from Jan. 3 to 6, 1939, see Pelley FBI File, pt. 2, 104–12.

122 **"I am wondering whether"** McIntire memo to Assistant Director E. A. Tamm, in Pelley FBI File, pt. 2, 45.

122 **FBI agents from the Charlotte, North Carolina, office** For FBI interviews with Pelley, see Pelley FBI File, pt. 2, 50–52.

122 **"He can't see what it has got him"** Ibid., 129.

122 **"blabber-mouth"** Ibid., 151.

123 **Roy Zachary, was on hand for the interview** Ibid., 152.

123 **The FBI had asserted back in 1934** Ibid., pt. 1, 35–36. An Aug. 1934 memo heading: "Further investigation at Asheville, NC, discloses nothing to connect the Silver Shirt Legion of America, Inc., directly to the Nazi movement at the present time." And in body of memo: "During the bankruptcy investigation referred to above the writer had cause to examine the ledgers, journals, minutes and many files and nothing was found to connect the Silver Shirt Legion of America, Inc. with the Nazi movement; however, it was noted, of course, that the Silver Shirts were imitating the Nazis in some respects."

123 **FBI activity concerning George Deatherage** Deatherage FBI file, 5–9.

124 "I do not have time" FBI File, "Seditious Conspiracy," 455, accessed at archive.org.

124 "well poised, self-confident and apparently very well read" Ibid., 458.

CHAPTER ELEVEN: "THE HANDWRITING ON THE WALL IS CLEAR AS A BELL"

126 In the third week of May 1939 For the bizarre testimony of Gilbert and Campbell, see "Hearings Before a Special Committee on Un-American Activities [1939]," 5:3180–212, 3223–84, 3343–84.

127 "I should say *I* have" Ibid., 3200.

127 "neglect to provide" "Dudley P. Gilbert Sued by Wife," *New York Times,* Feb. 15, 1941, 8.

127 "Remember those who are finally successful" "Hearings Before a Special Committee on Un-American Activities [1939]," 5:3291.

128 "because we have a very inquisitive" Ibid., 3246.

128 In his letter to Campbell Ibid., 3275.

128 Deatherage's return letter Ibid., 3277–79; letter also quoted in the *Washington Sunday Star,* May 21, 1939.

129 Chairman Dies had sent subpoenas "Dies Reveals Plot to Seize Government," *Washington Post,* May 21, 1939; "Moseley Denies Plot Against Government," *Post-Press* (El Centro, Calif.), May 21, 1939.

129 Deatherage came out swinging For Dies-Deatherage "sit down" exchange, see "Hearings Before a Special Committee on Un-American Activities [1939]," 5:3455–56; "White Camellia Chief Tells of Looking for Funds at Newport," *Washington Evening Star,* May 24, 1939.

129 He then proceeded to slalom "Hearings Before a Special Committee on Un-American Activities [1939]," 5:3456–58.

130 "In 1867, during the Reconstruction Days" Ibid., 3460.

130 had just sought out the advice "White Camellia Chief Tells of Looking for Funds at Newport."

130 the same James True "Hearings Before a Special Committee on Un-American Activities [1939]," 5:3538.

130 This comment, unfortunately, drew laughter "Deatherage Tells of Reich Rebuffs."

131 "You have only one recourse" "Hearings Before a Special Committee on Un-American Activities [1939]," 5:3490.

131 "You are bound to concede" Ibid., 3511.

131 "I have been assured" Ibid., 3502–3.

132 At the very end of two days Ibid., 3542–43.

132 He was the victim of a "smearing campaign" " 'Smells Like Russia,' Says Moseley of Dies Accusations," *Washington Evening Star,* May 26, 1939.

133 if he could "guarantee" the water supply Associated Press, "Gen. Moseley's Aide Bars Him from Witnesses' Water Supply," *Washington Evening*

Star, May 31, 1939; "Dies Inquiry Strikes Out Moseley Text," *Washington Post,* June 2, 1939.

133 **Moseley later explained the reason** "Hearings Before a Special Committee on Un-American Activities [1939]," 5:3687.

134 **"All I am trying to do"** "Moseley Denies Plot Against Government"; for Moseley's full testimony, see "Hearings Before a Special Committee on Un-American Activities [1939]," 5:3545–703.

134 **"Is that necessary?"** "Hearings Before a Special Committee on Un-American Activities [1939]," 5:3545.

134 **"You are not here for the purpose"** Ibid., 3546–47.

135 **"We have something like twelve million syphilitics"** Ibid., 3701–2.

135 **"I was aware of the fact"** Ibid., 3548.

135 **"He struck me as just a two-fisted"** Ibid., 3570.

135 **"Those organizations on the right"** Ibid., 3578–79.

135 **"The handwriting on the wall"** "Dies Probe Recess After Striking Out Moseley's Words," *Washington Evening Star,* June 2, 1939.

136 **"The first thing I would do"** "Hearings Before a Special Committee on Un-American Activities [1939]," 5:3579–80.

136 **The committee ran through** Ibid., 3607, 3620.

136 **"I have an idea"** Ibid., 3602–3.

137 **At one point, the committee questioned** Ibid., 3651.

CHAPTER TWELVE: HOLLYWOOD!

139 **"Friends, tonight there's a very special"** Audio recording of *Good News of 1939* radio program.

139 **"the name Barrymore is money"** Louella Parsons, "Close-Ups and Long-Shots of the Motion Picture Scene," *Washington Post,* April 9, 1939.

140 **Mr. Mayer, who was taking home $1.3 million** "Personnel: Above Average," *Time,* April 17, 1939; Ross, *Hitler in Los Angeles,* 215.

140 **Mr. Mayer declared that attendance** Ross, *Hitler in Los Angeles,* 264.

140 **The megastars William Powell, Myrna Loy** For attendees and quotations from Lionel Barrymore birthday party, see audio recording of *Good News of 1939* radio program.

142 **Warner Bros. had prepared for outrage** Ross, *Hitler in Los Angeles,* 263.

142 **financial backers of Leon Lewis's** Rosenzweig, *Hollywood's Spies,* 67.

143 **Warner Bros. had closed all their offices** Steven J. Ross, "Confessions of a Nazi Spy: Warner Bros., Anti-fascism, and the Politicization of Hollywood," in *Warners' War: Politics, Pop Culture & Propaganda in Wartime Hollywood,* ed. Martin Kaplan and Johanna Blakley (Los Angeles: Norman Lear Center Press, 2004), 51.

143 **"lousy Jews . . . a rotten bunch"** Ibid.

144 **"To represent Hitler"** Ibid., 52.

144 **"Our fathers came to America"** Sheilah Graham, "Jack Warner Says There'll Be Changes," *Washington Sunday Star,* Jan. 22, 1939.

144 **"The Silver Shirts and the Bundists"** Otto Friedrich, *City of Nets: A Portrait of Hollywood in the 1940s* (Berkeley: University of California Press, 1997), 50.

144 **The two months of preproduction** "Warners Ban Role of Hitler in Film," *New York Times,* Jan. 6, 1939; Douglas W. Churchill, "Deep and Dark the Mystery and Great the Tension on That Spy Film Set," *Washington Sunday Star,* Feb. 26, 1939.

145 **"The German-American Bund, the German Consul"** David Welky, *The Moguls and the Dictator: Hollywood and the Coming of World War II* (Baltimore: Johns Hopkins University Press, 2008), 120.

145 **"The evening," wrote the** *Hollywood Spectator* Ross, "Confessions of a Nazi Spy," 49.

147 **"We have only scratched the surface"** Leon Turrou, "Spies Turn to Plane Tests and Aircraft Carriers," *Washington Evening Star,* Dec. 17, 1938.

148 **demanding damages of $5 million** "Kuhn Sues for $5,000,000," *New York Times,* May 13, 1939.

148 **hundreds of threatening letters** "Tempestuous Career of a 'Nazi Spy,'" *New York Times,* Jan. 2, 1940; Ross, "Confessions of a Nazi Spy," 49.

148 **One small-town operator in Hagerstown** "'Confessions of a Nazi Spy,' at Maryland Next Thurs," *Hagerstown Globe,* June 9, 1939.

149 **"I found it almost continuously engrossing"** Nelson B. Bell, "'Confessions of a Nazi Spy' Glorifies Americanism," *Washington Post,* May 23, 1939.

149 **a battle within the FBI** For the best account of the fight between Hoover and Turrou, see Rhodri Jeffreys-Jones, *The Nazi Spy Ring in America: Hitler's Agents, the FBI, and the Case That Stirred the Nation* (Washington, D.C.: Georgetown University Press, 2021), e-book, 141–44, 146–51.

150 **"Turrou can never get back"** Ibid., 149.

150 **"Virtually every studio in town"** Frederick C. Othman, "Nazi Villain Triumphs over Hoodoo Past," *Washington Post,* May 22, 1939.

151 **a full-time railroad clerk** Charles R. Gallagher, *Nazis of Copley Square: The Forgotten Story of the Christian Front* (Cambridge, Mass.: Harvard University Press, 2021), 54.

CHAPTER THIRTEEN: COUNTRY GENTLEMEN

153 **John F. Cassidy was not entirely unknown** Gallagher, *Nazis of Copley Square,* 38–39.

154 **"the grievance claims"** Interview with Gallagher, 2022.

154 **serializing the hoary and despicable** *Protocols* Father Charles E. Coughlin, "The Protocols of Zion," *Social Justice,* July 18, 1938.

155 **"When he talked about Judaism"** Interview with Gallagher, 2022.

156 **His sermon conveyed** Transcript of Coughlin's radio address "Persecution—

Jewish and Christian," Nov. 20, 1938, accessed at Catholic University of America, American Catholic History Classroom.

156 likely received financial support Warren, *Radio Priest,* 236.

157 "duly appointed representatives" Charles Coughlin FBI file, pt. 1, 204.

157 two thousand Christian Fronters picketed Theodore Irwin, *Inside the Christian Front* (Washington, D.C.: American Council on Public Affairs, 1940), 13–14; "WMCA Again Picketed," *New York Times,* July 10, 1939.

157 "Communism in America has formerly been" Gallagher, *Nazis of Copley Square,* 39.

157 "More than at any other time" Coughlin FBI file, pt. 1, 200.

157 "grows stronger, more courageous" Ibid., 201–2.

157 "It's not like he's conjuring" Interview with Gallagher, 2022.

158 "I do not think there is a man" Cassidy to Coughlin, Sept. 13, 1939, quoted in Coughlin FBI file, pt. 1, 198.

158 "the meanest, the toughest, the most ornery" John Roy Carlson, *Under Cover: My Four Years in the Nazi Underworld of America* (New York: E. P. Dutton, 1943), 75.

159 A two-thousand-strong "Buy Christian" "Crowd Battles Police in Bronx," *New York Times,* Aug. 14, 1939.

159 "Long live our Savior" Carlson, *Under Cover,* 76–77.

159 "For size and sheer dramatic color" Ibid., 80.

159 their featured speaker was a no-show Ibid., 78.

160 "I am not content to walk" Ibid., 79.

160 He also let the crowd in on Rogge, *Official German Report,* 200.

160 "This is the first day of war" Marc Wortman, "Famed Architect Philip Johnson's Hidden Nazi Past," *Vanity Fair,* April 4, 2016.

161 "appealed to weapons" "Hitler Gives Word," *New York Times,* Sept. 1, 1939.

161 the Supreme Soviet had hastily ratified "Soviet Ratifies Reich Non-aggression Pact; Gibes at British and French Amuse Deputies," *New York Times,* Sept. 1, 1939.

161 "If we had to fight to protect our lives" Joseph P. Kennedy Sr., quoted in David Nasaw, *The Patriarch: The Remarkable Life and Turbulent Times of Joseph P. Kennedy* (New York: Penguin Press, 2012), 442–43.

161 she pulled off a stunt "Miss Ingalls' Peace Pamphlet Flights Curbed by C.A.A.," *Washington Evening Star,* Sept. 27, 1939.

162 an article for *Reader's Digest* Charles A. Lindbergh, "Aviation, Geography, and Race," *Reader's Digest,* Nov. 1939.

163 "He was fêted by the German authorities" William Shirer, quoted in his Oct. 1941 interview with the FBI in Johnson FBI file, 37.

164 Bishop was a tough man to pin down "Cassidy Defends Anti-Red Activity," *New York Times,* May 23, 1939; "Cassidy Ignored 'Nazi Spy' Report," *New York Times,* May 25, 1939; "Bishop Testifies to Life of

Mystery," *New York Times,* June 1, 1940; "Bishop Testifies He Was a Stowaway," *New York Times,* June 5, 1940.

165 **"represented that Jews were called upon"** "Plotter's Ammunition Requested by FBI, Witness Testifies," *Washington Evening Star,* April 17, 1940.

165 **"the Little Führer"** Gallagher, *Nazis of Copley Square,* 39.

165 **"One or two members"** "Christian Front Witness Tells of Wide Plot," *Washington Post,* April 9, 1940.

165 **orchestrated sprints at the Roosevelt dummies** "Finding of Bombs Told at Plot Trial," *New York Times,* April 24, 1940; interview with Gallagher, 2022.

166 **A young editor from the local newspaper** "Says Bishop Spoke of Revolt in U.S.," *New York Times,* June 12, 1940.

166 **"better reverse themselves"** "Youth's Admission on Bombs Is Bared," *New York Times,* April 27, 1940; Gallagher, *Nazis of Copley Square,* 57–58.

167 **At that point, things started moving** For Bishop and his dealings with Prout and the 165th Battalion, see "Bishop Testifies to Taking Bullets," *New York Times,* June 5, 1940.

168 **"Instead of waiting for the Communists"** "Boast on Bombs Laid to Viebrock," *New York Times,* April 26, 1940.

169 **"My dear Friend," Moseley wrote** See Rogge, *Official German Report,* 287.

169 **"seemed to disregard these folks"** Interview with Gallagher, 2022.

170 **more than four hundred New York City cops** "Duty Comes First," *New York Times,* Feb. 16, 1940.

170 **"The journalists at the time didn't see it"** Interview with Gallagher, 2022.

CHAPTER FOURTEEN: SMALL WORLD

171 **"[FBI director J. Edgar] Hoover came to New York City"** Jan Hoffman, "Lawyer's 50-Year Journey to the Bar; Christian Rightist from Long Ago Says It's Justice, Finally," *New York Times,* May 31, 1995.

172 **"more frightened than revolutionary"** "17 Held in Plot Against U.S. Jeered, Cheered at Court," *New York Times,* Jan. 16, 1940; "More Arrests Promised in Revolt Plot," *Washington Evening Star,* Jan. 15, 1940; "12 in Congress Marked for Death, Says Hoover," *Washington Post,* Jan. 15, 1940.

172 **The suspects had in their possession** "15 Partly Finished Bombs in Supplies Seized by Agents," *Washington Post,* Jan. 15, 1940.

172 **"We expect more arrests"** "More Arrests Promised in Revolt Plot."

172 **"it took only twenty-three men"** "17 Held in Plot Against U.S. Jeered, Cheered at Court."

173 **"The club planned among its early acts"** "18 Arrested in Bomb Plot Against U.S.," *Wilmington (N.C.) Morning Star,* Jan. 15, 1940.

173 **Father Coughlin's first instinct** "Coughlin Condemns Group," *New York Times,* Jan. 16, 1940.

174 **"I don't think the United States government"** United Press, "Sixteen

Christian Front Members Held in Bonds," *Waterbury (Conn.) Democrat,* Jan. 15, 1940.

174 **"a classic example of the indirect"** B. R. Crisler, "Last Week in the Cinema," *New York Times,* Jan. 21, 1940.

174 **"crackpot conspiracy"** For floor statement by Representative Emanuel Celler, see *Congressional Record,* House Proceedings, Jan. 23, 1940.

174 **marksmanship as "awful"** "17 Held in Plot Against U.S. Jeered, Cheered at Court."

174 **"The great plot to seize America"** Quoted in Coughlin's Jan. 21 address, "Father Coughlin Takes His Stand," *Tablet,* Jan. 27, 1940.

174 **Bishop told reporters he was wearing** Gallagher, *Nazis of Copley Square,* 60.

174 **Cassidy was passing time in the holding tank** Ibid., 72–73.

175 **"We are defending ourselves"** "17 Held in Plot Against U.S. Jeered, Cheered at Court."

175 **in his first Sunday radio sermon** Transcript of the entire sermon in "I Take My Stand," Father Charles E. Coughlin, Sunday radio address of Jan. 21, 1940, reprinted by Coughlin, Royal Oak, Michigan, 1940.

176 **"to teach a lesson to other citizens"** "Group Charges N.Y. Police in Christian Front," *Washington Post,* Jan. 18, 1940.

176 **"childish attempt to shield"** Associated Press, "Thorkelson Makes Statement," *New York Times,* April 30, 1940.

176 **Two days later, the defense lawyer** Gallagher, *Nazis of Copley Square,* 73.

176 **found a memo from President Franklin Delano Roosevelt** Ibid., 61.

176 **Jackson scrambled the newly appointed head** Statement by Robert H. Jackson issued on Jan. 21, 1940, in *Congressional Record,* House Proceedings, Jan. 23, 1940.

177 **The director could not shake the memory** Gallagher, *Nazis of Copley Square,* 67.

177 **The biggest cache was at a house** "Finding of Bombs Told at Plot Trial," *New York Times,* April 24, 1940.

178 **More worrying was the telegram** "Cassidy's Letters Read at Plot Trial," *New York Times,* May 1, 1940.

179 **"There was a cover-up"** Interview with Gallagher, 2022.

179 **"This is a hell of a country!"** "Charges 17 Plotted to Overthrow U.S.," *New York Times,* Feb. 8, 1940.

180 **"surged toward the defendants"** "Christian Front Men Deny Guilt amid Uproar," *Washington Post,* Feb. 8, 1940.

180 **One newspaper reporter who ambled out** " 'Front' Trial Jury Carefully Chosen," *New York Times,* April 5, 1940.

180 **Even the normally placid process** Ibid.; " 'Front' on Trial, Kennedy Tells Jury," *Brooklyn Daily Eagle,* April 5, 1940.

181 **The prosecutors, alas, had failed to ascertain** Gallagher, *Nazis of Copley Square,* 69.

181 **"He is kind of tasked with"** Interview with Gallagher, 2022.

181 **Denis Healy was the crucial witness** For Healy's testimony at the trial, see "Christian Front Witness Tells of Wide Plot," *Washington Post,* April 9, 1940; Associated Press, "Collapse of Healy Causes Adjournment of Sedition Trial," *Wilmington Morning Star,* April 11, 1940; "FBI Agent Tells of Plan to Arm 'Front,'" *Washington Post,* April 17, 1949; "Plotters' Ammunition Requested by F.B.I., Witness Testifies," *Washington Evening Star,* April 17, 1940; "Defense Grills FBI Agent in Plot Trial," *Washington Post*, April 18, 1940; "Entrapment Laid to Agent of FBI," *New York Times,* April 18, 1940.

183 **Peter Wacks, described by one newspaper** For Wacks's testimony at trial, see "FBI Man Testifies He Heard Plotting," *New York Times,* April 19, 1940; "Boast on Bombs Laid to Viebrock."

184 **Captain John T. Prout Jr. had instructed** "Guardsmen Accuse Capt. Prout in Plot," *New York Times,* May 7, 1940; "Prout Gave Bishop U.S. Ammunition," *New York Times,* May 10, 1940.

184 **Special agent Arthur M. Thurston** For Thurston's testimony and Viebrock's cellar, see "Finding of Bombs Told at Plot Trial"; "Boast on Bombs Laid to Viebrock."

184 **"showed Viebrock smilingly pointing at bombs"** "Boast on Bombs Laid to Viebrock."

185 **"I asked [Viebrock] what he thought"** Ibid.

185 **a Christian Front partisan and local priest** Gallagher, *Nazis of Copley Square,* 72.

185 **"The British Expeditionary Force"** Drew Middleton, "B.E.F. Means to Die Rather Than Give Bases to Germany," *Washington Post,* May 21, 1940.

186 **On May 29, the headline** Felix Morley, "Is Invasion of Great Britain Hitler's Present Objective?," *Washington Post,* May 29, 1940.

186 **"Sentiment for going to war"** Dr. George Gallup, "The Gallup Poll," *Washington Post,* May 29, 1940.

186 **Boettger explained that he would** "Plot Witness Bars Serving U.S. Abroad," *New York Times,* May 21, 1940.

186 **Sure, defense counsel admitted** "Sedition Case Held a Plot by the U.S.," *New York Times,* June 14, 1940.

187 **Cassidy walked right up to the judge** Interview with Gallagher, 2022; "Nine Acquitted of Sedition Plot," *New York Times,* June 25, 1940; "Coughlin Praises Sedition Acquittal," *New York Times,* June 26, 1940.

187 **"The so-called conspiracy"** For Coughlin's statement, see "Coughlin Praises Sedition Acquittal."

187 **Coughlin's closest ally in Brooklyn** Sam Marcy, "Christian Fronters Boast How They Fixed Treason Trial," *Socialist Appeal,* July 13, 1940.

188 **"There is one matter connected to the jury"** Ibid.; also Gallagher, *Nazis of Copley Square,* 69.

188 **"At least ten members of our jury"** Marcy, "Christian Fronters Boast How They Fixed Treason Trial." There may be those who argue that Marcy is

hardly a disinterested observer, but whether Boettger's statement is accurate or not, it is certainly in keeping with his character, such as it was.

CHAPTER FIFTEEN: TRIP 19

189 **When Dorothy Everhart stepped out** For testimony of Dorothy Everhart, Viola and Richard Thompson, Lydia Jacobs, H. O. Vincell, and other witnesses regarding Trip 19, see "Report of the Civil Aeronautics Board, of the Investigation of an Accident Involving Aircraft of United States Registry NC 21789, Which Occurred near Lovettsville, Virginia, on August 31, 1940," Dec. 31, 1941, 9–17.

190 **"The pilot seemed to have"** "Other Witnesses Give Accounts," *New York Times,* Sept. 1, 1940.

190 **strange pieces of airborne flotsam** "Report of the Civil Aeronautics Board," 20–21.

191 **The rest of the wreckage** For details of the debris field, see ibid., 18–20.

191 **The Loudoun County coroner** "25 Dead in Crash of Air Transport, Lundeen Is Killed," *New York Times,* Sept. 1, 1940.

191 **"The bodies of the passengers and crew"** Ibid.

192 **"We walked through this cornfield"** Audio of interview with Renace Painter provided by John Flannery.

192 **"Shoes neatly tied sat in the field"** Interview with Flannery, 2022.

192 **Virginia state troopers** "Report of the Civil Aeronautics Board," 1.

192 **difficult process of making identifications** "Bodies Identified in Plane Crash," *Washington Post,* Sept. 2, 1940.

193 **"Among the Pittsburgh passengers"** "Duquesne Track Star Dies," *New York Times,* Sept. 1, 1940.

193 **what made this disaster especially big news** "Senator Lundeen, 15 U.S. Workers Among 25 Killed in Airliner Wreck," *Washington Evening Star,* Sept. 1, 1940.

194 **The senator's remains got preferred treatment** "Bodies Identified in Plane Crash," *Washington Post,* Sept. 2, 1940.

194 **"It is a fitting name"** "Friends Take Body of Lundeen Home," *Washington Post,* Sept. 3, 1940.

194 **"rugged build and marked physical vitality"** "Death Balked Lundeen Plea for Neutrality," *Washington Post,* Sept. 1, 1940.

194 **"He dared to do the unpopular thing"** "Career Is Cut Short," *Askov (Minn.) American,* Sept. 5, 1940.

195 **"The shocking death of Senator Lundeen"** "Lundeen Is Mourned by His Colleagues on Capitol Hill," *Washington Evening Star,* Sept. 2, 1940.

195 **"The country is deeply divided"** Interview with Hart, 2022.

195 **the enraged citizens of Ortonville, Minnesota** "Anti-Leaguer Gets Cold Storage Ride," *New York Times,* November 18, 1919.

196 **"Roosevelt's foreign policy"** Rogge, *Official German Report,* 109.

197 **"the last crossroad before plunging"** "Lundeen Issues Call for Anti-war Party to Be Formed in Chicago by Farmers, Labor," *New York Times,* Aug. 2, 1940.

197 **one of only seven senators** "Senate Vote on Guard Bill," *New York Times,* Aug. 9, 1940.

197 **in an August 10 speech** "Address by Ernest Lundeen," Aug. 10, 1940, NBC Archives, Recorded Sound Section of the Motion Picture, Broadcasting and Recorded Sound Division, Library of Congress.

197 **He gave the keynote address** "Congress of Mothers Hears Senate Debate Selective Service Bill," *Washington Evening Star,* Aug. 20, 1940.

198 **"see no difference between the democracy"** "Draft Bill Upheld in First Test Vote in Senate, 54 to 29," *New York Times,* Aug. 28, 1940.

198 **"Such figures are fantastic"** "Acquiring Islands Was Lundeen Dream," *Washington Post,* Sept. 1, 1940.

198 **"The words he used so often"** "Death Balked Lundeen Plea for Neutrality."

198 **Two weeks after the crash of Trip 19** Except where otherwise noted, all details of the initial crash investigation are from the "Report of the Civil Aeronautics Board."

199 **The Douglas DC-3 was one** "Struck Ridge, Line Reports," *New York Times,* Sept. 1, 1940; "Report of the Civil Aeronautics Board."

199 **"The terminal of the stroke"** "Lightning Studied as Crash Cause," *Washington Post,* Sept. 12, 1940.

201 **Miss Harriet Johnson's salary** "Lundeen's Aide Hurls 'Lie' at Hint of Pay Information," *Washington Evening Star,* Feb. 24, 1942.

201 **"We handed the money directly"** Ibid.; "Senator Lundeen Only a Friend to Viereck, Widow Testifies," *Washington Evening Star,* Feb. 25, 1942.

202 **She received a memorable visit** "Says Mrs. Lundeen Took Viereck Data," *New York Times,* Feb. 25, 1942.

202 **"Mrs. Lundeen directed us"** "Lundeen's Wife Took Viereck File Out of Office, Jury Told," *Washington Evening Star,* Feb. 24, 1942.

203 **Pearson published his exclusive scoop** Drew Pearson and Robert S. Allen, "G-Men Were Shadowing Sen. Lundeen When Plane Crashed Mysteriously—Was Under Investigation," *Waterbury (Conn.) Evening Democrat,* Sept. 13, 1940.

203 **"I had my eyes open"** "Lundeen's Aide Hurls 'Lie' at Hint of Pay Information."

CHAPTER SIXTEEN: "PROMISCUOUS USE OF HIS FRANK"

204 **A dangerous tide was surging** For Hoke's testimony at Dies Committee on Aug. 26, 1941, see "Hearings Before a Special Committee on Un-American Activities," House of Representatives, 76th Cong., 3rd Sess. (Washington, D.C.: U.S. Government Printing Office, 1941), 4:1719–36.

205 **"Do you receive any compensation"** Ibid., 1734.

205 **Henry Hoke Award** "Echo Chamber: Sounds of Success Reverberate from 70th Annual DMA Awards," *Chief Marketer,* Nov. 30, 1999; "Pizza Box Delivers Results for WebEx," *AdAge,* Nov. 8, 2004.

205 **Picture—Promise—Prove—Push** Maxwell Ross, "How to Write Direct Mail Letter Copy," courtesy of the Direct Marketing Association, accessed at www.jcmanheimer.com/blog/1/35/how-to-write-direct-mail-letter-copy/.

206 **"didn't think it was serious"** Henry Hoke, *Black Mail* (New York: Reader's Book Service, 1944), 3.

206 **Local clergymen, for instance** Ibid., 4.

206 **"War in the Mails"** Ibid., 4–6.

207 **The debut issue of the Forum's new magazine** The title page of the first edition of *Today's Challenge* is reproduced in Sayers and Kahn, *Sabotage!,* 160.

207 **"The third piece on the cures"** For letters from Dennis to Auhagen, see Rogge, *Official German Report,* 181–82.

208 **Hoke sent his May 1940 article** Hoke, *Black Mail,* 4–5.

208 **"Interesting," they told him** Ibid., 6.

209 **Soon after the publication** For the threat from Schmitz and Hoke's response, see ibid., 6–8.

210 **"An agreement between us"** "Lindbergh Urges We 'Cooperate' with Germany if Reich Wins War," *New York Times,* Aug. 5, 1940.

211 **Congressman Jacob Thorkelson** "Hearings Before a Special Committee on Un-American Activities [1941]," 4:1732.

211 **"Only the country in which the mail"** Ibid., 1720.

211 **"Our theory of freedom of press"** Ibid., 1728.

212 **"so shocking that only the least repulsive"** "Secret U.S. Nazi Party Chief Held," *Imperial Valley Press,* Oct. 2, 1940.

212 **"Seldom directly, but by consciously directed indirection"** Dorothy Thompson, "On the Record: Dr. Auhagen," *Washington Post,* Oct. 23, 1940.

212 **the Dies Committee made a public report** "Disclosures Link Embassy and Consuls to Propaganda Agencies; Describe Efforts to Slant Press, Radio," *Washington Post,* Nov. 21, 1940.

213 **hate mail he received at his home** Hoke, *Black Mail,* 12–13.

213 **"plow under every fourth American boy"** Rogge, *Official German Report,* 356.

213 **Senator Wheeler banged the gong** "Lend-Lease Bill Assailed by Wheeler as Open Door to War," *Washington Evening Star,* March 4, 1941.

214 **When Hoke ran forensics on envelopes** For the story of the stamp machine forensics and outcome, see Hoke, *Black Mail,* 15–16.

214 **"Insolent agents and propagandists"** "Arm for a Thrust, Woodward Warns," *New York Times,* Sept. 15, 1940.

216 **Hoke was good at following the clues** Hoke, *Black Mail,* 17, 19, 20, 32.

217 **"We learned from a girl"** Ibid., 26, 32.

217 **When America First called a rally** "Lindbergh Joins in Wheeler Plea to U.S. to Shun War," *New York Times,* May 24, 1941. Full texts of Lindbergh and Wheeler speeches are printed in *The New York Times,* May 24, 1941.

219 **New York City Coordinating Committee** From a copy of the special interim report made by the New York City Coordinating Committee for Democratic Action, Charles Lindbergh FBI file 7b, 23–30.

219 **"Today, street rioters have merged"** Ibid., 28.

219 **In the final days of that summer** Full text of Lindbergh's speech in Des Moines, Sept. 11, 1941, accessed at charleslindbergh.com.

220 **Senator Robert Rice Reynolds** Sarah Wildman, "Meet Robert Reynolds, the Senator Who Wanted to 'Build a Wall' 70 Years Before Trump," *Vox,* April 4, 2017; *Congressional Record,* Senate Proceedings, June 5, 1941.

220 **"We cannot and do not intend"** Hoke, *Black Mail,* 21.

221 **Henry Stimson was appalled** For the Stimson-Wheeler exchange, see Charles Hurd, "Stimson Accuses Wheeler of Actions Near Treason," *New York Times,* July 25, 1941.

221 **"The insertions in the *Congressional Record*"** Henry Hoke, "Behind the Scenes in the Fight Against Nazi Mail Propaganda," *Reporter of Direct Mail Advertising,* Oct. 1941.

222 **"If I ever told my story"** Hoke, *Black Mail,* 28.

CHAPTER SEVENTEEN: "I'M NOT SUPPOSED TO BE DOING THIS KIND OF WORK"

223 **On one unseasonably cool** For the story of Sept. 19 and Dillard Stokes, see Dillard Stokes, "Fish's Office Helped Remove Data Wanted in Nazi-Agent Inquiry," *Washington Post,* Sept. 26, 1941; Dillard Stokes, "8 Bags of Evidence in Nazi Probe 'Turn Up' at Rep. Fish's Bin in House Storeroom," *Washington Post,* Sept. 28, 1941; "The Press: Sherlock Stokes," *Time,* Jan. 11, 1943.

224 **"Hustling young William Power Maloney"** "Business: Yaleman," *Time,* Nov. 18, 1935; "Maloney Resigns as U.S. Attorney," *Daily Home News* (New Brunswick, N.J.), Feb. 15, 1940; "Witness for His Client," *New York Times,* Dec. 19, 1964.

225 **Dillard Stokes had been on the trail** "The Press: Sherlock Stokes"; "The Rise of the Washington Post," *Fortune,* Dec. 1944.

226 **"The smear of the America First Committee"** Dillard Stokes, "Fish Admits His Office Sent Truck to Take Evidence Away," *Washington Post,* Sept. 27, 1941.

226 **The headliner was the powerful** Ibid.

227 **Too bad for Fish** Stokes, "8 Bags of Evidence in Nazi Probe 'Turn Up' at Rep. Fish's Bin in House Storeroom."

227 **Stokes raced up to the sixth floor** For the story of Stokes's discovering the

mailbags, see Dillard Stokes, "New Evidence May Shed Light on How Dennett Got Franked Envelopes," *Washington Post,* Sept. 30, 1941.

228 **Stokes answered the next day** Ibid.

229 **Burton Wheeler arrived in Los Angeles** " 'America Next' Advocates Honor Senator Wheeler," *Los Angeles News Letter,* Oct. 8, 1941.

230 **He made a twenty-two-minute speech** For quotations from Fish's speech, see Dillard Stokes, "Grand Jurors Call Viereck in Nazi Probe," *Washington Post,* Oct. 3, 1941.

231 **The indictment charged Viereck** Dillard Stokes, "Viereck Held, Accused of Using Frank," *Washington Post,* Oct. 9, 1941.

231 **"Small, slender, and graying"** Ibid.

231 **"If I had worked for war"** Ibid.

232 **his reluctance to produce** Dillard Stokes, "Bring Bags, Court Tells Fish's Clerk," *Washington Post,* Oct. 10, 1941.

232 **A bigger problem was Hill's refusal** Dillard Stokes, "Fish's Aide Indicted for Perjury, Jury Asks Where He Got $12,000," *Washington Post,* Oct. 25, 1941.

232 **"The ashes still warm"** Dillard Stokes, "Prosecutors in Nazi Inquiry Study Ashes for Use in Evidence," *Washington Post,* Oct. 24, 1941.

233 **"the keyman of a propaganda machine"** Stokes, "Fish's Aide Indicted for Perjury."

233 **"is an unimportant person in the picture"** For Hill's indictment and the O'Connor-Maloney exchange, see ibid.

234 **Fish harrumphed to a reporter** Hoke, *Black Mail,* 31.

CHAPTER EIGHTEEN: TO TELL THE TRUTH

236 **Headlines were full of war talk** *Washington Post,* Aug. 26, 1939; *New York Times,* Aug. 25, 1939.

236 **The Nazi foreign minister hosted Fish** "Hamilton Fish in Oslo Fears an Early War After Talking with Ribbentrop in Germany," *New York Times,* Aug. 16, 1939; Rogge, *Official German Report,* 270.

236 **"The European situation is so tense"** "Hamilton Fish in Oslo Fears an Early War After Talking with Ribbentrop in Germany."

236 **Germany's claims were "just"** "National Affairs: Idle Hands," *Time,* Oct. 23, 1939; Fish's comment was reported by an American wire service and later read into the *Congressional Record* by a fellow U.S. representative.

236 **The American then accepted a ride** "Hamilton Fish in Oslo Fears an Early War After Talking with Ribbentrop in Germany"; Eric Pace, "Hamilton Fish, in Congress 24 Years, Dies at 102," *New York Times,* Jan. 20, 1991; Rogge, *Official German Report,* 270.

236 **He departed Berlin** Johnson, *George Sylvester Viereck,* 195–96; Rogge, *Official German Report,* 130–31, 134–35.

237 **"will more easily fall victims"** Rogge, *Official German Report,* 63.

237 **"racial controversies, economic inequalities"** *German Psychological War-*

fare, ed. Ladislas Farago (New York: Committee for National Morale, 1941), 50.

238 **"My Jews are a valuable hostage"** Hermann Rauschning, *The Voice of Destruction* (New York: G. P. Putnam's Sons, 1940), 69, 236; Rogge, *Official German Report,* 66.

239 **The Nazi agent, as the senator's ghostwriter** Correspondence between Viereck and Lundeen at www.msnbc.com/ultra.

240 **"I think in the long run"** Hart, *Hitler's American Friends,* 103.

240 **Lundeen's top Senate staffer** "Witness Says Viereck Called Nazis Here from Lundeen's Office," *Washington Evening Star,* Feb. 21, 1942.

240 **The staff member who was charged** Ibid.

241 **So Viereck set up the Make Europe Pay** Rogge, *Official German Report,* 152–53; Henry Hoke, *It's a Secret* (New York: Reynal & Hitchcock, 1946), 94; Julian M. Pleasants, *Buncombe Bob: The Life and Times of Robert Rice Reynolds* (Chapel Hill: University of North Carolina Press, 2000), e-book, 174.

241 **They fitted out the office** Dillard Stokes, "Linked to Nazis, Dennett Activities Are Many," *Washington Post,* Nov. 14, 1941.

241 **A typical item mailed out** Rogge, *Official German Report,* 158.

242 **"I think I can report"** Ibid., 159.

243 **"drug[ging] the American people"** Chris Yogerst, *Hollywood Hates Hitler! Jew-Baiting, Anti-Nazism, and the Senate Investigation into Warmongering in Motion Pictures* (Oxford: University Press of Mississippi, 2020), e-book, 37.

243 **When he asked the aide** Rogge, *Official German Report,* 155.

243 **"Representative Fish," Viereck wrote to Lundeen** See *Ultra* website, www.msnbc.com/rachel-maddow-presents-ultra, episode 4, "Read: Letters Between Sen. Ernest Lundeen and Nazi agent George Sylvester Viereck," 53.

243 **Fish introduced the German agent** For the description of Hill meeting Fish, see "Hill Tells Jury Fish Introduced Him to Viereck," *Washington Evening Star,* Feb. 19, 1942; "Viereck Opposed Foreign Policy, Hill Testifies," *Wilmington Morning Star,* Feb. 20, 1942; Dillard Stokes, "Hill Testifies Fish Ordered Him to Mail Out Nazi Propaganda," *Washington Post,* Feb. 20, 1942.

244 **Viereck and his Nazi friends** Rogge, *Official German Report,* 59.

244 **"a mammoth mailing list"** Dillard Stokes, "Grand Jury Digs for Source of Hill's Cash," *Washington Post,* Nov. 4, 1941.

245 **a Nazi agent handed over** Rogge, *Official German Report,* 300.

245 **Viereck's Nazi-funded Flanders Hall** Ibid., 135–36, 167, 266.

246 **"George Hill is 100 percent OK"** "Not Fish, but Foul," *Time,* Jan. 26, 1942.

246 **"The Japanese have a right to Hawaii"** "Voices of Defeat," *Life,* April 13, 1942; "Ellis O. Jones, 93, Radical, Is Dead," *New York Times,* Aug. 2, 1967.

246 **Lawrence Dennis, for example** Horne, *Color of Fascism,* 143.

247 **One professor who knew Johnson** Johnson FBI file, 48.

247 **"The period of democratic debate"** Wayne S. Cole, *America First: The Battle Against Intervention, 1940–1941* (Madison: University of Wisconsin Press, 1953), 195.

248 **"I was at the communion rail"** "O'Connor Advised Him Not to Tell Truth, Says Hill," *Washington Evening Star,* Feb. 25, 1942; Dillard Stokes, "Hill, Ex-aide to Fish, Will Not Appeal," *Washington Post,* March 7, 1942.

248 **"a poor, little insignificant clerk"** "Maloney Calls Hill Cog in the Gestapo," *New York Times,* Jan. 15, 1942.

249 **He offered no defense** Ibid.

249 **"The main thing I recall"** "Court Orders Dennett Bond Lifted to $3,500," *Washington Evening Star,* Feb. 19, 1942.

249 **"was to put words in the mouths"** Dillard Stokes, "Nazi Speech Viereck Wrote Was Franked by Rep. Fish, Jury Told," *Washington Post,* Feb. 18, 1942.

CHAPTER NINETEEN: "MR. MALONEY WOULD HAVE PULLED NO PUNCHES"

250 **Maloney had also successfully prosecuted** For background on Laura Ingalls and her trial, see Rogge, *Official German Report,* 307; "Laura Ingalls Nazi Agent, Jury Decides," *Washington Post,* Feb. 14, 1942; "Laura Ingalls Says She Hoped to Expose Spies," *Washington Evening Star,* Feb. 12, 1942.

251 **her pro-Nazi sentiments** "Laura Ingalls Nazi Agent, Jury Decides."

251 **"I could tear the skies apart in triumph"** Rogge, *Official German Report,* 307.

251 **Baron Ulrich von Gienanth** For the relationship between Gienanth and Ingalls, financial and otherwise, see ibid.; "Laura Ingalls Says She Hoped to Expose Spies."

251 **"the best thing you can do for our cause"** Sayers and Kahn, *Sabotage!,* 214.

251 **"had a special liking"** "Interrogation of Dr. Heribert von Strempel by Capt. Sam Harris," Feb. 14–16, 1946, IMT Nuremberg Archives, H-3471, International Court of Justice.

252 **Maloney's federal prosecutors unleashed** For text and details of July 1942 indictment, see *United States of America v. Gerald B. Winrod et al.,* from FBI Office Memorandum to Director Hoover, April 12, 1956, 138–65; Dillard Stokes, "Jury Reveals Scope of Plot to Undermine Army's Morale," *Washington Post,* July 24, 1942; "28 Organized Groups Linked to Fascist Plot," *Washington Post,* July 24, 1942.

253 **"When the first special Grand Jury"** Hoke, *It's a Secret,* 53.

254 **"B-b-baloney"** "Mrs. Dilling Twits Adversaries with Songs in Court Lobby," *Washington Evening Star,* Oct. 19, 1942.

254 **not as vicious as the outlandish rumors** Glen Jeansonne, *Women of the Far Right: The Mothers' Movement and World War II* (Chicago: University of Chicago Press, 1996), 24.

254 **"the best-fed, best-housed"** Jean Lightfoot, "The Daffy Doings of Mrs. Dilling," *St. Louis Post-Dispatch,* Aug. 2, 1942.

254 **Maloney called her a "stooge"** "Mrs. Dilling's Bond Raised to $5,000 at Hearing Here," *Washington Evening Star,* Oct. 27, 1942.

254 **"Those rumors have their origin"** "Morale Indictment Challenges Are Taken Under Advisement," *Washington Evening Star,* Jan. 16, 1943.

254 **met in person every weekend** Hoke, *It's a Secret,* 55.

255 **He then took a full hour** For the full text of Hoffman's floor statement and the back-and-forth that followed, see *Congressional Record,* House proceedings, Dec. 8, 1942, 9396–405.

256 **"as long as a single Jew"** Jeansonne, *Women of the Far Right,* 155.

256 **"All of these individuals"** Interview with Ross, 2022.

257 **The damage, according to some estimates** "Production: Accident or Villainy?," *Time,* Nov. 25, 1940.

258 **Nye chimed in too** "Wheeler, Nye Deny They Fear Nazi Evidence," *Washington Post,* Jan. 15, 1943.

258 **"In that he may have been right"** Hoke, *It's a Secret,* 53.

258 **"plain, unadulterated lie"** "Wheeler, Nye Deny They Fear Nazi Evidence."

258 **William Power Maloney was named** "Maloney to Direct Trial Section of Criminal Division," *Washington Evening Star,* Jan. 27, 1943.

259 **a stormy and violent session** "Biddle Silent on Charges of Appeasing Defeatists," *Toledo Union Journal,* Feb. 12, 1943.

259 **First he heard of it** Hoke, *It's a Secret,* 51.

259 **"In this case the public"** "Appeasement Is Folly," *Washington Post,* Feb. 8, 1943.

259 **The U.S. Supreme Court, in a 5–2 decision** *Viereck v. United States* (1943), accessed at supreme.justia.com.

260 **Langer had been convicted** For background on Langer's legal troubles, see John M. Holzworth, *The Fighting Governor: The Story of William Langer and the State of North Dakota* (Chicago: Pointer Press, 1938); Agnes Geelan, *The Dakota Maverick: The Political Life of William Langer, also known as "Wild Bill" Langer* (Fargo: Geellan, 1975). There is also a nice little thumbnail of Langer's transgressions in "Expulsion Case of William Langer of North Dakota (1942)," accessed at the senate.gov web page "Powers & Procedures: Expulsion." Huey P. Long and Burton K. Wheeler also take star turns in "Expulsion."

261 **After his supporters filled the streets** "Langer May Seek to Impeach Olson, Other Officials," *Daily Banner* (Greencastle, Ind.), July 20, 1934. The article quotes Langer supporters urging the crowd to "yank him out and shoot him at sunrise."

261 **"Senator Langer, praising the decision"** "Viereck 'Persecution' Inquiry Is Sought by Senator Langer," *Washington Evening Star,* March 3, 1943.

CHAPTER TWENTY: BEDLAM

262 **Rogge was a prodigy** O. John Rogge, *Our Vanishing Civil Liberties* (New York: Gaer Associates, 1949), 12–14; "O. John Rogge, 77, Anti-Nazi Activist," *New York Times,* March 23, 1981.

263 **Rogge showed up in New Orleans** Harnett T. Kane, *Louisiana Hayride: The American Rehearsal for Dictatorship, 1928–1940* (New York: William Morrow, 1941), 312–13.

263 **"You will die before Wednesday"** United Press, "Death Threats Follow Charges in Louisiana," *Imperial Valley Press,* Aug. 14, 1939.

264 **Rogge put him in jail** "Smith and Weiss Get 30 Months in Louisiana Fraud," *Washington Post,* Sept. 16, 1939; "Seymour Weiss, Four Other 'Long Boys' Are Sentenced," *Tacoma Times,* Sept. 15, 1939.

264 **pocketed almost $500,000** "Leche Convicted by Louisiana Jury," *New York Times,* June 2, 1940; Kane, *Louisiana Hayride,* 403.

264 **the "hot oil" scandal** For excellent background and detail on the hot oil operation, see Kane, *Louisiana Hayride,* 319–31.

265 **Shaw committed suicide** United Press, "Key Witness Kills Self in 'Hot' Oil Case," *Washington Post,* Aug. 21, 1939.

266 **had an "educational function"** Kane, *Louisiana Hayride,* 337.

266 *The Saturday Evening Post* **did a whole series** Alva Johnston, "They Sent a Letter," *Saturday Evening Post,* June 22, 1940; Rogge, *Our Vanishing Civil Liberties,* 14.

266 **Rogge announced that he was headed to Michigan** "The Leche Conviction," *Washington Post,* June 3, 1940.

267 **"Time began to grow heavy"** Rogge, *Our Vanishing Civil Liberties,* 16.

267 **"bring to trial only those defendants"** "Biddle Silent on Charges of Appeasing Defeatists," *Toledo Union Journal,* Feb. 12, 1943.

268 **Among the gems in the book** Carlson, *Under Cover,* 486.

269 **In the first week of January 1944** Joseph Paull, "30 Charged with Trying to Nazify U.S.," *Washington Post,* Jan. 4, 1944.

269 **"Lindbergh had too much popular appeal"** "Reminiscences of Lawrence Dennis," 89.

269 **"unlawfully, willfully, feloniously"** "U.S. Indicts 30, Alleging Nazi Plot to Incite Mutiny and Revolution," *New York Times,* Jan. 4, 1944.

270 **George Deatherage, as a stunt** "Deatherage Is Arrested," *New York Times,* Jan. 10, 1943; "Deatherage Wants Willkie to Return $10 'Retainer,'" *Washington Evening Star,* Jan. 12, 1943.

271 **He claimed to the arresting officers** "Missing Smythe Enters Trial," *Imperial Valley Press,* April 19, 1944.

271 **One defense attorney, James Laughlin** "The Sedition Trial: A Study in Delay and Obstruction," *University of Chicago Law Review* 15, no. 3 (1948): 696.

271 **She once arrived** "Trial's End," *Time,* Dec. 11, 1944.

272 **he just didn't feel well** James E. Chinn, "Sedition Defendants' Tactics Irritate Judge, Entertain Spectators, and Pile Up Bill," *Washington Post,* April 30, 1944.

272 **even weirder inquiries** Michael Sayers and Albert E. Kahn, *The Plot Against Peace* (New York: Dial Press, 1945), 217; Leo P. Ribuffo, "The United States v. McWilliams: The Roosevelt Administration and the Far Right," in *American Political Trials,* ed. Michael R. Belknap (Westport, Conn.: Greenwood Press, 1981).

272 **The list of *proposed* voir dire questions to prospective jurors** "Criminal Case Files, 1863–1992" (Entry 77 in Record Group 21, Records of the District Courts of the United States), National Archives and Records Administration; Jeansonne, *Women of the Far Right,* 160.

273 **Until then, they argued, their clients** "Sedition Trial: A Study in Delay and Obstruction," 697.

273 **"That's a damn lie"** Carter Brooke Jones, "Shouts from Defense Interrupt Prosecutor at Sedition Trial," *Washington Evening Star,* May 17, 1944.

273 **"John Rogge tried to talk"** "Six O'clock WEAF News," May 17, 1944, NBC Archives, Recorded Sound Section of the Motion Picture, Broadcasting and Recorded Sound Division, Library of Congress.

274 **"I demand a mental examination"** Jones, "Shouts from Defense Interrupt Prosecutor at Sedition Trial."

274 **The defendants, Rogge said, "intended to impose"** For quotations from Rogge's opening statement, see "Opening Statement on Behalf of the United States, by Mr. John Rogge," *United States v. McWilliams,* Cr. No. 73086, "Criminal Case Files, 1863–1992" (Entry 77 in Record Group 21, Records of the District Courts of the United States), National Archives and Records Administration.

275 **"They probably should have held"** "Six O'clock WEAF News."

275 **Lawrence Dennis told the court** James E. Chinn, "Dennis Calls Sedition Trial 'Corny Farce,'" *Washington Post,* May 19, 1944.

276 **"complete loss of self-control"** "4 Defendants Wrote to Nazis, Gissibl Says," *Washington Post,* June 6, 1944.

276 **"resorted to every legal trick"** James E. Chinn, "Sedition Trial Defense Asks Delay 'to Let Hitler Testify,'" *Washington Post,* April 18, 1944.

277 **He had left the courtroom** Nancy McLennan, "Left City for Rest, Says Smythe, Brisk at Sedition Trial," *New York Times,* April 20, 1944.

277 **one of *Time* magazine's rewrite men** "Fairy Tale," *Time,* Aug. 28, 1944.

278 **"It's just impossible to estimate"** "Sedition Trial: A Study in Delay and Obstruction," 700.

CHAPTER TWENTY-ONE: "PARALYZE THE WILL"

279 **"an avalanche of motions of mistrial"** "Sedition Trial to Be Resumed Tomorrow," *Washington Post,* Sept. 4, 1944.

279 **Langer "was not someone who practiced"** Interview with Young, 2022.

280 **Wild Bill threw his arm around** J. L. Martin, "I Cover the Sedition Trial," *Sentinel,* Oct. 5, 1944; Carter Brooke Jones, "Langer Denounces Sedition Trial, Calls for Release of 26," *Washington Evening Star,* Sept. 9, 1944.

280 **Wild Bill was back in the Senate chamber** *Congressional Record,* Senate Proceedings, Sept. 8, 1944, 7620–26; Jones, "Langer Denounces Sedition Trial, Calls for Release of 26"; Martin, "I Cover the Sedition Trial."

281 **joined his mother in attacking** "Senator Langer Demands Dismissal of Sedition Charges," *Southern Jewish Monthly,* Sept. 1944.

282 **a juicy little feature** "Jail Serves Steak Semiweekly to 8 Sedition Defendants," *Washington Evening Star,* Sept. 12, 1944.

283 **pleaded with Judge Eicher** "Sedition Defense Asks Trial Between 3:30 and 9:30 P.M.," *Washington Evening Star,* Sept. 20, 1944.

283 **the actual cost to date** "Sedition Trial Cost Estimated at $65,819 by District Auditor," *Washington Evening Star,* Sept. 17, 1944.

283 **The headline stories were about the war** "First Army Reaches Big Highway Within 26 Miles of Cologne," *Washington Evening Star,* Sept. 12, 1944.

284 **"It is a sizzling document"** "The New Books," *Washington Sunday Star,* Sept. 10, 1944.

284 **"I admit, publicly, that my defeat"** "Isolationist Pair Is Humbled," *Monitor Leader* (Mount Clemens, Mich.), Nov. 9, 1944.

287 **"Adolf Hitler said," Rauschning explained** "Defense to Quiz Hitler Ex-aide in Sedition Trial," *Washington Evening Star,* Oct. 12, 1944.

288 **"Later on we will have baseball bats"** Carter Brooke Jones, "Sedition Jury Given Details of Plan for War on Jews, Reds," *Washington Evening Star,* Nov. 10, 1944.

288 **"the inevitable day of reckoning"** " 'Fascist State' Urged in Deatherage Paper, Sedition Jury Told," *Washington Evening Star,* Nov. 15, 1944.

289 **"regional commander of the Confederation"** "Allen Testimony Ends After 9 Days on Stand in Sedition Trial," *Washington Evening Star,* Nov. 28, 1944.

289 **"The time has arrived"** " 'Fascist State' Urged in Deatherage Paper, Sedition Jury Told."

289 **Allen testified before Judge Eicher** Carter Brooke Jones, "Attempts to Justify Anti-Semitism Kept from Sedition Jury," *Washington Evening Star,* Nov. 21, 1944.

290 **One of the few "regulars"** Hoke, *It's a Secret,* 65.

291 **three million words entered** Frederick R. Barkley, "Death of Justice Halts Mass Trial," *New York Times,* Dec. 1, 1944; "Sedition Trial: A Study in Delay and Obstruction," 700.

291 **"For more than seven months"** "Trial's End."

291 **Judge Eicher's law clerk noticed** "Justice Eicher Dies; Sedition Mistrial Seen," *Washington Evening Star,* Nov. 30, 1944; Melvin Gingerich, "Edward C. Eicher and the Sedition Trial of 1944," *Palimpsest* (State Historical Society of Iowa) 61, no. 1 (1980).

291 **Died in his sleep** "Justice Eicher Dies; Sedition Mistrial Seen"; Barkley, "Death of Justice Halts Mass Trial."

291 **Some of the alleged seditionists** Selden Menefee, "America at War: Little Hitlers on the Loose," *Washington Post*, March 8, 1945.

292 **A replacement judge took the bench** "8-Month-Old Sedition Case Ends with Mistrial Order," *Washington Post*, Dec. 8, 1944.

CHAPTER TWENTY-TWO: "WISE CHOICES"

294 **he and his small team spent eleven weeks** "Rogge Leaves for Nuremberg to Study Nazi Files," *Jewish Post* (Indianapolis), April 5, 1946; Dale Harrington, *Mystery Man: William Rhodes Davis, Nazi Agent of Influence* (Dulles, Va.: Brassey's, 1999), 205–6; *Meet the Press*, Dec. 6, 1946, NBC Archives, Recorded Sound Section of the Motion Picture, Broadcasting and Recorded Sound Division, Library of Congress.

295 **Clark suggested the removal** Rogge, *Our Vanishing Civil Liberties*, 19–21.

296 **When he submitted the final draft** Ibid., 22–23.

297 **"Truman essentially decrees that this report"** Interview with Hart, 2022.

297 **On his "vacation," Rogge** "Rogge Calls Aim Exposing Fascism," *New York Times*, Oct. 27, 1946.

298 **"had not attempted to restrain him"** Ibid.

298 **"chose the placid Quaker College"** "Rogge's Accusations," *Washington Post*, Oct. 24, 1946.

298 **"A political science class"** "Rogge Ties Lewis to Nazis in Politics," *New York Times*, Oct. 23, 1946.

298 **Hermann Göring, had told Rogge** "Nazi-Backed Scheme to Beat Roosevelt in '40 Related by Rogge," *Washington Evening Star*, Oct. 23, 1946.

299 **"The success of the isolationist Republicans"** Rogge, *Official German Report*, 262.

299 **the full-page advertisement in question** The full-page ad ran on p. 19 of *The New York Times* on June 25, 1940.

300 **one particularly problematic person** "Rogge Ties Lewis to Nazis in Politics."

301 **A very angry Burton Wheeler** Truman's daily appointments calendar for Oct. 24, 1946, is available in the digital collections of the Truman Library; Drew Pearson, "Merry-Go-Round"; *Waterbury (Conn.) Post*, Oct. 31, 1946.

301 **What happened next is hardly surprising** For details of Rogge's firing, the lead-up to it, and the reporting in the aftermath, see "Rogge Ousted for Speech on Nazi U.S. Plans," *Washington Evening Star*, Oct. 26, 1946; "Rogge Calls Aim Exposing Fascism," *New York Times*, Oct. 27, 1946; Drew Pearson, "Merry-Go-Round"; Rogge, *Our Vanishing Civil Liberties*, 28–31; Albert E. Kahn, *High Treason* (New York: Lear, 1950), 259; Clark's handwritten calendar in Tom C. Clark Papers, Appointments File, Box 96, Calendars, 1946 (June–Dec.), Harry Truman Library, Independence, Mo.

303 **"When I was first preparing the report"** "Rogge Calls Aim Exposing Fascism."

303 **Rogge went even further** O. John Rogge, "Fight Against Fascism: Rogge's Report on the Fascist Threat to the U.S.A.," *PM*, Oct. 29, 1946.

304 **"The list is probably not complete"** Ibid.

305 **"When I fired Rogge"** "Interview with Tom C. Clark," Oral History Transcript, LBJ Presidential Library digital collections, Oct. 7, 1969, 13.

305 **inundated with angry letters** Quoted letters are from the White House Central Files, Official File, Box 87, OF 10, Misc Rogge, Truman Library, Independence, Mo.

305 **A week before Rogge began** "Goering Ends Life by Poison, 10 Others Hanged in Nuremberg Prison for Nazi War Crimes; Doomed Men on Gallows Pray for Germany," *New York Times*, Oct. 16, 1946.

306 **Rogge got an absolute grilling** *Meet the Press*, Dec. 6, 1946.

308 **"The present manuscript"** Leonard Lyons, "Manhattan Memos," *Washington Post*, Dec. 26, 1946.

308 **"[Rogge's] practice of presenting the names"** W. Phillips Davison, "Thunder on the Right: The Nazi 5th Column," *Washington Post*, Sept. 4, 1961.

309 **At this writing, in 2023, Freedom House reports** "Freedom in the World, 2023," Freedom House, 16.

EPILOGUE

311 **Philip Johnson fully expected** Lamster, *Man in the Glass House*, 193.

311 **Johnson was officially suspected** Schulze, *Philip Johnson*, 142.

311 **the secretary of the navy** Lamster, *Man in the Glass House*, 195.

312 **"Every young man should be allowed"** Tomkins, "Forms Under Light."

312 **the burning question among the cognoscenti** Steven Kurutz, "With a Legend Gone, What Fate for Table 32?," *New York Times*, Jan. 30, 2005.

312 **"I am a United States Citizen"** Kaiser, *Gay Metropolis*, 42.

314 **Lonnie Lawrence Dennis** There is some dispute about the race and identity of Dennis's father. There were rumors that his birth father was actually his uncle, who had impregnated his wife's sister, but the truth was pretty plain: his father was a white man. Dennis probably never knew his biological father. He once described him as French and Indian. See "Reminiscences of Lawrence Dennis"; Horne, *Color of Fascism*, 18–22; Dennis FBI file, 10–12.

314 **Lonnie Lawrence enjoyed a brief celebrity** "Black Boy's Mission Ended," *New York Times*, Jan. 11, 1899; "Reminiscences of Lawrence Dennis," 1; Horne, *Color of Fascism*, 17–19.

314 **"I decided I had to go to college"** "Reminiscences of Lawrence Dennis," 1.

314 **Dennis renounced his family** Ibid., 25–26, 35, 36; Dennis FBI file, 10–12.

314 **"What jolts me is that over sixty-two years"** Horne, *Color of Fascism*, 171–72.

315 **In an interview he granted** "Charles Coughlin, 30's 'Radio Priest,' Dies," *New York Times,* Oct. 28, 1979.

316 **The 1995 profile of Cassidy** Hoffman, "Lawyer's 50-Year Journey to the Bar."

316 **he became a mentor** Stephen E. Atkins, *Encyclopedia of Right-Wing Extremism in Modern American History* (Santa Barbara, Calif.: ABC-CLIO, 2011), 84.

316 **Deatherage himself contributed** George Michael, *Willis Carto and the American Far Right* (Gainesville: University Press of Florida, 2008), 43.

317 **Pelley was convicted of sedition** "William Dudley Pelley, 75, Dies; Founded Fascist Silver Shirts," *New York Times,* July 2, 1965.

317 **"Jews, murderers and liars"** Ernest F. Elmhurst, *The World Hoax* (Asheville, N.C.: Pelley, 1938), 6–7.

317 **He made multiple appeals** Drew Pearson, "Capital News Capsules," *Washington Post,* Jan. 26, 1951.

318 **Moseley supported a convicted Nazi** Joshua Kastenberg, "The Crisis of June 2020," *Nebraska Law Review* 99, no. 3 (2020): 615.

318 **chaired the Texas Education Association** "Georgia Alumni Backs Prexy Who Refuses Bias Dollars for University," *Southern Jewish Weekly,* May 25, 1951.

318 **In 1949, the disgraced general** "Moseley, Self-Styled Fuehrer, Begins Hate Campaign from Atlanta," *Southern Jewish Weekly,* June 10, 1949.

318 **serious contender for army chief of staff** Joseph W. Bendersky, *The Jewish Threat: Anti-Semitic Politics of the U.S. Army* (New York: Basic Books, 2008), e-book, 311.

318 **"Let's Rescue Uncle Sam"** Michael, *Willis Carto and the American Far Right,* 34.

318 **President Eisenhower was a secret Jew** Jeansonne, *Women of the Far Right,* 166–67.

319 **"run her out of the state"** Carter Brooke Jones, "Guffey and Phillips Blocked as Viereck Trial Witnesses," *Washington Evening Star,* March 2, 1942.

320 **"We are indeed unique"** Anna Quindlen, "Hamilton Fish: A Congressional Saga," *New York Times,* April 6, 1977.

320 **impossible for him to get to** Eric Pace, "Ex-Rep. Hamilton Fish, Roosevelt Foe, Dies at 102," *New York Times,* Jan. 20, 1991.

320 **"I know he hated me"** Eric Pace, "At 100, Hamilton Fish Has Plenty of Kick," *New York Times,* Dec. 8, 1988.

322 **Dearborn's mayor responded** Sarah Rahal, "Dearborn Museum Protests Editor's Firing over Article on Henry Ford's Anti-Semitism," *Detroit News,* Feb. 1, 2019; Sarah Rahal, "Dearborn Mayor Defends Quashing Article on Henry Ford's Anti-Semitism," *Detroit News,* Feb. 19, 2019.

322 **"Still a lawyer and still exuberant"** "Witness for His Client: William Power Maloney," *New York Times,* Dec. 19, 1964.

322 **Rogge represented Ethel's brother** Peter Kihss, "F.B.I. Yields Rosenberg Files in Bid by Sons to Prove Parents Were Innocent," *New York Times,* Dec. 4, 1975; Robert D. McFadden, "David Greenglass, the Brother Who Doomed Ethel Rosenberg, Dies at 92," *New York Times,* Oct. 14, 2014.

323 **The rest of his life's work** "F. Dillard Stokes Dies; Award-Winning Reporter Covered High Court for Post," *Washington Post,* Dec. 17, 1980.

324 **Henry Hoke's 1970 obituary** "Henry Hoke, Author and Trade Editor," *New York Times,* Nov. 23, 1970.

324 **the death notice in the *Los Angeles Times*** "Leon L. Lewis, Jewish Leader, Succumbs at 65," *Los Angeles Times,* May 22, 1954.

PHOTOGRAPH CREDITS

INDEX

Page numbers in *italics* indicate photographs.

ABOUT THE AUTHOR

RACHEL MADDOW is the host of the Emmy Award–winning *Rachel Maddow Show* on MSNBC, as well as the #1 *New York Times* bestselling author of *Drift* and *Blowout,* and the *New York Times* bestselling co author of *Bag Man.* Maddow received a bachelor's degree in public policy from Stanford University and earned her doctorate in political science at Oxford University. She lives in New York City and Massachusetts with her partner, the artist Susan Mikula.

ABOUT THE TYPE

This book was set in Sabon, a typeface designed by the well-known German typographer Jan Tschichold (1902–74). Sabon's design is based upon the original letter forms of sixteenth-century French type designer Claude Garamond and was created specifically to be used for three sources: foundry type for hand composition, Linotype, and Monotype. Tschichold named his typeface for the famous Frankfurt typefounder Jacques Sabon (c. 1520–80).